D1477485

A CELEBRATION OF POETS

CANADA
SPRING 2009

creativeCOMMUNICATION

A CELEBRATION OF TODAY'S WRITERS

A CELEBRATION OF POETS
CANADA
SPRING 2009

AN ANTHOLOGY COMPILED BY CREATIVE COMMUNICATION, INC.

Published by:

1488 NORTH 200 WEST · LOGAN, UTAH 84341
TEL. 435-713-4411 · WWW.POETICPOWER.COM

Copyright © 2009 by Creative Communication, Inc.
Printed in the United States of America

ISBN: 978-1-60050-254-5

FOREWORD

Earlier this year I received a phone call from an individual who was sending in a poem written by a friend's son. Through the conversation it was revealed that the person I was talking to was the author, poet and playwright, John Tobias. His poem, "Reflections on a Gift of Watermelon Pickle Received from a Friend Called Felicity" is one of my favorite poems. Starting with the line "During that summer, when unicorns were still possible..." his poem takes me back to all the magical summers that I had where anything could happen. I was given a treat in that Mr. Tobias recited his poem and related the story that inspired it. What I gained most from the conversation was that the inspiration for any writing may seem to come from an event, but it is really written from a lifetime of experiences.

I also received a letter this spring from a young lady who was published in one of our anthologies in 1999. Now a published author working on her second novel, she took the time to write and thank Creative Communication for giving her the start for her writing career. The poets in this anthology are beginning writers. Yet, as they continue in their writing, the experience of being a published author will hopefully be an inspiration to them. As they gain a lifetime of experiences, I hope they will continue to write and share themselves through poetry.

As you read each student's poem, realize that every famous author started somewhere. I hope that I will continue to receive letters from authors who relate that we were the first place they were published. Will one of these authors become famous? Anything is possible.

I hope you enjoy this anthology and the poets who share their lives through words.

Thomas Worthen, Ph.D.
Editor
Creative Communication

WRITING CONTESTS!

Enter our next POETRY contest!
Enter our next ESSAY contest!

Why should I enter?

Win prizes and get published! Each year thousands of dollars in prizes are awarded throughout North America. The top writers in each division receive a monetary award and a free book that includes their published poem or essay. Entries of merit are also selected to be published in our anthology.

Who may enter?

There are four divisions in the poetry contest. The poetry divisions are grades K-3, 4-6, 7-9, and 10-12. There are three divisions in the essay contest. The essay divisions are grades 3-6, 7-9, and 10-12.

What is needed to enter the contest?

To enter the poetry contest send in one original poem, 21 lines or less. To enter the essay contest send in one original non-fiction essay, 250 words or less, on any topic. Each entry must include the student's name, grade, address, city, state, and zip code, and the student's school name and school address. Students who include their teacher's name may help their teacher qualify for a free copy of the anthology. Contest changes and updates are listed at www.poeticpower.com.

How do I enter?

Enter a poem online at:
www.poeticpower.com
or

Mail your poem to:
Poetry Contest
1488 North 200 West
Logan, UT 84341

Enter an essay online at:
www.studentessaycontest.com
or

Mail your essay to:
Essay Contest
1488 North 200 West
Logan, UT 84341

When is the deadline?

Poetry contest deadlines are August 18th, December 3rd, and April 13th. Essay contest deadlines are October 15th, February 17th, and July 15th. Students can enter one poem and one essay for each spring, summer, and fall contest deadline.

Are there benefits for my school?

Yes. We award $15,000 each year in grants to help with Language Arts programs. Schools qualify to apply for a grant by having 15 or more accepted entries.

Are there benefits for my teacher?

Yes. Teachers with five or more students published receive a free anthology that includes their students' writing.

For more information please go to our website at **www.poeticpower.com**, email us at editor@poeticpower.com or call 435-713-4411.

TABLE OF CONTENTS

Spring 2009 Poetic Achievement Honor Schools

* Teachers who had fifteen or more poets accepted to be published

The following schools are recognized as receiving a "Poetic Achievement Award." This award is given to schools who have a large number of entries of which over fifty percent are accepted for publication. With hundreds of schools entering our contest, only a small percent of these schools are honored with this award. The purpose of this award is to recognize schools with excellent Language Arts programs. This award qualifies these schools to receive a complimentary copy of this anthology. In addition, these schools are eligible to apply for a Creative Communication Language Arts Grant. Grants of two hundred and fifty dollars each are awarded to further develop writing in our schools.

A J McLellan Elementary School
Surrey, BC
Twyla Koop*
Cindy Zaklan*

Ascension of Our Lord Secondary School
Mississauga, ON
Maureen Ahmad*

Bernard Elementary School
Chilliwack, BC
Ieva Alger*
Grace Jones*

Blundell Elementary School
Richmond, BC
Erin Gebbie*

Chiganois Elementary School
Debert, NS
Ronda Parker*

Colby Village Elementary School
Dartmouth, NS
Lynn Coolen
Mrs. W. Mercer

Collège catholique Franco-Ouest
Nepean, ON
Jean-Auguste Gravel*

College Prep International
Montreal, QC
Mrs. L. Bogante*

East Selkirk Middle School
East Selkirk, MB
Deanna Cameron
Karen Potosky*

Ecole Akiva
Westmount, QC
Jen Fraenkel
Stacey Smilovitch*
Helaine Tecks*

École Renaissance
Burlington, ON
Lynn Kennedy*

Falmouth District School
Falmouth, NS
Karen Mulloy*
Tara Warner

Forest Hill School – Senior Campus
St Lazare, QC
Grace Henderson*

Gordon Graydon Memorial Secondary School
Mississauga, ON
Mrs. Manny*

Heather Park Middle School
Prince George, BC
Christina Furlan*

Hillside Jr/Sr High School
Valleyview, AB
Larry Magnusson*

Holy Cross Regional High School
Surrey, BC
John Prescott
Susan Sousa*

Homelands Senior Public School
Mississauga, ON
A. Cooper*

Islamic Foundation School
Scarborough, ON
Saheda Hafejee
Madeeha Mahmood
Sr. Fareena Masood
Sr. Mehrunisa Rendelia
Nusrat Sacranie

John T Tuck Public School
Burlington, ON
Claire Eggers*

Kennedy Langbank School
Kennedy, SK
Denise Singleton*

Khalsa School - Old Yale Road Campus
Surrey, BC
N.K. Dhillon
Ms. Pagely*

Kingswood Dr Public School
Brampton, ON
Amanda Bennett*
Ms. Millar
Karen Noel
Crystal Parks

Linden Lanes School
Brandon, MB
Susan Sambrook*

Linwood Public School
Linwood, ON
Mrs. Enns-Frede*

Macdonald High School
Sainte Anne De Bellevue, QC
Karen Jones*

Mary Montgomery School
Virden, MB
Audrey Harvey*

Menno Simons Christian School
Calgary, AB
Dayle Vienneau*

Merritt Secondary School
Merritt, BC
Laurie-Anne Barisoff*

Milford Colony School
Magrath, AB
Tarrell Harris*

Mornington Central School
Newton, ON
Linda Schurter*

Ormsby School
Edmonton, AB
Toni Sartorelli*

Park West School
Halifax, NS
Trish Gibbon
Joanne Walsh

Seminaire de Sherbrooke
Sherbrooke, QC
  Julie Cruickshank*

Silver Star Elementary School
Vernon, BC
  Mrs. P. Couch*

Sir Isaac Brock Public School
London, ON
  Miss A. Kirkness
  Debbie Ruebsam*

St Alphonsus School
Winnipeg, MB
  Taras Veryha*

St Anne School
Fort McMurray, AB
  Nadine Armbruster*

St Mary Choir and Orchestra Program
London, ON
  Susan Gosso*

St Mary Separate School
Niagara Falls, ON
  Mrs. DeProphetis*

St Patrick's Elementary School
Vancouver, BC
  Bill Wicken*

The Country Day School
King, ON
  Gillian Orr*

Tisdale Elementary School
Tisdale, SK
  Diane Burningham
  Jack Fulton

Webber Academy
Calgary, AB
  Mariaan Camp
  Bonita Ting*

Westside Academy
Prince George, BC
  Sherry Breck
  K. Nava

Westwind Elementary School
Richmond, BC
  John F. Knight*

Language Arts Grant Recipients 2008-2009

After receiving a "Poetic Achievement Award" schools are encouraged to apply for a Creative Communication Language Arts Grant. The following is a list of schools who received a two hundred and fifty dollar grant for the 2008-2009 school year.

Acushnet Elementary School, Acushnet, MA
Benton Central Jr/Sr High School, Oxford, IN
Bridgeway Christian Academy, Alpharetta, GA
Central Middle School, Grafton, ND
Challenger Middle School, Cape Coral, FL
City Hill Middle School, Naugatuck, CT
Clintonville High School, Clintonville, WI
Coral Springs Middle School, Coral Springs, FL
Covenant Classical School, Concord, NC
Coyote Valley Elementary School, Middletown, CA
Diamond Ranch Academy, Hurricane, UT
E O Young Jr Elementary School, Middleburg, NC
El Monte Elementary School, Concord, CA
Emmanuel-St Michael Lutheran School, Fort Wayne, IN
Ethel M Burke Elementary School, Bellmawr, NJ
Fort Recovery Middle School, Fort Recovery, OH
Gardnertown Fundamental Magnet School, Newburgh, NY
Hancock County High School, Sneedville, TN
Haubstadt Community School, Haubstadt, IN
Headwaters Academy, Bozeman, MT
Holden Elementary School, Chicago, IL
Holliday Middle School, Holliday, TX
Holy Cross High School, Delran, NJ
Homestead Elementary School, Centennial, CO
Joseph M Simas Elementary School, Hanford, CA
Labrae Middle School, Leavittsburg, OH
Lakewood High School, Lakewood, CO
Lee A Tolbert Community Academy, Kansas City, MO
Mary Lynch Elementary School, Kimball, NE
Merritt Secondary School, Merritt, BC
North Star Academy, Redwood City, CA

Language Arts Grant Winners cont.

Old Redford Academy, Detroit, MI
Prairie Lakes School, Willmar, MN
Public School 124Q, South Ozone Park, NY
Rutledge Hall Elementary School, Lincolnwood, IL
Shelley Sr High School, Shelley, ID
Sonoran Science Academy, Tucson, AZ
Spruce Ridge School, Estevan, SK
St Columbkille School, Dubuque, IA
St Francis Middle School, Saint Francis, MN
St Luke the Evangelist School, Glenside, PA
St Matthias/Transfiguration School, Chicago, IL
St Robert Bellarmine School, Chicago, IL
St Sebastian Elementary School, Pittsburgh, PA
The Hillel Academy, Milwaukee, WI
Thomas Edison Charter School - North, North Logan, UT
Trinity Christian Academy, Oxford, AL
United Hebrew Institute, Kingston, PA
Velasquez Elementary School, Richmond, TX
West Frederick Middle School, Frederick, MD

Grades 10-11-12

Top Poem Grades 10-11-12

Limitless Sky

My dreams are only imitations of an unforgotten memory
Blinded by visions of what I wish I never did see
My certainty strays so far out of reach, in a limitless sky
Through all the tears that choose to recklessly defy
In a world that can't prevent scars from becoming permanent
With returning tears that seem to form in an instant
And sudden flashbacks that deepen the scars intensity
The inability to forget them, proves to be only a mystery
I walk through each storm, losing another piece of my heart
Trying to forget every moment in life, that so viciously tore me apart
With each set back, molding into another reason to create hope
In a world that doesn't always make it so easy to cope
As my certainty fades deep, within this limitless sky
I carry no other choice, but to let these reckless tears defy

Sophia Affleck, Grade 11
Killarney Secondary School, BC

Top Poem Grades 10-11-12

Checkmate

My life is sixty-four black and white squares.
An eight by eight construct.
Here I am king, here I am powerless.

A soldier of destiny
One predetermined move after the next
Free will is an illusion.

The reality is sixty-four black and white squares
I am playing a losing game
Fate's game, but it is my life.

Check
I am vulnerable.

Why won't they help me?
They cannot move, their paths do not cross mine.

No, I refuse to let it end.
I have free will, I can choose.
I can live.
Checkmate.

Nour Ashour, Grade 12
Earl Haig Secondary School, ON

Top Poem Grades 10-11-12

The Storm in Me

Trying to find myself
while standing in the rain
my heart beats with the thunder
and the lightning highlights my pain

My heart beats faster
the rain pours down
and the wind blows my emotions
around and around

As the lightning illuminates the sky
and the thunder resonates around me
I ask myself why I've locked my heart
and thrown away the key

Erika Decock, Grade 11
Ecole Secondaire de Pain Court, ON

Top Poem Grades 10-11-12

Second Time the Fool

Repetition by memory
when it's the only thing known true
and when nothing seems to fall together
the lesson I've unlearned, is you.

I'm supposed to have learned the hard way
I'm not what you hold dear
but with everything falling through these days
It's only you I want near.

They say the second time around
— that's when it's me that plays the fool
but in the end you can't erase
what you don't truly want to undo.

Ashley Ferguson, Grade 12
Vegreville Composite High School, AB

Top Poem Grades 10-11-12

Loss

Her steps were light. Her mind was free.
She danced with sun. She read under the tree.
Then one day, came the Time, when the little girl,
Saw the world with another eye. Then she wondered, for what and why,
Do men take up cold steel, in their fight?
Was it not said, that life was everyone's right?
She shook her head and pondered on while her hair grew lustrous and long.
Then she opened a magazine to find, a woman, not of her kind.
Golden hair, fair skin, blue eyes, a body for sin.
Then, she looked in the mirror, and repeated a familiar line,
"Mirror, mirror, on the wall," but, the mirror does not answer,
Who's the fairest of them all. She sighed, she cried.
She looked at her waist, and stepped off the scale in a haste.
Such was the Time, when the little girl saw the world,
With a different eye in another light, all the while I wonder,
For what and for why?

Jing Han, Grade 10
College Prep International, QC

Top Poem Grades 10-11-12

The Pen Is Not So Mighty

When my thoughts are a burden, too hard to understand,
I pick up my pen and put it in my hand.
The ink flows like a river, my words are the bends,
Scribbled and etched across the papery land,
Creating a new world, one where I can command!
My pen is my sword and my shield too,
To fight for inspiration, to push my way through,
To defend my ideas, my words are my choice,
To conquer my fears and fight for my voice!
A world filled with the words of Hughes, Frost and Poe,
Where upon a balcony, climbs dear Romeo!
Where the question is: to be or not?
Those are my characters and that is the plot.
But alas, it cannot last!
My pen comes to an end,
It loses its life and power to fly,
When the ink from its tip runs out and goes dry!
My thoughts have no refuge; I'm alone in the dark,
I'm afraid of the shadows without my inky spark!
No shed of hope or hint of some light,
My pen has been killed, and lost all its might.

Janelle Martin, Grade 12
Ecole secondaire catholique Algonquin, ON

Top Poem Grades 10-11-12

Marina

For what hath thee? 'Tis a summertime tale,
Of love and a mystified man at sail.
'Twas June's steamiest day, with cloudless skies,
When a gorgeous damsel first charmed his eyes;
Swiped the jack's heart, with an eternal hold;
Held sapphire-like eyes, and locks of gold.
Fair as Aphrodite, she is man's sole wish,
Alas! The belle was part maiden, part fish!
Her emerald fins disrupted the sea,
She swam away, abandon ship did he.
Pursued the sea nymph, sought her forever,
A mirage's fool, heart deeply severed.
Like Bermuda's ships, swallowed by the sea;
Agonized vanquish, David Jones claims thee.

Victoria Morena, Grade 11
Collège catholique Franco-Ouest, ON

Top Poem Grades 10-11-12

Winter's Storm

Dark night skies hang above my head
Storm clouds brewing with news of the dead
And every night I stare up ahead
Trying to glimpse life outside my head
The cold winters passing but I want it to stay
So the blazing white sun doesn't brighten my day
Being locked inside darkness makes it easier to rest
With the overwhelming emptiness, heavy on my breast

Tonight I wait for the coming storm
So that my sorrow takes on a fleeting form
The murmurs of darkness filled with fear
The unknown won't find me here
Amongst the silver white branches of snow
The bright eyes of life won't show

And when the clouds have come and passed
The stars will show themselves at last
The moon will be full and bright
Glowing through the storm cloud night
Waiting here the fluid song ignites
The beating of my heart to take flight

Hollie Toms, Grade 11
Penetanguishene Secondary School, ON

Top Poem Grades 10-11-12

Garden of Stone

On a cold winter's night,
I lay my head to sleep.
I dreamt I walked a garden
To a nipping autumn breeze,

And on the ground were crested
The coloured leaves of elms.
And all around me loomed
A million and one gravestones.

Some were old and some were new
Of blue and marbled stone,
But on every one there could be read
A child's forgotten dream.

I bent my head and wept
When my eyes beheld the last,
A lovely, bright gravestone
Of an old familiar past.

For all at once I saw,
The name upon the grave,
Wondered how it could have been
That my dream should end this way.

Jennifer van den Bogerd, Grade 11
Home School, ON

Top Poem Grades 10-11-12

Love Beside the Mill Pond

On a cool clear night among the whisper of the leaves
I stood beside the mill pond, my thoughts wandering to the time when I first saw you
The moon sat high in the dark heavens casting its glittering glow on the waters of the pond
And the moonlight on the mill pond. The owl in the nearby tree
Watching closely as you snuck up behind me,
Taking my hands and making me fall into your dark eyes
Eyes darker than the heavens where the moon sat watching
I'd never seen you, yet I'd known you all my life
I stood beside the mill pond, soaking in the vision who had stepped out of my dreams
The moon sat high in the dark heavens watching our hearts smile, while jumping within our breasts
And the moonlight on the mill pond. Crickets singing in the grass a sweet lullaby of ever lasting love
As you took me into your heart; into your arms of shelter
Arms more warming than the soft sparkling glow of the moon
The guardians were enraged and refused to lend an ear
They gave me no chance to explain I saw behind the bad boy everyone took you for
The moon sat high in the dark heavens casting its mysterious glow down on the mixture
Of blonde and brunette as they were wed beside the mill pond

Kathy Waldner, Grade 10
Twilight Colony School, MB

Winter
Piles of snow block the road, many people are not in their joyous mode.
Until they see the beautiful flakes, that the clouds so delicately make.

It looks like icing sugar on desserts, but I know that it will hurt.
When I take a bite into that crunchy ice, there would be germs and it would not taste nice.

A snowman on my neighbor's lawn, if I were it, I would yawn.
All he does is stand right there, and have to deal with the freezing cold air.

When I come in from playing in the snow, my body seems to move quite slow.
When I get the warming hot apple cider, I get through that tuff rough radical rider.

When going down the hill, I feel like I am going 100 miles an hour, I lean my weight feeling like I have power,
Oh no! There came another bump! I immediately landed on my rump!

The winter will sadly come to an end,
But in the next season, I will see my best friend!

Lizette Gatlabayan, Grade 10
Holy Cross Regional High School, BC

Thoughts of the Past
Well there was this girl and this guy.
Everyone said that they made a cute couple, and she thought so too.
Even though there were other people in the room, he was all she could look at.
Did he know how she felt?
Did he feel the same way?

Years later, he's changed into someone she doesn't know any more and they have grown apart.
But no matter how far apart they are, he is still all she can look at.
Does he still think of her like she still thinks of him?
Sadness fills her heart as she sighs.
She knows that what once was will no longer and never will be again.
These are just thoughts of the past.

I don't know how you felt, but it was no mystery as to how I felt.
Everyone could see it, so why couldn't you?

Kaitlyn Bruce, Grade 12
Bishop Carroll High School, AB

Milky Way
Shall I compare you to the Milky Way?
You are more mysterious and unfathomable.
Your mystery colors and ribbons of dusty light are like the gateway to the great unknown beyond, a space which in this life we'll never know, but catch sparse glimpses of within the veil of sleep. Your influence is subtle, yet governs our destiny and thought from distant border realms of existence, whispering to us through light years and night years, iridescent pinwheels of white bright sound which soak the ears we use not in the day, but in the world of half awareness. Each night we sink into the vast depths of space, so cold and mournfully magnificent, and fall beyond the limits of comprehensible perception to a place where gravity is substituted by emotion, where we can tread the content of eons and transcend the watery deepness of the starry space. Yet in our time man has forgotten the unending potential of your gifts, the raw energy in your voice, which calls to us each night from beyond the curtain, as they have forgotten the power we can obtain from gazing into the light fields above our very eyes in the skies of ink-black nocturnal solitude.
But you who we call Dream, shall not fade so long as there's a place to go when eyelids start to fall, so long as there's a color and a light burning like a celestial chandelier in the sky for us to gaze upon and pass the time away until to those distant worlds where we repair to for the remaining eons of our time.

Nathaniel Hillaby, Grade 12
Vancouver Waldorf School, BC

Dream in the Dark

In a difficult position, nowhere to go,
unable to do something and able to do nothing
life looks at you on the downside,
you are now washing away in the tide.
Mother says get out and find a place.
Father says you're not good enough.
Acquaintances and friends look at you differently.
You don't talk to anyone deliberately.
You must be hated by all,
but that doesn't stop you.
You try every day to understand the world around you.
They say you're not going to make it,
You must follow your dream, no matter what,
even though you get stabbed in the back
by someone you may know.
It's time for that test.
It's time to give it your best shot.
You have a Dream in the Dark.

Alexander Kozlowski, Grade 11
St Marcellinus Secondary School, ON

I Once Called Her My Mother

The night life of her past
I see the pain that will forever last
Broken promises, hearts and tears
Her young children crying despaired in fear
The bitter taste of a soul, so empty
In a home so cold, frightened and lonely
She touched the face of a child once sad
Then her heart and see the life she once had
The smell of alcohol lingers those scarred memories
The smell of blood will always follow me
I am a scarecrow in a field alone
I am dead, scared, damaged and controlled
From a mother in a place I once called home

Natasha Longpre Nadeau, Grade 11
Collège catholique Franco-Ouest, ON

No Goodbyes

The time has come to leave this place behind
Inexpensive valuable paper
Sums up four past years, now future I'll find
Like baby bird's courageous departure

High school has been my relish, my retreat
My sanctuary where I am welcome
From the bus to the halls, and where I eat
Classroom, mentors; a magical freedom

When the sun is born again, I enter
Heavenly gates, floating on red carpet
Some ask how here I can be in rapture
Our colors are my pride as a poet

No goodbyes to this picture perfect place
It'll forever leave in my mind a trace

Brittany Lucky, Grade 11
Collège catholique Franco-Ouest, ON

Tear

I am crying
My lips quivering
My body aches

Sniffling,
Eyes watering
A tear escapes

Running down my cheek
Where it meets a dimple
Pressed against my skin

Continues its journey
To the corner of my lips
Curved upwards

I am not sad
Can you see?
The tears of joy

Because as sad as it is
That you're no longer here
I know you will always be with me

Sarah Paradis, Grade 10
École Secondaire Catholique Franco-Ouest, ON

Diving Blind

I haven't been that afraid since grade one.
When I stole crayons and the teacher caught me.

That time was guilt.
This time was fear.

But the same ice was in my veins.

This had something to do with pride,
But I know better now.

I should have walked away.
The cliff was too high,
And the water, a glassy eyed charlatan.

Hidden rocks.
            An undercurrent.
                        Shallows.

I dove blindly.

Next time,
I'll see.

Rose Karithanam, Grade 12
John Cabot Catholic Secondary School, ON

The Song That Feeds My Soul

This song fills me up
With infinite emotion
I cannot translate
Just experience the rush
Every way it turns
With every note, every word
My body and soul
Flow with the music
My breath starts to follow
The pattern of sounds
It seeps through my skin
And travels throughout
It reaches my heart
And explodes with sensation
My feelings are endless
All mixed up and crazy
Laughter and anger
Fear and longing
Fighting to keep back tears
It's wonderful.

Alex Friedman, Grade 10
Earl Haig Secondary School, ON

A Starry Night

The stars are a beautiful sight
what a pleasant night.
The clear blue skies
makes you want to die.
A nice night to take a walk.
To be with a friend and have a talk.
The stars make the sky bright.
It covers the darkness with some light.
Lying on the grass, to see
I hope my friends are with me.
This is what I live for
just to see more
of this beautiful sight,
on a summer night.

Cecile Ehman, Grade 10
Holy Cross Regional High School, BC

Time

Time, a force of nature,
leads us to our future.

You can't stop it;
you can't control it;
you can't see it;
yet you live in it.

So don't try to be a mime,
and stop wasting your time.
You might think you are someone,
but time waits for no one.

Shayne Li, Grade 10
College Prep International, QC

Together Forever

I know I've done something which is wrong
And we haven't talked about the situation in so long
We need to come to a conclusion about this
So I can feel your famous kiss
I'm the one that did the wrong thing
Just please don't take off that wedding ring
All we need right now is time
And I'm sure everything will be fine
I haven't seen you in almost 10 days
So all I can do now is clasp my hands and pray
I promise you, I'm done with all the lying
This is killing me inside, and I feel like dying
I've been here trying to call
And all you do is try to shut me out and make me fall
But you can't get me out of your life
You know that because I'm your wife
I'm not giving up on the future we were supposed to have together
Remember? You were supposed to be mine forever

Sonia Sheechoria, Grade 10
Ascension of Our Lord Secondary School, ON

Sending Love

It rains on me, blunt needles exploding into tiny crystals, shattering
with minimal sound, shimmering shimmering until they fall into puddles.
The waters are angry dark and roiling, clawing at the cliffs
of Dover, so white like a pontiff's robe so holy, found only in an abbey.

The winds are whistling, high and low they go, I stand my ground and breathe
inspire, expire, I unsheathe all that's in me into the flow.
I sing out to you, and I hope you hear across the strait, across the continent,
across the ocean and the stringent turrets by the beach, lovely Seer.

When you hear my song, encase it in a jar
and throw it afar, to where the winds are strong.
Then shall it come back to me, and I'll catch it with my hand
and bury it in the sand when the sun smiles down idly.

Twila Marie Amato, Grade 11
Sir Charles Tupper Secondary School, BC

Beauty and the Beast

I know I am doomed to wander alone for all eternity,
so why is it this charming girl declares she's in love with me.

She is so young, what would she know about the life she'd have to live.
I am too old, have no money, nothing but trouble can I give.

For I'm a creature of nightmares altered by the full moons pure light;
the beast harbors a strong blood lust which the man has no strength left to fight.

She does not think of dangers, she cannot even comprehend,
miserable is what she'd be, and she'd regret it in the end.

Sadly, I must push her away, though I see she hurts when I do,
but the thing that hurts most of all, is that I'm in love with her too.

Kyla Konecny, Grade 10
Mother Teresa Catholic Secondary School, ON

Hidden Release

I could write page after endless page
With the bleeding ink of this pen
This robotic hand flying over a sheet of nothing
Fallen words on the page, fallen from a mindless soul

Hidden underneath the scratches
Hidden underneath the spidery scrawls
Hidden underneath the entrancing curves

Roars the "truth"
Unraveling sweet confessions
Scripted are the words of a grateful heart
Not a blemishing "lie"
Rotting the perfection of my passionate release
Sinning this truly purified peace

Here descends words of serenity
Here descends words of dominance
Here descends words of corruption

As I sit at the window of my thoughts
Looking through the shattered glass, motivating inspiration
While paying heed to the lifeless clock
I could write page after endless page

Sultana Majid, Grade 12
Lester B Pearson Sr High School, AB

My Life as Rain

Life starts as a cloud,
With only the slightest intention to rain
The first drop is the first year
New and exciting with a sweet fresh scent
Then another drop falls
Then another
And another
Soon the memories of drizzle have disappeared
Replaced with a beautiful, powerful storm
But the storm soon softens
And treads lightly on the Earth
Giving life to flowers, trees, puddles
The rain gives life, and in return
The life gives meaning
But the rain cannot last forever
It slows
It weakens
It rusts
It filters off into nothingness, and eventually comes to an end
But the rain will forever be remembered
Through the life it has created.

Liana Curell Thorstenson, Grade 12
Merritt Secondary School, BC

together

they had a wonderful life
they had many kids
they lived in a beautiful house
they loved each other more than everything
now, they are lying in their bed
old and tired
love and soul,
walking slowly to heaven
forever and ever
together

Emy Brindle, Grade 10
Seminaire de Sherbrooke, QC

Time

Time is our most precious bequest
Moments spent before we lay to rest,
Time is our period of triumph and strife
As we make the journey that we call life.

Time is made up of elapsing seconds
A chance to explore our planet that beckons,
During which we will cry, laugh and share
As well as love, hope and care.

Life is like an irreversible hourglass
Time will never cease to pass,
What we can control is how it is spent
As we never know how much we were lent.

So instead of staring at the ceiling above
Spend time doing something you love,
So that when you finally reach Death's day
You would never want to have spent it any other way.

Alexandra Markus, Grade 12
Marianopolis College School, QC

New Year

New Year is the day not like other days
It is the time when the earth dress by the snow
When the river stops flowing
When the sun hides by the clouds
It is a day for peace, fun and love
It is time for celebration of one year left
And New Year comes with hope of better life
I love to see smiles on the faces of all people
Waiting for the sun to rise again
Waiting for the river to flow and the ground to be green again
The birds sing happy New Year, happy new life
Looking for the peace and happy for all people
I invite all kids all over the word to sing
For peace and love
Life is so short
No place for war and hate
Stop to destroy our dreams
Try to build a beautiful future
This is my hope, my dream, my message of New Year

Ahmad Abd al Hadi, Grade 12
Hillcrest High School, ON

Holy Cross

H ome to the Crusaders
O f much diversity
L oving atmosphere
Y oung people with potential

C ATHOLICS! Tournament
R ed and white
O pens doors for us
S ports teams and clubs
S chool spirit!

Hailey Olson, Grade 10
Holy Cross Regional High School, BC

Caged Hearts

My heart flutters when you walk by
Each beat strains towards you
I make it a caged bird
And clutch it close to my breast
I'm on an emotional high
I can't seem to get enough
Every glance is stolen
And my mind is at unrest
It chastens my poor heart
Every time it goes back
I try and reason you away
You have more important things
Than a young girl's hold
I'm a distraction
And every time
I try to talk
I fail
And yet each glance is a rush
Each word arouses a small hope
That maybe it's more than a frail heart
And a silly crush

Kara Wheat, Grade 12
Northern BC Distance Education, BC

Search

It is the dark of night
The moon is hidden
In the black-ridden world
A loneliness I dwell in

Joy give way to anger, despair
From tonight shall I be
Apathetic in my life
Callous in my heart

Emptiness is the emotion
Against time's running sand

Awaiting freedom from desolation
How can I feel fulfilled again?

Mujtaba Khan, Grade 10
College Prep International, QC

Will She Ever Understand Why?

She enters the school; why couldn't it have come sooner?
Surrounded she is by people too oblivious to notice.
Not wanting to be lonely she makes a friend or two.
Will she ever be cool?
Her mind is racing but she doesn't understand why.

She enters the party; why hasn't anyone taken note?
Surrounded she is by people too drunk to care.
Not wanting to be unseen she has a drink or two.
Will she ever be noticed?
Her head is spinning but she doesn't understand why.

She enters the bedroom; why hasn't he come?
Surrounded she is by people too infatuated to bother.
Not wanting to be lonely she kisses a man or two.
Will she ever be loved?
Her heart is breaking but she doesn't understand why.

She leaves all the insanity; why didn't she leave quicker?
Surrounded she is by people who want her to change.
Not wanting to go back to her old ways, she stays for a day or two.
Will she ever be normal again?
Her body is healing and she understands why.

Valerie Laplante, Grade 12
Glenforest Secondary School, ON

Finding Reality

One single frozen tear breaks free
And trickles icily down my cheek
But I turn away to hide it from the rest of the world
Not a single soul should see me crying
Sometimes sadness has to be kept a secret untold like lies
Sometimes love and sadness are the same
Just like pain and happiness
Facing reality I move on

The partly cloudy day turns into an overcast sky
With colder winds stirring
I can feel winter crawling up my spine
Its icy fingers sliding over my neck and shoulders
The wind is blowing harder
The sky is looking bruised and angry reflecting my mood
I can feel the cold rain threatening to shower down on my misery

Not regretting anything I'm moving on forgetting the past
Hopefully seeing my future clearly
Healing I can beat this cruel unforgiving world
But maybe for now I will try and find my inner soul
Finding who I truly am
Finding reality

Amanda Gadwa, Grade 10
Kehewin Community Education Centre, AB

Ink

Black ink is the language of the soul
it speaks to me and whispers in my ear at night
it runs a marathon through my open veins
and pulses in the unsteady chambers of my heart
the only real voice, when you take the time to listen.
It is mutual understanding
and unknowing mystery.
it is hello; it is goodbye.
Black ink is the blanket of the sky
home of the stars, canvas of the moon.
It is the portal to all places,
the clarity and the fog.
It is the sheen on my piano
the music in my notes.
It is universally recognized
but what nobody can see,
is that it is so often written on black paper.

Kristi Kwan, Grade 10
St Robert Catholic High School, ON

Paranoid

Paranoid
Close my eyes, and pretend not to hear
I try to keep my thoughts away,
The noises and feelings I can't bear,
There's not a word I can say.

It brings out an uneasy darkness
And you wish you couldn't feel the cold,
You open one eye and clench a fist,
Trying your hardest to become bold.

It is the one that you hate
Breathing heavily, gasping for air
Thinking that it's too late,
Calling for help, no one's there.

You cry a silent scream, and say goodbye,
You slowly and painfully, wither away and die.

Sarita Singh, Grade 11
Ascension of Our Lord Secondary School, ON

Diamond Gold

Last inning, they get two runs and we fail,
My team heads out to the field, I'm pitching.
A first batter comes up, it's a huge male.
Focusing on my target, deep breathing,
Swing my arm forward, surrendering the ball.
Three strikes twice, one more left, what pitch to choose.
Getting hit so far, will it ever fall?
Over fielders, home run, one more to lose.
Ball passed to me, and I try once more.
Bases loaded, it's now the final catch
But it's hit straight at me, I throw to four.
The catcher catches it, we win the match.
Hugs, high-fives, cheering, we run together.
Winning gold, we'll remember forever!

Stéphanie Goguen, Grade 11
Collège catholique Franco-Ouest, ON

The Rose

I am a rose, colder than death,
but I still save my last breath.
I sit here day after day…
waiting for something, but nothing to say.

These petals that I carry are weak, dry, and weary.
I am running out of time, what can I do?
I am tired of thinking, can someone send me a clue?
I feel old and heavy
as the petals crack off my body.
I am dying, can't you see?
Please…please set me free.
As I slowly wither, I start to ponder
about what I could have done to make my life fonder.

But wait…can it be?
A sign from God who planted this seed
that sits beside me?
This seed that lies here inspires me and it is clear
that I don't have to fear,
a friend is near.

Rebecca Laurenti, Grade 10
École Secondaire Catholique Franco-Ouest, ON

Melting Mirror

Sniffing glass
A field of burning grass
I fall back
Into a melting mirror

With every breath
I come closer to death
In this cold limbo
I watch myself drown

Ashes pour from my eyes
And screams turn into sighs
I am the victim
Of my own idiocy

I reach out my hand
As my throat turns to sand
But touch
Only my own fingers

Snorting glass
Smoking burnt black grass
Fade to black
In this melting mirror

Kevin O'Leary, Grade 12
John Cabot Catholic Secondary School, ON

You Are My Tree

Her roots stretch out grasping the limited rich soil,
while winding around rocks, sand, and gravel to secure a firm foundation.
Her bark, branded with memories left by the numerous elements, cover her soft interior.
Her leaves are plump and vibrant
as they absorb all the joyous rays of sunlight
that blesses her brow.

The rain begins to drip onto her supple leaves and down her mighty trunk.
Thunder and lightning swiftly rolls in striking the sky above
followed by the envious wind,
who threatens her strength.

That is when she is ever thankful for her foundation of experience.
She grows and endures through these troubles and pleasures
for a single immeasurable purpose.

She stands tall to acquire the necessities and knowledge,
to be strong enough for her seedlings so they may rely on her for:
shade, shelter, support, supplement, sunlight and surpassing love.

You are my tree
and I am your seedling.
I grow
because of You.

Dezirae Beck, Grade 12
Holy Cross Regional High School, BC

One Man Can Make a Difference

In a country far away, people lived in constant fray
With people so forlorn, a baby boy was born.
He started to see, problems in his country
He decided he would be the one, to see the problems were overcome
He started small, and moved till he conquered them all.
With his determination of success, soon problems were addressed.
His deed praised across the land, soon people began to understand.
One day he called his people together, towards him they all gathered.
He stood before them and said, "What will happen when I am dead?"
What makes me the right person to lead, my actions or my deeds?
You call me a hero, when I die will you be zero?
Is a hero formed through some change of body and soul,
Or someone who strives to achieve their goals?
What makes a hero I ask you now, their deeds, or sweat upon their brow?
So when I am gone, will my work go undone,
No — you must be the ones.
There is a hero in all of you, you cannot defy, you must be ready to spread your wings and fly
Find the heroes within yourself, and the work will finish itself.
Soon the people took charge, the difference was very large.
The young boy had taught them all, that a hero was someone who refused to fall.
The spirit has a strong influence, it just takes one man to make a difference.

Rehaan Khan, Grade 10
Delphi Secondary Alternative School, ON

Prison

My life is a test
A courtroom open to the public
Where I am judged on all I do
Expectations keep me behind bars
And disappointment locks my chains

I am an animal in the zoo
People come and stare
They tease and poke and shout all day
I have no escape from their sneers
Except to crawl inside myself and hide

My life is an open book
With chapters of fear and pain
Searching hands rip through the pages
Blotting ink and smearing words
Criticism leaves empty spaces
And tears smudge my lamentations

Life is everyone for themselves
No one cares for how others feel
Friends turn their backs
Enemies block all escape
I'm alone in this prison called life

Analea Styles, Grade 11
Abbotsford Traditional Secondary School, BC

Nature's Empathetic Greeting

When the sun lumbers out from the cold,
its magnificence alarms the world to enter a meditative state.
The sun has exhausted and aged old,
and it has caused our thoughts to deflate.
Flowers become bolted doves as they ascend,
their wings spread and flutter in a live tableau.
They shall never leave the soil and transcend,
for all they can do is grow and grow.
Rain streams through the sky,
with a gentle contort from a cloud.
Though the cirrus giants are shy,
their priority shall always be to shroud.
The ocean is both abundant and pure,
in its proficiency, does its best to cleanse the land.
Though no one is attracted to its allure,
forever, alone, it will stand.
Air weeps for and through us,
and remarkably achieves distant contact.
However, air is too ominous,
and must be forcefully held back.
The weather commiserates us in a myriad of opportunities.

Josh Wood, Grade 12
Port Hardy Secondary School, BC

Life Hides as the Sun Says Its Adieu

Life hides as the sun says its adieu;
Trees grow bald and their fallen hair wrinkles
Under the feet of critters, scampering away.
The world becomes a barren tundra,
A white desert with a gray backdrop.

Nature has closed its eyes for slumber
Yet bares its brittle fangs;
Water refuses to flow but waxes the ground.
The world becomes encased in an eternal shiver,
And solid tears fall with a yearning for the sun.

Sarah Gong, Grade 12
Gordon Graydon Memorial Secondary School, ON

Pressure

Sometimes my life is just too much to handle,
And I feel myself dripping, like wax from a candle.
Dripping and flipping and slipping away
Anything to be far from where I am prey
To hunters like parents and teachers and friends,
Cliques and homework and friendships I can't mend.
So away I slip, quietly and reserved,
Hoping no one will notice, hoping I'm not heard.
And I tuck away my smile, my laugh and my light,
So that my body is vacant 'cause it simply can't fight
Against all the pressure to be the best it can be,
It gives up because it can never be skinny,
Or smart or beautiful or cleaver enough
To measure up to those who don't have it so tough.
But until I am perfect like the people on TV,
I will continue to wage this war against me.

Alexandra Gregory, Grade 12
St Joseph School, AB

Light Breaking Through

I'm trapped in the unlit part of my mind;
I cannot think,
And I do not know what to do.
I feel lost,
Searching for a way out of this labyrinth.
Crying and calling out for help,
Hearing nothing but the savage beating of my heart.
It is bitterly cold,
And I'm benumbed;
The loneliness slowly creeping onto me.
Suddenly, Light;
Breaking through the gloomy darkness,
Appears before me.
A hand;
Stretched out for me;
Heat radiating from it,
Warming me and giving me my life back.
A voice;
Pleasantly disturbing the silence
Whispers
"Don't worry, I'm here."

Bashar Abdallah, Grade 10
College Prep International, QC

Flux

Like the ocean tides
You never could stay at home
Forever roaming
Nicole De Schutter, Grade 10
Holy Cross Regional High School, BC

Purgatory

The silver bird flies
Unhindered
Across the golden stars,
Cold frosted upon its white wings —
Held up by crimson-stained chains
Rooted to the darkened sky
Where its silvery reflection mocks it.

Alone within a world of snow:
A halo of decadence surrounds it;
Perdition burning through the air;
A rusted cross lying
Within a circle of broken light,
Illuminated.
A ring of lilies nearby.

Softly descending into insanity
Where demons await its arrival.
The gates to heaven are frigid;
Banished it is towards a frozen hell.
The jagged crystal calls beckoningly,
Seeking the pieces of its shattered heart
Forever.
Cindy Loo, Grade 12
Webber Academy, AB

Where Are You?

Where are you?
Or, where am I?
As a part was lost,
When I said goodbye.

So, where am I?
A zephyr on the Azure?
A Leveche through Gibraltar?
All I know is that I am not here.

When you passed, what did you
become?
A celestial shard of infinite beauty?
Or, maybe caught in nonexistence
That only the dead can see.

Death is not the end.
If only our time had passed less rapid
I might have known you better.
And that is all I ever wanted.
Chris Masternak, Grade 12
Webber Academy, AB

Hallway Warfare

Alone in the hallway, quiet for the first time
Faint sounds of learning heard through closed doors
Shut off from the inside world, the connecting hallway is a peaceful border
Keeping the worlds apart until it's time
Collecting my thoughts my mind knows no boundaries
While they learn math science and history
My mind wanders as I unravel the mystery of the world
The bell rings like a siren alerting the troops
Filing out creating complete chaos
Like a bullet through my chest my mind is put to rest
And I file in line with the uniformed soldiers
Following orders
Until the next time I desert this war
Brandon Macpherson, Grade 12
Crescent School, ON

candle life*

it was lit like a candle, the life you were given,
with concealed intentions, that remain hidden.
as the candle's flame glows, the clock ticks time away,
and the thread slowly burns, as the wax melts into the tray.
keeping the fire alive is a great task,
feeding it with oxygen, hoping it'll timelessly last.
one moment the flame looks like forever it'll survive
but a simple breath can end the spark and there goes the light.
recreating the thread is not possible, the chemical reaction has been done.
thus live each day as your last for tomorrow may never come,
choose your words and actions wisely, life has no reruns.
"Tomorrow may be your last day, don't let your candlelight fire get blown away."
Patricia Saad, Grade 10
École secondaire catholique Renaissance, ON
*Inspired by my sister Léa and Trooper Marc Diab (1986-2009).

How to Conquer a Snowstorm

Cruising on the highway
when madness occurs; the sky has a temper tantrum
and stiff, sticky snow starts to dispense.
Cannot see more than two meters ahead
therefore decrease speed of vulnerable vehicle
and switch to four wheel drive.
Move carefully, slow as a turtle.
Activate the newly installed window wipers
on high speed.
Subsequently, set heat control to defrost the foggy windows.
Turning on the helpful high beam will not do any good;
snowflakes will only shine brighter
in the pitch black darkness, like looking straight at the sun,
blinding the driver.
Pull over to the side of the road;
it is the logical thing to do,
for there are no other travelers daring to pass by.
As a snow plough strolls closer, clearing the trail,
play follow the leader, keeping a fair amount of distance behind it,
as if it is a mentor, until destination is reached.
Simren Hara, Grade 12
Merritt Secondary School, BC

Sometimes

Sometimes I have a sleepless night.
I toss and turn
with thoughts racing

Sometimes I wonder.
I question terrible things
that perhaps, the answer is best left unknown

Sometimes I go insane.
Living things within
that vex me till I let go

Sometimes I am honest.
I know the truth
harmful or not

I hate the nights
Where sometimes happen
reality crashing down.

AlexAndria Douglas, Grade 10
Melfort & Unit Comprehensive Collegiate Institute, SK

Enmity

Associates upon learning grounds,
In ev'ry class brought them captured moments
and crumbs of time still delivered shared sounds.
Spilled ink, so toxic, came and formed a dent.

His words meeting her ear in a grand blur,
thoughts of slipping away left her quelling.
Those unreal sensations made her unsure
and these empty hallways left her running.

Nile's flowed from her eyes and down her round cheeks.
With the lust lost, in came the bitterness,
thinking so anxiously this could last weeks,
but shattered glass came with no happiness.

Battling against fading ecstasy,
hosting her ultimate enmity.

Marie-France Langlois, Grade 11
Collège catholique Franco-Ouest, ON

War

I don't understand
    Why governments can't agree
    Why some people are afraid of differences
    How some people sleep at night

But most of all
    Why they dropped the A-bomb twice
    Why $E=mc^2$

What I understand most is
    Why some wounds don't heal
    Why war drives men mad

John Bass, Grade 10
Seminaire de Sherbrooke, QC

Being a Princess

I am a princess,
It's not as pleasant as it seems,
Take it from the person,
Who has been ruling since half past three:

My throne is a toilette,
My court is the smell,
My country is the sewer,
And my idea is the swell,

First step in my plan,
Is to get a fan,
The second it would be nice,
Is to find some sort of device,
To clean up all the mess,
That my country gave me to address,
And the third in my idea,
Is to apply a little less onomatopoeia.

How will I do it?
I don't even know!
But I'll solve all the problems,
As I go.

Christina Berti, Grade 10
Villa Maria High School, QC

Received a Ring But Lost a Finger

Don't cry my dear, thy finger has gone.
A story of lust, the beginning of dawn.

Had it not started, with a simple request.
Marks of beauty, shattered by guests.
Embracing the floor, once dance of the night.
When ye gave me thy hand, the story took flight.

Lustering smiles, my thorns take the lead,
Growing too fast, each pierce do they bleed.
Three bells of horror, as we walk down the aisle,
Stiffen our backs, hold for a while.

Gentle kiss, the room says farewell,
A ring past my grasp, hearts begin to dwell.
Not a story, or either a book,
A moral nor lesson, but a past that had shook.

Say goodbye, once again it is dawn,
An exchange for a ring, but thy finger has gone.
For it has ended my love, a sorrowless shrine,
Next for a head, a bride which is mine.

Amani Barrie, Grade 10
Islamic Foundation School, ON

Always Another

For every one smile there's 100 tears nobody knows about
For every 10 good situations there's always one more terrible unheard about
For every problem you think just couldn't become any worse in your life
Someone had overcame the unthinkable and survived through it twice
For every thought that you wished there was something you would have said
Were the words that another wishes their words never would have been spoken outside their head

Jessica Gordon, Grade 11
Dartmouth High School, NS

Perfect Stillness

As I inhale a large gasp of the warm air of my bedroom, and release a heavy breath,
There is nothing even mildly comparable to the tranquility I feel now.

My fingers run across the tiny beads of truth,
Of compassion, of suffering.
My voice reciting the words of the Virgin,
The expression of her utmost affection for her Son.

Each repetition is an adventure;
A deeper insight into the comprehension of His mystery,
Witnessing to her prevailing love and dedication to the Father.

Every decade amounts to ten years worth of knowledge,
Consequently growing in abiding faith.
The serenity is overwhelming, but I am blissful as I become consumed by the perfect stillness.

I release the miniscule ivory pearls that are so flawlessly intertwined within my fingers,
Lingering on the shape of His crucifix.
I have completed the journey of the rosary, and I am completely at peace.

Abby Zaporteza, Grade 10
Holy Cross Regional High School, BC

Fanatical

These words will never sleep.
They are active running through my mind, like a dictionary out of control.
They swirl through the air, testing frigid waters of unknown fantasies.
Flying by and flying high.

With the unfurling of fantasies that never leave the recesses of my mind,
They capture my last breath of air, as I chase away the sheep of sleep.
Running paces as the night hits high, dancing out of my control.

Sweet relief from weights on my mind lifts my soul on high, I smell of austere air.
I wish these words were in my control, as I lose my wits in sleep.

In fanatical worlds of unwritten fantasies redundancies are out of my control,
And in the liberation of my mind these words are one with the sheer air.
As the dreams of dreamers go to sleep, and through the picturesque fantasies that send the expectancies high.

I crave a better peace of mind that will float my soul on air, and send me up higher than high.
In worlds where wake exists through sleep, and sends me back into control like my unwritten fantasies.

Time to wake from this sleep, I say awake.
On high I stand, awaiting my mind to find, fantasies of untold riches spinning out of control, in the air.

Danelle Scharringa, Grade 11
Oxford Reformed Christian School, ON

Mistakes Happen

Mistakes happen, that's a part of life
It's when we acknowledge it that makes the difference
And learn from it as if it were nutrition
We can't let it be the reason we fall
We need to stand tall and take back the ball
That was originally in our court
Mistakes should be seen as our support
For making us stronger
So we could deal with conflicts longer
Rather than accepting defeat and giving into our minds
We've got to become the soul and have faith in time
Have hope that we will one day become mature
And not have to face the same mistake again
Not having to deal with the same pain by then
Because we'll be on another level
And marvel at the fact that we ever made such a mistake
We need to realize that it's all innate
We're not meant to be perfect
But we are given the ability to correct it
Mistakes happen, but so do achievements
It's all apart of life; dealing with God and demons

Pooja Jaiswal, Grade 12
St Francis Xavier Secondary School, ON

Love

Love is warm, yet cold.
Love is fierce, but bold.
Love mends broken hearts together,
Yet causes us to feel under the weather.

Love is a passion felt from deep inside,
A feeling that many of us try to hide.
Love has the ability to lock us down,
And some may even say it has the ability to drown.
Love has the fascinating power to save,
And requires for those who endure it to be brave.

Love is for both the young and old,
And is described to be more precious than gold.

Love is a creation
That requires determination.
It is like an equation
That may cause humiliation,
But it is not a delusion,
And has no easy solution.

In the end love can make you feel complete
In a world where hate can make one feel obsolete.

Peter Kahama, Grade 10
King's Christian Collegiate, ON

You'll Be Missed

I saw her today,
Lying there so peacefully.
Her head laying on a soft pillow;
Her hands folded neatly
On top of a flowing white gown,
Looking so peaceful, floating on the clouds.
She was there,
Then gone in a flash,
Leaving a husband,
A newborn child,
And an amazing family behind her.
Instant tears from all,
Realizing she's really gone.
The tears that still flow today,
And will flow forever
So sudden,
So tragic,
And so unfair
Blossom in heaven…

Jaime Curtis, Grade 12
West Country Outreach School, AB

Hatred

Shall I compare thee to a devilish storm?
Thou seemest far more violent and unforgiving.
If hearts can fill with fire's form
Then in thine eyes they're living.
Black clouds encase your soul,
You spit cyanide and spite,
I hear destruction's church bell toll,
And you have stolen my sight.
Yet you who we call hatred shall never hope to fade,
As man is man and beast,
And I am at thou's aid,
So long as man must blunder,
Continually refuse to see,
So long lives this and pain
And both give life to thee.

Ceara Boyer, Grade 12
Vancouver Waldorf School, BC

Change

Many living in the cold street,
No family, no shelter, no food to eat.
We have no memories from the past,
We live each day as if it were our last.

Police chasing the troubled everywhere,
Men killing men with no care.
A baby is found with no parent around,
Her cries are only just a sound.

The world has become such a different place,
With no regard for human race.
My homeless life has become very strange,
So keep your coins, I want change.

Eric Colobong, Grade 10
Holy Cross Regional High School, BC

Shattered

Crystal clear
Delicate as a flower
Precious as a diamond

A previous friend
Able to read me like
An open book

Nothing but a pool of darkness
I let myself fall into

A victim to it's web of lies

"Too big"
"Hideous"
"Pretty ugly"
"Too thin"

Trapped, isolated.

Willing to risk seven years of bad luck
For freedom
No longer bound to nothing but mere
Shattered glass

Tiffany Wong, Grade 10
Little Flower Academy, BC

Fight

Tempers flared
Voices raised
Punches thrown
Bruises formed
Open wounds
Panting breaths
Dripping blood
Regretted actions
Sorrowful tears
Heavy hearts
Apologies exchanged

Michelle Truong, Grade 10
McNally Sr High School, AB

One Tough Problem After Another

the road goes upwards
conversation stops, puff, pant
the silence of hills

close eyes and focus
mustn't let burning legs stop
finally, the peak

downhill bicycling
forty, fifty miles per hour
should have fixed my brakes

Keiji Nakatsugawa, Grade 11
College Prep International, QC

A Whisper from the Heart

I gave you all I had to offer, but even you couldn't see that.
So then, I forgot to mention
There was another before our correlation
You had no idea how much I felt his connection
Like, for instance, I did not need to be in any relation
Because I fell short of my own insecurity, I apologized and reaccepted
Now, I would say we'd contradicted
By forgetting myself I became what you hunted
And I honestly admit that it was a fine visage to be wanted
But even that came to a level I could no longer stand —
I've learned that you could never be satisfied with what you had
And so you left, saying you had "to do this, to be free"
And not long after that, there was She.
Tired of the waiting, tired of the aching,
I'd appreciate it if you would do some of the begging.
No, actually, I reprimand that,
You had (at one of our points) wanted me back
Your reason for retrieving:
You had to be the one leaving.
Had I listened to my heart, it would never been broken
But then again, this experience would not have brought out a woman.

Regilyn Chudyk, Grade 12
Holy Cross Regional High School, BC

She Was Water

Her hair, like red streaks of wind in a painting
lifted the water of her body into a powerful cascade
Yet she was of the nimblest sort
Translucent, as she would pour herself into the shape of a glass
I could drink her
In want of her to float in the quay of my stomach

But she would surge all through my arms, neck, breasts and spine
Tearing my veins apart for their heat
to boil herself into a sort of liquor

My blood diluted with alcohol becomes a still stream
And then she is lifted, like a tidal wave
With red streaks of wind in a painting
out of me
The tide of her tugs at my limp body with her ocean fingers

She draws me into her embrace,
Bathing me in her affection as she cradles me in her arms
But quickly I drown in the cataclysm of her potency
I wither away into pieces
Drifting through her, like the fins and gills of a torn fish
And the entire time I thought I had her
She really had me

Annu Bangar, Grade 12
W J Mouat Secondary School, BC

To Flip Through Her Pages

The sky is red from the sun's great light,
The pages flip through a midsummer night.
Her voice, it calls from within,
Her branches sway on the wind.
Soft footfalls are heard in the castle's keep,
And cries of agony and torment from the dungeons deep.
Men from afar come ponder her words,
Though none comprehend what they have heard.
She is lost within the city's people.
Only some know what she used to be.
Adventure and perils are her fortes,
Knowledge and wisdom are what she portrays.
Great men and women are bound to her pages,
Where they stay to inspire the young from all ages.
They take you away into the night,
Where brave knights come fight for their right.
Fair maidens atop the castle's wall,
Dance freely below in the great hall.
To turn her pages, you must be willing to let go,
To dance, to sing, to ride through her adventure.

Katherine Luyten, Grade 10
Holy Cross Regional High School, BC

Persistence of Memory

Time: unchanging event
that is never late
each soul it takes
after a few thousand wakes.
For I dare
someone to take
Time's last wake
  Persistence of Memory
   left the world
    with melted faces
     lack paces
      and the rest is left
       alone

Spencer Mathurin-Ricks, Grade 12
Applewood Heights Secondary School, ON

Life

Life is like a car.
Brain working like an ECU system,
Telling the parts what to do.
Engine working to provide power,
Just as our lungs and heart do.
Everything working in perfect coordination,
Performing each and every task asked.
Replacing tires as the humans do their shoes,
Keeping it upright and balanced.
Engine burning the fossil fuel for energy,
Like the body digests and burns its food.
Life is like a car in so many ways,
Maybe that's why we name them.

Derek Webster-Dinney, Grade 11
Westcliffe Composite School, SK

For You Daddy

I wasn't perfect, but neither were you
You had high expectations
Whereas I only asked for a hug and a kind word
Once in a very long while
So when you hurt me the way you did
When instead of a warm embrace
I got a cold word and a painful slap in the face
I ran, ran from your anger, from you

You're forgiven though Daddy, for all your mistakes
Because you've suffered enough for me
I've put you through a lot
Sorry for not being the child you wanted me to be
But I am your little girl
I always have been, and I know that
You're still the man that never left my side
The lion that has protected me my entire life

So come back home Daddy
The place that you were never supposed to leave
I'm still waiting for the hugs you've withheld
The words you've never had the courage to say
Come back and be the father I've always wanted you to be

Sarah Shahid, Grade 12
Glenforest Secondary School, ON

Between the Crowds

I see you and you see me,
It's been a while you see,
but I cannot help but be regretful of the day,
that I pushed you away,
not knowing any other way.

You see nobody has ever made me feel this way,
And I believe this each and every day.
Leaving such a footprint on my heart,
You will remain in a very special part.

When you look me in the eyes,
I realize they say no lies.
Every day I wish that I could say,
thanks to you,
I push everyone else away,
Waiting for something that will never come.

No matter what happens,
In a long time from now,
I promise that when I look upon a star,
I will remember exactly who you are.

Alyssa Castracane, Grade 10
Heritage Regional High School, QC

The Future
We should be thinking about the future
Teach our children to love
Teach them many languages
So that they may live together, up high
We'll see how life goes
Try to make it better for the future
At first it might look like a show
In the end it will be all good
Arshia Hirbod, Grade 11
College Prep International, QC

Morning
Sunrise,
The yellows, oranges and pinks,
Glowing on the horizon.
The perfect start,
To a new day.

Mountains and trees are colourless.
Gloomy,
And yet elegant.

Stars are fading.
High up above.
Clouds are looming,
In the graceful sky.
Josh Drake, Grade 10
Holy Cross Regional High School, BC

Your Inner Winner's "Circle"
Intangible, yet clearly seen
This stain of fame is always clean
Both malleable, yet rough and mean
It sings a tune to fight to

Immeasurable, yet still you hold
This circle can't be bought or sold
You fight, you sweat, you bleed for gold
And soon it grows within you

Unbreakable, yet prone to shrink
This circle's shaped by how you think
Your brain will dictate if you'll sink
While actions cause a breakthrough

Unmovable, yet seems to spread
Your circle is forever read
This circle even holds the dead
For time can't take its virtue

Un-killable in every way
Each circle burns with things to say
So hear its praises every day
And watch success surround you
Ubong Umoh, Grade 11
Oakridge Secondary School, ON

Beast of Metal
Oh Beast of Metal
Why have you given me, a desire to ride upon you?
As I wait my turn in line, butterflies arise and flutter — trying to come out of me.
As I come closer and closer, the hairs on my neck stand up — proof that I am afraid.
It's finally my turn.
No use turning back now.
I sink into the seat, thinking why am I doing this?
The seat belt straps me in — I'm paralyzed with terror.
Then the beast moves on its metal track.
It swoops, curves, turns, drops, and my heart halts to a stop.
Then I noticed the ride was put to an end.
So was my fear.
Paulina Laszkiewicz, Grade 10
Ascension of Our Lord Secondary School, ON

Without Saying Goodbye
You leave without saying goodbye.
Confusion and sadness rips through me as I search for you.
You are no where to be found and tears creep up to my eyes.
They stream down my face like a river in a storm.

You leave without saying goodbye.
Despair rips me to the core as I realize you are gone.
The perplexity makes my nerves freeze, leaving me still.
I have hope, but the suspicion that you are gone overrules.

You leave without saying goodbye.
Here I thought you cared, or maybe you care just that much.
My last strain of tolerance leaves me, anger is released.
You could have put the effort to say it, but you left without saying goodbye.
Stephanie Marsh, Grade 10
John Rennie High School, QC

Mortality
Two entities float above the stars
Higher than order, higher than time
One the embodiment of an ideal
The other the envisionment of a god
Destiny dictates they shall fight a winner-take-all battle
And the world watches with bated breath

Underneath it all however, they are both mere mortals
Subject to weakness and human emotion
And even though they know they are meant to be enemies
They are drawn to one another
So, when the sun sets and the world sleeps, they silently bind themselves to each other
Desperately hoping destiny is wrong

The earth continues to spin but its people stand still
As the epic battle before them continues on
And they take bets on which shall be the one to fall
While within the world of the two "enemies"
They stare into each other's eyes, hearts, souls
As they pray with all their strength that neither will have to
Emily Middlestead, Grade 11
John Taylor Collegiate School, MB

Control

To all who decide that life is confusing
that it is out of our grasp
no control fears that time
will not be kind to this weathered facade
these so called "damaged goods"
maybe religion is the answer
a chance to believe
a chance for us to feel like we have some sort of
control
but then again we don't
life is an untamable stallion
who runs by his own will
he will not stop for anybody
he will not stop for anything
he will simply continue
like this untamable stallion
nicknamed "life" so is religion in vain?
a cheap attempt at an easy existence
with the idea that if it is in someone else's hands
the pressure to succeed fades
like time until eventually we forget how to dream

Daniel Friedland, Grade 10
Earl Haig Secondary School, ON

The Shelter We Build

When it rains, it pours,
bringing woe to this small town,
and with the rain comes truth and lies,
that spread turmoil around.

Among the pain and heartache,
lies a poor and helpless child,
who's trodden dreams and hopeless screams,
have turned her young heart mild.

Each and every single drop,
marks the shattering of a dream,
crushed hopes, lives lost, upheaval true,
devastating, as it seems.

As the secrets surface,
and the chaos is engaged,
the failed attempt to mask what's wrong,
evokes a sense of rage.

So if you find that in your life,
the rainfall has begun,
just keep in mind a parasol,
won't mend the damage done.

Scott Rollo, Grade 12
Dunnville Secondary School, ON

My Black Abyss

I don't know what's wrong with me,
I've lost my will to live.
Now my fate's open to die,
Like an open book with the ending soon to come.
Everyone feels broken from time to time,
They say you have to live and die.

I don't understand their words,
They say them with twisted mouths.
I fear their words weaving a hard bound spell,
What if I were to fade away?
Into the dark abyss,
I could do it without dying,
Then hide from their evil kiss.

The light is fading now as I am willing to give in,
There is no one hear to save me from myself.
I'll hide deep down inside just like the last time,
Telling myself lies just to withhold this dark abyss.

Erin Sabourin, Grade 11
James Fowler High School, AB

The Unforeseen Love

You're the only reason I wake up with a smile upon my face
You make my heart skip a beat
You make my words confused, and my emotions weak
You make my love for you oh so real

I've loved you since that sunny day
I still loved you when you took my heart away
I loved you even though you hurt me so
I love you now, and I always will

You gave me back my heart
You showed me how to forgive
You showed me what love truly is

Ashalynn Fuller, Grade 11
North Hastings High School, ON

And So It Begins

Snow vanishing, sun vastly glistening
All delighted students scampering free
Ideal season for adventuring
Contemplating; "no better place to be"

Ecstatic! Exams concluded for all
Heading towards the beach wanting to tan
Girls and boys joining forces, playing ball
Musicians excited, ready to jam

No more summatives, time for traveling
Loss of ice hockey, let soccer balls fly
Skiing season over, time for surfing
Depression leaves as the summer comes by

Scholars' summers wonderfully begin
Students not discovered without a grin

Caroline Damiani, Grade 11
Collège catholique Franco-Ouest, ON

Untouched, Unloved, Unwanted

What happened to us?
We were perfect, at least that's what they all thought.
But little did they know how you really were.
You tricked me, into falling for you
And when you knew I fell, that's when you changed.
A change that nobody saw, only me.
You turned into something, something horrible.
Someone who didn't care, someone who played with my head.
Until finally one day you got bored of your little game,
And you ended it.

Now what? What now?
I'm here, alone silently screaming, crying, wanting you.
No one can hear me but you!
Yet there you are, everywhere I go,
I can't get away from you, I can't get over you.
But yet you seem so content, at peace almost,
As if you don't care still and it kills me.

Because I love you to death and you didn't even give us a second chance.
Now I'm faced with the truth. I have to live with your lies, and like you always said,
"A promise is something made to a fool."
Well I must be the damn fool because I believed you when you promised and said "I love you"…

Brittany Murphy, Grade 11
Ascension of Our Lord Secondary School, ON

Romantic Olfaction

The smell of blizzards and tornados and hurricanes makes me think of all my pains,
But luckily, one whiff of your scent can spark images of the times we've spent.

The smell of snow and rain and foggy days provokes me to look for all the sun's rays,
But happily, one sniff of your flair can bring happiness back into the air.

The smell of fires and tsunamis and deserts impels me to ignore all of my hurts,
But soothingly, one snuff around you, my loved one can remind me of the things we've done.

The smell of freshly-cut grass and prickly pine trees induces me to feel weak at the knees,
But fortunately, just one breath in your vicinity can cure and cheer and strengthen me.

The smell of you, your hair, your body, your face causes me to feel warm inside and my heart to race,
And surely, whenever I'm around you, my dear, all of my troubles completely disappear.

The smell of you, your energy, your aura, your force lets me conceive where we are, of course,
Because no matter where you are, I know that you will never be far.

The nose is a powerful tool
Only neglected by the biggest fool.
Toucan Sam's words are never listened to
So I will follow my nose and say: "I love you."

Eric Chow, Grade 12
Glenforest Secondary School, ON

What Does Love Feel Like?

What does love feel like? Is it…
Looking into someone's eyes,
And seeing your future with them
Feeling fireworks in your hands when you touch
Getting butterflies in your stomach when you kiss
Is it that feeling?
That you never want to let go
Watching their every movement
Shaking with happiness,
When their name pops up on call display
Or is it all those feelings combined
Love is all those feelings and more,
A great feeling, that makes your day brighter,
And makes you smile bigger

Jennifer Muchowski, Grade 12
Merritt Secondary School, BC

I'll Take the Time to See You There

In the clear blue sky my heart will soar
How fast, how far, how high
I cannot tell for sure
I'll take the time to see you there
Over the mirrored lakes and rainbow hills
With distant glow where skyline towers
Radar patchwork velvet fields below
I'll take the time to see you there
Checklist screening the highs and lows
Align my soul upon your wings
And grasp my goals safely ahead
I'll take the time to see you there
A dream of glory guides the way
Shifting the thrust forward
Roars the splendour of your power
I'll take the time to see you there
The many things I need to know
Will guide me above the distant yonder
Gliding and climbing the sky's the limit
I'll take the time to see you there

Justin Slack, Grade 12
Gordon Graydon Memorial Secondary School, ON

A World Unknown

I traveled to a world,
An unknown world,
Where peace reigned, and everyone was free,
Where a smile and a hug were many.

I traveled to a country,
A peaceful country,
Where men were equal, and they could decide,
Not letting the color of their skin preside.

I traveled to a home,
A beautiful home,
The people living there were a sight to behold,
They loved and cared and everything was cherished and shared.

Jennice Colaco, Grade 11
Ascension of Our Lord Secondary School, ON

Endless Light

The sunlight came from beyond the falling leaves,
Caressing the dying and broken pieces of summer;
"It's autumn again," you said,
"Ah, so it seems," I replied, nodding.

We walked quietly together
Along that deserted path, sheltered,
Talking and laughing and loving,
Being content with each other, and needing no future.

But where are you now? Where is that smile,
Those eyes, the gentle laughter, that
Always seemed to paint the world a kinder shade
And seemed all too evanescent?

Yes, youth is always so; a blind thing
That stumbles by and is gone, taking with it
Some essential moment that can never be
Recaptured, and that will never be the same.

I wonder if this can be called happiness?
Still I stand in the shadows of that weary path, while you
Turned into endless light and soared and flew and
Became too bright for my eyes to bear.

William Fung, Grade 12
Markham District High School, ON

Love Myth

She is the angel in the sky
She is the lights in my eyes
When I see her I feel like flying
Never want to feel like dying.

That night I saw her in the dance
I fell for her in a glance.
I told her "how can an idiot guy like me
Dance with a beautiful girl like thee"
She then hugged me,
And at that moment I knew who my true lover will be.

Every second that passes I miss her more
When I don't see her waiting for me beside the school door
It pains me hard core,
Makes me always think of her more.

She wears dresses so divine
I want her love to be mine.
My love to her does not need a sign
When I'm with her, everything will be fine.

Mostafa Sheteiwy, Grade 10
Robert Bateman High School, ON

A Depressed Smile

Alone, in the darkness
I see no one but me
I sit at the corner…
And almost hear the sea…
It calls me for life
And to fly like a bee
That'd taste real honey
And would pay no fee

What's real life mean?
Is it falling on the knee
Or it's the touch of tomorrow
That we always see

Life is a smile,
That causes us to cry
That whenever we fall
We stand up to try

My friends…I'm calling you
Come…and be my best,
For life is short
And we live it just to rest…
Hoda Mustafa, Grade 12
Glenforest Secondary School, ON

One Window Is All I Need

One window is all I need

To watch the rain falling
To see what's waiting for me
To imagine myself saving the world
To see the good side of life
To protect me from my fears

To escape my problems
And be able to start over!
Josiane Bernier-Lessard, Grade 10
Seminaire de Sherbrooke, QC

Old Age

Viewed as useless
Because you are old
Dreaming about the past
Alone in the dark

Until you pass away

Limited capacities
Health problems
Confined to a bed
It hurts to live

But that's the way it is.
Vincent Ouellet, Grade 10
Seminaire de Sherbrooke, QC

Caught

Curiously,
He walks towards mom and her new toy,
Step, stumble, fall; he gets up and tries again,
A gift

Seriously,
The concentrate on the task at hand,
Pedal, pause, pedal; he learned how to ride a bike,
A moment

Shyly,
She buries herself into his shoulder,
Blush, hide, laugh; she peeks at the camera,
A feeling

Proudly,
He presents his winning trophy,
Cheer, boast, excite; he smiles at the awesome victory,
A celebration

Subtly,
The quick shutter captures the memory,
Simple, significant, precise; each one tells a story with a glimpse of the past,
A photograph

Boriana Gantcheva, Grade 12
Glenforest Secondary School, ON

One More Day

Such a remarkable man, he has become,
Living a life he has always dreamed of;
Until one day when the sun stopped shining
And the world froze.
For one moment when our eyes met,
I wasn't so fond, at first,
But the way he showed his love for me, made me love him more;
The trust he showed in me, made me grow more entwined.
The more we fought, the more I realized,
That I love him, endlessly;
We dreamed our dreams, together
We fought our fights, together.
But most of all we lived our lives, together
Only falling for each other.
No one else but us;
No one will share the bond, he and I had together.
We stayed in the fairy tale until his minutes of life went dry,
His time on Earth disappeared.
If I had one more day with him,
I would remake our first moments, the happy moments,
And recount the love we have for each other.

Alicia Young, Grade 11
Bluefield High School, PE

I Walk Alone

"I walk alone.
My shadow is the only one who walks beside me."*
I need no one, no one depends on me.
I am a mountain,
steady, stable and strong.
No one can influence me,
nothing can move me.
I have the power, all control is mine.
I don't need a shoulder, I don't need to cry.
I can make it through the journey of life.
I am as I am, a woman among others.
Unafraid to stand out, to be different.
Independence is power,
individuality is an asset,
strength is a quality.
No one will wait, life will not slow down.
On this long winding path that we call life,
that is full of obstacles and challenges,
I walk alone.

*From "Boulevard of Broken Dreams" by Green Day
Carmelle Mongeon, Grade 11
École Secondaire Catholique Franco-Ouest, ON

Ode to Gardener

The smile of flower glows bright like sunshine;
While stepping over a garden so fine
I only think of colors of blooms, yet,
Forget the gardener and her sweat.

A gardener does not sing, but she hums;
The joyful song to birds of spring she brings
Who sways old winter with pure white wings.
To her joy, cold snow leaves and green life comes

She cheers the pallid daisy bud to bloom,
She bids the weak ivy to crawl the wall;
Her wish is to see them be strong and tall,
Regardless of heat or cold, light or gloom.

A gardener is no harvesting reaper,
Her passion is not the golden crop,
But to gather the freshest raindrop
For the young tree to grow and to prosper.

In summer colors tint her little yard,
Fresh green grass like landscape on a card,
With true heart and effort she builds a dream
Where flowers can bloom and stars can gleam.
Feng Xin (Cindy) Lai, Grade 11
Ecole Antoine Brossard, QC

Her Angelic Tears

What torments you Miss?
How can this beauty weep such
tears of distraught emotions?

What evil could corrupt your lovely presence
and cause your radiance to be dimmed by sadness.
Your broken heart tears my mind apart
to see such perfection distressed.

It disturbs me that I can only wonder from a distance.
And only when your worried eyes glance upon my safety
can I ask,
"Is everything all right miss?"
Randi-Lynn Crawford, Grade 11
On-Line Learning Centre, BC

Cramp

Things left unspoken I'll yell at the trees
Of course, without you, I'm never at ease
Feet on the road at the end of the night
Breaking through darkness 'til I reach daylight
Lingering memories of moments past
I'll always remember when I saw you last
Who spoke odd words I wouldn't hear;
Yet painfully were crystal clear.
You weren't a constant, no "Northern Star"
I know my feet can't carry me far
From you.

I hate this.

Alexandra Bella, Grade 12
St Thomas Aquinas School, BC

The Elements

Fire, earth, air and water
All elements of life
The one I share the most
Changing with the sun, seasons, and weather
Water flows through rivers and oceans
Feeding man and giving life to nature

A whole world by itself
Containing thousands of species
Incomparable landscape made of rocks, corals and sand
With man's treasures form the past
Allows humans to travel and discover
Building ships and improving them to confront the fury of water

Having this great resource in our hands
We must work together to preserve it
Finding ways to protect it from ourselves
And sharing with those who don't have as much
I dream of a world where pure water is everywhere
Future generations will thank us…
Gabriel Veilleux, Grade 10
Seminaire de Sherbrooke, QC

Failure Made Me Strong

My teachers, my big support, how can I make you proud?
My school, my little home, I yearn to make you well-known
I appreciate your trust in me to represent you out there
Determined, diligent, and persistent as I worked almost non stop
Finally, the moment had come when the results were to be announced
Keyed up, confident and eager, as I waited to attain my awards
Suddenly, everything just went wrong mind confused and completely lost
Heart stopped and body froze when they passed over my name
Now, I realize that this is reality once I leave my school, my home,
Every day will be a challenge and an experience, where every problem is a lesson and a tolerance
This is finally the time to mature and to strengthen my mind and soul
I must continue to keep up the fight to win, to stay strong and to visualize my dream.

Ruotong Wang, Grade 11
College Prep International, QC

Graduating Love

It was in elementary I saw you first, we teased, we fought and gave each other names.
Running in the halls even on the stairs, searching for each other and hiding from one another.
Somewhere in those games I wanted to make you mine, yes that was a first time I felt a love so divine.
Elementary passed junior high came, but still nothing changed until one day.
It was your birthday and you were with a few girls, and I wondered why my heart cried.
After that event you treated me like any other day, but stupid me ignored you and made you turn away.
Slowly we moved on to the high school, and I would still think of you at nights.
anyhow we now were complete strangers, but still when our eyes met I could see you questioning why.
Come to think I was just blinded with those green eyes, that started when we were in the middle of junior high.
Now we are graduating and I can see you in front, I heard you are going overseas during this month.
Slowly I realize it wasn't your mistake, but to make up those five years is now too late.
You start walking towards me and I wonder why; so you hand me a note and tell me goodbye.
I heard a word for me from you, but why are my emotions coming out so few.
In the note it reads; it was in elementary I saw you first, we teased, we fought and gave each other names.
Running in the halls even on the stairs, searching for each other and hiding from one another.
Somewhere in those games I wanted to make you mine, yes that was a first time I felt a love so divine.
Elementary passed junior came, nothing changed until one day,
after my birthday I teased you from behind, you gave me that look which couldn't be read from my mind.
Slowly I realized my one word was enough to damper your day, so I stopped talking to you and just turned away.

Jesmin Subba, Grade 11
Foundations for the Future Charter Academy-Dr Norman Bethune Campus, AB

When I'm Around You

As we sit at the end of the dock, we both have our feet in the water
And the sun is setting in the distance.
Every day, he tells me, that he takes at least 5 minutes out of his days
To remember the past 2 summers that we spent together.
Meaning, canoe races, paddle boat wars, and shooting stars.
He looks at me, noticing the tears trembling down my cheeks.
I turn quickly, looking at everyone sitting around the campfire.
They are the people I spent my days with, and it's been 2 years to this night
That they spend their last moments enjoying the place they've known for so long.
He puts a shaky arm around my neck, as he knew it would be the last summer of our lives,
As we spent the last couple of days like we were dying.
That's not always a good feeling, faking your own death.
But this summer was already the death of all good things.
As we sit at the end of the dock, we both have our feet in the water
And the sun has already set.

Melissa Tryon, Grade 12
North Addington Education Centre, ON

Dark Summer Dream

The waves swimming made my mind drift away
As the clouds drew some anger, he appeared
The weather turned black, your ice soul stands near
Shivering in fear, confused for it's May

In this dark place, the boy ran for the day
His severe yells like the sounds of a gun
Fear said he, becoming the only one
In fright all that's in sight, the stones that lay

Sensing the green flesh that stands behind me
Glimpsing at the creature, feeling no fright
Seeing this monster before shed some light
My soul and mind feeling suddenly free

My eyes awake to the rays of the sun
Light coloring my skin, the dream is done

BriAnne Lafleur, Grade 11
Collège catholique Franco-Ouest, ON

Once in Love

Once in love,
Blinded by the brilliant magnitude,
Together forever, on and on,
Marriage and kids, happy family life.
It falls apart,
Never speaking, never looking,
Once in love,
On and on, side by side,
But not as one.
Once in love,
Now barely friends, strangers in one bed,
Drifting apart,
Lawyers come, papers signed,
Belongings split, along with little hearts.
Once in love,
Forever apart.

Joëlle Levasseur, Grade 10
École Secondaire Catholique Franco-Ouest, ON

War and Peace

It feel a shame to be alive.
When men so brave, are dead
Leaving family behind.
Since when, a man was great, brave, strong when he killed.
We can kill, torture, and steal. But where is the pride?
When will all believe in peace?
Time has come for fire to cease.
A cease that grants children to live
As plants can grow and flowers can breathe
It should never end
It shall not freeze
Let peace blow in our direction.
Let it touch us, melt and mold on us.
No war, no violence and lots of silence.
Why destroy when we could create.
Lets keep peace and erase the hate.

Abdulrahman Al-Khoudari, Grade 11
College Prep International, QC

The Passage

The news came
Like a gush of an icy whisper
On the napes of our necks,
Freezing us into statues
Of stone filled with sorrow,
But undying acceptance of your fate,
Our fate.

Then your arrival approached
As clear as a night sky during a gale.
But the course of your life had been won.
You were blessed as all vessels ought to be.

But again you started another passage
You set sail through unforgiving waters
This only caused your sails to rise in utter defiance.
We rowed beside you bracing every wave.

Then the waters calmed
Once again you had been victorious
You are now in full swing.
You have been melting all the ice in your path
Just like the salt that you sow
In each person you touch.

Julia Pedota, Grade 12
Hawthorn School for Girls, ON

Genuine Doesn't Deserve Punctuation: An Excerpt

we've found ourselves in the same old place
flashing each other a familiar face
forgetting to present our forgotten grace
we place ourselves in this dangerous state
in which to blame is what we call fate
the voices tell us stories while our lips verbalize
words to them which they then turn into lies
honesty has been erased from their eyes
and now we've given them one too many tries
bath yourself in genuine lands where we know that we can
do whatever we planned and we'll make ourselves grand
and stand with our toes in the sand knowing that
we'll always understand when we make ourselves grand
now here we bury our lies as we look up into the sky
and deny all of the goodbyes and replies
and look into each others eyes and we both imply…
I've found myself in the same old place,
Flashing you this same old face.
Forgetting to present my forgotten grace,
I've placed myself in this dangerous state
In which I can only thank what I call fate.

Allena Nguyen, Grade 10
Little Flower Academy, BC

Sun

Up in the sky
Farther than the clouds
The solemn star stands
Spreading light to the Earth
Making life possible

Martin Rodriguez, Grade 10
Seminaire de Sherbrooke, QC

You and Me

You look at me
Don't know what to do
But look away
The truth is you always
Have had a key
A key to my heart
It's almost too late
For you to see
Soon we shall be
Millions of miles apart

Jasmine Skye Bainbridge, Grade 12
Beaverlodge Regional High School, AB

Me

One window is all I need
To show who I really am
To see through lies
To understand the truth
To feel emotions
And to face reality

Antoine Dessureault, Grade 10
Seminaire de Sherbrooke, QC

The Beginning to the End

In the beginning,
The roses are red.
The violets are blue.
But something has changed.
The dawn is dead
And the sunset splits.
The breaking waves are making hits.
The sun is black
So it's time to act!
All the pretty things are gone,
They say
"No one leaves without the keys."
The cry of desperation
Races through my veins.
Time is ticking
Slipping
Escaping my grasp.
I find myself falling without a past.
No future. No present.
Only
The End.

Heather MacDonald, Grade 10
Bashaw School, AB

Why Me?

I raise this question in confusion that I have apparently seen
Due to the fact I had everything from the ground to the sky
I have made bad choices or maybe the choices chose me
But in the end I am going to be left with the question why me
Maybe I love the feeling of regret maybe I thrive on pain
But I am the only one to blame and clearly nothing to gain
I have happiness and sadness so does everybody, am I any different
My incantation of fear is what controls me
It controls everybody but it has such a grip on me
That my last breath might just be the one to save me
We all try to break our fears from us and most of us think that we are free from it
But it is so deep within that it might be next to your conscience
My name is Ishaq Albiz and I clearly hate this disease
Of fear that has drawn me to ask this question why me

Ishaq S. Albiz, Grade 10
College Prep International, QC

Procrastination

Oh, you evil one-eyed monster,
So myopic your eye must be!
Sense of logic you do so lack,
Carefree days you snatch from me!
Why trap me in your constant game
Of debate and negotiation
For more worrisome time just to play?
Why do you have to turn my precious time into fuel for your game?
Do you enjoy making me frantic, anxious, even paranoid
When I complete my tasks while burning the midnight oil?
Why do you still continue to haunt me even in my little hours of sleep
When you have already overtaken my entire waking life?
Oh, my deepest failure,
Why do you have to make my life such a misery,
When I should be the one in control of you?

Karen Jin, Grade 11
Sir John A MacDonald Collegiate Institute, ON

Your Everything

I can be the stars, that light up your night sky.
And I can be your shoulder, if ever you need to cry.

I can be your words, if ever you cannot speak.
And I can be your eyes, if the truth you ever seek.

I can be your conscience; that whisper in your ear.
And I can be the one, the one that you hold dear.

I can be the laughter, that puts the smile on your face.
And I can be the beauty, that makes your heart beat race.

I can be the girl, that you just can't get off your mind.
And I can be the perfection, that you've searched so long to find.

Boy, I can be your anything; and to you I'll always tend.
I want to be your everything, but never just your friend.

Holly Marie Caron, Grade 11
Ecole Secondaire de Pain Court, ON

Live Your Life as if Life Ends Tomorrow

Sometimes it's the little things in life that makes one happy
Like a smile, a helping hand or anything dandy.
In life we have choices, to go for the good or for the bad
For where we decide to go, that's where we will stand.
Life's as if we were on a ride,
It goes up, down, and sometimes side to side.
Depending on our mood,
We say life's not worth it.
But when we think about fortune
Why is it easier to show it?
The most difficult challenges ones face,
Can sometimes be referred to as a race,
With everyone wanting to win first place.
Life is like magic
It has its surprises,
Life's also tragic
It has its disguises.
We must all come together
And reunite as one,
To make life better
And let it shine like the sun.

Melissa Greco, Grade 12
Laurier Sr High School, QC

Zest

Minute after minute, the clock ticks
The sound of the alarm clock blares in my brain
I run downstairs and put on my kicks
I can't wait to ride in the pouring rain

Minute after minute, the drops fall
They quench the thirst beneath my skin
Sometimes the Earth makes me feel so small
I can't wait to get on my bike and begin

Mile after mile, my heart races
The sunrise begins to warm the sky
I feel the fresh air and all nature's embraces
I do not know where I'm going or why

Mile after mile, my feet pedal
The street begins to slowly unwind
I feel the creaks and cracks of rubber and metal
I do not know where I'm going or why

Muscle after muscle, my sweat gleams
A sudden zest fills my body and mind
I feel so calm, so cool, so clean
I do not care where I'm going or why

Ana Cabak, Grade 12
Glenforest Secondary School, ON

The Morning Rush

I awoke to emptiness in my ears
As I rose from my bed with a sight unclear
Opening the curtains I tried to see
Upon the horizon the light as sea

Natural brightness illuminating
Helped me find my towel for bathing
Refreshing my body in the shower
Leaving me with a smell to empower

Throwing on clothes ready to skedaddle
Trotting down the steep stairs with a dazzle
Running out the door challenging the world
Wait! I'm so nervous I want to hurl

Not knowing what's going to hit you next
A bird, a plane, perhaps by a vortex.

Samuel Neelin, Grade 11
Collège catholique Franco-Ouest, ON

To My Big Sister

Someone we once knew,
we hear you're voice and know it's you.
Also we could never forget your name,
but things have changed you're not the same.
We think in these past years we've lost you,
a sister, daughter, and best friend we once knew.
When times got rough you chose to get high,
but when this happens mom really does cry.
We thought you changed and you'd be all right,
but nope you're still messed up awake all night.
Now all we can do is hope you'll stop or might,
be my sister I used to know and get some sleep tonight.

Samantha Magee, Grade 10
Whytecliff Education Centre, BC

The Stranger Unknown!

You look forward and see someone you haven't before.
They seem familiar, you need to know more.
But this person you see as you look straight ahead.
Is tormented and hurt their eyes appear dead.
Remember when you lived, cared and fought.
Fought for your life; now living? You are not.
Your face is creased with hatred and defeat.
This person you see now you badly need to beat.
In the battle of living and your utter demise.
You believed the evil and all the horrible lies.
Think of the road so treacherous and rough.
A blood curdling scream and you cry, "Now this is enough!"
You've forgotten all the joys and happiness you had.
No longer sweet but in your mouth is a taste sour and bad.
The shadows under your eyes give away your sleepless night.
You grasp your face and try to hold on to your sanity tight.
No longer will you feel the cold fingers of defeat.
Break free now, there will be no more demons you will meet!
You stare ahead at the stranger unknown.
You look in the mirror, the stranger is you and you alone!

Rachel Helten, Grade 10
Holy Cross Regional High School, BC

Solar Affair

She begins
Her climb in the morning,
Reaches her crown 'round noon.
Now she gravitates down
And beckons,
Moon.

Denon Wilgosh, Grade 12
Webber Academy, AB

If You Never Knew

Sometimes, there are things
you'd wish you never knew,
you could never visualize,
you could never see.
Sometimes, you are better off
with a sense of unknowing,
a sense of controlling,
you could change the story,
to make it more bearable,
but once you know,
you lose your hold, the ability
to keep the situation your own,
to control the happenings,
the way it goes down,
now you just have to accept it
and move on.
The way it is now,
the way you wish
you never knew it was.

Lerissa Suite, Grade 10
Holy Cross Regional High School, BC

Us

We are born dead
And resurrected by love
Drowned in a sea of darkness
Given breath by a mother's cry

We are nothing
In silence we learn
The sound of speed
Engulfs our hearts
With unspoken words

With a kiss our lips are sealed
The taste of memories
Fading on the tip of our tongues

In the growing absence of light
The sun, an orange disc
Plunges into the night
Its explosion turns into
The eyes of the universe
And we die living

Kimberly Tsan, Grade 12
Pinetree Secondary School, BC

The Losing Battle

There have been battles and wars since a long time ago,
They fought for status, territory, or even just show.
They fought bloody fights with a spear and a shield;
Some men didn't have proper weapons to wield.

Later on there were arrows to pull back on great bows,
Men died fighting proudly on horses in rows.
Later still, in the trenches, out on the front line,
The hidden picked off their opponents one at a time.

Then machines came along, more powerful still,
Some could erase the enemy from the top of a hill.
War is different now; it's not man against man,
It's people knocking down buildings 'cause they know that they can.

The tactics got smarter, the weapons got stronger,
But things can't keep going this way any longer.
When we get nuclear bombs going off all around,
It won't be long before we burn this place to the ground.

In the conflicts today, no rules or morals are clear,
It's easy to see that no endings are near.
They say if you fight fire with fire, you're going to get burned,
But it seems that some lessons just aren't going to be learned.

Johanna Boyce, Grade 12
Sir Robert Borden High School, ON

Warped

I guess it's always been with me,
A part that needs to breathe.
I've found myself in the worst places to be,
Stuck with the hope of feeling nothing,
Planted like a seed.
I was too young to know the difference
That was shadowing what was real.
So I learnt much too fast,
That the high I was clenching to,
Would not last.
How could I have known that the good times would pass?
And that fear would overcome everything.
And so I distanced myself
And distracted my mind from anything.
All the small efforts that I made,
Couldn't surpass this empty state of mind.
I knew that I probably should have stayed,
In that life where all I knew was time.
But now I know that I prefer my new mentality,
Because I feel like I can finally breathe,
And never once will I regret that my skeletons got the best of me.

Shanna Luis, Grade 11
Pierrefonds Comprehensive High School, QC

One Little Flaw

As the wind was whistling
Over the top of the trees
And the lake was glistening
A beautiful spirit ran free
It was a handsome man
Lost in the breeze
An intelligent young man
Who loved to tease
But there was one little flaw
In this spunky teen
He had a knack for getting into trouble and never being seen
People say he moved at the speed of light
But the truth is
He was more than lightly into speed
And loved to fight
Only one day he took it too far
And now he's among the trees, among the wind
And forever in my heart.

Mireille Lacasse, Grade 10
École Secondaire Catholique Franco-Ouest, ON

A Life of Calculus

We add years, to multiply friendships
We subtract the obstacles
To divide tiles towards the golden gates
We add years, to multiply ourselves
To divide families
To subtract relatives
And round up on special occasions
We add years, to subtract the hair
To multiply the losses
To divide the pairs
We add pain, to subtract calcium
We multiply the pills
Only to divide them daily
Then comes the day, when a whole person
Adds the memories and loses them
Multiplies the tears, to finally divide body and soul
A life of calculus, we add all the years

Melissa Mallette, Grade 11
Ratihente High School, QC

The Performer

An object
Patted and tucked in tight
Cared for and kept warm at night
Smothered in something they call love
This sickly adoration of themselves
Through me
Is it really my fault?
When I am expected to perform
Pampered to please
A product of the search for a second chance
Perfection of course
The lights were shone on me
I put on a show

Julia Phillips, Grade 11
Burnaby Online School, BC

The Puddle

The door it opens, I jump out.
A new adventure? There's no doubt!
The air feels lovely, warm and sweet,
The scent of raindrops, what a treat!
A look to the left, a look to the right,
I look up and down, to see what's in sight.
And lo and behold! Just down the front steps,
A scene of delight lays waiting for me.
Shimmering colors, with magical light;
They dance with such brightness, and swim with such ease.
I hop down the stairs, while bouncing with song,
Stopping right at the edge — a sea of water.
My rain boots are ready, my heart is all steady.
I bend my knees, and touch the ground:
And with a big sound, a shout of glee, "wheeeee!"
I jump.
A mighty splash, a tremendous crash!
I part the waters, quite easily too!
And with great joy, I stand up straight.
My little secret:
I can fly.

Enoch Weng, Grade 11
Burnaby North Secondary School, BC

From Death to Life, from Life to Death

The last breath we take.
The last move we make.
The last cloud we see,
the last smell of the sea.

From death to life,
from life to death.
God works in a mysterious way.
He gives us life and He takes it away.

The first breath we take,
the first move we make.
The first sight of light,
the first morning sight.

From death to life,
from Earth to heaven.
From our birth on Earth,
to our last moments on Earth.

God works in a mysterious way.
He gives us life and He takes it away.
But when He takes it away,
He gives us life again with Him in heaven.

Matt Hein, Grade 10
Holy Cross Regional High School, BC

The Power of Love

Love is selfless, love is kind. For me love is my Lord personified.

In moments of doubt when you cease to believe in yourself, your loved ones trust you like God.

A single expression of love wipes off all your tears and makes you smile.

The whole world rests on its mighty power,

Love of my beloved guides me every hour.

It can't be described. A four lettered word, too deep in meaning,

Shines in cold weather, like sunlight beaming. Unconditional and pure, no language it has.

Yet is the loveliest expression of all.

The only emotion with the strength to lighten the world of all its ugly loads, cleanses and purifies the tired dark souls.

God rests in each one of us, just learn to see the gifts you have.

Everyone wants loves and care.

Trust me the evil souls crave for attention and time to spare. To be a true lover stand up and dare.

Imagine how Almighty wanted us to be.

Be the best of what you can be, to be a better being to reciprocate his love for us.

This life is a gift from God.

To thank Him best, just love everyone and don't think about the rest.

Forgive oneself and others.

The world is rude and unkind, does not know the secret of a happy life.

What I discovered in my own little way and what I know is just to love and smile.

The way to true happiness is to reach out to soothe and heal, the poor, helpless and needy.

Harjasleen Kaberwal, Grade 12
Ascension of Our Lord Secondary School, ON

Survival*

In the beginning, God created night and day, the plants and the animals, and saw that it was good.

He then created people to take care of His world and each other.

When He was finished, He concluded that all of His creation was good.

Peace and harmony between all of His creations, that was His intention.

Hitler, Jews, Concentration camps, War. Starvation, Abuse, The Final Solution. Death. Lifeless.

Shutting down emotionally in order to keep living from day to day.

What was once a person filled with love, dreams, expectations, and emotions, is now an empty, hollow shell,

With only one goal, one purpose. Survival.

Father, Son, sticking together, staying alive so the other may hold on for just a little bit longer.

Feeling enough to make sure the other doesn't give up, and blocking out the rest.

Moving, one step after the other, following orders, robots, don't think just move, keep pushing, don't give up.

Fading into the background, trying your hardest not to get noticed.

Conflicting thoughts: can he leave his father, does he dare face life on his own.

Will his father survive, can he make it on his own?

Encouraging each other, pushing the others on, not giving up.

What was once a feeling of hate and revenge for the people who did this to them, is now just an aching need for freedom, for the end.

The End. Freedom, Life, a human corpse, dead but alive, emotional, physical, psychological damage.

The person who you were before, so innocent, happy, and uncorrupted,

Now Dead, buried along with all of the people that didn't make it, forever to be a memory.

Katelyn Jansma, Grade 12
Burstall School, SK
*Based on "Night" by Elie Wiesel

The Journey

Every day you get up
And you do the same old thing
You never know when things will change
Or what tomorrow may bring
They always say:
"Live today like it was your last"
But that's so hard to do
When the world moves so fast
What about your future?
What does it hold?
Is it happy and bright?
Or is it dark and cold?
The way you live life is completely up to you
In every choice you make
And in everything you do
Do what you know is right
You can always tell in your heart
Because in the end
You don't want to wish that you could restart
So get up each day with a new thought in mind
That each day is a journey with something new to find

Katrina Budgell, Grade 10
King's Christian Collegiate, ON

Fear

Fear of something new,
of letting go of the old.
Fear of getting hurt,
from the stories that I'm told.

Fear of opening up,
and letting someone in.
Fear of loving you,
and getting hurt again.

Fear of testing you,
to make something that will last.
Fear of not being able,
to let go of my past.

Fear of hurting you,
or you changing your mind.
Fear of breaking up,
and being left behind.

Fear of our first kiss,
and possibly our last hug.
Fear of getting hurt,
but mostly of falling in love.

Trisha Lamothe, Grade 11
École Secondaire Catholique Franco-Ouest, ON

My Love

Time is stopped when I'm with you
Nothing else can be more true
Then the feeling I have when I'm with you
I need you here to help me through

I understand our friendship
Might be more important
But in my heart
You'll always have a special place
Always ready to love you.

Lyel Elemquies Girerd, Grade 10
Heritage Regional High School, QC

Morning at the Beach

Entering this framed picture, my escape.
My mind is long thrown away, I capture.
The ocean is never-ending landscape
Filled with fluffs, light warms the vast sky azure

Strolling upon sand banks tickling my toes
Salty, refreshing mist fills my dry mouth
Wind, like harmonious melody blows
Birds fluttering, tiny crabs crawling south

Gentle waves caress the shore from the sea
Here, there, exquisite shells are left restful
Energizing water dances calmly
This scene is a dream, serene and peaceful

Into another world slowly diving
This splendid nature beauty is whis'pring

Charline Dubois, Grade 11
Collège catholique Franco-Ouest, ON

Time's Up

A million years that I've spent searching
For a fairy tale life
Just a happy ending like an open story book
I've spent so much time seeking…
Tick Tock Time's Running Out

A beautiful mess surrounded me
Pieces of my dream world
Seeped into reality…
Tick Tock Time's Running Out

A white dress with a black bouquet
Nothing was ever perfect
My book kept kicking me out…
Tick Tock Time's Running Out

Broken down, the clock winds
A carriage without a wheel, I didn't move
I searched for my happy ending all my life
How ironic — for a perfect life
I threw mine away
And now…
Tick Tock Time's Up

Janessa Collins, Grade 12
Merritt Secondary School, BC

Ignorance

As we stare into a solid wall,
seeing nothing,
but life.
As we stare into a mirror,
seeing everything,
but death.
As we stare into ourselves,
seeing anything,
but care.

David Beshay, Grade 10
King's Christian Collegrate, ON

Eagle Eyes

Sarcasm thickly laced
Glares shot down from sides
Can't hold up to what I'm faced
These partially insane carnival rides
Watching me from the sides
Oh, she still abides
To these conspicuous lies
Wait…surprise!
Watch the eagles rise…

Demi Lee, Grade 11
Earl Haig Secondary School, ON

End

Frightened, Yet
Fierce.
Captured, Yet
Complete.
Lonely, But
Living.
Why does this have to be,

The way of life for one that has
The breath for the habitat of trees.

Exiled.
Entitled.
Extinct.
Endangered.
Evaporating.

Renishaki Kamalanathan, Grade 12
Victoria Park Collegiate Institute, ON

The Widow's Sorrow

I looked through the window,
To see a widow behind the willows,
Walking toward a meadow,
Her shadow haunts me with sorrow,
For she's fit for a pharaoh,
But she fell for a hero,
He, who struck by an arrow,
Left her heart hollow.

Bonnie Han, Grade 12
John G Diefenbaker High School, AB

Trees Are Like Us

The Earth containing the seed is the mother waiting for her child to be born
The rain falling on the trees is the water of life flowing through our lips
The sun shining down on the woods is the happiness after darker moments.

The forest is the grove of friendship
Where we make friends and keep till the end
The forest is a land of peace and serenity
Where we can feel secure next to our family.

And still, life only hangs by a thread
Lumberjacks can slash their lives in two
Diseases can strike us like predators
So men struggle to survive
As trees pray to be spared.

It is the way it goes everybody
We grow
We live our lives
And finally we lose our leaves
When the sun goes to sleep
The night may be settled forever.

Louis Philip Pelchat, Grade 10
Seminaire de Sherbrooke, QC

Confusion

I see how upset he gets at the world,
I want to help him concentrate on him but it's such a challenge,
They are always yelling at him,
Telling him how stupid and wrong he is,
But in my mind the question left behind is "who are they?"
They are described as the ones called your family and friends.
No one appreciates him for who he is and I don't understand,
The amount of effort I see he puts into life is worth more than one's heart.
This is why I shall give him mine,
So until he reaches the end of the road he has my heart to guide him.

Caroline Grillo, Grade 11
Ascension of Our Lord Secondary School, ON

I Am But a Shadow

Her glittering gleamy greenish eyes in the morning,
 A blooming beauty mark on her right cheek that blends on her face
 Like the sun in the sky.
Her gregarious laugh when she's in a crowd,
 Her cute voice that makes me shiver in embarrassment.
I'm licking the same flavor of ice cream that she's licking so peacefully,
 It tastes twice more luscious just cause she's eating the same thing as me.
I touch her shoulder as she deliberately gades by me,
 Her hair then caresses my face like summer wind
I can smell her replenishing perfume of heavenly pomegranate,
 Her hair has the aroma of lavender that has just bloomed.
It feels like I'm in love but we're just so distinguished,
 Well at least she's the girl I once said "hi" to,
 So stupid cause I've never really talked to her but…
 I wish that one day I'll find the spirit to finally talk to you.

Billy Alcine, Grade 12
Collège catholique Franco-Ouest, ON

Poetry Is…

Poetry is…
a blooming butterfly,
a plain, soft, vibrant, booming melody of thoughts,
an external rainbow lacking, a pot of gold,
a cocoon of steel; brittle, light, not easily moved.
It is an illustrious puzzle,
never complete without all the right pieces.

Poetry is…
unsolvable, as all cries for help are.
Puzzling, it holds never-ending meanings from my soul,
helping me to solve problems I do not control.

Poetry is…
fairy dust,
one can fly if he believes.
It is, altogether, untaught, identical, original, artistic —
It is freedom disguised as words.

Taylor Olson, Grade 11
Quesnel Secondary School, BC

The Forest

So many beautiful flowers,
Wonderful big and tall trees
Luscious natural fruit that gives me power
With sweet water from the river
Pleasant "piu-piu" of little birds in the morning
But scary Black Panther paces in the evening
When I look around carefully there is
Amazing flying motions of little birds
Surprising rare trees that have pursing,
Breathing fresh air from the forest
That makes me feel supernatural, scent of purity
Powerful breeze on my body
Relaxed, like I am, in the Paradise.

Alex Rema, Grade 12
Collège catholique Franco-Ouest, ON

My Green Friend

Waking up to the unbearable heat,
Lying in a sea of perspiration,
Desiring a sufficient position
The sun has brought my body to slow defeat.

Out my window stand figures still as night,
Roots growing bellow the outdoor carpet.
Live statues drawing a vast silhouette,
Body meeting an unreachable height.

Trapped in dry earth, seeking fluidity,
Though satisfied to regain his jade mane;
The glorious sun prohibits the rain.
Wishes to slurp the waters of the sea.

Sitting beneath the azure atmosphere
With my natural friend I hold so dear.

Giulia Marcoux, Grade 11
Collège catholique Franco-Ouest, ON

Just to Love You

How do I love you?
I love you gently and effortlessly,
like a slow flowing stream

How do I love you?
I love you with warmth and kindness,
that shines on your skin like the gentle moonlight
when the sun sets behind the mountains

My thoughts are about you
as you sit outside
on a cool summer's night
thinking…
Why does she love Me?

I love you because of the passion
that gives me a reason
to wake up the next day

Your love is so gentle and yet…
so painful if left behind
I love you just to love you

Amanda Sprinkle, Grade 11
College Prep International, QC

Revision

"Accept your fate,"
They said.
The world will never, never change
"Our destinies cross the threshold and orbit then fade."
So I sighed.

I smiled, closed my eyes
Feeling the wind push back a curl,
Hearing the silent, sunlit music of the world,
Seeing a globe that they could only dream of.
And so I thought.

To turn the other cheek if I am struck, I will not.
To be stuck at the crossroads and turn back, I will not.
To look at a map and choose no road to take, I will not.
Wherever I am I will pick my place or else be free.
Why? Because reality is worth the risk!
And so I chose.

Now I open my eyes,
Unlock my lips and say,
"Accept not your fate,
Accept only yourself."

Sarah Beale, Grade 10
Lisgar Collegiate Institute, ON

My Grandpa

We all really miss you Grand-dad,
But we know you would not want us to be sad.

From kings in the corners, to walks in the parks,
Grandpa your kindness has left great marks.

All the memories are so clear,
Oh how I wish you were still here.

Holiday dinners will never be the same,
But there is no one to blame.

In my life you have been such a big part,
You will always remain in my heart.

We realize Grandpa that you never did go,
Your soul will always be with us, even if it doesn't show.

Every night I will sit by my bed and pray,
That I will see you in Heaven one day.

There are no more tears to cry,
Grandpa I love you, goodbye.

Tessa Beauchamp, Grade 10
Holy Cross Regional High School, BC

Valley of the Dead

As I walk through the valley of the shadow of the dead
I can see all the innocents that don't know why they are here
They can't remember, won't remember
For they are walking in the valley of the dead.

As I walk in the shadow of the dead
I can start seeing all the pain they are in
When they start to remember why they are here
For they are in they valley of the dead.

As I walk through the valley in the shadow of the dead
I can see all the fear that these people feel
I know why they are here but wish they weren't
For I am walking in the valley of the dead.

As I walk in the shadow of the dead
The dead realize that it wasn't by choice
They did not choose this life they see
They are forever in the valley of the dead

As I walk among the dead
I will remember them.

Andrew Reed, Grade 10
Seminaire de Sherbrooke, QC

Misgivings

Disguised imprints leading to masked dismay
Protesting monsoons impelled me away
Scorning, ignoring, warnings all proclaimed
Unwilling love with Satan was attained
True nature discovered with passing time
Foul actions a plenty, so few sublime
Offensive slander spoiled many a day
Imbuing all colors with ashen gray
Unspoken gestures provoked shattered hearts
An abyss consumes me as he departs
Profound sorrow transforms to pure outrage
My feelings for you never did assuage
Exchanged love for eternal seclusion
Summer romance, man's greatest illusion

Gabrielle White, Grade 11
Collège catholique Franco-Ouest, ON

What Is Perfection?

Perfection has been wrongly defined.
All through time it has seen as good,
but what if there was perfection of bad.
What if a dinner was perfect,
then it would be good,
but a disaster could be a perfect bad.
Perfection is a scale,
where everything must be equal.
Perfection should be when there is no difference,
when there is no better or worse but equal.
So when life seems good,
think of this,
if there is a consequence for every actions,
than a good action must have a consequence.

Jonathan St-Arnault, Grade 10
Heritage Regional High School, QC

Natural Experience

Leaves floating
Slowly onto the ground
Crisp
Cool autumn air swirls around me

Snowflakes drifting
Down like a blanket
Numbing
Cold winter air blows around me

Rain falling
Loudly onto the roof
Warm
Wet spring air stirs around me

Sun shining
Bright like a spotlight
Sweltering
Dry summer air hangs around me

Seasons bring amazing weather every day
To everyone in the world
And to me

Anne Huang, Grade 12
Glenforest Secondary School, ON

Vancouver

The wind snarls its whistling whip,
Cars slide and patience slips.
The snow has fallen an inch or two.
They panic and cry; they think they're screwed!

They say their streets are piled high,
They should see ours they reach the sky.
Vancouver panics as they watch
Their city be buried, their dreams are scotched.

Our cars will make it they always do,
Deep in snow we'll make it through.
We get a foot we make it work,
From shoveling our backs do surely hurt.

When we see an inch we moan and sigh
When they see that they start to cry.
Their city falls into a frenzy.
They should take a look at MacKenzie!

They never do their lesson learn,
For warmer times they surely yearn.
We patiently wait for it to melt,
For the cold to no more be felt.

Taya Vos, Grade 12
Kelly Road Secondary School, BC

Cannot Be Replaced

There is no laughter
In this cruel, cruel world
It was the most precious thing
Made of gold.
And now it's gone.
I lift my head up
Thinking, why oh why
This thing of gold had to die
Broken toys, broken hearts, broken homes
All casualties of war
A tear appears, sliding down my cheek.
A child walks by…no, not a child.
A woman in girl's clothing.
The face of a lost and confused kid.
It haunts me; day and night…
The war has ended
But, that precious thing
Made of gold
For some piece of land, it was fought over and sold
It can never be reclaimed
Childhood was its name.

Yuliya Malyk, Grade 12
Applewood Heights Secondary School, ON

My Childhood Lover

It feels like forever…
Since I last saw your face,
Since I last heard the heartbeat in your chest.
I miss the warmth of your arms around me,
And the smile that always made me melt.

Your music drew me towards you, your words made me stay,
And the feeling of your lips on mine, drove me insane.
The months we spent together went by without a care.
And I began to dream that you would always be here.
How did it come to end like this,
After all the times we've shared?
I still remember our first kiss…
When I thought you really cared.

I cried myself to sleep again, hoping to never wake.
Thinking that dream would last forever was just a big mistake.
The wounds of my numbing heart, will they ever mend?
But if they did how would I know?
You took it when you left.

Lovejeet Bhatti, Grade 12
North Albion Collegiate Institute, ON

Swift Summer Haze

Voyage commenced, plunging into unknown
Treading multiple scholastic treasons
Loathe pressure during temperate seasons
Leaping towards adventure, so alone
Anxious butterflies cascade through organs
Diverse faces, places: such are my needs
Camaraderie growing like shy weeds
Mother Nature vs. Miss Metropolitan
Her gentle perfume purifying night
Star studded sky, contouring bedtime sheet
Day: insane scorching heart bruising skin's meat
Dim curtailed light, at summer's ending sight
August classrooms, an absent minded daze
Sunny memories revived in swift haze

Julie Houde, Grade 11
Collège catholique Franco-Ouest, ON

Stroll Through the Sticks

Lingering in woods aimlessly alone
I hear surrounding waters meet wet stone
Embracing the remains of summer's air
As a painting, the view is oh so fair
Although birds gaily chirp their melody
Like a coverlet, sun beams and warms me
As if it were Christmas, I smell the pine
Come to terms with weather truly divine
Lying here, I see the trees and flowers
Giving the forest its life and color
Foliage swishing with wind that calms my soul
All of this coming from a simple stroll
Beep! Beep! Beep! Alarm rings, announcing day
Snow's on the ground, summer's still far away

Minhthi Bui, Grade 11
Collège catholique Franco-Ouest, ON

The Canucks

I'm so excited I cannot wait to watch my Canuck team versus the team I hate
Out of the tunnel I see them come their determined faces will look scary to some

I pushed and shoved my way to my seat I feel sticky gum under my feet
The smell of buttery popcorn fills the air I send my friend to go get us our share

People are out of their seats, the anthem is going the music stops and the horns start blowing
My friend returns with a bunch of food nothing in the world tastes this good

The new addition to our team the amazing player Mats Sundin
Along with Henrik and Daniel Sedin half of Swede nation is on our team

We shoot and score and the crowd cheers jumping up and down and spilling their beers
We win the game, putting the other team to shame

The player of the day, Mats Sundin skates on the ice smiling in gleam
Playoffs to come, what will happen next we will see who's the best!

Nicholas Campagne, Grade 10
Holy Cross Regional High School, BC

The Profession

If I were a teacher I'd show kids they can learn, show the power of knowledge and teach of respect they can earn.
If I were a doctor I'd make sure all hearts were beating, comfort those who are sick and attend all doctor meetings.
If I were a lawyer I'd defend those in the right, express opinions in public and put up a good fight.
If I were a zoo keeper I'd give the animals their food, give tours to school children, and say things like "Hey dude!"
If I were a business man I'd carry a briefcase on the subway,
Call important meetings and work with people so that they could get more pay.
If I were a dancer I'd invite everyone to my show! Receive bouquets of flowers and do ten pirouettes in a row.
If I were a cleaning lady I'd read every diary I could find, know every secret in the entire household but keep them in my mind.
If I were a movie star I'd act as a role model for all, make every fan feel like they know me and sign autographs at the mall.
If I were a philosopher I'd read large complicated books, all about Reality and Idealism and give people strange looks.
If I were a scientist I'd discover a cure, for all life threatening illnesses and folks would say "We love her!"
And if I were a mother I'd be as happy as can be, that way there's a little bit of every profession inside of me.

Beck Lloyd, Grade 11
Earl Haig Secondary School, ON

The Side I Never Knew About

Long forgotten sunlight
Never before seen disorder

The heartwarming happiness that kissing dolphins brings me
Is destroyed by the sight of homeless hounds and poverty

Surrounded by classic run down vehicles putt putting there way along
Our talented chef dances and sings as Echale Salsita glorifies jams of the Kings

Curiosity before tasting the freshly cooked Mahi Mahi
Reminds me of the rotten jelly fish that sleep on the beach shore that have lost their spark

Reminiscing about sipping refreshing Mai Tai's quickly fade
As I eat the food that a poor Cuban man has made, in a sweat shop with no glorification

I am thankful that I don't live in this beautiful nation
My eyes have been widely opened at this historical vacation of exploitation

Michelle Laforest, Grade 11
Collège catholique Franco-Ouest, ON

Save Me

I always came to wonder
if there were people who even bothered
To consider me part of their lives
or someone that they had left behind

'Cause I hate to see people passing by
turning their backs without saying goodbye
I hate the feeling of being alone
never wanted even at home

It hurts to know
that you've got nowhere to go
But it hurts more
that you're not needed anymore

That for all of them
you're just a burden
Just someone to be left in the dark
just someone with a broken heart

Amanda Weir, Grade 11
Ascension of Our Lord Secondary School, ON

The Race

I felt the cold air rushing into my face
As I ran in the race
My hands were numb and cool
Who thought of winning it, was a fool.
In the beginning of the race I was energetic
I could not breath properly; like an asthmatic
Now my lungs were quickly vibrating
As if it was the end of my breathing
When I looked back I saw my friend
The two contestants were near the end
As I dragged myself across the finishing line
I saw the whole big crowd cheering behind
On the victory stand I had the sensation
Of a great winner who got standing ovation.

Saqib Pervaiz, Grade 11
College Prep International, QC

Blacksmith Blue

Worn hands to be blamed on love spoken too late,
Welding each day, he works with unwavering fate.
Submerged in his shadow that hunches like the old,
Damned is his heart of lead, feeling solely with cold.

The moon yawns, sun awakes, stretching its arms through,
The splintered boards planing his cabin coloured blue.
The shade never forgotten, of his dearest Lise,
Who drowned from the breath and hiccups of seas.

With a ball-peen hammer, the sound of impact cries,
Bending steel of spirit, unveils what underlies.
Without a word to speak, he screams for one last look,
As nature plays the shameless thief, love she then took.

Wrinkles tell the tale with no apparent end,
Of Blacksmith Blue's heart, never could he mend.

Danielle Robert, Grade 11
Ecole Secondaire de Pain Court, ON

Hey It's Friday

It was a beautiful morning,
I was still in my lovely sleep,
Dreaming lovely dreams,
The light was peeping,
Through the window into my room.
I had to get up,
Then the sweet Friday refreshed my mind,
The last day of the tiring week,
Bringing a satisfying smile on my face,
I kissed my cute little bear,
Started the whole new day with a new beginning,
I went up to the window,
Looking through it,
I saw,
A beautiful spring morning,
With colourful flowers and their sweet fragrance,
Flocks of birds flying in the sky,
Little kids going to school,
Looking smart and smiling,
I love Friday morning.

Jatinder Multani, Grade 11
Ascension of Our Lord Secondary School, ON

Don't Go

DON'T GO.
It is too soon.
Give me a minute.
NO, not even a minute.
In that minute I would give you a hug that would last forever.
You are the sun,
That always gives us warmth and light.
DON'T GO.
Without you our hearts will shatter.
Loving you has brought so much pain.
If I had that minute,
I would hold your soft, gentle hand for the last time,
Never wanting to let go.
NO, not even a minute.
You left so fast,
All that is left is the past.
Stories and pictures,
But I will never be able to hug you again.
DON'T GO.
Just one last minute.

Amy Kullar, Grade 11
LA Matheson Secondary School, BC

Little Girl

Little girl, with skin as thick as stone
No one ever knew she was really all alone
Little girl, had everyone demanding the best
Leaving no room for her tired heart to rest
Little girl, not expected to breakdown and cry
Little girl, forced to live a lie
Perfect on the outside: that's what she had people believing
But everybody knows, appearances can be deceiving

Caitlin Kelley, Grade 10
Heritage Regional High School, QC

Midnight Dance

Take my hand and come with me
We will dance beneath the moon
You and me, together, we
Savour the midnight tune.

Time is but a trifle
In this world of ours
And you mustn't stifle
What you feel beneath the stars.

You and me, together, we
Our hearts shall beat as one
So set your spirit free
And ignore the rising sun.

Rosemary Greer Trost, Grade 12
Sir Robert Borden High School, ON

In All of Us

The devil hides in all of us
Satan and pure evil plus
All the lies and hate we hide inside
All used to protect our precious pride

Heaven lives in all of us
Goodness and happiness plus
All the joy and love we feel inside
All taking us on a wild ride

Heaven and Satan inside of us
Pure goodness and evil plus
A mixture of love and hate inside
Both trying to take full stride

Confusion lives inside of us
A need to understand everything plus
A mixture of emotions swirling inside
All wishing we had a wonderful guide

Ahsha Williams, Grade 11
John McCrae Secondary School, ON

I Am Standing

I am standing here alone
In the middle of the road
With blank paper in my hand

I am standing here with anxiety
Not knowing which way to go
Worrying if it is too late

I am standing here with fear
Watching others decide their way
Still have no idea about my way

I am standing here
Still not knowing the direction
Looking for a solution

Yun Noh, Grade 10
College Prep International, QC

The Harsh Reality

They wrap around you, and encase your soul;
making you listen to the lies they weave.
They hold you tight, and sing sweet songs,
forever binding and forever silent.
The iron grip, the whispered lies, the sugary stories, the subtle ties.
The truth they hid, a story untold,
forever replaced by another.
The harshest truth, the sweeter lies,
the nectar of simple demise.
The shocking truth, the disbelief,
the doors that open wide.
The sands of times, leak swiftly by, lost to the gaping hole.
The harshest truth, the sweeter lies,
the nectar of simple demise.
The fall from innocence, a devil's crime,
the tainted heart, the blackened soul.
The world today, a shrouded veil,
The time has come, for a faithful day, the day of utmost judgment.
So come, you sinner and non-believers, your web of lies end here.
The truth laid bare, for all may see and you cannot survive.
The harshest truth, the sweeter lies, the nectar of simple demise.

Angela Luan, Grade 12
Sir Winston Churchill Secondary School, ON

A Dreamer's Dream

With an eye, an eye so blue (why so blue they ask in wonder?)
Staring, gazing out towards the moon
(It's full round shape glaring white and new)
The dark tresses, the curls of satin
(Once gold but now brown, they shine with luster)
Fall harmlessly upon thin, pale shoulders
Spotted with faint freckles on the skin

Something old, something new, something borrowed, nothing blue
Except the eyes shining out towards the shimmering lake
(Across the sea to where they ask?)
Now it has become my task to pull the face so upward-lift
Down to earth where it must stay-forever on this twisted bay.

In the early months of May
The eyes again look upwards so
To the stars where fireflies go
And stick on the black ebony sheets.

Here, (they say with white-rimmed lips)
Look toward where the horizon meets
The sun so yellow in the blue.
(With this she's stuck on land for good)
With this she's stuck on land for good.

Caitlin Lamb, Grade 12
Burnaby Mountain Secondary School, BC

I Am

I'm the pain in your heart
I'm the tear in your eye
I'm the mystery in the days that the time flies by.
I'm the star in the sky that always catches your eye
I'm the whisper in your voice when you say goodbye.
I'm the voices in your head
I'm the lyrics to the song
I'm the thing that keeps you going, all day long.
I'm the words that you said
I'm the tears that you shed
I'm the sunshine when there's rain
I'm the colors in the sky
I'm the red in the cheeks, when you get shy.
I'm the heat when you're cold and the wisdom when you're old
I'm the sweetness in the sugar and the cherries in the pie
And the magic in the wings that makes the birds fly high
I'm the love note passed in class and the smile on your face
I'm the adrenaline in your veins
I'm your favorite place
I'm the butterfly so bold and blue
But I'm nothing without you.

Megan Taylor, Grade 12
Tobique Valley High School, NB

Abandoned Love

I see you and I go crazy
my heart starts beating faster and faster
so fast that I can't breathe
I try to talk but only air comes out
I am left wordless,
breathless and in a world of you.

Shazeen Hirani, Grade 11
Burnaby Mountain Secondary School, BC

Converter

I am a converter, I am a remote
I control everything
but sometimes the converter controls me
I am a converter, I am a remote
people may push my buttons
but that doesn't necessarily mean I will carry out the actions
sometimes my battery is low and everything starts to go awry
people seem to be pushing all my buttons at once
sending me different signals
and I don't know what to do, how to act
I am a converter,
frequently flipping through channels without a care,
turning the volume up when I feel like it's important
turning it down when I don't want to listen
I am a converter
pressing the rewind button when I recall
the memories, the laughter
fast-forwarding when I want to forget
I am a converter
controlling what I want to see
controlling actors in a play called life

Najmah Siddiqui, Grade 11
Silverthorn Collegiate Institute, ON

The 16th Year

So here it comes,
The sixteenth year,
Sixteen candles on the cake,
Sixteen years of my life finished
The big leap towards adulthood
Am I ready?
I don't know,
So many expectations,
What have I achieved in all these 16 years?
Nothing major, a normal life I guess
I expected greater, then again it was all in my hands
I don't know if I'm ready
If I take this leap who will take it with me?
Take a deep breath and jump.
So here it comes,
The sixteenth year.

Cornelia Baptista, Grade 11
Ascension of Our Lord Secondary School, ON

Family Stays, the World Goes On

As the clock ticks,
Friends come and go.

You get a new job,
You get a new house.

You buy her a blouse,
You spend your savings.

She leaves for him,
You are alone.

You look around, and there they are.
To comment on how much you've grown.

Your family puts you on a throne.
God gives you everyone else as a loan.

Mohsin Khandwala, Grade 11
Gordon Graydon Memorial Secondary School, ON

Fall

Diamond rain and mist fall together
Whispering the sordid symphony
Of bittersweet eternity
Beneath a purple sky
Chaining in his delirious scream
As weak vision recalled,
And breast ached,
For some time gone away
When it was spring.
Light and beauty,
Blackness and lies
Madness robbed men of dreams
Powerful shadows repulse essential love
Leaving the want of a friend
In the winter, after the music dies.

Madison Reid, Grade 12
Langley Christian Middle/High School, BC

Lines
Behind the lines is an unseen tale.
Caught beneath what used to be.
Struggling for life, reaching for air.
Desperation consumed by hope's desire.
Moving forward but wishing to go back.
Confronting the lines.

Alix Ehrler, Grade 12
Foundations for the Future Charter Academy-Dr Norman Bethune Campus, AB

Leaders
Leaders see and leaders do, they are unique; some different too.
Standing out from the crowd, they can be both soft and loud.
Through actions and words can you truly see, the light that they shine, it is how they be.
Taking part in anything; completing almost everything.
Being there in times of need and comforting those who bleed.
Leaders are among us all; within our people they seem small.
Open your eyes, look twice if needed. They are the ones who have succeeded.

Our nation now is blind. By those who choose to unwind.
They lash out fear and cause us to cry. No more should we stand by!
Waiting for fate, how it moves so slow. Instead we ourselves should emerge from below.
Destiny is on our side; hearts may leave that notion to hide.
Free from war, along with hate. To that moment, from this date.

Passion is an odd emotion. It is greater than the largest ocean.
Love it seems is far from reach, together now we must preach.
Speak of peace to the world, announcing that the time has come.
To lay it all down, say peace has won.
To forgive our enemies and love them as friends. To put aside the hurt and fix all of the bends.
Our people are the key, and with them we shall see.
Our past may seem a bust; Now our future, this is a must.

Katherine Janota-Bzowska, Grade 12
Elphinstone Secondary School, BC

Feeling for You…
I want to start straight from the inside of my heart.
If I gave you a flower, and a heart with that too, could I make "Love" mean something to you?
Could I be your dream come true, until the skies turn blue, and the day has gone through?
Let's take a walk in the park sitting on that bench, thinking, cuddling in the dark.
It's you who makes me smile, even if it was just for a little while.
I want to be the first to call, want to be the last to fall,
And mean the world to me, can't you see?
I want to be with you, never break your heart into two.
Is it okay to call you my "Boo?" Honestly, you know I'm in love with you.
I think of you every day, when we're on the phone, I don't know what to say.
When you're laying on your bed, after every phone call do you remember what I said?
You're glued to my heart, I don't think anything will tear us apart.
It's that one touch, and no one can describe it, no such.
I'm so tired of running away, and would it be okay,
If I said I want a chance, even if I end up asking for just "one last dance?"
I'm trying to make you feel number one, it's one of those infatuations that can't be undone.
Breaking your heart is one thing I won't do, giving it away is number two.
"It might be you?" You're starting to love me too.
I love this poem, it's just for us two. I want to end it with — "P.S. I love you…"

Ralph Torres, Grade 10
Holy Cross Regional High School, BC

Wanderers

Cold trails of thought snake through my mind,
Searching for that which will make it real.
What makes it real?
What makes anything real?
Is it the warm glow of emotion, the promise of
Feeling and humanity?
Logic screams for the whispering gentleness of sentimentality,
And it screams without realizing it;
An impulsive and silent longing.
A blizzard of icy thought-trails, forever trapped in my mind.
Forever wandering.
Forever searching for the warmth of feeling to defrost in.

To be voiced with.
To be heard.
To be loved.

Matthew Hudson, Grade 12
Webber Academy, AB

Once by the North

It was first the wind that obscured daylight;
the clouds they battered put up no fight.
The sun sank down in scarlet hues,
and bloodied the entire avenue.
The torrential snow was a conniving trick
to drive the flames from every last wick.

The trees had whispered their warnings high.
No creature stirred in land or sky,
except the human, the piteous soul,
deaf to the prophecy the breeze foretold.
The frost would crack its own shelled life;
no use remained in preparing for strife.

The trap, the lock, the chain was broken;
the rage, buried deep, had finally woken.

Anjali Gopal, Grade 12
Gordon Graydon Memorial Secondary School, ON

Echoes of Life

You can take the good, while you keep the bad,
Worry about your mood, but don't get sad.
You can envision an end, while you strive,
Dream of round the bend, it keeps you alive.

Fight for the living, don't forget the dead,
The point in caring, because hearts aren't lead.
Learn from your trials, and keep fast your pride,
The sun's on its dials, life is a short ride.

There are many devils and a hell inside,
That's for holy men, thoughts I cannot abide.
You can have your virtue and all your sins,
Not noble intent's curfew or few of kin.

We might be the source of all human strife.
There's still more joy than pain in this life.

Akbar Khurshid, Grade 12
The Woodlands Secondary School, ON

Retrospection

My sweet memories down memory lane
Are like patches of moonlight illuminating a forest trail.
Standing in a crowd, thinking back in time,
I lose myself in my past crimes.

All the things I did wrong,
All that I ever wanted to say,
All the people I've hurt,
All those who I took astray,

If only I could wind back the clock,
I'd have another shot.
To heal all the deep wounds
I gave to those who were mine

There, I've lost myself in my memories again.
It takes no effort or time
For one to lose oneself
In his own special rhymes.

Ghazal Mir Masood, Grade 10
College Prep International, QC

Coming in Last

You could have all of me, if you knew how to get it.
I would be irrevocably yours, if you would but try.
To repeatedly ask, to then be denied,
It's a little too much to keep inside.

I would be your everything, if you would but ask.
If you gave me a reason I would make this last.
Please don't push me away, give me a reason to stay.
I've had all I can take of coming in last.

Jennifer Starmer, Grade 12
Webber Academy, AB

By the Edge of the Earth

We stood by the edge of the Earth
   And witnessed the wondrous birth,
Of a world rid o' hate
   Together, sealing our fate.
No more fire, cold and darkness
   Love wrapped around us, like a harness,
A mere dream, possibilities unknown
   I stand here waiting, not to be alone.
We are lost in the fires o' doom, slowly dyin'
   How did we come here? Cheatin', lyin',
Our children face the burden of our guilt
   The oceans dry up, the flowers wilt.
What do we do from here?
   Take my hand, wipe your tear.
Together we make new ties
   Renew our souls, erase the lies.
We shall stand together at the edge of the Earth
   And witness the wondrous birth,
Of a world rid o' hate
   Together, sealing our fate.

Jyotsna Venkatesh, Grade 12
Gordon Graydon Memorial Secondary School, ON

Michelle Kwan

When Michelle skates
She does it with radiance and grace.

She always believes,
And dared to achieve.

She is my inspiration
Even in times of desperation.

Michelle, come back and compete!
So that one day we may meet.
Leanne Butler, Grade 10
Holy Cross Regional High School, BC

This Loss

When my heart for you
begins to sway,
It's hard to come back,
you're so far away.

The thought of you gone
brings nothing but pain,
But maybe, it's fate
this wanting in vain.

For some are so carefree,
no worries abound.
But the loss of your love
is one that's quite sound.

Some don't care what you think,
for me it's my life,
to know I am loved,
and safe through the night.

So maybe it's fate.
Maybe that's life.
But, no matter what,
It's the end of this strife.
Lauren Griggs, Grade 12
Webber Academy, AB

Every Time

Every minute of every hour
Every hour of every day
I will always think of you

Every day of every week
Every week of every month
I will always be with you

Every month of every year
Every year of my life
I will always love you.
Catherine Dionne, Grade 10
Seminaire de Sherbrooke, QC

We Have Forgotten

To those who never came back…We are sorry
To those who were never the same…We are sorry
To those who fought for us…We are sorry
To the families who received a box instead of a loved one…We are sorry
To those who still hang on…We are sorry
To those who must leave their loved ones behind to go and fight for us…We are sorry
To those who are left behind and must deal with the loss of loved ones…We are sorry
To those who begged, prayed, and died hoping we would remember…We are sorry
To those who still utter "Lest We Forget"…We are sorry
We are sorry because…We have forgotten
Because we continue to kill even though we do not have to…We have forgotten
Because we continue to settle disputes and arguments with a gun or a bomb
Instead of a kind word…We have forgotten
Because we thoughtlessly throw our poppies to the ground…We have forgotten
Kyle Reeves, Grade 12
Hon W C Kennedy Collegiate Institute, ON

Life Is a Roller Coaster

Life is a roller coaster
When you get on, you can't wait for what the future holds
You get in the seat and look at the ride ahead
with anticipation and wonder
As the cars start their journey up the hill
you look down and realize there's no getting off
When you get to the top you close your eyes and hold your breath
then the wild ride begins
There are twists and turns, drops and loops
and to your surprise, you find yourself enjoying it
There are times of horror and despair
then times of laughter and joy
As the ride draws to a close
you look at the end with sadness and relief
You don't want to get off but you realize
there are more people waiting to ride the roller coaster
Ashley Bond, Grade 12
Westcliffe Composite School, SK

Like the Waves

As we sat on the sandy shore, the cool water licking our feet
And glancing at its speckled surface, the stars almost in reach
Cymbals were crashing, sounding a warning as clouds gathered overhead
I sat and dug my heels deeper into the sand, hoping the calm weather would hold
But you coaxed me as the moon does the tide,
Hands clasped we waded further into the deep unknown
It was serene, letting the calm engulf us but it was just the quiet before the storm
The waves began to rock to and fro
I reached for your soft, yet calloused hands
I held on tightly, never letting go
As the waves grew violent your hold grew weaker
And I searched to find your hand
A wall of blue then took me under
When I surfaced all was calm again
I could see your smiling face; the storm had nothing on us
With your smile I then realized the current had pulled you under years ago
Jessica Milette, Grade 12
John Cabot Catholic Secondary School, ON

Two Faced Stranger

A puppet master with strings made of words,
You put on the greatest show of them all.
Blinding the world left and right,
Dazzling me with that crooked smile.

Painting a picture with colors of deceit,
I fall helplessly into your work of art.
You knew what words to use on me,
Playing with all my hopes and dreams.

Speaking words of love and adoration,
Singing a song that hypnotizes my soul.
Once I am caught in your web of music,
You break me like a string on that beat up guitar.

Unfortunately you're the fool in this little play.
Full of flaws; you're just a fake.
Alone you will remain upon center stage,
Continually playing your two-faced masquerade.

Cheria Xavier, Grade 10
Strathroy District Collegiate Institute, ON

A Stark Truth

Bright colors paint this radiant sight
And birds sing warm ballads
As a diamond sky glows;
What a vision.
A vision that is almost just a fantasy
As our world slowly shuts down,
Bound in a cloak of pollution, it is crumbling.
Simply craving salvation
But what is, will subsist
This stark truth.

Lianne Copeman, Grade 10
Heritage Regional High School, QC

Giving a Thought

Do you ever think about how you'd die
Did you ever think of how time'd fly

Do you ever wonder, what you would give
Just to live

Would you want to know
When your time's come to go

Are you scared or do you fear
Of what is far yet seems so near

We fear so we lie
To death we always deny
We run thinking that from death we could just pass by
We love and bleed
This Earth we don't want to leave.

Would you die for true love
Would you leave here for above?

Mariam Aziz, Grade 10
Ecoles Musulmanes de Montreal Campus Secondaire, QC

Graduation

Scalding afternoon rays blanket my peers
Fearless, yet afraid. Anxious, yet assured
Aged regrets have always been deferred
Now linger in their minds, launching out tears
Names announced singly, an orderly beat
Possessing that piece of parchment, our prize
Observing the surrounding glee-filled eyes
This hour, minute, second; bittersweet.
Then brief silence and the whole takes a stand
Eagerness and mirth leave distinct traces
on familiar, soon-forgot faces
Like death/birth, old and new are hand in hand
Gazing up at the cloudless sky, I cast;
my cap. Ready to venture out at last

Brianne Clouthier, Grade 11
Collège catholique Franco-Ouest, ON

Seasons

Spring colours are the best,
They are much more colourful than the rest!
It's nice to see the flowers grow,
And I like to see the pollen flow.

Summertime is so warm,
But there are mosquitoes that always swarm!
You can go to the beach and wake up late,
Because waking up early is what I hate!

In autumn the leaves fall,
From the trees that are quite tall.
Thanksgiving and Halloween are very fun
But I get sad when all the food's done.

Winter is so very cold,
And the white snow is so bold.
I love it when there is a snow day
Because it's the time when all the children play!

Brenda Lee, Grade 10
Holy Cross Regional High School, BC

Picturesque Paradise

Chirping birds at dawn brought me back to life
As the welcoming sun, showers its rays
The horizon purges nocturnal strife
Reveals an oasis of golden haze.

I then made my way out, pulled up my sleeves
Observed in silence nature's true duty
The dew that lay upon the glistening leaves
Bright blossoms blooming, oh, floral beauty!

Deep distressful silence was to be heard
Till interrupted by murmuring bees
And the wings of hawks and doves who fluttered
As the pines whispered to the gentle breeze.

This aura, this scene, I cannot explain
Though one thing for sure, I cannot complain.

Isabelle Aubry-Boyle, Grade 11
Collège catholique Franco-Ouest, ON

Depression

Early morning the sun rose
A wave of joy floods the air
The warm summer breeze blows

With the wind, happiness spreads through
The sunlight was affectionate
But still remained a drop of dew

The birds were cheery
The hope remained
And still that drop of dew was weary

The sun slept while the moon awoke
Sparkling stars filled the sky
And still that drop of dew spoke

Violently the rain fell
The storm was vicious
The drop of dew bid its farewell

The drop of dew had been replaced
However, never will it be erased

Lindsay Morgan, Grade 12
Webber Academy, AB

Do Not Fear Me!

You cannot see me
Because I am free
Right through me you can go
Yet you won't know
Mysterious I am

A short while I may be gone
But I am surely not done
When one member departs
I aim for their heart like I was to play darts
But you have nothing to fear

This happens during life
And I may have even taken your wife
"Tick, tick, tick" as the finial minutes pass
Your family holds one last mass
As the clouds welcome you with open arms

Do not fear me
For I eventually create beauty
In the end you will be reunited
So please don't feel frightened
I am the angel of death

Melissa Omaga, Grade 10
St Boniface Diocesan High School, MB

I Am

I am the sky.
I stand before the sun. I am the wind.
I am as red as fire, yet as green as grass.
I am strong, yet weak. I am winter. I am summer.
I am the future. I am today. I am the past.
I am me, you are you.

Josh Celaje, Grade 12
Holy Cross Regional High School, BC

Night in September

That unrecognized reflection.
Thoughts confused. Crazy? Maybe.
Heartbroken to the core. That's for sure.
Torn from the roots, manifested to nothing more.
Once innocent, not a worry bestowed upon her gentle soul.
Now looking into the eyes that are now invisible to her.
Remembering that man when her family was happier.
Leaves change, seasons change. The sky too has its change. The world.
But people change too, so is what she was told.
She stands alone, another fallen tear.
There's something dearly wrong I fear.
Seems like she's stuck.
Lift your head, wave, smile. Here comes the pain. Duck.
All her fairy tale lies.
She's missing her sunrise.
Can't stop crying, her emotions flicker like the weather.
Sinking, pull her out. Falling, catch her!
A message to that girl, staring back at her reflection,
Everyone has been in that direction.
I have to remember, to forget that memory, in September.

Shanice Bailey, Grade 11
Lincoln M Alexander Secondary School, ON

Abstraction

The walls were never another colour
They were always white
They were always void of colour
The windows were never open
They were always closed
They were always black and dirty
The room in which I stayed in
Was always locked
The door was always stuck shut
I remember them yelling out,
"You shall pay for your sins against humanity!"
All their voices screamed in my ears!
All in one chorus, all in one harmony,
"You will rot in Hell! You will rot in Hell!"
Their words stuck onto my skin like tattoos.
"I haven't done anything to hurt you!
All the blame is yours!" I retorted.
They shook their heads in disgust and threw away the keys.
The sun doesn't shine here, nor does the moon illuminate the room.
It's just my shadow and the endless ticking of the clock.

R. Dhadwal, Grade 11
LA Matheson Secondary School, BC

I Believe
I believe in the greatness of our country
The joy of love
The sadness of death
The difficulty of learning
The satisfaction of a job well-done,
of the sweetness and of legitimate sacrifice

But I don't believe that money can solve everything
I believe in human capacities
I believe that we can change
I believe in life

And I believe that I am maybe too optimistic
Roxanne Beauchemin, Grade 10
Seminaire de Sherbrooke, QC

I Am
I am the leaves and the wind
I wonder how many hurricanes will hit the coasts again
I see the whole world getting fixed
I am the leaves and the wind.

I pretend to not know what's going on
I feel that it's getting worse and worse
I touch the feet of an angel
I worry the scientists can't help our earth
I cry the tears that feed the trees
I am the leaves and the wind.

I understand why I am so anxious
I say that it won't end soon
I dream of the perfect world
I try to remove the sadness
I hope for peace and health everywhere
I am the leaves and the wind.
Emile Gendrone-de Vette, Grade 10
Seminaire de Sherbrooke, QC

The Sun and the Storm
Harmonious humid summer, midday
When wild winds swished emerald treetops.
So mellow, sun don't surrender today
Feeling moisture as mad murky raindrops.

High as the sky, with the gracious climate
I turned, scanned, shadowy clouds behind me.
Down from the sky hasty as Jack rabbit,
Storm's hands seized the sky, vast obscurity.

Up to flee, Death's wind pushes me, such ail!
His lunatic tears a vicious cascade.
His malicious tears become ghostly hail.
Storm conquers sun, all worlds begin to fade.

Alive! Heart beating! Sweat splashing I sit,
Rouse from a deranged dream, then relive it.
Byron McRae, Grade 11
Collège catholique Franco-Ouest, ON

I Do Not Know
I try my best in all I do,
But what do you want from me?
I do my best just for you.
Cannot you see?

I have so much potential.
I have so much passion.
But I want to explore what is beyond,
To be able to take action.

I love you so.
I love you much.
But please let me go,
So I can do such.

But until then,
I am confined to this chair.
Forever to see,
Only this door with you and me.
Yvette Kuo, Grade 10
Father Michael McGivney Catholic Academy High School, ON

The Judgment
My attempts are embarrassing,
She scoffs when she sees me.
He.
Beautiful boy standing behind her,
Laughing at me.
Her lips form a smirk as she mocks me.
Smoke curls around the room.
The French Inhale,
Leaving her mouth in delicate wisps.
I cough.
He laughs with her, his perfect teeth showing,
Her red lips judging.
I try to release the tension.
It's evident.
I chew and gnaw and bleed.
Looking down at me
They both torture and tease
Until I surrender
And give in to the disease.
Karly Wilson, Grade 12
Webber Academy, AB

Deceit
Despite tiny lies and a touch of deceit
You stole my heart, my love for you is all so deep.
Always in the end did I tell you the truth.
You didn't question my love, that was your proof.
Take a deep breath and may the sun bring you energy by day.
Exhale and may the moon gently restore you by night.
Let the summer breeze soothe your soul with new strength.
I think God made you just for me,
A mixture of passion and fidelity.
So dry your eyes my love so sweet.
I gave you my heart, it's yours to keep.
Cheyenne Simon, Grade 11
Ratihente High School, QC

The Gift of Humanity

Being human is about making discoveries and acquiring knowledge. Learning about things you never thought possible and some you wish weren't true. Being human is about feeling hopeless like all is lost, then realizing you
can make it through. Being human is about believing in a higher power, that affects all the things we do.

Humanity is our ability to think and reason. To love and be loved. To consider the consequences of our choices and learn from the bad decisions we make. Being human is about having to endure travesties in our life but also about experiencing the miracles. Being human is about beating the odds when they're stacked against you.

It is about having the courage and endurance to face extraordinary difficulty. It is about falling flat on your face and being able to pick yourself up again. Being human is also about knowing when to give in. A human recognizes defeat but also the chance of victory. Being human is to cherish memories, good and bad.

The gift of humanity is one that should be embraced as it takes us on a journey through life, to challenge us, benefit us and ultimately claim us.

Elizabeth Hrib, Grade 11
John Paul II Catholic Secondary School, ON

City Streets

See the city streets, see the city lights twinkling like mass numbers of stars.
Over the bridge, through the windows, around the Christmas tree which was put up a few days ago.

Hear the city streets, hear the city sounds. Listen to the cars going over the wet drains.
Rain and snow falling on sidewalks and roads.

Smell the city streets, smell the city scents — the pollution and smoke, the food and drinks.
Around the corner, on the streets, in the houses, brushing by your nose.

Taste the city streets, taste the city weather — the snow on your tongue, the ice air in your mouth.
Soft and cold, cool and minty; brings back memories of childhood

Feel the city streets, feel the city air. Touch the icy air both day and night.
Today, tomorrow, next week, next year. Every day during winter.
What is that sight? What is that sound? What is that smell? What is that taste? What is that feeling?
The city streets.

Ruth D'Souza, Grade 11
Philip Pocock Catholic Secondary School, ON

Great Grandmother

The warmth of your smile, your soft but cold hands
You're up in Heaven so far away, many miles, I wish we could go and put our feet in the sand

I miss you, where are you? Please, here I am if you're wondering
We used to be a team, but here I am alone

The woman in you was amazing, you fought for love, you were strong
The fire around me is blazing, are you happy? Am I wrong?

I know you are all right, I feel it in my heart, deep down inside
We will see each other someday, again, you will be by my side

I'm becoming older every day, it seems like yesterday we were playing cards together
I have changed in different ways, I will always miss spending time with no other

You are a part of my life missing, but I know in a way you're looking down on me
Smiling, laughing maybe screaming, I hope our love will make us see

The wonderful great grandmother you were to me.

Danielle St-Onge, Grade 12
Cite-des-Jeunes-A-M Sormany, NB

Deep Thought

During an exquisite summer sunset
In a field with grass as tall as statues
Stars elucidate with their silhouette
Wishing a dream, I start to have the blues

First let's jump to the space continuum
A few moments ago, I'll try to show
But I must not lie, it will be random
A thought of mine came to mind oh soooo slow

Dazed and confused I tired to puzzle out
The world is just like a black and white take
Pff! And we thought we had it figured out
Wished I was original, what's at stake

Now I snap back to the tedious flick
Why must our lives lie when we cry and die

Simon Kou, Grade 11
Collège catholique Franco-Ouest, ON

Music Past

I'm turning around; turning my back on yesterday.
Finding that our love lies within the lines of music past.
We search to find the strings that held us up.
The echoes cut them down,
and the silence cleared you out.
As smoke you follow me back in and cloud my vision.
The sun has set.
Lightning strikes and thunder rolls.
I can't hear my heart.
Truth fell from our lines and the music stopped.
Erase and replace.
Fresh notes read new headlines,
"Fractured Love."
Broken on the floor,
Where were you?
Lost in music past.
Fractured in the lines of music past.

Victoria Boleak, Grade 11
Burnaby South Secondary School, BC

Friendly Farewell

In August my skin welcomes sunlit tears
entranced by summer's fulfilling outcome.
Meaningful friends I have not seen in years;
friends I will seldom see for years to come.
Friends I have never uttered "goodbye" to;
but a rather cowering "see you soon."
Behaving hesitantly to debut;
we then blossomed with ease past splendid June.
Running about once more through sparkling streets
as we would within resplendent playgrounds.
July's deadline kissed my playtime's retreats au revoir.
Time it was to turn around.
As I challenged forth, head raised to the sky,
I turned to my friends and released "goodbye."

Navid Rahemtulla, Grade 12
Collège catholique Franco-Ouest, ON

The Night of Day

A more peaceful sound, one will ne'er hear,
Than the morning call of the joyous bluebird.
For though the dreary wake of sleep doth keep,
The fast of night does break away
And joy does reap.

Though tranquil the times of peace and mirth,
His omnipotence does yet prevail
And light o' day does bring sight of early morn,

At first dull gray, but cloudless
Skies do seem. But when His winged servants
Do feel remorse of times gone by,
The tears o' heaven; of cleansing from above
Do bring regret and dampens spirits too.

Of peaceful sounds, and foul sights,
Of joy and failed spirits it doth bring
The light of darkness, yet darkness light;
Of kindred souls, to sing unto the night.

Samantha Hossack, Grade 12
Notre Dame High School, AB

Yourself as a Jigsaw

pieces.
colors and patterns.
singularly: an unrecognizable picture.
fit together, producing a beautiful work of art.

bodies.
flaws and experiences.
alone: a misunderstood being.
loving and being loved, producing beautiful works of art.

Abby Hodgins, Grade 10
Kipling School, SK

My Castle in the Sky

My dreams are difficult to form,
considering they are not the norm.
I imagine myself back in time,
with many adventures and happenings all mine.

When I am in that magical trance,
I believe that I can actually dance.
My dreams are hard to make,
just like baking a double decker cake.

In reality my dreams can't come true,
due to the fact that the realistic ones are few.
Just like the task of bait,
my dreams hook their fate.

As you can tell my writing skills are short,
so I will go back to dreaming as my first resort.
For in my mind everything is as smooth as cream,
that is why I love to dream.

Hannah McKinnon, Grade 10
Holy Cross Regional High School, BC

Harvest

The crops are golden
The pods are all full of seeds
Combines everywhere.

Michelle Hale, Grade 10
Worsley Central School, AB

The Wind

The wind is a wolf
Ravenous and snarling
Prowling its way across the meadow,
Pushing out of the way
All obstacles
Then quieting as it stalks and waits
For the opportune time to strike again
Ripping to pieces
Everything in its path
And continuing on an endless journey
Light on its feet
And soundless at times,
But heard from far away at others
It is soft fur on the face
On a warm summer day
And a bite on the skin
In the harsh of winter
It is unpredictable, untamable
And ultimately wild
Those who try to stop it
Never succeed

Samantha Reid, Grade 11
Norwood District High School, ON

Lives for Sale

Lonely, they await,
They know you'll come.
As much as they run, hide or cower,
You'll find them.
You don't care where they're from,
Where they are,
Or where they're headed.
All you know is you have the power,
You have the gun,
A license to kill whomever you choose.
They can't stop you, nobody can.

You see their black and orange,
Moving speedily behind the grass,
Three of them so close,
You can't miss,
You load your gun,
Point the end,
And fire: once, twice, three shots.
Three heavy thuds,
You stole their lives,
Only to sell their hides.

Cheryl Noon, Grade 10
Ideal Mini School, BC

Inner Voice

The brokenhearted girl couldn't stop sobbing;
Nobody was there to be her crying shoulder, her punching bag, her listener.
How lonely she felt at that moment,
Seemed like the world was crashing down,
Flooded by a deep ocean of salt water.

The athletic boy couldn't stop stressing;
Somebody should be his leaning shoulder, his mentor, his role model.
How pressured he felt to be the best.
Seems like everyone had their eyes on him,
He was flooded with the expectations of everyone.

The wrinkly man couldn't stop screaming;
Anybody take away his pain, his aging years, and his poor health.
How useless he felt to be in this world.
Seems like his children thought he was a burden.
He was flooded by disappointments but keeps moving on.

I couldn't stop pretending;
Who could take away my pride, my conscious, my inner beauty?
How peer-pressured I felt to be like the rest.
Mean, cruel, obnoxious.
I lack inner strength. Sinking slowly.

Jessica Sit, Grade 12
Glenforest Secondary School, ON

I Am Who I Am

Who am I?
Am I the moon or the stars
That sit in the dark sky during the night,
Or am I the sun and the heat
That choose whether or not to come out,
Maybe I am just an average person
That acts to please other people instead of myself,
NO!
I am neither the sun, moon, stars nor heat,
I am definitely not one to please others,
Well, Who am I?

I feel like I am the music, always unpredictable with a twisted beat,
I think I could be a picture
One that gives laughs, but slowly fades,
Maybe I am just your average person
Instead of pleasing other people I please myself,

Who, really, am I? I am just an average person
One who wants peace, kindness and forgiveness,
I am one to stand strong
One who knows to choose the right path and follow it,
There is no definition of me, but I am who I am.

Samantha Bruneau, Grade 12
Leoville Central School, SK

I Want to Know

What does life mean? What does love mean?
We see them anywhere, they're always everywhere
Few know the key to happiness,
Those who don't are full of bitterness
I look to notice, I hear to acknowledge
What does it all mean? I want to know

How do you explain why you take a chance?
When all the confusion will put you in a trance
You try to understand your purpose in life
But failing so much adds on to your strife
My heart aches to understand this, I want to know

Ask yourself, are you happy?
Do you know what you want? Do you have what you need?
Have you found Love? Have you discovered Happiness?
Knowing why you exist will always be a mystery
Life that we go through can make you unhappy
Figuring this out is no simple game
It is all clear and simple, I want to know.

Michael Jordan Yong, Grade 11
École secondaire catholique Renaissance, ON

A Frail Winter

Fallen leaves, painful icy air.
Looks like Winter is back on the track;
Green meadows turn slowly into wastelands,
Looks like Winter is back on the track.

In this bleak season,
Life becomes unbearable,
Shivering cold right to the bone,
Because of Winter's raw blazing touch;

Beneath the frozen fields,
Lies sleep and death,
Waiting for the warmth,
To make its way back through this season of despair.

Mathieu Jette, Grade 10
Seminaire de Sherbrooke, QC

Succeeding

Nothing can prevent you from succeeding
yet you feel to become insufficient
The future is bright no one competing,
Your triumph is at a impediment
Who I question, who can this be standing
Barricading my fortress of knowing
Not a sound, no thought, the teacher speaking
My ears open, nothing clarifying
why are my thoughts still deriving elsewhere
The words I hear aren't to be remembered
Scholars screaming, excitement in the air
A substitute here, why should we be pleased
For the lack of knowledge we have to share
Or do we have a mystery to bare

Hani Mansour, Grade 11
Collège catholique Franco-Ouest, ON

High School Time

Throughout high school, time, one cannot befriend
Everything counted, beginning 'til end
Work stealing nights, studying 'til morning
Days inch by, while we count the remaining

Events, replacing calendars, fly by
Parties, dances, holidays, keeping time
Racing by like those countless reckless nights
Endlessly nagging like a fear of heights

Suddenly, this years long game is ending
Agonizing, questioning this training
The day was never thought to be so near
Proud mothers crowd the stands, fearing, in tears

To promising bright futures we look on
Have we yet to realize this time's gone?

Everett Delorme, Grade 11
Collège catholique Franco-Ouest, ON

Here

I'll stand in the room, you're there once and awhile
Whenever I glance over, I can see the pain in your eyes
You'll smile at me or give me a hug
But it's different, those hugs, almost strained
I tried to help, you pushed me away
I know things are hard, I've dealt with it before
I understand
Yeah, it's hurting me, and others too
To see you in so much pain
I can't figure it out
I have to help and yet I can't
I guess for now
I'm not mad at you
It'd be wrong for me to be
If you want to talk, without criticism
I'm always here, any time of day, or night
My phone is on
Just be strong, and remember…
You have friends, you're not alone, you have me

Samantha Seymour, Grade 11
Mount Boucherie Secondary School, BC

Arcade

The place is so full like a playoff game
Kids hypnotized by the machines
Metallic demons that steal
My money for the very last time
As I hear the sound of the winner
The coins getting swallowed by those living stones
The sweat of the players
The fragrance of the food being chewed by the crowd
The savor of the winner's joy so sweet and splendid
The loser's flavorless pain
I can feel the winner's concentration
And the loser's frustration
Game Over

Frank Zidona, Grade 11
Collège catholique Franco-Ouest, ON

The World's Faces
The sea is blue, the sky is gray,
the grass will be green day after day.
But in your mind you know it will change,
once the world has changed its phase.

The sky will be black and filled with stars,
but in the city all you see is streetlights and cars.
So as the world turns its face,
the sun will shine in another place.

But every day is a new opportunity.
People judge, telling you what you should be.
Just clear your head as the world spins round,
and fulfill your dreams, because the world is your playground.

Michael J. Mendoza, Grade 10
Holy Cross Regional High School, BC

Falling Through the Clouds
Falling through the clouds, with a deafening noise going through my ears
The awkward sense of peace falling towards earth is beautiful
Even though I am falling from the heavens
And heading towards a world filled with hardships
I couldn't be more happier that I have received such a bizarre moment of peace

I did not take a leap of faith and head towards earth
But rather was sent to the earth with a purpose
Once I reach the earth I will find it
My body reaches closer to the ground then…BOOM!

I wake up after a perfect slumber
it was all a dream
This dream felt so real
I will do anything to re-experience that moment of peace
Falling through the clouds, falling from the heavens.

Jason Kim, Grade 10
College Prep International, QC

Morphing
Ubiquitous sun…
Its roots envelop the ocean waves,
Which crash and disintegrate onto the harsh shore,
Repeatedly over without mercy.

Roots cage the saddened ocean,
Offers of protection and love.

Hardly does it crest and fall unexpectedly, given the remedy of time.
Instead, the rough cocoon hatches.

A silky pond emerges,
Flourishing with life yet ambiance,
Drip by drip fearlessly…
Smiling under the acceptance of the rays, bidding the clouds farewell.

Julie Tran, Grade 12
Lester B Pearson Sr High School, AB

Amid a Summer's Night

Evening gently conquers sunlit skies
Abundant colors mask'd by dusk's disguise
Stray from menacing obscurity's night
Charmed insects embracing blaze's light

Flee; jail's ruptured iron bars, demons try
Like dancing flames reach up to heavens high
Dazzling spirits, enchanted atmosphere
Suburban notions slowly disappear

Mother Nature's mighty essence captured
Profound desire newly discover'd
Tunes arise, out-pour tender furtive depths
To George, Ringo, Lennon, Paul's honored steps

Meaningful lyrics fill blank paper's white
Lift off reenacting mid-summer's night
Erika Schmitz, Grade 11
Collège Catholique Franco-Ouest, ON

Time

Time is the key to everything,
We sometimes lose ourselves in a dark hole,
Lose ourselves enough to find that there's no escape,
Sometimes we make it through,
But we are never the same,
We confine ourselves within four walls,
Time really does change it all,
Time takes it all,
Time gives us all,
Time bears it all away,
Time is the eternal test of a nonstop journey,
We find ourselves standing at a point against our wills,
Sometimes we shut out the rest of the world,
And yet still never seem to make it through,
We're still stuck in a single time frame,
Lost so far in the darkness, standing alone on our two feet,
Wondering if we'll ever find our way back again.
Misha Patel, Grade 12
Rick Hansen Secondary School, ON

The Day After

Settling into a gloomy class
Same faces, same teacher, same class, no more
Three seats as empty as a clear glass
Calling the names of those who came before
Sobs and weeping from the girls in the corner
The boys always mopped, never spoke
I spoke as if given an order
Three hollow chairs began to choke
All the girls missed the way Mary made them smile
And the boys mourned the loss of Greg's skill
I mourned the loss of our Genius, Kyle
The boy we never ever thought would kill
Such a price Greg and Mary had to pay
We were here all together yesterday
Paul Lanouette, Grade 11
Collège catholique Franco-Ouest, ON

I Still Believe

I believe in the magic of a wish,
The hope of a better tomorrow,
The destiny that guides us,
The heavens where my angel is,
The intensity of passion,
Fervor, desire, adoration

But I don't believe that you can understand
The way I feel about you.

I believe in the strength of a family,
I believe in the faith of a friend,
I believe in the power of love,
Vitality, fidelity, devotion.

And I believe that you are the person
Nearest to perfection.
Katherine Lacroix, Grade 10
Seminaire de Sherbrooke, QC

A Fool's Paradise

My eyelids gently dim out the light,
I gradually drift to an altered sight,
Of images invading my mind.

Figures travel within whispers of the breeze
Nothing distinct but all is at ease,
The darkness never seemed quite so adequate.

A sudden terror lurks in my path,
I am desperate for an escape of this wrath,
Thereupon reality came to see,
The world just as it should be.
Vanessa Ferreira, Grade 10
Heritage Regional High School, QC

Behold the Essence of Beauty

Behold the essence of beauty.
When a seed has fallen, the flower can bloom.
When the sun shines, the people can see.
When the wind blows, the trees can feel.
Behold the essence of beauty.
A time to love,
A time to hear,
A time to speak,
A time to remember who we are.
Behold the essence of beauty.
Oh arrogant nation,
Full of wants and envy,
Oh pitiful creation,
That stumbles and falls.
Crash. Shatter. Broken.
The flower cannot grow,
The people cannot see,
The trees cannot feel,
Our minds wonder, what is the essence of beauty?
Rolisha Walters, Grade 12
White Oaks Secondary School, ON

Our Beautiful Shiny World

Look at our faces now
We've got the happiness crow
So many colourful flowers blow
They're what we're looking at
Grinning like a Cheshire cat

We are losing something now
Did we ever notice that?
That's never thought about
Though we have no doubt
Of our beautiful shiny world

We'll see the darkness water
Soaking through from our feet
All the tears are into the boots
That is the exactly same world
With where we're living in

It's not too far away
From us and where we are
But we never see them
We never listen to them
Although they're same with us
Although we'll join them soon

Yunsun Noh, Grade 11
College Prep International, QC

Opposite Day

I woke up one morning
To an opposite day.
The world seemed somewhat different
In every single way.

Keeping my feet off the ground
Was a lot of trouble
Since the law of gravity
Decided to double.

I looked out my window
And saw a clown fish.
Was I in the ocean?
This wasn't my wish.

Walking to the bathroom
My head hit the floor.
For some strange reason
It was under my feet no more.

My eyelids flew open.
My feet hit the ground.
I'm back to reality.
What a sweet sound.

Jessika Porter, Grade 10
Holy Cross Regional High School, BC

Relationships

Things don't always work out
Sometimes you got to scream and shout
It's all what you make it
I'll give you my heart, but promise not to break it
I want to build trust and of course have lust
Friendship will lead the way
Kisses will leave you with nothing to say
All in all, just please be there to catch me when I fall

Sinead Byng, Grade 12
Whytecliff Education Centre, BC

The Moon

As the moon comes out at night
Blessing the people with their wishes
Many believe it might come true
But many think it is going to fly back with the moon
Many individuals ask for bliss
But some are already blessed with grief
As we all see the moon shining in the sky
Gives us anticipation and the strength of standing alone
Only because and only for *our dreams.*
Many do it for affluence, but many for identity
That somewhere was vanished among the stars
Soon it will come to us with the most significant obsession in the world *our dreams.*
As the dreams are about to come veritable
As the moon comes out at night, reveals itself and then vanishes
As we swiftly open our eyes to search for it
We find the sun that pervades our life with illumination
That is never meant faint
As the moon comes out at night to fulfill our dreams.
As the moon comes out at night to fulfill our dreams.

Naina Mehta, Grade 11
LA Matheson Secondary School, BC

What Happened?

I feel my fists clench and the blood rushing to my face.
My heart is skipping beats as I try to find a solution to this case.
What is happening to you?! Look at what you have become.
I see you for one second and the next, you are done.
What is that in your hand? Please let go of it now.
It is no good for you, you are just going to go down.
What happened to your attitude? You have become so moody.
What happened to us? We used to talk so smoothly.
I am so lost for words, I do not know where to start.
You know we care for you so much, but you have picked up this dark art.
I understand you did not keep your word, I know people make mistakes.
I just do not understand why you need to be so fake.
I miss the old you, the one I looked up to.
I hope you soon realize what is the right thing to do.
Remember that we will always be here.
We are your true friends, but we are filled with fear.
I know you are smart enough to know when to stop.
I just pray that it is soon, before the stop of the clock.
You are still my best friend, I just do not know what you are doing.
There is no one to impress, so just stop with the fooling.

Charisse Trinidad, Grade 12
Holy Cross Regional High School, BC

Life

Life is a gift from God
Life is passionate
Life is adventurous
Life is love
Life is cared for
Life is music
Life is art
Life is nature
Life is school
Life is books
Life is family
Life — is everything.

Joanna Paluch, Grade 10
Ascension of Our Lord Secondary School, ON

The Three Chinese Boys

One was short and fat,
Another was thin and cynical looking,
The third one looked like a deer caught in headlights.
Mumble mumble.
What were they talking about?
Not a single word would be understood.
Giggle giggle giggle.
The giggling goes on.
We cannot stop.
Three chinese boys.
They have a funny accent, weird looking glasses.
Snerk snerk.
The teacher looks at me, Sharma, and Kathy,
Disapproval in his eyes.
Giggle giggle giggle.
Can't stop.
Snerk snerk.
Can't stop.
Still can't understand them, but so hilarious.
Hey, I wonder if they can understand us,
The three Korean girls

Sylvia Jun, Grade 11
Earl Haig Secondary School, ON

An Aboriginal Cry

I cry myself to sleep each night
For I am Cree, I have no right
To carry any traditions, to hold any sign
Of my heritage, for it is a crime.
I was taken from my home to a residential school
Where the teachers and staff are very cruel.
I am forced to live in European culture
Or I will be beaten and left for the vultures.
This assimilation is not fair or just
And I need to make known my disgust
Of the horrible government in this "fair" land
That force us to follow their every demand
And get rid of our culture, wipe off our grin
They want us to become, European.

Zach Vogelhut, Grade 10
Dr G W Williams Secondary School, ON

Ending to Beginning

These varied emotions filling my head.
I'm feeling an unhappy sensation.
What should be the next step I take ahead?
I know it won't be the same direction.

Approaching more and more, near to the end.
Glancing at books I'll never see again.
Gliding that path that I've always taken,
After a long and torturous lesson.

Reaching the metal door, ten twenty-three,
A bright light reflecting from the shutters.
To see, my combination is the key.
Straining the panel, out goes the clutter.

Fiouf! No more teachers, school is now done
Summer has begun, and so has the fun.

Dana El-Sabbagh, Grade 11
Collège catholique Franco-Ouest, ON

Strength

The winds that expel from your mouth colour
The air with a transparent steam that I
Greet in hopes of not kissing a duller
Face; embracing your triumphs, joy, and sighs.
The mountains, however mighty and tall,
Caress the shadows clouds expel upon
Them; this darkness, seemingly benign, falls
Down along mountain walls to the green lawn
Below. Your strength I respect, but have no,
Inhibitions; the cancerous shadows,
That haunt your peace of mind, now present woes
And stress hinder growth of joyous meadows
Within the confines of thine thought, please find
Our hopes and hearts entwined, our strengths one kind.

Avery Parsons, Grade 12
Gordon Graydon Memorial Secondary School, ON

Summer

Great and wide is the sun of that magnificent season
With the light of dusk a deep red crimson

And in the blue glowing days
Loudly chirping are the blue jays

With hot and humid weather
Into the pool people go together

On a hill you will have a beautiful view
You could see the ocean sparkling blue

The trees tall and green
Are as high as anyone has ever seen

At the end of this season people wear coats of heavy leather
And leaves fall as light as a feather

Mahdi Bedrouni, Grade 12
Academie Marie Laurier, QC

Smile

A smile on your face
Gives glory to your face

A smile is a key to love
Without smile the world is dull

A smile is a jewel
That can be bought without money

So wear this jewel
And consider it as a gift from God
Yumna Baqai, Grade 11
Erindale Secondary School, ON

Whispers

A desolate landscape of secrets
unfolds around me,
enveloping me.

In grey as gray as the
concrete on which I step,
where all that is heard is the
Silence Whispers leave in their wake.
Behind the walls of grey
are skeletons, enjoying:
— the freedom of privacy
— of whispers being the only knives.
Truth made them
what they are:
afraid to be seen, or see, and
locked in their prisons of grey,
guarded by Whispers.
Anne Simonen, Grade 12
Rossland Secondary School, BC

I'll Be Near

I'll be there when you're screaming
I'll be there when you need me
When you're slipping through sand
I'll give you my hand
When you're blinded by fear
I'll hold you near
When you're silenced by doubt
I'll voice your shout
When you need a friend
I'll help your heart mend
I'll give you my voice
I'll hear your dreams
I'll lighten your burden
I'll set your soul free
Anything you want
Anything you need
But the door to my heart
Will remain without a key
Anneke Chambers, Grade 10
Ecole Secondaire Mille-Iles, ON

The New You — Increased in Hatred

Constantly you fill your life with hatred darkness,
and further regret the decisions you make.
Do not apologize; you're only hurting yourself in the end.

I pity the battle you live through (against yourself)
I cannot help you win until you learn
to respect yourself.

I pity your selfishness, your recklessness,
your stubbornness and your carelessness.
Get well, before we speak once more.

You've seemingly slammed the door of ignorance
in my face, while my hands stretched out towards you,
to guide you, to help you, to befriend you.

You slammed it closed, with force, and I understand
I won't get in the way of this new life you plan to attend.
But when you wonder what that feeling is, during your periods of darkness,
remember that the cold you're feeling
Was easily thrown away by us, whilst sitting hand in hand.

When all is said and done, what will you have in the end?
Chelsey Minor, Grade 11
École Secondaire Publique l'Odyssee, ON

Silence

The young girl runs away, to avoid the truth.
The abuse continues day after day,
No one is there to stop it, to save her, to protect her.
She runs to her selfish mother who turns a blind eye.
Who can she run to, when family is in silence?

The teen hides his face, to avoid the looks.
The cruel remarks continue day after day,
No one is there to stop it, to prevent it, to control it.
He runs to the police but sees no change
Who can he run to, when authority is in silence?

The innocent man hugs himself, to avoid the pain.
He ages in his cell day after day,
No one is there to listen, to stand up for him, to seek justice.
He runs to his lawyer who just wants his money
Who can he run to, when society is in silence?

You think about other things, to avoid reality.
You wonder about it day after day,
No one is there to change things, to voice their opinion, to show they care.
Thinking, fading, worrying; reality is becoming untrue
Who can you turn to, when everyone is in silence?
Justin Harvey, Grade 12
Glenforest Secondary School, ON

Just Below Your Throat

From the moment it was assembled
It performs its given labour
Tirelessly, for years
Keeping its one promise
So uniquely designed,
Draining life into connected streams,
Then traveling throughout the body
The Queen of the Circuit
The strongest man cries,
Only because it feels its sorrows, knows its desires,
Challenging the workings of the rational mind
The burdened one as small as a fist
Locked behind a cage, in supreme secrecy
So its beauty is protected
It is hidden
Yet never silent, never dares to stop
Maybe to remind us all that it exists
The sole architectural image of love
The battery of the human
Another artwork by God
The heart

Sanjida Hoque, Grade 12
Marianopolis College School, QC

Self-Proclaimed Intellect

Hypothesis of hippopotamus
Or other hysterical the-o-ries,
Haunt and hoard the core of my genius,
While the teacher questions me with expertise.

Are you spacing off in my class, young lad?
Howled the elder, with excessive sound.
Kind sir, replied I, how I would be glad
To explore Mars and reach the higher ground;

For I have never caressed apathy
Equivalent to this colloquium;
Oh, how my soul bathes in pure agony
When I enter this filthy asylum!

At that, without surprise, I sit…await…
For the principal to conclude my fate.

Alexandre Riel, Grade 12
Collège catholique Franco-Ouest, ON

Fake Friends

Today, they like you
Tomorrow, they hate you
Today, they care about you
Tomorrow, they do not even know you
Today, they want to share secrets
Tomorrow, they're telling everyone your secret
Today, they got your back
Tomorrow, they are the ones stabbing it
Fake friends are such
And such are fake friends

Isaac Geam-Worlanyo, Grade 11
Ascension of Our Lord Secondary School, ON

Forlorn

A world of complexity
Intricacy
Nothing comes easy.
Delusion, confusion
Lies, goodbyes
Faces pass by
One, two, three, four
Just another man to adore.
One, two, three, four
Just the same as before.
A flick of the wrist
A sway of the hand
An imagined kiss
A moment unplanned.
Feelings incontrovertible
Essence undeniable
Results indistinguishable
All inconsolable
For now.

Nicole Angelucci, Grade 12
Father Bressani Catholic High School, ON

A Day in Utopia

Floating, drifting upon crystal waters
fiberglass shuttle piercing the smooth flow
paddling along like nothing else matters
delight increases as time seems too slow

Mother Nature's marvels entice my eye
so chilling in stature, majestic trees
witness birds carve their path through open sky
life's problems flee like a cool summer breeze

As crescent moon substitutes solar rays
whilst constellations materialize
as stunning as day, the nocturnal phase
these night-time wonders seem to hypnotize

Assemble encampment, feeling so drained
But on this day, perfection was attained

Patrick McKee, Grade 11
Collège catholique Franco-Ouest, ON

Life and Death

Life
An ocean
A never ending sea
Dark as night near the bottom
Where death falls upon the unfortunate
While giving life on those who feed upon them
Near the surface is the blue stolen from the sky
Where abundant life flourishes within thee
Nature at its best until death comes
In a white boat on the surface
We come; humans
Death

Jennifer Newton, Grade 12
Merritt Secondary School, BC

Perfect

You brought me into a world which was perfect, now the only perfect thing left is you
The unfolding truth has turned it into a nightmare, but like you always say, "Dreams do come true."
All I could was stare, while the lively blue sky turned a dull gray.
All I could do was watch, when the "perfect world" went astray.
The stars would only shine at nightfall, the flowers died as soon as they came,
But you will always stay my mother, won't you always stay the same?
They say, "Time always wins the race over man," it stole all which I had so preciously kept,
Happiness merely turned into memories, and now you're all that I have left.
You held my hand back then, as I was staggering to take my first step,
But it feels as thought it's slipping away, as faster and faster time has swept.
As the number of my years grow higher, I stop showing I still need you,
That hand rarely shows up now, but know it needs me too.
But when those hands do reach out, to give me a warm welcoming embrace,
The world feels perfect again, time is flying at the perfect pace.

Swati Pareek, Grade 10
College Prep International, QC

Nightmares

Dark mountains far away
A swarm of bees coming my way

Dive into the water, I swim and pray those evil monsters won't get me today
Climbing a tree as high as I can, suddenly I feel a drop of rain

Overhearing young children's laughter then screams of pain shortly after
Listening to people run around followed by gun shots, they fall to the ground

The odour of fire fumes pass me by
The stench of dead bodies makes my eyes cry

My salty tears is all I have to get by, my stomach growls it's hard to keep my eyes wide
I pick leaves off a dying tree to satisfy my hunger, but all I feel is a weight pushing me down under

Never been more scared, this feeling makes me impaired
Physically and emotionally tired this nightmare has now been expired.

Monica McLaughlin, Grade 11
Collège catholique Franco-Ouest, ON

Vehicles and Human Life

Life is a busy highway,
        if you don't flow with traffic,
                you are singled out by everyone, and
sometimes get in trouble with the law,
        or end up dead
                People have their own life to live,
                        that is why you
sometimes go past them fast or they go fast past you.
                All around you,
                        you see the dangerous
decisions people are making with their life.
        Sometimes you see people,
                or know people that have lost
their lives going too fast,
        or making bad decisions.

Joshua Aaron White, Grade 12
Westcliffe Composite School, SK

Life and Death

Death is like the end of the road
While life is the path that follows,
Life can bring you home
And the unkind death strips it from you,
Life evolves day by day
So does the butterfly in the cocoon,
Death bares his hollow smile
Wishing decay in the tomb,
Some believe in life after death
Some believe that death steals your breath.

Tanner Turchak, Grade 12
Merritt Secondary School, BC

With a Twist

The overpowering light engulfs me.
The heat is unbearable.
I can feel the rays from the sun, burning my back.
Trapped in the haze of midday.

Suddenly a slight breeze whips through the air,
but then it's gone.
Where are the clouds?
I need protection.

I begin to feel dehydrated.
Water, I need water to quench my thirst!
Surrounded only by long dried grass.
Time is passing ever so slowly.

All is silent.
I am lost in my thoughts,
slowly slipping from reality.
Drowning in sweat.
As I lie outside to tan.

Cami Weiler, Grade 12
St Anne's Catholic School, ON

Nothing to Lose

Stepping up on the blocks
Looking down to the bottomless ground.
Still, my heart was at a pound.
I could hear the tick tock of the clock.

I hear the starter's bell
My heart started to race,
At an unbeatable pace.
Off my face the sweat fell.

Racing like I have nothing to lose,
The wall is not too far.
If I keep my pace could I be the star?
And if I do, I will try not to have the blues.

I am working so hard I started to thirst
I touched the wall
I know I cannot fall
Look I won first.

Emily Williams, Grade 10
Holy Cross Regional High School, BC

12:05

12:00 and awake.
Screams echoing throughout the night,
reverberating off of tee-pee poles
and million year old rocks.

Wanting to block it out,
defeat when you can't.
Voices drilling into your skull so willingly,
not knowing,
or knowing all too well,
that a thin layer of cloth
cannot soften the screeching.

At last, the final spell of
cachinnate laughter is thrust
into the quiet darkness.
12:05 and not quite dreaming.
Now all is quiet,
until the sun rises,
to kill the envious moon.

Christina Wutzke, Grade 10
St Dominic Catholic High School, AB

How Do I Work with You

How do I work with you in my mind?
You're all I can think about
There's no way I can get you out of my mind.
I gaze out this window
Wondering if I'm ever going to see you,
Talk to you
What do I have to do to get the time of day?
When am I finally going to be alone with you
When am I going to feel you arms around me?
I'm going insane without you.
I have nothing but feelings for you.
I don't think I can ever let you go.
My heart would break if you were not in my life.
When will I finally tell you?

Kimberly Harrison, Grade 12
Ascension of Our Lord Secondary School, ON

crying into ice cream.

tears and cookie dough should never be a flavor.
there's too much bitterness attached
to the sweet dough who tries to make it all better.

and yet.
here i am.
creating a whole new genre of ice cream
with my tears.

other things i could create now:
chocolate chips and hurt.
vanilla sob ripple.
now with swirls of fear
and regret.

Sarah Goldstein, Grade 12
Webber Academy, AB

Victim

Look into my eyes
And tell me what you see.
You don't see a damn thing
Because you can't possibly relate to me.

All my life I've lived in agony,
All your life you lived in harmony,
Do you see a difference between,
You and me.

You worry about your education
And the bills you have to pay.
I worry about my helpless life
And if I'll survive another day.

The peace agreement will be too far
Only the dead
Will see an end to war.

Ghaith Sabouni, Grade 11
College Prep International, QC

The Dawn Breaks Twice

Consider, if you will,
The sun shining down on the earth below,
Glancing at every dewdrop,
Every flower's petal,
Every bird singing its first morning's song.

Perhaps, then, the clouds roll in,
Slowly, but soon dramatically
As all the light is blocked.

Darkness.
Silence.
The world is in shock.

Gradually, the light starts to creep through
The world of black.

Earth sees light again.
This is a new day.

Rebecca Deutschmann, Grade 10
Holy Cross Regional High School, BC

A Life's Oath

I am as strong as a mountain,
As great as a raging sea,
But mountains crumble,
The seas dry,
And I will cease to be.

So I will live my little time,
As if it were a race,
For far too soon,
I will be gone,
Alone in a wooden case.

Erin Compeau, Grade 11
Bishop Allen Academy, ON

The Gilded Truth

Heaven's stores were told in vain
holding you close with no remorse or pain
Let it be said, I'm not one to stay
live your life neither happy nor gay
If that's who you were, that's all you can hope to be
You are just a man, not fit enough to see
All you are is everything I've ever been
So leave me here, save a sin

Tatiana Abdel-Malak, Grade 11
College Prep International, QC

The Fire of Words Unsaid

In a silent empty room I light the wood on fire
I let the flames surround me mistaken they're what I desire
Sitting by the fire, comforted by its heat
Staring deep into the light, not realizing my own defeat
Taking protection from the cold of the falling snow
Burning away the wood with words that they'll never know
The fire that I take comfort in is filling my lungs with smoke
Knowing what is truly burning is unlike the words that I spoke
The wood burning is covered, smothered with the utterance of my heart
I think of it as heating my body but really it's burning each part
Burning slowly in the flames I see a shattered reflection
I frantically wave the smoke away to make clear the imperfection
I look into the mirror and stare at myself staring back
The smoke the fire gave off has burned my face black
The fire has not helped me improve I now begin to realize
I know I should've told the truth I see it in my own eyes
I look at the wood and suddenly I know
These are the feelings from my heart, the ones I wouldn't show
I lit them on fire, to protect myself from pain
But now sitting in a burnt down room I see there was nothing to gain

Shradha Talwar, Grade 12
Gordon Graydon Memorial Secondary School, ON

homeless man

there's a homeless man who lives under my bed.
he wears no shoes and drinks wine red.
he's tiny and dirty and talks with sass.
he swears, he fights; he's got no class.
one day the homeless man took me aside and whispered in my ear,
"dear child, you live in fear.
i was never there, nor here.
i never lived under your mattress springs,
and i never heard you sing.
i never lived a day in my life,
especially not under this bed.
oh dear child,
you've lost your head.
you're thinking and imagining things that will never come into play.
i'm sorry, dear little child, but it's time to grow up now; it's just the way.
it's time to put all this in your past.
this is the last time, this is the last."
and the homeless man vanished into thin air.
"no, mother," i nodded my head. "the homeless man was never there."

Kym Couchie, Grade 12
St Joseph/Scollard Hall Secondary School, ON

The Fairytale That Came to an End

I never desired you, candidly
I found myself persistently wiser,
Blinded by your eyes that day of summer;
Or how mine locked on yours delightfully

It caught me off guard like a hurricane
As you kissed and held my hand lustfully
Dreams as a little girl came with glee
Sweet summer smells graved in memory lane

Bee's buzzing, blossomed lilies, splendid sea
Replaced by a cool breeze of crimson leaves
Running through my torn soul with expertise,
Every inch of my heart burning cautiously

Falling leaves brought a mountain of goodbye
You fell in the sea; I let my heart cry

Michelle Haines, Grade 11
Collège catholique Franco-Ouest, ON

Soul Cyclone

Wind picks at my shirt
My bare arms prickle with goose bumps
My hair whips, my eyes water
The cold air whistles down my throat with every breath
I feel like flying. I feel like a leap
Could take me anywhere, to anything
My feet are planted but I sway with every gust
My ears are closed
No sound but the sound of my own heartbeat
I do not think of anywhere or anything
My heart takes a jump into unknown territory
My body stays behind, dejected, alone
My mind watches them both and my spirit is torn to pieces
I go everywhere, become everything
A car rushes past
My dog pulls at her leash
The wind calms for a moment and I fall back
Together. My pieces settle
But I begin to walk home still full of cracks

Jocelyn Tennant, Grade 11
Okanagan Mission Secondary School, BC

Time

Each second that I spend in here
I count.
The day crawls by and I wish nothing more
Than to be free.
Fall, winter, spring
They are all endured
As I wait for the clock to release me.
I even count the years
Until this place will be a memory.
I only hope
That I will not look back and wonder
If for all my counting
I only slowed the passing of each day.

Mary Poelstra, Grade 10
Holy Cross Regional High School, BC

Promise

The sky is a beautiful place,
I always wonder, what's up there?
Especially in this certain case,
when I'm asking for you, where?
I feel this empty hole in me
where it cuts me to the core,
if there is anything I could be,
is to go back and to know you more.
But fate has left you up there
and me below,
though the thought of you in the air
with your radiant glow
makes my heart smile.
You are known for your beautiful ways,
in your own unique style,
so on those sunny days,
spread your wings and fly.
Even though you leave behind all earthly things,
there is no need to cry,
because we all love you forever
and you will never be forgotten…promise.

Natasha Cvitkovich, Grade 10
Holy Cross Regional High School, BC

True Disguise

Sour when sweet, sour when sour,
Incomprehensible, unaware.
Pleasant in company, grotesque with her,
Painful, disgraceful.
A heart painted gold by day and the blades of night beat it black,
Unstoppable, unalterable.
Mind grown of flowers, truly devices ever-scheming,
Harmful, horrible.
Gentle and soft spoken, forceful, words screaming,
Hurting, deafening.
Minimized liberty, livable, controlling, bound to the ground,
Isolated, unbearable.
Viewed as happy, steady relationship,
Lived as dangerous, broken connection.
Smelled as clean, fresh, honest,
Dig up the pungent odor of dirt, lies.
Heard as wonderful, lucky, perfect,
Deaf from disgraces, shrieks, problems.
Felt as soft, comforting, velvet and silk,
Felt as the wounds of yesterday,
Forever etched across her skin.

Valerie Amyot, Grade 10
John Rennie High School, QC

I Am Not Alone

The moon is bright,
The stars twinkle throughout the night,
A breeze sweeps by me,
My heart beats quickly.
I am not alone.

Stephanie Commodari, Grade 10
Ascension of Our Lord Secondary School, ON

Innocence

The jailer peers between the bars
The cage is in his eyes
He swallows the key and smiles at me
Then walks off amidst his lies

I sit in solitary captivity
The truth still lies inside
My ropes have no slack, he's not coming back
Why did I not tell my side?

(The killer smiles as he leaves the space,
You'll see no guilt upon his face)

(The framed man sits in the killer's place,
He was unable to plead his case)

(The killer disappears without a trace)

Jordyn Wear, Grade 10
Lake Cowichan Secondary School, BC

Wondering Pain

Tears don't come, I'm wondering why.
Not a sparkle in the eye.
Memories are passing by.
Not enough to make me cry.

Wondering why my legs feel weak.
Energy is what I seek.
Writing is a great technique,
but not enough to make me speak.

Wondering why my life is steep.
Concentrations hard to keep.
I'm trying things like counting sheep.
Not enough to make me sleep.

Wondering pain in my own land.
Memories vague, details bland.
A tear falls down into my hand.
Just enough to understand.

Michael Porfirio, Grade 10
Philip Pocock Catholic Secondary School, ON

Love, the Monarch of the Heart

The rusty gate closes,
And opens

Once forever locked,
The raging creepers of guilt wound,
Winds of belting nothingness pound,
Rain pours,
Rivers flow,
And after the night, the storm,
The key glistens on the stone,
Love, the monarch of the heart —
It opens the door to my soul.

Ishi Zachariah, Grade 10
College Prep International, QC

Can't Let You Go

I've been down this road before and it tore me apart.
I didn't want to feel this way afraid you'd break my heart.
I've felt the pain before and it left so many scars
But the world disappears when you hold me in your arms.
I've opened my heart before and gave all I could give.
But your smile makes me weak I find myself caving in.
I've made this mistake before and I'm scared of how I feel.
Loving the way you look at me you make me feel so real.
Holding back all the tears hiding deep in the shadows
Afraid that any minute this feeling will go.
Scared that you won't see and afraid I'll be alone
But no matter what, I just can't let you go.

Paula Pajar, Grade 10
Holy Cross Regional High School, BC

The Homeroom Blues

Why don't you love me?
Every time I walk to school
I run as fast as a cheetah, just to see you
Your golden blonde hair,
Is worth more than a billion dollars
Yet, I am an ant around you
I feel as if someone has put my life on shutdown
Nevertheless, your smile tells me a different story everyday.
Thump! My heart is a fast muscle car
One day, I will get my wheels
. Then, we can take a three year drive
Because it is just a high school fling.

Jeevan Ahuja, Grade 10
Merritt Secondary School, BC

Memories of Mother

I'm young, my mother is here with me, I close my eyes, go back to sleep.
I know that she will always care, I know she will always be there.
We draw, we read, we watch TV, she's always there to comfort me.
I love her, I need her, I will always keep
These fond memories with me while I sleep.

Middle school comes, I sew and reap, I close my eyes, go back to sleep.
My mother is always partying now, she stays out so late, I wonder how.
I draw, I read, I watch TV, I see more than I *need* to see.
I love her, I need her, I will always keep
These failed memories with me while I sleep.

Back from high school, I lay and weep, I close my eyes, go back to sleep.
I can, just barely, recall her face, she left me alone in this dreaded place.
Can't draw, can't read, can't watch TV, she doesn't return to comfort me.
I love her, I need her, I will always keep
These fond memories,
These failed memories,
These memories with me, while I sleep.

Shawna Smoke, Grade 12
Glenforest Secondary School, ON

Remember

Remember who you are
And where you come from
Remember the people who are there
And the ones who were there before

Remember the past
Because it's what created who you are
But live in the present
Because tomorrow it will be your past

Remember to look at the sky
It will reveal to you the stars
Just like love
It will reveal to you the guy

Dream about the future
And let the future be your dream
Believe in yourself
And everyone who deserves it

Remember that everything happens for a reason
And remember that anything that doesn't kill you
will make you stronger.

Jessica Gauthier, Grade 10
Seminaire de Sherbrooke, QC

About a Girl

Every night in bed she weeps,
While praying to God for her true love.
She wonders why he hasn't come,
And sadly cries herself to sleep.

Next morning she wakes up for school,
Not knowing what's in store.
Because on her way to class,
She meets the new kid in school.

To her surprise, they ended up flirting.
She was dazzled by his winning smile,
And the way he pulled off a black cardigan.
He was her soulmate, and she was for certain.

But his heart was one that did not care,
For he was too blind to see,
The love she was willing to lay on the line for him.
Because he ended up leaving town, and her heart in despair.

Now she cries, feeling as if her heart was left to die.
Her tears run down her cheek like a waterfall.
He meant everything to her,
And he will never know why.

Kevin Mariano, Grade 10
Holy Cross Regional High School, BC

Las Vegas

The deafening silence
resonated from the
distant mountains,
whose appearance
loomed over the
sand paper ground.
Not affected by a
moist heat.
But rather a heat
like a blowdryer,
that blew dry yet
solid air.
The sand reflected,
the blue bedsheet sky.
As an unwelcomed
sound was muffled,
by the pressing
silence.

Julia Pereira, Grade 12
Applewood Heights Secondary School, ON

Love

like a flower
    blossoming in the spring air
like honeydew
    as sweet as it sounds
like the bright sun
    bringing out playful souls
like the romantic moon
    unleashing passionate spirits
like a bird
    soaring high in the sky
like the carefree summer breeze
    subtle, but beautiful
what makes your eyes gaze upon the scenery of the city?
what makes your heart race?
what makes your fragile heart strong?
what makes you close your eyes and dream,
    dream a dream…
        so soft and pretty, sweet and silly?
what is it, this essence of beauty?
        …Love

Kiran Bhachu, Grade 11
LA Matheson Secondary School, BC

Rollercoaster

Rollercoaster climbing higher,
Falling down again.
Stomach turning, head is reeling,
Close my eyes and scream.
Rollercoaster, hold on tighter
Make another spin
Feeling lighter, much too high now
Wish for ground beneath my feet
Rollercoaster lose control
I can't even breathe.

Emily Piperni, Grade 10
Heritage Regional High School, QC

Raindrop
Ra
indro
p raind
rop raindr
op falling fro
m the night sky,
So damp and pure,
Going no where, just
Falling, falling, falling
From the night sky
So cold and wet
drop
Kirsti Langen, Grade 12
Victoria Park Collegiate Institute, ON

Song of the Drifter
Over there is the one
Holding his ancient guitar
Standing between the crowds
Playing a series of chords

And there he is with a bad voice
Hoping for a spare of change
In the ever lasting crowds of metro
That is the story of the drifter
Philip Chan, Grade 10
College Prep International, QC

My Baby
When I see you…
 My heart jumps
 My body shakes
 My eyes sparkle

When I'm with you laughing is easy.
If you look in my eyes
You'll see they are shining
Like the starts in the sky
When I see you…

You don't know
How lovely you are,
I guess I need you baby…
Can't stop thinking of you

Imagine…
Would you lie with me
And just forget the world?
'Cause baby we belong together.

Soon, I hope that
I will be the girl
You point at
And say…that's her.
Sarah Lussier-Roy, Grade 10
Seminaire de Sherbrooke, QC

Celestial Sandbox
The day they tore the old school down, I stood and watched the sky fall into fireworks.
And I listened to the crumbling mar
the imperfect silence of a summer night
like explosions in the stars.

And that was the night I decided I talk to myself because I don't listen anyway;
That I couldn't keep your secret, so I'm giving it away.
They paved the playground years ago and left the school still standing.
We used to play there, an age ago, and you were so

Demanding that it all goes your way,
and I tried to keep nodding in lieu of leaving you alone.
Because no one else doesn't smile like you do.
And we crossed our hearts and hoped to die
or at least get out of here
(step on the cracks or you might come back)
and so I wondered, when it all disappeared
in that fading summer light —
Is that halo chafing your ears?
I miss the way you used to glow,
but not the way it kept me up at night,
like all those stars we used to know
exploded.

Devan Kreisberg, Grade 12
Webber Academy, AB

Teardrops
Teardrops are falling right down my cheek
Falling and falling every day of the week

My eyes are red and are almost dry
But I keep on going letting myself cry

Every day I think to myself where did I go wrong
Must be somewhere or I wouldn't think for so long

I want to open up but I find it hard to do
It's not easy speaking your mind through and through

I see you get frustrated as you are pointing this out
But you don't understand how hard it is while I sit there and pout

You say I always think and never talk out loud
But how can I speak up when I always have a doubt

I know I have no reason for feeling unsure
But I can't help it after what I have endured

Tears continue to fall right down my cheek
Falling and falling every day of the week

Avani Mehta, Grade 11
Woburn Collegiate Institute, ON

Hopeful Faith

Her dress has slowly fallen from her limbs
Her fragile frame quivers
She's gathered the remains around herself
To give her strength when it is needed
Yet her strength insists on drifting off
But she uses what remains
To pull herself together when the time comes

And one day
The time does come
The howling wind has ceased
The sun is teasing her with its warmth
Her limbs ease and thaw

She gently digs her feet into the ground
As the cool earth envelops her toes
Slowly, she pushes green buds out from her fingertips
And once again
Her beauty shines

Alysia Lor, Grade 11
WL Seaton Secondary School, BC

Jonas Brothers Concert

I am shining and smiling
I wonder why it takes so long to start
I hear the rhythm of the drums rolling
I see the lights glowing up around
I want to scream with all my heart
I am shining and smiling

I pretend to not be excited
I feel the music taking control of me
I touch the floor with my burning feet
I worry about my excitement coming out so fast
I cry as they come on stage
I am shining and smiling

I understand why people said it was amazing
I say I cannot be in a better place right now
I dream to meet them after the concert
I try to think about how many smiles they put on those faces
I hope I'll remember this moment all my life
I am shining and smiling

Cindy Pratte, Grade 10
Seminaire de Sherbrooke, QC

Life

Street lights, strictly afternoon.
Breathe in, winds from out of June.
No way, watch the birds fly high —
we go by, let the rainbows rise,
throughout the sky so high.
Tidal waves, clear the world of content.
He sees, He knows, we're all different.
We all try to pretend,
live our life
before it's the end.

Karana Ferreira, Grade 11
St Marcellinus Secondary School, ON

Nature

N aturally shaping the
A ppearance of
T he earth,
U ndeniably
R esembles an
E ternal sculptress.

Mary Yang, Grade 12
Woburn Collegiate Institute, ON

Return Policy

My hamster died and I got a refund.
He was an artistic genius, my hamster.
He would shred his hamster hay into a million little
hamster hay shreds.
He would make statues and sculptures.
Tunnels and caves;
with his shredded hamster hay.
One day, my little genius,
my hamster,
he ran.
And ran.
And ran.
He was in great hamster shape.
He ran.
And his little hamster leg
got stuck.
Got caught.
In the wheel.
And it broke.
My genius died,
and I got a refund.

Mackenzie Smith, Grade 12
Sacred Heart Catholic High School, ON

Life of a Cheerleader

Walking to my position
too nervous to even think
the music starts to play
too afraid to blink
this is our only chance
as I start to cheer
one, two, down, up
people in the crowd are so loud I can't even hear
it's getting harder and harder
my heart's beating too fast
trying not to fall
as I see Parris flipping past
hitting my bow and arrow
then it's done the music's over
my coaches screaming so loud and proud
I see everyone around me starting to lower
looking around hoping we weren't the worst
screaming to the top of my lungs we were first place

Connie Limcolioc, Grade 10
Holy Cross Regional High School, BC

Breaking Point

She tells it all when she's drunk,
Truth coming out with tears,
Showing how low she's sunk,
Drowning in wasted years,

Wishing on stars long since fallen,
Slipping on her old lies,
She regrets ignoring her calling,
Seeing through unfocused eyes,

She should have been a model,
She could have went to college,
It doesn't take a genius to tell,
She's thrown herself off the edge,

Stuck in this town with her time,
Living for the end of the day,
She searches the bottom of her glass,
For some relief from the pain,

It's not living, just existing,
A cage without a door,
And if someone were to listen,
They'd see she can't take anymore.

Erica Craigie, Grade 11
Gravenhurst High School, ON

Silent Heartache

Looking out the foggy glass,
she drifts away.
Thousands of daydreams
will die today.

Her best friend's in love with
the girl she hates.
And they get together
to laugh at her fate.

Her lips are locked.
Her eyes are dead.
She can't say a word
through the storm in her head.

Her life fell to pieces by
her own fair hands,
and there's nothing left here
for her to stand.

This was the story
of one lonely girl,
the one who was lost
though she was a pearl.

Pia Sengupta, Grade 10
Vincent Massey Secondary School, ON

My Eraser

Staedtler my eraser comes in handy when I need her
Helps me fix up the mix up on an assignment paper
Free of latex made of mars plastic
She's fantastic
Never leave home without packing her with my pen and paper
Staedtler completes my stationary supply
My eraser my ally
Without her I'm lost
No lie

David Assedo, Grade 11
College Prep International, QC

Changing Seasons

The spring rejoiced; reborn again, new life begins to grow
The buds begin to escalate as flowers start to show
And though at times the rain comes down to cleanse the waiting earth
The shrubs shall blossom beautifully: the cycle of rebirth

The summer beamed with glory and the clouds could not conceal
The purest form of beauty — light; perfection that is real
The warmness still surrounds me on the coldest winter day
Sensations indescribable, no words can justly say

The autumn: changed and colourful — much more than falling leaves
Some would call it beauty — Mother Nature's masterpiece
Although the trees are left alone to shiver in the cold
The dying leaves are beautiful — all yellows, reds and golds

The winter crept upon us with a frosty angel glow
The freshly fallen blanket of the purest, whitest snow
Upon which moonlight shines and so the sparkles catch our eye
But the beauty is forgotten as the short months quickly fly

Jaclyn Hodsdon, Grade 12
Holy Trinity High School, ON

An Ending to Hold Onto

Five a night, a deathly drink, a life he's known too long,
He risks his life and rarely thinks, to whom that he belongs.
His loved ones seek to find him help, they think that he can change,
He treats them like they're something else, he starts to act deranged.

His daughter knows of what comes next, a smart one she can be,
She leaves the house just in time, she's lucky she broke free.
He's done this once or twice before, he begins to overpower,
He hits until mom's red and sore, he leaves then for an hour.

While he's gone mom cries for help, but help's not what she gets,
But yet a phone call saying that there's been an accident.
On highway five not far from home, a car has hit a tree,
A fender bender from behind, it's the daughter's Mercedes.

The accident was not her fault, but of the man behind,
Who seemed to look familiar, to the mothers eye.
The father says he'll never drink, he'll never hit again,
But for his girl it was too late, he brought her to an end.

Cameron Fowler, Grade 11
Sir Winston Churchill Secondary School, ON

One Day Left

Twenty-four long hours.
But will anybody remember
That I once walked upon the soil?
No, for I am
Alone.
Nobody saw past my loose mask
Of happiness and joy
To find my invisible soul.
But there is just one day left
Until I make my mark.
One day.
One life.
One rope.
One fall.
Now will I be remembered?

Samuel Quan, Grade 12
Webber Academy, AB

Silence

Shall I compare thee to a summer's day?
Thou are more precious and more delicate.
June, July, August have not strength to stay,
Are blown headlong while autumn lies in wait.
Though time swings slowly through the summer hours
It does bent to rest beneath the sun
Whose fiery heat does often end in showers,
But shortly makes the season dead and done.
The passing din of summer's noise must bow,
For you that we call silence shall ne'er die,
And fall to Death, his scythe to mow
The fields of green, the sun-filled clear-blue sky.
    So long as man can breathe and eyes can see,
    So long lives this, and this gives life to thee.

Aiden Brant-Briscall, Grade 12
Vancouver Waldorf School, BC

A Taste of High School

Sometimes it feels so surreal in this place,
With many situations we must face.
Rumors spread like a viral infection,
Often getting you some bad attention.

A growing experience it may be,
It can also be a catastrophe.
Great friendships formed for many years to come,
Although, this is not always true for some.

Minds take shape as they make new discov'ries
Starting to fill a box full of mem'ries.
Smiles and laughter, tears and heartache meet here,
Stoic'ly pushing aside all our fear.

A stepping stone this is, under our feet,
One thing's for sure, high school is bittersweet.

Anika Dilawri, Grade 11
Collège catholique Franco-Ouest, ON

Love

The flight of a dove
Brings a message of love,
Forging a bridge between two hearts
Like the shot from Cupid's dart.
A deep connection
That creates infinite affection.
Proof that real beauty is internal
And that friendship can be eternal.
A lifeline of support
That should never fall short.
Always desired
For everyone deserves to be admired.

Jesse Brame, Grade 12
Webber Academy, AB

Am I Loveless?

Tears glistening like diamonds were dropping,
On our fragile, naive world made of glass,
The night sky shattered and without stopping,
Shards of sorrow in my heart they did pass.

Crimson tears wept, my promise was not kept,
A haunting melody sung by a wraith,
My mad desire, a beast that never slept,
Was killed by my shameful lack of faith.

A gaping wound in my heart left bleeding,
This scar is so it's you I shan't forget,
Immensely painful yet I am breathing,
The blazing sun shines rays with no regret.

We will meet again soon my dearest one,
Cherish past love, yet life has just begun.

Mehrunnisa Khurshid, Grade 10
The Woodlands Secondary School, ON

Entering into the Darkness of Death

The woman is holding a lamp
A lamp so bright
She is saying goodbye,
The darkness hugs me; pouring me all its love
The pain, the sorrow starts to heal
It is an enchantment that cannot be expressed
A sleep clamps my wondering mind;
It is a dream!
A dream of darkness; a mystical dream
Waking up seems pointless
Nothing is seen; nothing is heard
Yet, plenty is felt; it feels calm
As if I am staring at a speechless lake
The echoes of silence all around me
It is the loneliness; the loneliness so steady
Nothing is heard, and nothing can be said
As if I am the silent evening sky…
No, I am not asleep, neither am I in an esoteric dream
It is my soul,
It is my soul that is done being fed…

Chathurika Gamage, Grade 11
Ascension of Our Lord Secondary School, ON

Who Am I?

They say I was born on Friday the 13th; However, I was never born
They say my favorite number is 666; However, I can't have a favorite number
I am whatever you let me become
I created darkness; I invented terror, tears, and torture
When all is wrong, everyone turns to me
I can control you; I can control everyone, that is if you allow me
I represent depression and suicide even death
I can be the star-splattered night sky
I can be full of vengeance, I can be aggressive, I can be full of deception, and I can be abusive
I am the gothic side; I am the final unpaved path everyone walks on
I am the dark trail in the forest that others curiously wonder through
However, not one of them make it out alive
I am your hollow shadow that haunts your every move
I am a fragment of your identity, you can even say I am a state of mind
There are many of us that are hidden within you
One color cannot define you, I am just the one being used for the moment
There is a rainbow waiting to be unleashed in you; The rainbow that releases your brighter side
Keep in mind I should only be used once or twice; Otherwise, I might control you
Try not to use me, unless it's your last option
So, who am I?…I am just a color
I am BLACK

Khalida Aliazhar Braid, Grade 10
Foundations for the Future Charter Academy-Dr Norman Bethune Campus, AB

You Promised Me Daddy

I open my eyes, my tender fingers gripped onto his. He comforts me nicely and draws me back to sleep. "I'll never let my baby go."
I see a blur image of his smile, while my eyes drowse.
No one is listening Daddy; but, I know only you can hear.
You have a grasp of my finger. I am frightened; Daddy never let me go.

I struggle with my shoes, my left hand laced into his. He leads me safely and walks me to school. "I'll never let my little one go."
I see a blur image of his nervousness, while I take further steps.
No one believes in me Daddy; but, I know only you can understand.
You have a grip of my hand. I am nervous; Daddy never let me go.

I graduate from high school, my head lifted as high as his. He sits in the third row and watches me receive my achievement. "I'll never let my angel go."
I see a blur of his pride, while I climb up to the podium.
No one is satisfied Daddy; but, I know only you can acknowledge.
You have your head lifted high. I am eager; Daddy never let me go.

I walk down the aisle, my arms swung in with his. He marches me to the front of the ceremony and kisses me on my forehead. "I'll never let my daughter go."
I see a blur image of his strong posture, while I watch him walk back to his seat.
No one is concerned Daddy; but, I know only you can comfort.
You have a grasp of my arm. I am excited; Daddy never let me go.

I walk near motionlessly with my hands tightly pressed together. He lies here peacefully, his soul as somber as mine.
I see a clear image of him and nothing around me. I cry as loud as I can, and everything flashes right before my eyes.
Everyone can hear me Daddy. Can you? I miss everything about you: your voice, your touch, your patience, and your comfort.
Today, I have a strong grasp of your hand Daddy: I feel alone. You promised me Daddy and you said you would never let me go.

Sahana Gnanathurai, Grade 12
Glenforest Secondary School, ON

A Bitter Vice

You happy fool:
the lying smile that says yes.
they say money makes a man deceive,
but from you, more lies spring than rich men have dollars.
I do think — that while my teeth glisten,
my tongue is poison.
my mind drinks you down, takes you like a drug;
your smoke clouds my head and stings my eyes,
but blindly I breathe in to calm my electric nerves.
while I indulge, bitter vice,
you spread your lying lullabies.
I'm happy though I don't know better
(better than the dreams you paint).

Julia Robins, Grade 12
EL Crossley Secondary School, ON

Grades 7-8-9

Top Poem Grades 7-8-9

When We Couldn't Wait to Grow Up

Remember when we couldn't wait to grow up?
When the fastest kid in the grade was the coolest kid in the grade?

And when you got hurt
it was most likely because you skinned your knee
playing tag on the playground.

When all you had to do was walk up to someone
and ask them if they wanted to be best friends.

When people didn't judge
and race didn't matter.

When our homework was to write down
what we did on the weekend.
Remember when we couldn't wait to grow up?

Cara Blair, Grade 8
Mulgrave School, BC

Top Poem Grades 7-8-9

I Am the Lamp Post of McKenzie Avenue

I am the lamp post of McKenzie Avenue,
I stand here, through night and day
There is the story of Jane Davidson, she was diagnosed with pancreatic cancer
She lost all her lovely hair, but at the time when you least expect,
She slowly grew it back

I am the lamp post of McKenzie Avenue,
I stand here, through night and day
There is the story of Mrs. Lothe, the old lady that went to buy groceries every week
On Saturday, at 3 o'clock, but on one Saturday she lost her glasses
And a car thudded against her frail body

I am the lamp post of McKenzie Avenue,
I stand here, through night and day
There is the story of little James, he was a fan of superheroes
But received a dog for his fifth birthday, the dog was named Eddie Brown
And Eddie's children were given away

I am the lamp post of McKenzie Avenue,
I stand here, through night and day
A thousand stories have been on this street, and a thousand more will come here
But sadly, I will not be the one to read the plots, I have been signed for replacement
I will leave quite soon
I am the lamp post of McKenzie Avenue, I stand here for one more day

Yichu Dai, Grade 8
Mulgrave School, BC

Top Poem Grades 7-8-9

So Write Me

Writing. So crazy.
So choose, so mark, so win.
Make words, score thoughts, write fin.

So pen it.
Move pencil, move paper, move mind.
Show product, show working, make find.

And cast it.
Role phrase, role vowel, role word.
Release it, sing forth it, fly bird.

With feeling.
Cast odd, cast mad, cast great.
To finders, drop gold, words fate.

Pen verse. Confusing.
Roll eyes, roll mind, roll pen.
Create thinking, make peace, find Zen.

So write me.
Choose words, choose paper, choose cast.
Find endings, sweet nothings, to last.

Laura Edwards, Grade 8
Mitford Middle School, AB

Top Poem Grades 7-8-9

Moonlight

The soft glow
Beautiful simplicity
A million white diamonds sparkling

Dancing around the dark shadows
It is a flicker of hope in a black world
A promise for an ailing child

Igniting a joy from the deepest gloom
The flame spreads
A single ripple in a dark sea

Encircling the cruel shadows
Awakening the light
Until the day breaks
Moonlight

Sylvie Glisinski, Grade 7
Westwind Elementary School, BC

Top Poem Grades 7-8-9

The Poetry of Art

The dark ink flows across the page
With elegant sweeps and lines
The vibrant brushstrokes illustrate
The rhythm of design

With the flow, the feel, of poetry
Art liberates closed minds
Abstract hues and imagery
Tell verses of different kinds

Bold paint swirls through pale canvas
It's a portrait of success
For a picture can speak so poignantly
What a thousand words cannot express

RuiLin Guo, Grade 9
Innisdale Secondary School, ON

Top Poem Grades 7-8-9

Imagination

My sister and I
Have a magical forest
In our backyard.

The snow tastes like cream.
All plants taste like candy —
Licorice rosehips
Peppermint pine needles,
Cinnamon bark.

Chipmunks whisper
From their hiding places.
Can they trust us?
We fill our pockets with peace offerings —
Nuts we cracked from the bowl
On Grandma's kitchen table.

We walk carefully,
Apologizing to any plants we step on
Before they start to cry.
After a time, they know us
They accept us.
We are welcome in the forest.

Rhiannon Hatch, Grade 8
Hillside Jr/Sr High School, AB

Top Poem Grades 7-8-9

My Morning

I lie in my bed, as the seconds tick by
I stare at my clock and I almost cry
It's almost 7 o'clock why oh why?
I shall have to get up from my warm bed
I have to walk around my cold room instead
I crawl in the shower hoping the water's hot
And I jump right out after I find out it's not
Once I'm all clean, it's off to the table
To have a tasty breakfast, if I am able
After I eat, it's back to my room
To put on some clothes, and a bit of perfume
When I come out, I'm ready for school
Dressed to kill, looking all cool
I then go out to see who won hockey
I see Ovechkin the great, and Sid being all cocky
I am almost in a good mood until I realize it's 8
Which is the time of morning that I really hate
So we head off for another day of sorrow
And I sadly realize I'll have to do it all over again tomorrow.

Tyler Jones, Grade 9
Netagamiou School, QC

Top Poem Grades 7-8-9

The Fool and the Swan*

There she stands in snowy silk,
With seraph wings as white as milk.
Chained by day to fate and flight.
Her only hope; the frozen night.

When moon and stars hang in the skies,
She opens her glowing onyx eyes.
Away melts her beak and wings and down
Till the princess remains with her golden crown.

Her prince boldly gave her his undying love,
Unaware of the sorcerer watching above;
The villainous monster who cursed the young girl
And forced two white wings from her back to unfurl.

The prince was so smitten, he stumbled half-blind
Into the arms of a trickster sent to poison his mind.
He heard his love cry and he woke with a start.
He realized too late he had broken her heart.

He chased her through branches, over root, over hedge,
Till he found the swan princess at the lake water's edge.
They made one last promise and then, hand-in-hand,
They plunged to their fate, to their bright promised land.

Emily Lehune, Grade 9
Worsley Central School, AB
*Based on the ballet, "Swan Lake"

Top Poem Grades 7-8-9

Spring

I smelled it in the breeze,
I saw it in the sky,
I heard it in the little birds,
That went quickly flitting by.

I peeked at it in the snow,
I swept it in my net,
I scooped it off the hazy sky,
That cradles the lazy jet.

I felt it in the trees,
I caught it in my hand,
I heard the whole Earth sing it:
Spring's come to the land!

Maddie Trottier, Grade 7
Blind River Public School, ON

Top Poem Grades 7-8-9

Bounce, Bounce Weeee

My mama says I'm hyperactive
Whatever that may mean.
I prefer super active
It comes from too much caffeine.
My mama warned me about candy
And all the sugar it brings
But I paid no attention
And ate the dandy things.
It started as a tingle
Way down at my toes
Then as it began to rise
I felt it in my nose.
As the adrenaline increased
So did my speed
Everything became a blur
As I started to proceed.
The energy was so extreme
The only thing I could think
Maybe Mama was right
As I flew around in flight.

Kiefer Winters, Grade 8
Community Bible Fellowship Christian School, MB

Dark Wild
There is always a quiet breeze in the wild
rare species lurk
dust blows on the quiet ground
no house in sight
no love to be seen
the stream trickles
as the fire burns
the young lilacs
this is
the dark wild
Jacob Henderson, Grade 7
Menno Simons Christian School, AB

The Hunter
The hunter moved steathly
Through the barren trees.
His glowing eyes like lazers,
Searching, scanning.
The bright moon lighting his way
Through the shadowy trees.
Not a sound was heard
As he slithered like a snake,
His muscles tense and strong.
As he turned I saw a flash of white teeth
Like rows of sharp knifes.
His feet moving skillfully
Through the moonlight.
He sang a long mournful song
The hungry predator unsuccessful
In finding both meal or mate.
He sang his sad, lonely song once more
Ears forward listening for an echo
But there was none.
The hunter had failed —
The Great White Wolf.
Emma Martin, Grade 7
Linwood Public School, ON

Peaceful at Last
She lay there pale and tired,
Helpless and unmoving,
With her family and friends beside her,
Grieving and praying.

One night God called her to his side,
And she left this world peacefully,
Now she is with God up in heaven,
Rejoicing with all the angels.

She left all the pain and weakness
To be in a better world.
Levi Kleinsasser, Grade 8
Milford Colony School, AB

My Best Friend
You magnify my happiness,
When I am feeling glad,
You help to heal my injured heart,
Whenever I am sad.
You're such a pleasure in my life,
I hope that you can see,
How meaningful our friendship is,
You're a total joy to me.
Thanks for listening with your heart,
For cheering me when I'm blue,
For bringing out the best in me,
And just for being you.
Thanks for concern and understanding,
You give abundantly.
Thanks for in-depth conversations,
That stimulates my brain,
For silly times we laughed out loud,
For things I can't explain.
For looking past my flaws and faults,
And for all the kind things that you do,
Thank you very much my friend.
Abrar Dabbagh, Grade 8
Laurelwood Public School, ON

A Fly's Life
sit
still
on
sill
sees
light
must
fight
bright
light
can't
fight
ZAP!
Anne Hessler, Grade 7
Signal Hill Elementary School, BC

Fire
The flames flare up
There's no where to go.
I can't get out,
When all I can see is flame.

There's no way out.

At least I get to see
How hot fire really is.
No way out.

No way out...
Andrea McDonald, Grade 8
St Anne School, AB

Snow
The whiteness of snow
One will never know
Crystals sparkling in the sun
Snowballs making lots of fun

One will never know
The secret of snow
Snowballs making lots of fun
Nice unlike ice

The secret of snow
Drifting slowly earthward
Nice unlike ice
The perfect Christmas present

Drifting slowly earthward
Crystals sparkling in the sun
The perfect Christmas present
The whiteness of snow
Elijah Santos, Grade 7
Menno Simons Christian School, AB

From Dawn to Dusk
Day/Night
Light...Dark
Warm...Cool
Lively...Slow
Loud...Quiet
Awake...Sleeping
Shannon Garbauski, Grade 7
St Anne School, AB

Acceptance
As I lie here, I think of all
The things that block out
Sunlight, and how I will
Never accept my death
How I will never let
Myself die
I look out the window and all
I see is black darkness and no
Light
I cry, never being able to
Accept the fact that my
Eyes will see no Sunlight,
But only Darkness
And then as my hands
Start to go numb, I realize that
Acceptance is how to find peace
After Death
I close my eyes, and breathe my
Last breath
I have accepted Death, and
As I feel myself slip away, I smile and cry
Darren Pooni, Grade 8
LA Matheson Secondary School, BC

Rain Forest, My Land

I am a tiger, peering at my foes.
A big cat, roar! I watch their every move.
I see them with their big machines, tearing up my home.
I see them with their laughter, loving every minute.
I roar with outrage! I know just what they've done.
I see their faces go blank, oh, they feel sorry for it now!
I think of the other creatures, know what I'm doing is right.
I take in things around, I want to remember this moment.
I feel the dirt beneath my paws,
see the canopy of trees above my head,
the moment is just right.
I see them load their big gun as I have three times before,
I scream as I pounce. Not this time.
ROAR!

Jake Roslyn, Grade 7
Linwood Public School, ON

Summer Will Come…Right?

As I stare, standing up, at the bright shining moon,
I knew that summer would end too soon.
Then would come the chilly autumn wind;
Brush our cheeks and we would have to go in.
The weeks fly past and the days grow colder
We know spring will come, only much, much slower.
But then the groundhog will wake and see his shadow,
And spring would come, with saplings handled.
Yet my favorite season summer would still have to wait,
Spring passes solemnly and the squirrels end their mate.
The fruits nearly ripen and get much larger,
Now I hope this year's summer will be longer!

Zihan Cai, Grade 7
Lower Canada College, QC

From the Heart

Where would we be without our dreams?
Our hopes to make it a reality
To make the world, a better place,
A culture with every single race.
A place where we can visualize,
A whole new world, in our eyes.
Where we can do anything without a care,
With smiles, laughter, hugs, and cheers.
We should try to dream about,
A place where voices are heard aloud.
To improve our growing society,
To reduce fear and anxiety,
To welcome hope, and aim for the top,
To believe in yourself, and never stop.
And in some events, people succeed,
To fight for rights, and to be seen.
Because in the end, we will come through,
And the world shall learn of the things we do.
For no one is complete without a heart,
A heart with a dream, that never parts.

Joy Zhou, Grade 9
Thornlea Secondary School, ON

Stallion

Tearing up the rocky mountain trail
Swiftly running with out a break
Jumping over boulders, following the winding path
Galloping ever faster, speed increasing rapidly
Until the proud, mighty stallion
Is a speck in the colorful sunset

Peter P. Kleinsasser, Grade 7
Milford Colony School, AB

The Magic of Nature (Cedar Wax Wing)

I jump, I slide, I fly,
I glide, and I soar,
Through the wind
Like a roaring tide.

I sit on my tree
With my smiles and glee,
Awaiting the snow
In anxiety.

I love the smell
That Nature brings
When snow comes tumbling
Down on things.

My family and I like to sit
In the trees, singing and chirping
Awaiting the breeze.

It's not often you see
Us bonding in glee,
But still we're important
To nature and fleas.

Arianna Froese, Grade 8
Hillside Jr/Sr High School, AB

I Love You, Mom

Since we were very young,
Mothers have played a big part.
They taught us how to walk and write,
How to talk and love others by heart.

She has taught me so much,
That's what I want to tell her;
About how many feelings we've shared,
And how close we were.

Mothers are essential part of our lives,
Even though now we're grown.
She's my role model, my hero.
Mom, you're the best of the mothers ever known!

I love you, mom.

Sahiban Katari, Grade 8
Pleasantville Public School, ON

Apple Pie!

An apple with eyes,
Struck me with a great surprise.
He smiled and waved,
My stomach growled and ached,
Now he is baked in a pie.

Spencer Cameron, Grade 7
Homelands Senior Public School, ON

Emotionless

Single minded he stands
Ball in hand
Eyes on the basket
Swift
Fast
Resilient
The ball swishes through the net.
The crowd cheers
He stands
Emotionless

A stitched ball flies through the air
He grabs the ball
Dog piled
Tough as a brick wall
Unstoppable
Sprints
Crosses over the line
The crowd screams in enjoyment
He still stands
Emotionless

Michael Xu, Grade 7
Blundell Elementary School, BC

Runaway Love

When I saw run away love,
I mean don't come back.
Caused me a lot of pain
Left my mind depressed
By your side I left like an angel.
Now you're gone.
I find the news too hard to digest.
You took me apart
And at that part of impact
You shattered my heart.
Love is dangerous,
'Cause it leaves you dead.
For the devil in disguise
Whispering tempting thoughts
In your head.
Leave all my loved ones,
And left alone.
So if I erase all feelings
Love will always be gone
And shall never be known.

Kariya Manichoose, Grade 8
Hillside Jr/Sr High School, AB

God's Creation

The lunar moon, the blazing sun, the celestial stars
Are the extraterrestrial wonders of God's creation
Such wonders and curiosity, its boundaries set far
A mass of mysterious beauty, made by God's dictation

The evergreen firs and the mightiness of the great mountain
Are signs of the precise and vigorous attributes of God
Such beauty of the great wonders sets our minds and soul astrain
The spectacular oceans of blue are filled with frogs and cods

The free minded deer frolic in the midst of the green meadows
While the exotic birds and the queer-minded bugs praise in joy
The Garden of Eden is filled with spectacular rivers
A wonderful, celestial site, a treasure and joy

But God's majestic and spectacular creation out of them all
Was us, the stewards and children of God, we are proud and tall

Jennifer Tabon, Grade 7
St Patrick's Elementary School, BC

Before I Hit the Bucket...

I'd like to ride and drive the biggest bomber that gives
And I'd also like to ski-jump off a very high plane.

I'd like to own the fastest jet in the world
I'd also like to own the fastest race car there is.

I cannot go unless I'd ride on the highest roller coaster I find
I'd also like to win the cash that would buy me the things I need and want.

Before I'd go I'd like to be the one who could
Fly to the moon in a matter of just two hours.

Before I go I'd like to walk on the biggest planet
And make the record of touching every planet in the universe.

There are so many things I'd like but there's one I'd especially want
Is to get the powers that I could move from one place
To the next by saying the desired word.

Ryland Wipf, Grade 8
Decker Colony School, MB

Boredom

Boredom is like a boat in the calm ocean waiting until the wind comes.
Boredom can be;
Color like white, empty space with nothing to do.
Hot like desert, no where to go.
Cold like ice, sitting in the refrigerator waiting to get used.
Sounds like a cat sitting in the couch.
Tastes like spaghetti without a spaghetti sauce.
Smells like nothing, I'm hungry and bored.
Looks like house without furniture.
Feels like Friday at school waiting school to be over.
Moves like a turtle it takes forever.

ChanWoo An, Grade 7
St Anne School, SK

What Am I?

Hair as white as the clouds
Eyes as blue as the sky
Lips the colour of my stuffed bunny's nose
Skin the colour of peaches
Loud or quiet
I come in many sizes
Big or small
Need milk to grow
Big and strong
I am a baby

Megan Bozykowski, Grade 8
Heather Park Middle School, BC

A Whole New World

When you hang upside down,
what is the first thing you see?
The sky, the clouds, the trees?
The first thing I see is the beauty;
a new way to look at life.
So still and gentle
yet, it's taken for granted day after day.
We forget about how amazing our world could be,
when looking at it in a different way.
Our world is such an amazing place,
with nothing we can ever replace.
When I look at it in a different way;
it really and truly is,
a whole new world.

Selene Mallone, Grade 8
St Margaret Mary Separate School, ON

Our Lives in Time

Time
We are all born in it
And live life in very different ways
But crumble away to it all the same
We think the hours pass by slowly
But when we look back at the years
Our lives in time have gone by so quickly
As we watch the news
Great achievements are made
While crimes make regretful memories
And disasters bring grief and sorrow
Why is the world at war
With violence and blood
Spilled from innocent civilians
When we could cooperate
And have peace and happiness
Flowing from all four corners of the Earth
So in the time that you are alive
Live it well and don't waste it
Because you only have one
Life

Kim Tran, Grade 9
Smithers Secondary School, BC

Bring Us Down

It's amazing how when we are young
We feel as nothing could bring us down
But as we grow older and things begin to change
The happiness around us falls to the ground

I lived a life
Filled with today and tomorrow
But the way the world works is strange
Because now it's just the loneliness and the sorrow

I had a dream
And it filled my skies
But because of all the changes
It was chased away by my cries

I had been surrounded
By many beautiful things
But God is merciless
And only pain he brings

It's amazing how a child
Can be so apart from the rest
And then fate comes crashing down on them
And they never pass that final test

Alexandra B. Mikell, Grade 8
Homelands Senior Public School, ON

Inescapable Desert

The scorching, hot sun heats up the grains of sand,
Provoking crimson burns on blistering hands.
Streams of trickling water come into distant views,
Yet they are streams I find I never get to use.
My muscles ache from walking, day by day on my journey,
Trying to get away from this death land.

This is what some may call an inescapable desert.

But, knowing someday I'll face this world
Without your loyal eyes to watch out for me,
Without your listening ears to hear me out
Even when I am wrong,
Never again would I see your beautiful smile and wagging tail,
Or see you come running to greet me at the door.
To look ahead, only into cold, relentless sorrow,
Because you'd not be there to comfort me.

Now that would be my inescapable desert.

Kate Anderson, Grade 8
Laurelwood Public School, ON

Joe Carter

There was a ball player named Joe Carter
No matter what, he could always hit harder.
He was a huge fight starter.

Josh Slater, Grade 7
Homelands Senior Public School, ON

What I Can Become…Do…And Be

Before I, die, there are many things I'd like to do
Things I'd like to become and many things I'd like to know

Explore the universe through a telescope and getting involved in some exciting adventure
(I'm not sure about this one) it might get to be too exciting

Understanding what hunger, thirst, and being poor really means
So we can feel and experience what a large population of the world's people go through every day of their life

Discover something completely new and foreign, like finding a world within this one
(We do this often without realizing what it is) like the way people in different countries contrast
And the way each family or colony of people differ from others

Doing something no one thought possible before; making time slow down
So we can stay young, but 'mature' in knowledge and understanding without getting any older

Learning to understand all manners of people so we can get along well
Being able to change the way I speak and watching the stars blinking slyly at you by night,
As if they knew all the century old secrets of the world shining like pinpricks
On a domed black blanket covering heaven.

Charity Waldner, Grade 9
Decker Colony School, MB

We Thank You

You're the ones that stood and fought for the country we now call home.
We thank you, for standing on the lines for something we believed we'd win.
Some have fallen; some have lived to see the day of peace,
the day we showed hands and stopped the madness, stopped the killings.
We thank you, for being brave running into combat with nothing but a gun and a heart to show for.
It's because of your bravery that we have a country without people running into the streets
and shooting innocent women and children.
We thank you, to you, it may have been a job something you did not want to do but in my eyes you are a hero.
The ones that died came home in a Canadian flag to show what they fought for,
to show what they did for us, the Canadians.
We thank you, for doing the best you could to keep the peace in our country.

Jacqueline Cauvier, Grade 7
École Séparée Lorrain, ON

One Litre of Tears*

You're always thinking of a way out of this nightmare instead, try to find a dream.
But that dream you keep wanting will never come true.
You want someone to help you but no one's going to come, no one's going to help you.
You can't go back to how it was before because you cannot go back to the past.
You can't build a time machine, but should you really stay focused about those things?
Because as long as you're still here, shouldn't you enjoy what's going on now?
If things can't be the way they were before, then make a new path for yourself.
Use your will and live on, live forever, you still have the time.
So don't look back, but look forwards to the future.
If you write down what you're feeling now, then people will surely understand you.
Because not having others understand you and not understanding others, they're both terrible choices.
If you want others to remember you from time to time, then they will remember you for sure.
No matter how much time may pass, here is the place that you belong because you still exist here on Earth.
I've already cried One Litre of Tears

Kimberley Chow, Grade 7
James S Woodsworth Senior Public School, ON
*Inspired by the diary and drama.

The Road to Insane

Each morning begins with obscurity and gloom
As if every second the world were in doom
Every moment my head's in torturing pain
My life is spiraling on the road to insane

My mentality is conveyed to ludicrous thoughts
Individual ideas are binded in knots
Anguishing pangs cascade down like acid rain
My life is spiraling on the road to insane

Demented notions cause devastating actions
All error is aimed at me; there are no retractions
I'm burdened by immense mental strain
My life is spiraling on the road to insane

A mind's free will is forcefully seized
Nothing is left here for it's been diseased
A mere heart has relinquished; a psyche's been slain
My life is spiraling on the road to insane

Kathleen Acena, Grade 7
St Patrick's Elementary School, BC

I Love You!

You were just another friend
but when I got to know you
I let my heart unbend
you were everything and I need you to know
I miss you
everything about you was worth while
it was heartfelt to see you smile
my heart won't let you go
and I need you to know
I miss you
I will never let you go
my feelings are true
just remember one thing
I love you!

Isra Hussein, Grade 7
Laurelwood Public School, ON

Element of Nature

People are the elements of nature
Who create and destroy creatures,
We are another form of 'the Almighty.'

If we want to survive
We need to have pity.
Have pity on humanity, not nature,
So our future will have serenity.

Why not pledge to beautify nature,
With our combined effort.
So that when we look forward to our future,
We see a world filled with nature's essence.

Kayla Smith, Grade 8
Hillside Jr/Sr High School, AB

Cancer

Cancer
A poisonous snake
Lurking in the corner
Waiting to wrap itself around its next helpless victim
Slowly sucks the breath away
Leaving pain, dead or alive

Cancer
A ferocious grizzly in hot pursuit
Charging behind a back
A shocking surprise attack
Quickly destroys a life
Leaving scars, physical or emotional

Cancer
An unfair disease taking over the world
Stealing happiness
Extinguishing dreams mercilessly
Bringing tears to faces
Leaving sadness in weak or strong hearts

Cancer

Alexa Wiskin, Grade 8
Heather Park Middle School, BC

Good Old Tippy

Smells like musty, moldy hay,
He barks a shrill, mournful bark,
His fur is like a handful of thick, tangled sand,
His baggy, dropping, drooling, dull mouth,
is hanging open like a fierce wolf.
Good Old Tippy
Woof! Woof! Sometimes he barks
like a whining puppy,
He runs and jumps like a leopard,
He smells like a stinky skunk.
I am so happy to have a dog.
Good Old Tippy

Elvina Hoover, Grade 7
Linwood Public School, ON

A Furtive Secret

There is an introverted girl in class
She's deaf, but can hear
Using other senses, as her small pink ears.
Only I know of this furtive secret.
While others don't fathom her.
They believe she can't hear
Saying negative words about her each year.
But she reads their pink lips
And knows all they say
And she will end up
Telling them all she's heard one day.

Aliya Tariq, Grade 7
Blundell Elementary School, BC

My Weather

My happiness is the sun
As it kisses my back
My sadness is the wind
As it weeps through the trees
My anger is the hail
As it pounds the rooftops
My excitement is the rain
As it jumps happily from the sky
My happiness is the sun

Danielle Seiter, Grade 8
Heather Park Middle School, BC

Snow

When snow falls
It reminds me
Of confetti at a wedding.
So white and so beautiful,
I like how many things
You can make with snow.
Snowmen
Snow angels
Snow forts
And snowballs
I absolutely love
Winter and snow.

Jolayne Goodswimmer, Grade 8
Hillside Jr/Sr High School, AB

Kid

Young, energized
Laughing, playing, screaming
More skills, grow bigger
Working, kids, success
Older, smarter
Adult

Zachary Milne, Grade 7
St Anne School, AB

Love

I tell about it
I show it
But I just can't find it
Do you, do I
Will I ever find it?
I don't know
but, but, I, I feel alone
I feel unloved
It feels like the God of love
pierced my heart
I need, I need
someone to cuddle and love
but I will know
when I find
my one true love.

Kevin Myrie, Grade 8
Royal Orchard Middle School, ON

Liquid Sunshine

A beating heart in the rain.
Pressed against my side.
And it skips a beat,
As the sun shatters the clouds.
Green grass, tinted with water
Explodes
Into flame.
The once gray life is now afire,
With the colour of my sun.
Lightning strikes,
But not here, not close.
A beam of light
Shrouds
A heart.
A beating heart.

Taylor Goldsmith, Grade 9
Foundations for the Future Charter Academy-Dr Norman Bethune Campus, AB

Anger!

Who am I?
I'm like a thunder that flows within your body.
I'm like an earthquake that would never stop, and I shake like a baby's rattle.
I make you turn red and burst into tears, like lava flowing out of a volcano.
I'm another word for fire.
I burn you up and then you turn into ash!
Who am I?
I am anger!

Shangavy Sackthivel, Grade 8
Royal Orchard Middle School, ON

My Horse

When things go wrong, and I am down,
I simply just take a walk outdoors,
To where I find a great creature on four legs.
I walk up and explain my problems,
As he stands there looking at me as if he agrees,
I walk up closer, give him a hug and let out a cry.
When I stop and look up at his big, bulgy, brown eyes,
It makes me smile to see they are full of joy and happiness.
As my problems slowly disappear, I take a hold of the mane
That he has there to hold; I take a step, and vault myself onto his back.
The next thing I know, when I'm settled on his back,
We are racing down the luscious, green meadow.
The wind whistling through our hair,
As the ground thunders loudly in my ears.
The speed of our pace makes the wind so cold, my eyes begin to tear.
When I take another look, I realize we are back at the barn.
I give him a pat and tell him, "good boy."
Before I walk to the house I turn around,
Blow him a kiss and tell him goodnight.
On my way in I think, my horse is the very best!

Breezi Helmus, Grade 8
Hillside Jr/Sr High School, AB

What I've Been Waiting For

My heart pounds like a repetitive punch in my chest.
Coarse whisper like breaths spill from my lungs,
Every muscle I have tenses up with adrenaline.
I'm ready to go now, just let me go!
The barely audible announcer calls my name,
It sounds so perfect, there for everyone to hear.
It's what I've been waiting for!
Now I can go. I'm ready to compete.
I tighten up the cinch on my saddle.
I stumble clumsily on to her back.
My horse gives a triumphant shout-like neigh,
She gallops down the dirt path,
This is it,
It's time to go!

Beth Prouse, Grade 8
Grayson School, SK

Him

As I sit alone in this empty hallway
holding the necklace he gave to me.
Tracing the diamonds with my fingertips.
I start thinking about what he meant to me.
And realizing how I meant nothing to him.
When the pain that I thought was there, never was.
I did something that I never thought I could.
I got over him.

Kimberly Gilmore, Grade 7
Macdonald High School, QC

The Lock and the Key

I am the lock
And you are the key
Without you, I am nothing

You give me security
And you enable me to hold on
To all the treasures
And to all the pain

With you, and only by you
Can I be set free
From the responsibility
And all the worries

I cannot function alone
And my heart hangs hopelessly without you
But when we are together,
Does my broken heart become whole again.

I am the lock
And you are the key
Without you, I am nothing
— Useless —

Alvin Kim, Grade 9
Fraser Heights Secondary School, BC

Day Dreamer

Wandering in my own carefree pastime
lost in space,
not willing to be found,
for this is my place,
the place where I do not need to search,

How much they try to lure me back,
to their home,
not mine,
but I,
am not as careless as you think,
and I shall not be pulled,
for I am here,
calm in the clouds,
stretching out into the cosmos,
at peace,
peacefully daydreaming.

Maggie Smith, Grade 9
Sir John Franklin School, NT

Cellphone

I was walking down the street one day
just by myself, just walking the path.
The sun was strong, the trees wouldn't sway,
but the quiet was broken by my cellphone.
I answered the call with a cheery hello,
but the end was silent, not a single moan.
What use was this object, if not to talk,
so I continued along with my morning walk.
I got to the corner and what did I see,
there were so many people not talking to me.
I quickly realized I was really alone,
everyone else was talking on their cellphone.

Kristina Stark, Grade 8
Macdonald High School, QC

A Bond, So Strong

A feeling, a sensation, unbroken
By scandal, by heartbreak, by hate and rage
Despite arguments there is no notion
That bond will break, their hearts remain unscathed

The wonder, the amazement, to her grace
The kindness, the awareness, of this boy
When near her, he never feels out of place
When around him, she no longer feels coined

Spills her heart into this young, growing man
So much she reveals, nobody else there
He listens, takes in as much as he can
Never will he see a woman as fair

Yet, after all that has been said and done,
They are unbreakable, mother and son

Hussein Chmaissany, Grade 9
Hon W C Kennedy Collegiate Institute, ON

Nature

Nature is great
Buzz
There goes a bee
I zip
I zap
All around the trees
I step in the leaves
Crunch
I hear the swish in the sea
Nature is great

Andie-Lynn Deak, Grade 7
Menno Simons Christian School, AB

Wild Mustang

Black as the night,
Fast as the wind,
Running wild and free
Out in the prairies,
Holding his head high,
Mane blowing in the wind,
A mustang running free.
Feeling life in his veins,
Never accepting capture.
Freedom is his!

Joe Kleinsasser, Grade 7
Milford Colony School, AB

My Dog

My dog likes to dig
Straight through the earth's core
Like a mountain, he's big
Won't fit through my door
He eats like a pig
All down his throat
He jumps a quick jig
Then he sleeps on my coat.

Davy Parker, Grade 7
Bella Coola Adventist Academy, BC

These Eyes

These eyes they hold a darkened sin,
Buried deep, deep within.
Dare not tell the words unspoken,
Though I seem a soul wide open.
The eyes shall never give away,
The way I feel day by day.
The happiness inside shines so bright,
My heart no longer pale and white.
I allow it to shine, no longer caring,
Passionate and smiling, oh so daring.
Soul returning happy and bright,
Happiness never losing sight.
No eyes hold back an unspoken sin,
No longer afraid, I let my heart win.

Katie Phillips, Grade 8
Odessa Public School, ON

Trapped

Cold and trapped
Like an animal in a cage
Not sure where I am
I open my eyes
But nothing is there
Just the darkness
I start to panic
Start to struggle
But my hands are tied
I start to scream
Like in a horror movie
Get me out of here
But no one comes
I start to cry
Not sure where I am
Not sure what's going on
All I know is that I'm
Trapped.

Fontana German, Grade 9
Westcliffe Composite School, SK

Delicate Duck

The bright green head glinted in the
dazzling afternoon sun,
The fresh odour of clean water
drifted up my nose,
"Quack, Quack, Quack!"

The soft feathers were like a
live suit of velvet
It looked majestic as it glided
through the open water
"Quack, Quack, Quack!"

Cleason Martin, Grade 7
Linwood Public School, ON

A Popcorn's Life

Drop me into the soft, brown, dirt
of the warm earth's surface.
I grow with the help of wet watery
raindrops and bright, beaming sunlight.
The full grown stalk stands proud as a
statue from long ago.
Kernels!
Squished, squashed I sit on a shelf,
hard as a rock
Bought
What will happen?
I am dumped into a hot cooking pan.
I start to get fatter and fatter
Until...
POP!
I explode loudly into a puffy white
Popcorn!

Rachel Martin, Grade 7
Linwood Public School, ON

Leafy McGhee

I am a quiet little leaf.
I am a small green,
And partially eaten leaf.
I am a very beautiful
Part of the forest.
I help make the wonderful colors.
I am 1 out of 1200
Leaves on the trees;
There are lots of leaves
With all sorts of colors —
Green, brown, orange, and red.
I am not just a leaf,
I am a beautiful part of nature.
You may think I am just a leaf,
Just a no good waste of material.
You just wait until there
Are no more trees with leaves on them.
You will see how much better
The trees look with us on them.
We'll see what you think then.

Hayley Ashley, Grade 8
Hillside Jr/Sr High School, AB

White

Faith is white,
Sounding like the laughter of joy,
And feels gentle like a feather.
It smells tangy and sweet like fruit.
But tastes delightful and heavenly,
like a buffet at a 5-star restaurant.

Patricia Gutierrez, Grade 7
St Anne School, AB

Crocodile

How this crocodile swims
With a cheerful grin
How little birds clean
To make his smile gleam.

Aliecia Smith, Grade 8
Hillside Jr/Sr High School, AB

Home

What is my home?

My shelter from crazy weather
My safe haven
A place where I can eat, sleep and play
My family
A place to be left alone
A place to have friends over
Storage for my belongings
A place for comfort

That is my home

Amitoj Chahal, Grade 7
John Campbell Public School, ON

When Darkness Falls

Darkness has fallen, the light grows dim
The world grows still, and all is calm
Across the land, the light fades out
The sun retreats, and shadows emerge,

The night has come, the shadows dance
Weaving through fields of green blades
Licking up the light left behind
Predators of the night swim through pools of shadows,

From the stifling mist, boogeymen crawl out
Feral beasts race across the yard
Shadowy claws slip silently, ripping through the darkness
Slithering down the streets all is silent, but not calm,

Do not fret, the sun will rise!
Sensing a change, the beasts retreat
They sink through the maw of darkness
But soon even that will be gone, giving way to righteous light.

Gavin Grochowski, Grade 7
Westwind Elementary School, BC

I Wish You Could Understand

Dreams are lined up against the wall,
The problem is I can't see them all.
All these thoughts in my head,
They're telling me what to do instead.
Sometimes I wish I could scream,
But that wouldn't help because no one would hear me.
All these thoughts and dreams,
Are fighting their way out.
I want to tell everyone,
But I can't.
There's no one I can trust,
No one who will understand.

Alexis Chislett-Rowsell, Grade 8
Netagamiou School, QC

Precious

The shiny old me
My heart is full of gold
Everyone loves me
Why?
My diamond locket just hangs on me
The outside of me is rough
The diamond makes me stony
Someone makes me precious
Not only with money
I bring back so many memories
From the past
Some even make me shed a few tears
The rusty old jewelry box is my home
Maybe someday I will melt from gold to silver
When will someone place me in their heart?

Sukhmandeep Aulakh, Grade 8
OV Jewitt Community School, MB

The Lighthouse

The lighthouse,
The guardian angel of the night.
She shines her light for all the poor souls
Lost at sea.

Her beam is bright, even to the sun,
Flashing through the night sky.
Her light piercing through the storm
Like sharp knives.

During the day, she sleeps.
Her light, a silent deer not wanting to be found.
In the darkness of the night, she warns the sailors
Of the dangers around her.

Leslie Ho, Grade 7
Westwind Elementary School, BC

Sanctuary of Darkness

Trying not to give in
to the craving gray of fog.
The sun warmed the Earth,
but I could not feel it.
At my touch, light shattered,
hearts bled, love ended.
Love could not live in me.
My hate, like a deeper void,
was being built, stronger and stronger.
My hate, uttered again and again
in the eaves by spirits;
spirits touched and consumed by my darkness.
Love was a mirage,
all day long I would fake it,
but at night, I was consumed.

Sam Sjerve, Grade 9
Avalon Junior High School, AB

Untitled

Comrade, can you hear me?
Did you forget your name?
Have you lost your trust in yourself?
Did you deepen all desire to live no more?
Has the sun gone down?
Do you feel no pain?
Did fear strike you cold?
They took it all.
Left you for dead.
Are you left to question it?
To wonder why?

Brother, can you hear me?
Hold on strong.
They say you're doing fine
Just fine.

Louis Bursey, Grade 7
Homelands Senior Public School, ON

Never Is an Understatement

Consistent repetition,
Of the same lecture.
Doubtful of the possibility,
Of a consequential mistake.
Never thought of a decision;
For more than a blink of an eye.
One choice.
To determine your future.
One will.
To diminish the probability.
But when recognition strikes,
And realization penetrates,
It's too late.

Julia Kang, Grade 9
Webber Academy, AB

Skiing

Yes, I'm glad school is over!
As I pack my books from class.
I race outside to the car
Across the snow covered grass.

Down the school lane Mum drives,
Up the mountain road.
Until we are in the car park
Then on the ski slope.

On the freshly fallen snow
I have so much fun.
Going over jumps
And snaking down the run!

The stars have come out now
So I stop to see the view.
I can see Vancouver,
And what about you?

Emma Moulton, Grade 8
Mulgrave School, BC

Wall Jumping

A fellow jumped off a high wall
And had a most terrible fall
He went back to bed
With a bump on his head
That's why you don't jump off a wall

Skylar Dunning, Grade 7
New Horizons School, AB

Mountains

I climbed
the mountain
of life. I made it to
the top and died. Now I lay
in peace with the people I love.

Amanda Devoe, Grade 7
St Anne School, AB

Before My Ever After Comes

Before my ever after comes I'd like to do a lot of things,
I'd like to surf through the ice cold water before the water chokes up my lungs

I'd like to explore the under world seeing all the weird creatures
Staring at me, with popping green eyes

Before my lifeline ends I'd like to sky dive
Seeing the world million miles below me wondering what I am

I'd like to drive a huge airplane others wondering why it's me driving the plane
I'd like to be part of the Olympics and win gold for my country

Hey I can't go yet there's still a lot to do before
I'd like to watch the National Hockey League (NHL) playoffs
Seeing the Sens kick out the Wings that would be awesome

Before I die I want to do what I can 'cause I am what I am
I want my best friend always close to me when I am gone
There will be just one space for someone new and I could go on and on forever
Listing what I would like to do before ever after is calling for my name.

Mikayla Wipf, Grade 7
Decker Colony School, MB

Finally Falling

Perhaps tonight the stars will plummet from the sky
Maybe next spring the ocean will recast into nothing but dust
Conceivably tomorrow the color yellow won't exist
Subsequently today the sun will shine
Later tomorrow the past will be the future
The following year, all of our bad memories will *finally fall*
A dream that is crushed won't come alive in the material world,
But a dream that is crushed will end up in your soul, mind, and in heaven.
If only good intentions rise up in your life, then love will present itself in front of you.
"Rise, take up your mat, and walk!" — Jesus Christ (Matthew 9)

Olga Jablonski, Grade 7
Lower Canada College, QC

Before I Go

There are many things I would like to do, see or become before I go
But there are some things in peculiar that
I would like to do even before all my other
Smaller steps in my life are taken before I go
I would like to see a place where ancient history becomes alive
And where smart people combined their ideas
To make their civilizations as safe and as organized as possible
Seeing all the seven wonders of the world would be truly wonderful before I go
I would like to fly in a military helicopter and feel the angry rumble of its motor
To hear it growl and moan, to ask the pilots many question before I go
There is much more that I could say,
But the best wish on my list is tour a rocket station
And see the inside of a huge space rocket, before I go
As it looks down at me as if to ask me for a ride that I'd never regret
Do simple things like ride on the back of an ostrich, elephant
And maybe even something as crazy as a giraffe before I go.

Sheldon Wipf, Grade 9
Decker Colony School, MB

The Same Old Episode

I can still see you
In my mind
I see your face
And the emotion on it
The day I broke your heart

I hurt you
Without knowing
What I was doing
And it hurts me too

It hurts to wonder
To wonder what we'd be
If I chose the other path
It hurts to remember
Remember all that happened
It runs through my mind
Over and over
Like a movie that can't stop playing
Like an episode
That keeps rerunning
With nothing new to play
To write in

Stephanie Donath, Grade 9
St Thomas Aquinas Catholic Secondary School, ON

Invisible

Am I invisible?
Or am I not important enough to be seen or heard?
Do I have to be an over-achiever to be noticed?
To be acknowledged?
Being compared over and over to everyone else.
Always feeling 2nd best.
Can you imagine trying to be you?
Feeling like it's the only way to earn your approval.
For you to be proud to call me yours.
Am I still invisible?
Maybe I always will be.
Invisible

Eliza Ma, Grade 8
Bishop Lloyd School, SK

Best Friends

This poem is about my cousin Dylan,
every weekend you can find us chillin'
He is my best friend
and we're in this until the end
We've been together through the good times and bad
and we're there for each other whenever we're sad
I've got his back and he's got mine
We make each other laugh all of the time
Every moment with him I treasure
We will be best friends forever

Brandon Morris, Grade 8
Macdonald High School, QC

Is It So?

Is it so?
The ice beneath my skates,
The sound of leaves falling, sticks breaking,
Waves hitting the side of the boat.

Is it so?
The goal everyone talks about,
Ten antlers in the forest,
The swirl after my lure.

Is it so?
The cheers as you skate off the ice,
The sound of the gunshot,
The splash in the water.

Exciting,
Subtle,
Adventure.

Is it so?
So it is.

Fraser Duhaime, Grade 7
St Joseph Separate School, ON

I Have a Dream…

I have a dream,
That there will be love and peace on Earth
That war does no longer exist
That we would no longer hear the sound of gun shots
That everyone could stick out without being made fun of
I have a dream…
That there was no more bullying
That we cared about our earth and would stop polluting it
That everyone should be f r e e
That everyone should be allowed to express themselves
I have a dream…

Shannon Hunt, Grade 8
Bloorlea Middle School, ON

Left Behind

A road hidden in moss and fern
Where will it take me, what will I learn?
I need to get there, I need to find
The part of me I left behind

They say I need to change my ways
But I cannot see through the haze
It should stand out, be clear and defined
The part of me I left behind

When will they understand, it's not a sham
I cannot change who I am
So there is nothing left to find
No part of me I left behind

Olivia Pink, Grade 7
St Patrick's Elementary School, BC

Relief!

I awake to the sound of the loud alarm clock, a normal day awaits, with school at eight o'clock.
As I slowly exit my sleepy state, I think ahead to what, in the afternoon, will await.
Maybe I will go skating, or perhaps just watch TV, I feel a sudden chill and cry out, "Oh no, not me!"
Today is Tuesday, not a normal day at all. No, today is the day that makes me want to bawl.
After school I won't be just hanging out, I will be playing the piano, badly, without a doubt.
The rest of the day goes by so quick, I wish with all I've got, "Please, let me be sick."
Nothing results from all of my prayers, I prepare for the agony; it's a sad state of affairs.
I get off the bus, and slowly trudge up the driveway, I take my time getting into the house to try and delay
Practicing the piano; an activity I am forced to endure. I tell myself to just get it over with and be mature.
And so I take a deep breath, and sit at the bench, my playing is so bad, like a terrible stench.
My mom calls me over, the phone in her hand, she says, "Piano is canceled. I hope you understand."

Madison Riddell, Grade 9
Webber Academy, AB

Beautiful Doom

They tricked me down
          down into the dark green water to find their lovely music,
                    their beautiful music.

But once I stopped at the bottom stair
    evil noise was everywhere,
        evil noises, bursting through my ears
    and I realized my worst fears.

            up the creaky stairs
      I had to run up
                  and try not to fall down
                        down.
      I had to escape those stubborn, tricky frogs, the
            tricky frogs.
But once I started to run
        run, the lovely music returned.

    I knew they wanted my doom
        and I knew it would be soon.
    But a life without their song,
          their lovely song, their beautiful song,
            means doom to me.

Kacie McLeod, Grade 9
Avalon Junior High School, AB

Moving

There I was, shocked, after soccer practice, just beginning to believe my mom about the big move to Canada.
    Canada? Fish, fish, bears, moose and more fish?
    — Great

    Leave all my friends, sports teams and my school? Move to another country?
    — Sure, why not.

    Now on the plane, I was scared, not knowing at all what Canada looked like.
    — Different.

    I like it here, have new friends, play rugby instead of soccer, speak English instead of German. Move back?
    — No way.

Constantin Wahle, Grade 8
Mulgrave School, BC

Would You?
Some say that they would kill for admission
To a tennis match, or a rock concert.
So reply. Need not be a magician.
Answer truthfully: Would you from good avert?
Would you ever sneak in to watch a crown
Being placed on top of somebody's head?
In your rush to be on time for Chris Brown,
Would you forget one who was left for dead?
This might sound silly to you just right now.
You have not done such things — at least not yet.
But maybe in the future, you will — wow!
Commit such a stupid act. Care to bet?
And now, before I lay down, rest a tad,
I ask you one more time: Would you be bad?

John Parkinson, Grade 7
St Patrick's Elementary School, BC

Ottawa
The first thing I see are the stars,
single souls in the sky
trying to compete against the charcoal black night.
We keep walking — with the snow like a
pillow under our feet.
and the cold scorching wind viciously biting our cheeks.
Now all we can see are ice sculptures,
glistening, as clear as diamonds.
In front of me a field of art work, —
exquisite masterpieces of ice,
each one a breathtaking, translucent piece of culture.
To the east I see a Beaver Tail shack,
with a sparkling lonely light.
I am hungry and chilled to
the bone as the wind crawls up my back.
I order a hot and scrumptious chocolate pastry,
and wash it down with a cup of sizzling cider
to heat me up.
We sit on the bench, my family and me,
then we walk through the cold,
smiling with glee.

Marty Metzger, Grade 7
Linwood Public School, ON

Sisters
They love us so
With their little pink bows
And their pink little dresses
All lined in a row
When they come out to play
On a bright sunny day
They sing and they shout
As they scurry about
Singing about the wonderful day
That has brought us together
Now and forever

Megan Moore, Grade 7
Community Bible Fellowship Christian School, MB

A Fireman's Job
The telephone rings with one big ping,
I pick up the phone and begin to sing.
I say "Hello, there's a fire I'm your fellow,
All black and yellow."
We jump in the truck,
And with a bit of luck there'll be no muck.
We finally arrive, we'll be lucky to survive.
The flames lick and curl and begin to whirl.
It's a beautiful sight with all that light,
I strap my boots on tight.
I go into the house and look for the lost spouse.
A board gets me tangled,
I feel like I'm being strangled
The smoke is so thick it makes me feel sick.
I find the lady whose name is Katy.
The flames getting hotter, I teeter and totter.
I find a door that leads under the floor.
I see a vent that looks slightly bent,
I kick it out without a doubt and am caught up in celebration
And begin my meditation to God.

Landon Kozak, Grade 8
Bella Coola Adventist Academy, BC

Eternal Love
The guards are running.
The alarm bells are ringing.
Love will conquer all, love will conquer all.
He looks into her eyes. And she cries.
He holds her one last time.
Close your eyes. Peace will come.
They are coming. They will take her.
His love. His all.
Embrace her for the last time.
Smell her.
Touch her.
And step away.
No words can be said.
His fate is set.
And one step closer, his imminent death.
"Forever," he whispers.
He leaps to his doom.
There is no worry.
There is no fright.
She will live.
And he will die.

Matthew Wizinsky, Grade 7
Constable Neil Bruce Middle School, BC

Changing of Seasons
Two worlds, one is up, one is down.
They both connect but do not.
One path leads to another and yet it is the same path
and I am in between both, yet still in one.

Philippe de Gaspé Beaubien, Grade 7
Lower Canada College, QC

Joy

Joy is
boundlessly yellow.

It sounds like
a kitten's
rumble purr.

It smells like
fresh earth
after a rain.

It tastes like
triple chocolate
cheesecake.

It looks like
a mountain of books
I haven't read yet.

Joy feels like
the unexpected recovery of an
injured animal.
                Savanna Lindley, Grade 8
Heritage Christian Online School, BC

Spring Has Come

With grass so green
And sky so blue
When wispy clouds pass
Overhead
I know that spring has sprung
Life has come
To end cold winter again
                Victoria Diederichs, Grade 7
                New Horizons School, AB

Going to French

Oh how I hear the buzzing
Buzz buzz buzzing
Indicates that it's next period
DREAD
Getting green binder, green binder
Click clack clacking
Mechanical pencil, mechanical pencil
On my binder
Shake shake shaking
On my toes
Walk walk walking
To my destination of
DREAD
Why so hard? Why do we have to learn?
I don't know, I don't know
What I do know is what is called...
FRENCH
                Henry Dao, Grade 7
John Campbell Public School, ON

Goodbye Home

As I fight for everything, my heart it begins to sing,
For the eyes are that of a bright morning sun.
Never forget a face: her words, elegant as lace
My brace, for life, and everything that I've won
Never forget her until I'm outdone
Never leave her 'til the lighting of the candles has begun.

Disappearing slowly; nothing more is holy
Gone forever is the lust for seasons.
Shots in the air; slipping off our blue mare,
But why care? Bandage these lesions.
Thinking has become treason
With this heat, I'm freezing.

The light is slowly dying; third eye is crying
Your scars are feeling the rain
Tasting the acid; relinquish the placid
Home has become pallid, but is running in the fast lane
Shove it away, see what won't come again

Goodbye, though it is a lie; truth is just another failed try
This is our doing, but fake the facts to save
A reputation, grinding this silencing creation
Wisps are all that is left of salvation, as we dig our shallow graves.
                Joe Byram, Grade 9
                Vernon Secondary School, BC

My Bucket List

Before I go home there are a couple of things
That I'd like to do just for the fun of it

First I want to fly up high in the air with a plane
And then jump out and feel the winds lift me in my parachute

And then I'd like to visit the moon, jump up and around in a suit
Visit the ocean bottom and see the whales swimming around me

Ride on an elephant's back in the hot sun of Africa
As it thunders through the desert with a long train behind it

And drive in an orange race car and forget the world around me
Without being afraid, just enjoying the thrill

Next I'd like to see Celtic Thunder live in action, as the
Crowds erupt in cheering and they give out the bouquets

Last I'd like to have a jet, so that I can fly quickly
Through the sky and leave a trail of dust behind me

That's all for now, but tomorrow I am sure to have more
Because the world changes and so do I
                Barbmaria Waldner, Grade 9
                Decker Colony School, MB

Dream

Water lapping at my ankles
Gulls screeching above me
I close my eyes and dream
Flying effortlessly above the world
Above troubles, wrongs, sorrows, hurts
Floating in space
Among the stars and galaxies
Happy and free, I want to stay
Feel this calmness for eternity
My heart sighs,
But taking a deep breath,
I pull myself back
Sucking my soul back into the world
When it longs to dream in endless bliss
Back to reality
The sunset cuts through the clouds
Exploding in hues of red, orange, and pink
And I breathe in the beauty around me
My soul is at peace, and I start out for home
Because there I can do just the same
Dream.

Natalie Lim, Grade 7
Dr George M Weir Elementary School, BC

Friends Forever

Friends will pick you up when you are down
They'll make you laugh when you frown
We went through times that were good and bad
We even had moments that were happy and sad
Take my hand, we shall move on
To a place that we can bond
When the time is right to choose a friend
I have mine that I will lend
But in my life I will always choose
To have a friend that is just like you

Victoria Sobol, Grade 7
Macdonald High School, QC

Love

Should I compare you to a shining star?
That is very lovely and attractive.
Baby, please tell me who you really are.
I could be nice and very sensitive.
Sweetie pie, I love you so much girl.
From the first time I met you until now.
I promise I would give you the world.
Even though I'm struggling to know how.
I am so hypnotized by your beauty.
I would give you anything, my lady.
Your smile makes you look like a cutie.
So come on and ride on my Mercedes.
So don't be shy because I'm a nice guy.
You can trust me because I never lie.

Victor Danh-Tran, Grade 9
Hon W C Kennedy Collegiate Institute, ON

Lost: Memory

LOST: MEMORY
Location last seen is a mystery
For what is lost is a memory
Date and time remain unknown
Maybe we'll never really know
Memory has a greater value than gold
Even more than your grandmothers old, shiny broach
If found, please locate the one who's wandering the streets
Missing that spring in her step
The shine of New York City at night in her eyes
And kindly return,
You will be rewarded.

FOUND: MEMORY
Card for a digital camera
Photographs of a shiny broach worn long ago
New York City late at night
And a person walking away from the location discovered
Call if it jogs your memory

Kristen Love, Grade 9
Hon W C Kennedy Collegiate Institute, ON

Cavalry

The sound of the army marching (running).
They move as one (herd).

Nothing else can be heard.
It seems as if they swept everything away (speed) and are
headed to the battlefield (valley).

As people (animals) run and try to find cover (safety) the
sound gets bigger and louder each step (stride).

They go past rocks and step (jump) over anything.
Their only thoughts are conquer (graze) that land.

They act quickly (spook) to what's thought to be an
ambush. And keep moving.

They move (gallop) over the horizon and glance down at the
battlefield (valley).

Their commander (stallion) walks up and sees that this is
their stop (rest).

Stephen Berard, Grade 7
St Joseph Separate School, ON

Horses

As they run through the grass
Their mane soaring behind them
Like a flag that says wild and free
But the sun goes down
And they become a black shadow against the
Calm, fiery sky

Rosie Schick, Grade 8
Kennedy Langbank School, SK

Amazing Poetry to Write
Poetry
Triplets, Tonka
amazing, rhyming, writing
Poetry is jolly to write
There are so many ways
to write Poems
Sylvie Dzafic, Grade 7
Homelands Senior Public School, ON

Snowmobiling
Racing across the fields
Two lengths to go
Jumping in and out of the snow
Almost there
I see a big hill
I can conquer it
Try the best I can
Oh no he passed me
But
I'm determined to catch up
Winner!!
Aaron Case, Grade 8
Heather Park Middle School, BC

Music
Music is played,
And it fades
To the sound
Of the ground.

The Music's sound
Is finally found
With a tune
Like the moon.

The wind blows.
The sun shines.
But music will play.
Until the end of time.

Till the dawn of day.
The music plays.
Kirsten Raccio, Grade 7
St. Paul School, SK

Fear Is Like
Fear is like a red hot fire in a house.
Is cold like a winter day.
Sounds like a wasp flying near your ear.
Tastes like dog food.
Smells like rotten fish.
Looks like an angry man.
Feels like a rocky mountain.
Moves like a snake.
Logan Blackstock, Grade 7
St Anne School, SK

A Tree
A tree is a very majestic thing.
And what you see is what you get
Because a tree is like me
A very majestic being that stands TALL
Daymen Ashmeade, Grade 7
St Anne School, SK

Camping Trip
We're going on a camping trip
I wonder what we'll find
We're going on a camping trip
Just can't get it off my mind.

We just set up the tent
And we did it without a fight
I'm so glad that we went
On this camping trip tonight.

As we all sing campfire songs
We start to do a jig
And as everyone sings along
Aunt Judie lost her wig!

Well it's getting pretty late
And we just put out the fire
I think we should call it a day
Because I'm feeling really tired.
Morgan Reiber-Mason, Grade 7
St Anne School, SK

Parents
Your parents love you
And care for you
They also discipline you
You're sometimes grounded
Which is no fun
All you do is stay at home
Can't see or call friends
Or go out for a movie with them
Sometimes parents are no fair.
Tiffany Twiss, Grade 9
Elm Creek School, MB

Life Is a Song
Life is a song,
Every beat is something
that happens in life.
Every chorus is a
favourite dream.
Every lyric is an adventure.
Every note is something that you
will remember forever.
That is why everyone walks to their
own rhythm.
Samuel Gaudreault, Grade 7
Macdonald High School, QC

Dreams
Dreams are everyone's desire.
They're the things we all acquire.
They're all of our inspiration
Mixed with our imagination.
Fatima Farrukh, Grade 7
Homelands Senior Public School, ON

Take the Time to Look
Take time to look
The world is big
It's huge, so huge.
Something new to see every day,
Even in the same spot,
You can see something so spectacular.
That you are taken aback by,
So all you have to do,
Is take the time to look.
Joe Duda, Grade 8
Hillside Jr/Sr High School, AB

Wind
The wind is blowing
Wind going through my thick hair
Past my shirt it comes
Wind is flowing everywhere
But I will never see it
Easton Foley, Grade 7
Homelands Senior Public School, ON

That Girl
I gaze upon her
She settles on a chair there
Looking admirable
So gleaming was her hair
And she is very popular
Antoine Saddler, Grade 7
Homelands Senior Public School, ON

My Home
Home, Sweet, Home
The fresh morning air,
Bringing an appetite.
The little birds singing,
Their daily songs.
With wooly flocks of sheep,
Grazing in the glorious meadow.
Home, sweet, home
Strong, willing work horses,
Pulling loads of hay.
Clouds as fluffy as lambs,
In the clear blue sky.
A cool breeze whispering in my ears.
The sun is a stove.
Home, Sweet, Home.
Naomi Bowman, Grade 7
Linwood Public School, ON

Grandma's Cancer

Was a bright and cloudless day,
Little did we know, a horrible storm was coming soon.
She was so beautiful, and full of life
But that would not be the case for long.
One day, she took me alone into a dark closet,
She told me the news,
I didn't believe it,
Grandma had cancer,
That wasn't going away.
I cried and cried tears of sorrow,
For days I didn't stop.
She went to the hospice,
Just for a day,
For when I came home,
Sorrow filled the rooms and people.
I know what had happened
No need to explain,
She was dead,
Never to come back again.

Melissa McFadyen, Grade 7
Westside Academy, BC

Smoon

The sun rises up in the morning,
With the yellow, orange, and pink sky.
Then it stays up in the sky,
Thinking of the evening when it has to say good-bye.

The moon's way up there in the sky,
Waiting for nightfall to arrive,
With its great big craters,
I don't know anybody who hates her.

The sun starts to set,
Now it's being put back to bed,
The light starts to fade,
The night wants her to stay.

The moon is up with its yellowish tinge,
Ready to play all night but not the day,
It's up in the sky thinking of the sunrise,
Thinking it will start all over tomorrow.

Megan Rice, Grade 7
St Joseph Separate School, ON

Sick Day Blues

Oh no, oh no what a horrible day,
The fluids aren't helping, if I may say.
The coughs, the groans, the awful sneezes,
And how I feel those shivering breezes.
Oh what, oh what could get me healed?
Just darn those germs that were not sealed!
They wrecked my day, of fun and play,
So now with a scowl in bed I shall lay!

Christina Penkov, Grade 7
Aurora Charter School, AB

Hide and Seek

Tick-tock
Of the clock
Bong, bong
I jumped at the sudden sound,
My heart leaps into my throat with anticipation.
Tick-tock
I was never good at waiting,
Waiting…
Waiting to become one of them.
Tick-tock
I can hardly stand it,
Not moving, just sitting like a stone statue,
A death warrantee.
Tick-tock
The clock is a reminder,
Banging around my head in a steady beat,
The precious time.
Tick-tock
"Got you!"
With those two words,
I become the enemy.

Jana Wagler, Grade 7
Linwood Public School, ON

The Beginning

Floating, falling, gliding, prancing
I can hear the heavy laughter and joy
The echoes of carols that bring love and joy to the world
The lights are radiant, while trees smile.
Dozens of hands cover the tree
with an illuminated glimmer at the tip of the tree.
The cheery sounds of carols are quiet
The angelic brightness is gone,
The snowman's face is melting,
And the birds are chirping.
…It is the beginning
Of spring

Gloria Feng, Grade 8
Mulgrave School, BC

Mexico

Sounds of tropical birds in the morning
Bright blues, yellows and pinks
Fresh seafood, with twist of hot sauce

Sights of monkeys, toucans, and iguanas
Coral with a pinch of beauty and pain
Warm water washing upon my feet

Tropical flowers, smelling of the richest fragrance

Forever love, forever
Mexico

Robyn Durst, Grade 8
Rutland Middle School, BC

Holland Lops

Small bundles of joy.
Fh, fh, fh, a quiet whispering sound,
as it hops to the front of its cage.
Small bundles of joy.
Cuddly little 'Kleenex boxes',
loonie-like front paws,
large thumping back paws.
Small bundles of joy.
Fluffy as clouds,
wide as the spine of a phone book,
soft, cuddly, little teddy bears.
Small bundles of joy.
Thick, soft, fur,
happy, quiet,
crunchings as it munches on a carrot,
turning its lips orange.
Small bundles of joy.
Fast, fluffy, friendly.
Small bundles of joy
Holland Lops.

Kristen Joy Harris, Grade 7
Linwood Public School, ON

Today

I came home from school
I have homework
So here I am
On a Wednesday night
At 10:00 pm
Sitting at the kitchen table
Writing this poem for LA
It's almost done
Then I'll go have some fun
I missed watching hockey
And the Flames won
2-1

Dylan Enns, Grade 7
Menno Simons Christian School, AB

Lost and Found

When the cold frost bites,
And you're lost at sea,
When you are eager to just be,
Let your spirit be free,
And you will soon see,
That the horizon looks warm,
And through that storm,
Is the rainbow of life,
A mystery of colors,
And shine,
Hold on to your faith,
Believe in who you are,
And that morning burst of sun,
Will light up your window.

Madison Meyer, Grade 8
William A Fraser Middle School, BC

Remember When…

Remember when cooties were the only things we thought guys had?
When you couldn't sleep, you climbed in with mom and dad
And spending time with friends was playing a hand game
But now they're just memories that will stay the same

Remember when 'fat' was a man in baggy pants and skinny was nothing?
And playing the card game 'speed' was addicting
When we didn't think much about fortune and fame
But now they're just memories that will stay the same

Remember when 'scary' was a small spider on the wall?
When you thought about Disneyland above all
And when candy was everything and learning was lame
But now they're just memories that will stay the same

Joanne Nellas, Grade 7
St Patrick's Elementary School, BC

Friends

You're my friend and always remember that
If I could give you one thing, I would wish for you, the
ability to see yourself, as others see you
Then you'll see how amazing you are and your wonderful personality
I cannot even imagine where I'd be today were it not for that handful
of friends who have given a heart full of joy and delight
If I didn't have any friends, my life would be so dull
We've been friends in sunshine and shade, and I hope to keep it that way
Our friendship is the only rose with the petals that holds the world together
Some friends will just lie to keep you from getting hurt but
best friends will tell you the truth and wipe away your
tears and problems
I am very thankful to have such wonderful friends.

Jessica Tran, Grade 7
Blundell Elementary School, BC

My Dearest Friend

I know you'll always be there,
To stand by my side and care.
You're behind me to defend,
So I thank you, my dearest friend.

We laugh, we argue, we smile,
But never the less, for you I'd run a mile.
I'm here for you until the very end,
So I thank you, my dearest friend.

You and I are like jam and toast,
You're the one I run to the most.
I know you will never pretend,
So I thank you my dearest friend.

To me, in my heart I know you'll always be true,
And if you're in a time of trouble I'll eternally help you break through.
Our friendship hopefully will never end,
So I thank you, my dearest friend.

Rebecca Siglos, Grade 7
St Patrick's Elementary School, BC

For the Love of Dance

Spinning across the floor
Feeling like I can't stop
The blood racing through my veins
My heart beating like a hummingbird's

Sailing through the air
Landing on the scuffed floors
Happiness, laughing and smiling
Tears, blood and sweat

My feet softly stroking the smooth surface
Of the floors beneath me
The power rushing through my entire body
Unable to stop itself
Propelling me up above
Almost flying to the heavens

All of the pain
All of the joy
All of the training
All for the love of dancing

Elizabeth Wanstall, Grade 9
École Secondaire Catholique Mgr-de-Charbonnel, ON

Waiting for Tomorrow...

Waiting for tomorrow,
To see your smile,
Waiting for tomorrow,
To feel your touch.

Waiting for tomorrow,
To kiss your lips,
Waiting for tomorrow,
To hold your hand.

Waiting for tomorrow,
To feel your love for me in the air,
Waiting for tomorrow,
To be with you.

No matter where I am,
I smile,
Waiting for tomorrow...

Mélanie Veilleux, Grade 9
École Secondaire Catholique Franco-Ouest, ON

Black

I feel sorrow when I see black
I taste caster oil and salt water when I see black
I hear heavy breathing and crying when I see black
I feel sorrowful and scared when I see black
The color makes me feel
Like a black hole

Saakshi Dhingra, Grade 7
St Anne School, AB

It's Gone

You walk a lonely road, there is no end.
You ask yourself
Will this ever end, or will it continue forever?
The clouds come hide the sun
The dark creeps over, someone comes around
You see the light. You see hope. You see the end.
You start running, toward the end, it gets farther away
In a blink, it's gone.
You knew it was your way out of this misery
Away from these people who don't care.
The end is far
You still keep walking, as far as you've ever gone
The road gets shorter
But then you realize, it's never over
Not 'til your dying breath.

Emy Lafontaine, Grade 9
Ecole Secondaire Mille-Iles, ON

An Ode to Sydney

There's a place that I often ponder
Filled with koalas, lizards, and kangaroos
A place that is called down under
A place that is exotic and new

The plane ride was tiring and long
But when we landed, it was worth it
I thought I wasn't going to be tired but I was wrong
After landing I knew that this city was a good fit

The clear blue ocean is so warm and comforting
The soft sand went between my toes
The waves were perfect for surfing
When I was riding the waves on my board I had no woes

When we had to leave I was sad
I would miss this place a lot
I saw so much of Sydney that I was glad I had
I would miss the climate being hot

Jessica Pura, Grade 7
St Patrick's Elementary School, BC

Dreams

People wonder why we have dreams,
I think I know what it means,
Dreams are things you see in your sleep,
You can imagine things like a lion, a monkey and a sheep,
Anything is possible like a flying seal with wings,
You can be a hero and save the world and other things,
You can be the best at any sport,
And even if you're really short,
You can beat any game,
Things will be the same,
But most of the time I would wish it never ends,
Because all those times I would be with family and friends.

Christopher Angatookalook, Grade 7
Macdonald High School, QC

The Tiger

The great cat soundlessly stalks its unexpecting prey.
The careless prey knows nothing as the beast creeps.
It excitedly prepares to pounce.
From the skilled hunter's experience, it knows to wait for the right moment…NOW!
He attacks with amazing velocity; his prey has no chance.
The battle is quick and gruesome.
Its amazing speed, powerful claws,
Tremendous body mass and vicious jaws,
The battle is over before it started.
It's like the battle is between a hawk and a mouse.
The jaw is like a blade, devouring the prey.
It tastes blood, meat and triumph.
Wait! It sees a strange creature holding a long object.
It goes over to investigate it without care.
"Two meals in one night," it thinks as it approaches for the kill and then…
BOOM! A high speed object comes at him with great speed and goes through the tree behind him.
It needs to get out of there…NOW!
He runs for miles and miles until he's sure he's safe.
Even though tonight he was as close as a hair to death, he'll be out tomorrow night,
On the quest to survive.

Matt Ridge, Grade 7
Linwood Public School, ON

Guns Are Firing and All I Can Think About Is Home

I was in my early 20's (or so my fake I.D. says so) and excited to go to war.
I was told it was fun and a good thrill. Now I realize that they were lies.
The Nazis were defeating us in this battle.
There was constant gunfire and grenades going off.
I was hidden in a trench firing my rifle once every 10 seconds.
Only difference between me and my comrades was that I wasn't thinking about war,
I was thinking about home.
I was thinking about my parents, my carefree life and my closest friends.
Then I woke from my daydream, and realized that I was crying.
I was known as a rugged hell-raiser at home to some people.
And this was true, I had taken many punches in my life but — I had never cried before.
This realization hit me like a brick.
So war did bring me something good, that thrills cannot compare to being home.

Ryan Zacharias, Grade 9
Westcliffe Composite School, SK

The Hero

You were sent from a place, a place called heaven,
I listened to his heart pounding through his T-shirt and knew everything was going to be okay for now.
But, suddenly I broke out of my daze,
I took a deep breath and started coughing.
Then out of nowhere, a voice from the background was shouting, "Get Out!"
After that he fainted before he got out of the window.
Suddenly, he had hit me and saved my life,
That was my silent fear.
But I don't want to lose you,
You saved me.
I don't want to lose another person that I care so much for,
I wondered how I could ever have thought him hard and unfeeling,
But just remember this, you're not my brother, you're not my friend, you're my hero!

Samantha Canal, Grade 8
St Mary Separate School, ON

My Camera

Flash, goes the camera, taking its pictures,
The memory remains on a SD card.
You can go back and see what you've taken,
Were they happy, or were they sad,
Have you done good, or have you done bad?

A camera is similar to a dictionary,
Remembering your feelings and your meanings
It's always by your side, just like a friend
You can ask anything from A-Z,
And it will be there when going to bed,

It has no sound, but will help you out,
Being a teacher, no need to go to school.
Feeling like the past, you know you've done good
Colored to the words, working hard as you should.

Kay Yamashita, Grade 7
Westwind Elementary School, BC

Bozette

Such a small, lovable and feisty cat
She's constantly looking for something new
With her slyness being of some weird rat
There's no doubt that this could ever be true
Although she's seen the world for seven months
It's like she's a veteran of the earth
All the things she does gives me an odd hunch
But in our hearts it is not what she's worth
Throughout the day she likes to stay and play
This is of course if she is not sleeping
Those two activities keep her all day
Even if her body isn't leaping
Now I leave you with Bozette's mellow words
That's if she could talk she'd say "Chase the Birds"

Mitchell Bako, Grade 9
Hon W C Kennedy Collegiate Institute, ON

Raining Cats and Dogs

"It's raining cats and dogs"
Is something I've been told.
Raining cats and dogs?
That statement is very bold.
When I go outside
It's very plain to see
There are only raindrops
Falling down on me.
A question that I have
It really makes me thin
It's about why cats hate water
Outside of what they drink.
Dogs are big and fluffy
I have never seen one fly
I think it would scare me
To see one falling from the sky.

Ashley Brocker, Grade 8
Community Bible Fellowship Christian School, MB

Read Them

I'd prefer pen, but I can't seem to find one
With these walls watching,
Which is what I'd like to discuss
My walls are a form of art in their own way,
Collages of what people want to be
What people need to be
What people are and facts of life
But if you look at my walls,
And I mean really look,
You'll find me there
The pieces form a whole,
The drawings, poetry, pictures and past
All create a side of me that no one knows
A side that maybe I'll have to find for myself
My walls, unlike others
Speak up for themselves
They talk about
Reality, cruelty, fame, past, and future
They hold more than pictures,
They hold me.

Samantha Boisvert, Grade 8
Kate S Durdan Public School, ON

My Life

My life is complicated.

Full of peer pressure and people who spy.
Trying to tell the difference between the truth and a lie.
Rumors seem like they never end,
Making scars that never mend.
I don't know how my friends could be so mean.
Someone's shoulder I need to lean.
People with unknown souls.
Feeling like you're left out in the cold.
I have to scream what I want to say,
But we know the peer pressure goes away.

Our lives are complicated.

Madison Bowman, Grade 7
Dewberry School, AB

Thirteen

There's people in my school
There's so many new faces
And no one can find where their right place is
My friends won't talk to me for some reason this year
My teachers all hate me
Am I that insecure?
I'm getting dirty looks
And I can't find my books
Why oh why does this happen to me
And why oh why does it start the day I turn
THIRTEEN?!

Paige Anne Morgan, Grade 7
Worsley Central School, AB

If We All Took Time

If we all took time,
there would be no rush;
the world would for once be calm.
Nothing would unbalance.
If we all took time,
where would we be?
Would we see a different side of beauty?
If we all took time,
humanity wouldn't be the same.
The way things are now
wouldn't be how they would be,
if we all took time.

Samantha Stewart, Grade 8
St Mary Separate School, ON

To Whom It May Concern

This is a call to arms,
Trenches dug,
People snatched for training,

Armored war vehicles,
Over the enemies corpses,
Avoiding the circular death,

Men at the door,
Dressed in uniform,
Carrying remorse and regret,

But less we forget,
To whom it may concern,
This is a call to arms.

Matt Delosada, Grade 7
Devon Gardens Elementary School, BC

Death

There is a
Light, at
The
End of the
Tunnel.

I begin
To run towards
The
Light, not
Knowing

Where it
Leads, but I
Know that my
Soul
Shall go up to

Heaven.

Herbie Tait, Grade 8
Kennedy Langbank School, SK

'Till Now

I watch carefully to see as you get off the bus,
your face before it becomes the mask you put on for us.
Your smile is so wide your eyes are shining so bright,
It took me years to notice something wasn't right.

Like the way you get nervous when you're on your own,
And the way your smile fades slightly when it's time to go home.
I've known you since we were children and I can't believe how,
There were so many signs I didn't notice 'till now.

You've been to my house so many times but I've never seen yours,
When they pick you up your parents never come to the door.
The school isn't far from my house but still my parents always drive,
On the other hand you've taken a public bus since you were five.

You always wear a long-sleeve shirt no matter how hot or bright the sun,
We invite you to pool parties but you always say you cannot come.
I want to ask you about it but I'm afraid that you'll push me away,
And no matter how hard I try I can't find the right words to say.

I wish I could go back to before I realized any of this,
I now know what they mean when they say ignorance is bliss.
I don't know what to do to make things right or set you free,
I'll just be here for you and hope you find some happiness with me.

Emma Banwell, Grade 9
Thornhill Secondary School, ON

Free to Roam

When I first glanced at that letter, my heart had stopped.
I tried to catch my breath, but oxygen wouldn't reach my frozen lungs.
I just couldn't seem to take in the written words that they had wrote.
I was tainted with pain, anger, fear, and regret.
I should've held you tighter and not let you out that door.
It's not the same without you here beside me.
You held my hand, taught me what was wrong.
You wiped away my tears from my very first love.
My heart is empty, cold…I hate the fact that you had to go.
I used to look up to you, with my ever so youthful eyes.
My view had been changed…the world I had once known had grown dreary.
The warmth I once received from my father had now gone cold.
"Why him?" I thought. "He was mine."
I know I'm being selfish, but I have every right to be.
You were my dad, their dads, even the whole world can see.
He went off in his best suit — looking so brave.
I wanted him to hug me, and tell me everything was going to be okay.
It was gone now, back in the past, but the thought still tainted my heart.
So many lost in the war…but why him? Why my dad?
My dad was now free to roam the country he loved and once fought for.
"I love you Dad, and I think that's something you should know."

Brianna Bernhardt, Grade 7
Macdonald High School, QC

The Playground

Ring! The bells screams.
Feet run.
Mouths shout.
Hands push.
Who will get there first?
Each grade rushes to the playground.
Desperately trying to claim dominance.
The fastest students break away from the crowd.
It's between grade one, three, and six.
Grade one, too small falls behind.
Grade six too big, trips.
Grade three, almost there.
The wood chips fly.
The grade three's hand approaches the monkey bars.
An inch away in her hand.
She touches the metal, ever so urgently.
She has triumphed not only for herself, but her grade.
Groans and moans emerge from the defeated crowd.
As the grade threes begin to play.
Every kid knowing inside.
That time doesn't stop, for the playground.

Rachel Ingram, Grade 8
Mulgrave School, BC

Remember Me Always

So many memories that we made together
As the years have slowly passed by
The laughs that we had
Sharing my deepest secrets
But now I must leave
And you stay behind
Who will make me laugh?
Who will make me smile?
I will always love you as my friend
I want you to think about me
Remember the times we shared
And maybe I will make you smile
And since I can't take you with me
Take the memories that we had and
Cherish them as I always will and
Remember Me Always.

Anny Chislett, Grade 9
Netagamiou School, QC

My Sister

I have a sister, her name is Amrit.
She gives me blisters, like a twister.
Even though she's eighteen, she's still the drama queen.
She showers for hours and never smells like a flower.
Every day she watches *Friends* while I wait for it to end.
When she acts like a grown-up, that's when I throw up.
She may be annoying, boring and meddling,
But I don't mind her that much.

Inderpal Singh, Grade 7
Macdonald High School, QC

Who I Am

I am like a heart.
I don't like being apart.
I am like a deer.
I can tell when danger's near.
I am like a book.
There are always new chapters to look.
I am like a basketball.
Always bouncing off the walls.
I am like a dream.
I come and go as I please…
I am like a flower.
Always trying to get taller.
I am like a different type of music.
Always trying to find my own lyrics.
I am like a cool summer breeze.
While I blow through the trees.
I am like a little devil,
Sometimes a bit evil,
I am like someone that just died.
I'll always be there to say bye!
I am a lot of things, but I am who I am and that's me!

Megan Farmer, Grade 8
École Séparée Lorrain, ON

What Is Our Country?

Freedom and justice
A peaceful nation
Symbol of peace
Everyone's friend
A place of happiness
All cultures living together
Sharing and learning
A safe place to live and learn
Education for everyone
No fighting, bullying or violence
Celebrating different cultures and religions
Respected and honoured
Filled with helpful people
Proud and thankful
That is our country!

Princee Patel, Grade 7
James S Woodsworth Senior Public School, ON

Butterfly, Flutterby

Butterfly, flutterby, gliding on wing,
Beautiful butterfly announcing it's spring.
Your vibrant wings shimmer like delicate lace,
And never fail to put a smile on my face.
I watch you sip nectar from flowers bright,
From the first of dawn, 'til the arrival of night.
An exquisite pattern of random flight,
Upon a new flower your body alights.
Butterfly, flutterby, kissing the sky,
Goodbye butterfly, flutterby, fly away fly.

Adrienne Morgan, Grade 8
Odessa Public School, ON

My Friend

My friend
  We go sliding
    After school
      Up the hill
        Just for fun
Tyler Grinder, Grade 7
Sxoxomic Community School, BC

Reality

Money is falling from the sky.
That would be the dream of many,
But we must all face the facts of reality.

People living on the street
What do they have to eat?
We take the food on our plates
Like the sunshine on our face.

God has given us one chance,
Maybe one too many.
Soham Mehta, Grade 7
Greenbank Middle School, ON

Freedom

As I sat by the old river,
I heard a sound.
Footsteps were coming,
But who could it be?
I watched as fifteen wild horses,
Walked through the water.
They took off into the trees
Without a care in the world.
I heard the bell that tells me
I have to go home.
I always wished I could be
Free like those horses.
Briana Saville, Grade 8
Hillside Jr/Sr High School, AB

I Scream You Scream
We Scream for Ice-Cream

I love eating Ice-cream
Best flavor is milk chocolate
It is very cloying (maddeningly sweet)
It's really tasty great rich in taste
It gives me a brain freeze too.
Nawaid Jaffri, Grade 7
Homelands Senior Public School, ON

Love

Love is sweet and everlasting
It smells like fragrances
It tastes like sugar and sounds like
A sympathy that can never be forgotten
Sarah Thomas, Grade 7
St Anne School, AB

The Best

I am the best
Nobody can stop me
I go anywhere
I can catch anything
I could stop anything.
Todd McDougall, Grade 7
Kennedy Langbank School, SK

Patriots

Patriots,
Amazing, terrifying,
Running, hitting, catching,
Making football look easy,
Champions
Charlie Pinkerton, Grade 8
Odessa Public School, ON

Why?

Why is she getting bugged?
When bullies walk all over her like a rug
Why isn't the victim mad?
Instead, the victim is sad
The bullies were not thinking
As the victim's hope was sinking
The bullies were acting like fools
Yet they hurt her like it was their rules
Why?

Julio Lombardo, Grade 8
Macdonald High School, QC

Farewell to Winter

I hear birds chirping
The spring has blooming flowers
Farewell to Winter
It brings many rain showers
But summer is coming soon
Warisha Khan, Grade 7
Homelands Senior Public School, ON

Lost

My name is C.J.
I am lost on the dark streets,
No transportation.
The sound of wind comforts me.
Even though I am alone.
Hsin-Chieh Liao, Grade 7
Homelands Senior Public School, ON

Creatures in the Lake

The beautiful lake.
It glitters in the moonlight
Home to animals
Large and tiny, short and tall.
What lucky creatures they are.
Saadia Khatoon, Grade 7
Homelands Senior Public School, ON

Anger

Anger is like:
The color gray like a storm cloud
Hot like an egg boiling on hot cement
Cold like a stormy winter night
Sounds like water boiling on a stove
Tastes like Mac without the cheese
Smells like a rotten apple on the ground
Looks like sand on a beach
Moves like boiling water on the stove
Brandon Bortnak, Grade 7
St Anne School, SK

The Day I Got My Drums

The day I got my drum set
Was like any other day
I brushed my teeth and caught the bus
And then we drove away

I went through school not knowing
That today would be the day
That I would get my drum set
That I would love to play

Mom picked me up from school
And hid them in the trunk
I found the box and asked my mom
And she said "that's just junk"

I opened up the box
And found the drums inside
I set them up and played them
'til my brains had almost fried
Eric Redekopp, Grade 7
St Paul School, SK

Home

Home is love,
Home is warm.
It is not only where I live.
I could be anywhere,
But not with anyone.
With people I love wholeheartedly,
And that is called home.
Family, friends, works and education.
Which one would you choose over?
Which one is the most important?
Home is invisible,
Home is imaginable.
It is the place you love,
With the closest people you treasure.
No matter what has changed.
They will always stay the same.
There is no doubt in this question,
Because, home is home.
Summer Xing, Grade 8
Mulgrave School, BC

High Merit Poems – Grades 7, 8 and 9

A Teen's Life

They are always telling you
These are the best years of your life.
But what they do not tell
Is these years are full of strife.
You are judged on appearance,
Your friends speak rumors of you.
You are laughed at, you are joked at.
You are insulted. You are lied to.
You are pressed to drink and swayed to drugs,
You are bullied by the 'popular' crowd.
You are humiliated by teachers.
You are not confident, you are not proud.
You are teased for being too geeky.
You are too fat. You are too thin.
You are not athletic enough to be cool.
You are always 'out'; you just want to be 'in'.
You are focused on being liked,
You change you to be accepted.
You are scared of being yourself,
You just want to be who is expected.
So just what about these years is so great?

Delane Garner, Grade 9
Webber Academy, AB

Earth and Outer Space

The stars are shining,
And squirrels are gliding,
The moon is gleaming and dancing,
And humans are singing and prancing,
The planets are twirling,
And the wind is blowing,
It's happy down here,
And up there,
I'm talking about Earth and outer space.

Nitisha Iqbal, Grade 7
Samuel Hearne Senior Public School, ON

How Do I Love You? Let Me Count the Ways*

How do I love you? Let me count the ways
I love you more than I could measure
My soul as it flutters on a detour
'Til the end of time and for endless days
I will love you to the height of each
Morning light and breath of whispering wind
I love you simply like a baby's grin
I love you softly like sand on a beach
'Til the earth meets the sky my love will fly
When the soft fire glows your heart will know
I will love you as long as it needs two
I love you when you are here and when you go
With tears and smiles, wishes eternity
I love you as death calls us both to go

Jessica Olson, Grade 9
Westcliffe Composite School, SK
Inspired by "How Do I Love Thee? Let Me Count the Ways"
by Elizabeth Barrett Browning

Explosive Experience

The earthquake struck my brain.
There were miles and miles of details to memorize,
Only a small patch was possible.
I was driven to the end and
Overflowed with confusion.
My heart shouted out in pain,
As it was torn apart.
My head shattered like heated glass and
The leftover rash burned like fire.
These fumes were extinguished
By leaving behind the scent of blue cheese.

Andrea Iachetta, Grade 9
Centennial Regional High School, QC

Lies

I'm freezing in hot water,
I'm drowning in no water

The life boat that could have saved me
Left a long while ago

The more I swim
The deeper I sink

I could have escaped when I had the chance
But now I slowly drown in the water that wasn't here before

Nobody cares anymore
Because I'm the girl who kept crying wolf

Alyssa Panteluk, Grade 7
Kennedy Langbank School, SK

War

Crash!
Bang!
Boom!
The sounds they hear every day,
Before they have their last dream,
Their last breath,
Close their eyes
Forever.

Heart's broken
Shattered
Feels as if you are missing a piece of the puzzle
To your heart
Forever

The sun comes out
The rain stops
And the clouds drift apart
He shall remain in my heart
Forever.

Ali Poonja, Grade 9
Webber Academy, AB

Page 121

Moonlight

Moonlight.
Shines down on us.
It makes the night beautiful,
It lights the sky with an elegant glow,
It creates an unforgettable moment.
Moonlight.

Kelsey Calder, Grade 7
North West Central School, SK

Running Race

I step up to the starting line
My palms are sweating
My heart, racing
All that's left to wait for
Is the roar of the gun
Signaling the race to start
I wait and wait and wait until
BAM!
I push off as hard as I can
I'm not far behind
I'm catching up
The end of the track is near
I'm almost in first place
Desperately trying to pass
I speed up
Running beside him
The crowd falls silent
Slow motion and then
The crowd cheers like thunder
Exhausted, excited
I won

Daniel Merlo, Grade 7
Westwind Elementary School, BC

The Life of a Survivor

A child is crying out there,
And you're not trying.
A mother is dying out there,
And you're not believing
When we could have everything,
We have nothing.
Today I realized we're not living,
We're surviving.

Renade Younis, Grade 8
École Pierre-Brosseau, QC

Mirrors

You are the reflection
Of the same me
Glass is in my bathroom
With a frame
Dakota oh so handsome Dakota
Is in a two way mirror
He looks at me

Taylor Poulsen, Grade 9
Elm Creek School, MB

The Two Mermaids

Among the horizon on a far away land,
On a spectacular beach with oysters on the sand,
There lived a mermaid with sparkly fins,
She also had a sister and they were twins,
Together they lived in the deep blue sea,
Watching for sharks swimming carefully,
You must never go and try to find them, so be aware
Because sometimes they are hungry and will give you a glare
The mermaids like lots of food but their favorite is leaves
So if you gather them and put them by the water, they will soon be retrieved,
They are extremely beautiful with daisies in their hair,
But living in the water, these creatures will be found nowhere,
When they swim in the water and see you passing by,
They will spring out of the water and wave good-bye.

Dylaina Gollub, Grade 8
Abbotsford Traditional Middle School, BC

The Absence of Respect

I have never been so disappointed in this generation, especially my youth,
I truly am ashamed of them, a 15 year old speaking the truth.
What ever happened to being respectful? What has happened to them all?
They've lost themselves completely, their morals are so small.
But of course the youth aren't all the same, most are quite polite.
Sadly because of other bad seeds, the polite, for respect must fight.
But when I heard someone say, "I hope your baby dies,"
Never have I been so disgusted for this person with ungrateful eyes.
How dare you speak ill of a mother who has done so much more then you'll know.
She is carrying a miracle, a miracle that in months time will grow.
How dare you wish a mother's child's death, when the baby isn't even born.
What have they possibly done to you? Why wish for someone to mourn?
Rude, selfish and dishonorable, you are all of the above,
How dare you wish so hatefully. What ever happened to love?
You claim to be kindhearted. I see a lie to cover the true,
I cannot believe that I ever was, once friends with the likes of you.
As if you act this way on purpose, as if you don't regret,
Never again will I trust people like you, it would only waste my breath.

Krista Saumur, Grade 9
Ecole secondaire catholique L'Horizon, ON

Pizza

The oven heats up as it goes in,
The smell of melting cheese traveling corner to corner
And the dough hardening in the oven,
I look in and the dough is basking in the ovens sun beating down on it,
The family swarming around like bears,
Waiting for their feast of the night,
The bell finally dings like thunder waking you at night,
DING!!!
They scream and snatch the soft oven mitts,
They take it out as their eyes go as big as the sun on a hot day,
They wait like vultures waiting for their feast,
The pizza cools as the family is in agony,
The family snatches their plates,
Then gobble their feast.

Marissa Kurtz, Grade 7
Linwood Public School, ON

Ignorance

Ignorance kills with a sharp blade
All its victims are evenly paid
With a sad and lonesome life
That often is compared to strife

The blood that is shed from its thorn
Can never do anything except to scorn
Those who try and fight its power
Mostly end up as a frowner

Those who succeed and can control it
Are very happy and will admit
Their friends are ignorant this they know.
But because they're friends, they love them so.

Michael Cumbers, Grade 8
British Columbia Christian Academy, BC

Twisted

At Midnight's hour the sun was high
It's pouring outside but the grass is dry
I watch as invisible people walk past
They're all moving slowly while their feet move fast
I waited forever as three seconds went
Then opened the letter that I had just sent
I pace through my room while standing in one spot
When out the window I hear a silent shot
I peer through the glass to see two men with knives drawn
Each of them dead while they fight on my lawn
I run down the stairs and I'm tired from the climb
Then rush out the door while taking my time
I look around but the men I can't hear
So I walk for two hours though my house is still near
I hoped the dead men left the battle unharmed
This thought made me feel calmly alarmed
I sat on the ground while standing upright
And realized this day was a terrible night

Rachel Keilhofer, Grade 7
Homelands Senior Public School, ON

Is It Possible?

Is it possible to pack a tree's trunk?
Or drive a tank top?
Is it possible for a chair's legs to run?
Or to read a palm tree?
Is it possible to hear a tree's bark?
Or to measure using a country's ruler?
Is it possible for a unicorn's horn to make noise?
Or for a blinking light to see?
Is it possible for a baseball bat to suck a human's blood?
Or for a hot dog to bark?
Is it possible to seat belt a song?
Or to hammer nails with the head of a shark?
I wonder.

Kevin Yeung, Grade 7
Westwind Elementary School, BC

Hockey

Hockey is a team sport
Whether it's organized or just for fun
In my mind hockey is number one
Shinny has few rules
It's the game you play with friends
On the rink or on the pond
We never want it to end
The puck is dropped and we fight for it
When we get the puck we shoot it
The players on the ice pass the puck to succeed
As it soars through the air
The back of the net we hope to feed
As we fight to defend our players
The referee comes to break us up
As we hope no penalties
Will stop us from getting the cup
At the end of the game we shake hands
To show good sportsmanship
To some people hockey is a game
To the Char-Lan Rebels
It's the only game

Steve Bell, Grade 9
Charlottenburgh-Lancaster District High School, ON

Mysterious Person

As I look in your eyes I see,
Someone who is smart, beautiful, and does not show it.
Someone who is confused and will not ask for help.
A person like you is not hard to find,
But to make a person like you,
Smart, beautiful a person who shows it.
A non-confused person, it takes courage and time.
It takes help.

Collin Reynolds, Grade 8
St Mary's High School, ON

Love

Love, so tender and sweet
No other feeling can beat
So real but so strange
Many for you to exchange
Oh love what a treat

But yet with love there comes another
Hate Love's evil twin brother
Hate rampages spreading war, fights and deaths
As well as dark creations by the thousandths
Luckily Love is the big brother

Love rules over Hate
By a score of one to eight
Because of that there's no need to worry
No need to run no need to scurry
No matter what Love will always be your mate

Lisa Gingera, Grade 8
St Mary's Academy, MB

The Big Game

We're down.
Down by one point,
with 10.7 seconds remaining in our championship basketball game.
I'm staring,
surrounded by a huddled storm of sweaty, worn, exhausted, narcoleptic team mates.
Strange lines, X's and O's are being scattered all over coach's drawing board.
His blustering voice rings in my head, over and over and over again.
I'm petrified and unbelievably nervous, completely unaware of my surroundings.
Breathing becomes harder…my heartbeat pounds continuously like a powerful drum vibrating in my chest.
It is like I am staring into the face of pressure itself…as it mocks me.
I'm confused.
I feel nothing but the drop of sweat
crawling down the side of my cheek,
I attempt to swallow down my long, dry, hard throat.
I feel like a statue as our agitated team breaks from the huddle weakly, like old sick men.
There's no where to hide, nowhere.
Hopefully, I won't have to.

Sayaad Bacchus, Grade 8
Laurelwood Public School, ON

I Am a Champion

When coach blows his whistle, and points towards the end of the gym,
We know what's coming, we know what we are in for, we know suicides.
We line up along the baseline, waiting for the sound, the sound of the whistle.
Coach blows into his whistle for the second time.
The squeaking shoes, as each line is touched, means every player is working hard, working as a team.
Coach blows his whistle for the third time, we speed up.
Sweat is now jogging down each players face, as he continues.
Every muscle screams with agony, some players drop out in pain.
When coach blows his whistle for the fourth time, cramps form.
Only the best players are left, and they keep each other going. The whistle sounds for the fifth time, we are now sprinting.
The temptation is there to drop out, but your team is there, standing by you through everything, even your pain.
The sixth whistle sounds, two players are left.
The two players are waiting for the sound, the sound of the whistle.

Reece Fisher, Grade 8
St Mary Separate School, ON

Katie

With cream pale skin, chalky and smooth.
Her eyes, a rich, deep blue, the colour of the ocean.
So delicate, sitting on my shelf.
Very elegant, no precise expression.
Perhaps depressed? No way of telling of course, the doll cannot speak.
Silence.
Her dress is so proper, mannerly. As though from an old movie.
Burgundy in colour, but if you feel it, it's satin, with buttons up the front.
Silky, red locks of curly hair, down to her shoulders, with a muffin-high hat laying on her head.
Black nylons from her hips to her feet.
She's wearing beautiful, crystal, figure skates.
So *lifelike*.
I wonder what it would be like sitting on a shelf all day?
Every day. Looking gorgeous, perfect.
My, she is so peaceful.
My doll, Katie.

Breanne Ford, Grade 7
Linwood Public School, ON

The Power of One Word

One word can destroy your hopes and dreams
It can be your worst fear come true
It can be the word you never want to hear
Dying

One word can be your friend
It can lift your spirits
It can conquer anything
Love

One word can save you
It can shine light onto the dark
It can bring you another chance
Hope

One word will give you peace
It will make you believe
It will set you free
Faith

Danny Colavito, Grade 9
Laurier Sr High School, QC

My Attempt at a Poem

I am sitting here with nothing to write,
In this school under a horrible light.
It's hard to think because everyone is talking,
And outside the door people are walking.
The teacher expects us to write something,
But in my mind I can't think of nothing.
When it comes to poems I am pretty bad,
I don't know if I should write something happy or sad.
I am sitting here in this class,
Waiting at my desk for time to pass.

Jenna Cox, Grade 8
Netagamiou School, QC

Habits

They don't know what we can see
Behind closed doors
They don't know we can hear
The silent screams or the shuffling footsteps

They don't know that we know everything
That happens behind their door
They think we are sweet and innocent

What we don't know is that
They will never stop
Or that we can't stop them
Even if it means hurting someone

We get shoved aside
We are second,
Their habit is first

Skye Grant, Grade 8
Hastings School, MB

Illusion

What do you see when you look at me?
Do you think that I am restricted, reserved?
Possibly under lock and key?
Do you see fear in my bright blue eyes?
Do you see tears that I can never cry?
Do you see someone who crawls into the corner and hides?
Do you see someone who will never learn to fly?
Or maybe you think I'm dark and cold?
And that I never do what I am told?
The scars I carry show that I have no self-respect.
I always feel the need to think I am correct.
You could not be farther from the truth.
For you could never imagine the troubles I've seen in my youth.
How could you not see, the love I share with all mankind?
Are you sure that you're not blind?
Do you not see the strength and pride that shines from me?
The confidence and faith that helps me to be
Much more than I ever could
Before you set boundaries
Limiting me from choosing
To be what I am.

Sarah-Michelle Nemeth, Grade 8
St Raymond Elementary School, ON

More Than Just Boxes

Working, wood boxes,
12 inch by 12 inch.
At first thought, it's only just a box.
Thank-yous, stories, smiles,
Memory containers holding one short life,
They mean more to parents than ever.
Once hold in plastic baggies,
Grieving parents too depressed for their deceased child,
Boxes containing personal effects and certificates,
Now hold in beautiful boxes made by the caring.

Lyn Duong, Grade 9
Hon W C Kennedy Collegiate Institute, ON

I See a Fly

I see a fly,
it's stuck in the window,
the fly is small,
but makes a loud noise,
I want to go help it,
but don't know how,
and then I see it,
dark, small, and hairy,
it is a spider,
whose stomach growls,
it caught the fly,
and hurried off,
I felt very bad,
but a spider's got to eat.

Mathankey Jeyakumar, Grade 7
James S Woodsworth Senior Public School, ON

September

September
Colourful leaves
Full of excitement
Laughter fills the air
The wind blows past my face
Autumn
I love this season
Kimberlea Haggarty, Grade 8
St Mary's High School, ON

Mary Had a Little Lamb

The Johnson's had a sheep farm
They worked hard throughout the year
In the spring on their favorite eve
Mary had a little lamb

Mary had two big brown eyes
And a sunny disposition
Her lamb's name was Kate
Who's fleece was white as snow

Kate went everywhere that Mary went
She never stayed away
Around the hill and bend
And everywhere that Mary went

Mary's fleece was thick and woolly
As Kate grew she still followed Mary
When Mary went in to be sheared
The lamb was sure to go.
Laurel McMillan, Grade 7
Menno Simons Christian School, AB

Ravishing Colours

Purple mountains
I dream to climb,
White sparkling snow
Lying upon the peaks.

Blue bright sky
Which exalts the heaven above,
Gray clouds tumble in
With the clear expanse.

Green grass
Fresh from a spring rain,
Brown soil
Warm with spreading roots.

Red, Indian paintbrush,
Reflecting the glow of the yellow sun,
Which makes everything grow.

Nature, a living rainbow of colours.
Adina Kleinsasser, Grade 8
Milford Colony School, AB

Smoking

Why are you smoking?
That weed will mess with your head
It will kill you dead and I am not joking
Remember the first time you tried? Your lungs filled with it and you were choking.
You and your friends laugh it off.
They tell you it will pass.
So you take another try, now you're feeling high.
Listen to me, I am telling you, you are going to die.
Don't ask me why.
You take a smoke every day, just throwing your life away.
Smoking makes you feel good you say.
One day you turn fifty and then suddenly your system feels filthy.
You make a visit to the doctor to see what's wrong.
You say doc I am not feeling too good.
He said let's take a look under your hood.
He asks you, do you smoke. Yes doc I do.
Ok my friend this is what is going on
Your lungs are filled with tar; the cancer has spread too far.
I am really sorry sir but there's nothing that I can do for you.
You look in the mirror, and you see death staring back at you.
And then you say those darn cigarettes, all they do is stink up my breath.
Brandon Providence, Grade 7
Macdonald High School, QC

Love's Last Concerto

The very morning of your departure
sweet rice cakes in the trenches of revelation
a voice, low with dripping contention
tells me of better days.

dear Lover, I write with shaking fingers rapt
of alabaster moons and unkempt heartstrings
to your upturned back in the fishbowl's light: very very quite, quaint
in its exquisite sadness.

Time ticks, heavily unbound
blue cups risen to greater heights
you need not tell me of sweetness
nor hearts nor empty teacups, no,
I will live through this last concerto
with or without a conductor.

though You refuse to show me the pieces
of the celestial satin, the covenant that somehow
perished beneath the blade; darling!
stop when they come
I will tell them I need a new clock
I will think
I need a new Lover.
Michelle Jia, Grade 9
Markham District High School, ON

Alone

I remember that night
I remember her fright
I saw deep inside her eyes
She was like a hollow
She warned me not to follow
It was dark outside, it was raining
I was dark inside, I was aching
Something persistent made me go further
Something persistent brought me closer
I did not know where I was going
I was sure it was not my own doing
I was alone following her footsteps
So scared to take the next step
The road never seemed to end
I started crying all over again
Stronger and stronger
Yet I felt weaker and weaker
My head between my hands I was done
And then looking up I noticed she was gone
I knew at that moment I could go back home
I knew at that moment I was not alone.

Kuburat Abdulkadir, Grade 8
Ecoles Musulmanes de Montreal Campus Secondaire, QC

The Woods

I saw the trees lightly swaying in the wind
I heard the whisper of the trees
I smelled the sweet scent of pine
I tasted the sweet fresh air

Alex McIntosh, Grade 7
Menno Simons Christian School, AB

I'm Learning by Osmosis

"I'm learning by osmosis,"
Says Garfield, the comic book cat.
I'm leaning by osmosis
And I'm sure that Odie can't.

I'm learning by osmosis
It's very plain to see
That it's not smarts going into me.
It's my smarts going into thee.

And when Odie tried to do
What I could always do
It turned out quite funny.
He started to act like me.

And so you see, you see, you see
Be careful of which books you read
Because you might wind up like Odie
Always acting like me.

Lindsay Penner, Grade 7
Community Bible Fellowship Christian School, MB

Chocolate Kiss

A chocolate waterfall running down my throat,
A delicious teardrop,
With a silver coat.
Scrumptious, satisfying, succulent.
Tasty treasures for my mouth.
Outside there's a wrinkly wrapping,
Inside there's a smooth chocolate drop.
A little pointy top as if it were a mini mountain.
The smooth soft chocolate melting in my mouth.
Chocolate Kiss

Kelsey Barker, Grade 7
Linwood Public School, ON

Haphazard Happiness

So many faces
Each one different…
No two alike
One has wrinkles
Another is caked with makeup
That face is unknown,
Masked by layers of clothing
Trying to keep out the winter bite
A different thought is plastered on every face
Simple insights to their wandering minds
Did they leave on the coffee?
Did they forget their cell phone at home?
How will they find the money to pay this month's rent?
Their thoughts are on hold.
Everyone looks back at you, wondering
Why do you sit there, analyzing our every move?
Pen in hand, chilled to the bone
Pouring out the world around you through plain blue ink
On this chilly Saturday afternoon
They don't care anymore, they just remembered
They're late for life.

Hayley Aurora Dawn Galbraith, Grade 9
WP Sandin Composite High School, SK

Your Eyes

One time I had a dream
I flew up into the stars
I saw your eyes brighten in the dark
Feeling you an ancient before I saw you
Your eyes are the spirit of my life
Seeing them in the ocean, waterfall and fountains
Making my heart racing fast
Sit upon bank or river your eyes come with every wave
Secrets in your eyes are the meaning of the wisdom
Diving in the deep sea of your eyes is the reason
To share, to love and to touch her sweet heart
Through her eyes, her smile and soul
Her eyes show wondrous things in the winter day
It is the silent love of the birds to spring and green trees
This is the way we meant to be into snow

Zaidoon Abd al Hadi, Grade 7
St Patrick's Intermediate School, ON

Onza's Dynasty

Black as night the panther creeps,
Through the darkened woods unseen;
Rabbits tremble, deers will flee,
For she is this forest's queen.

Large paws do not make a sound,
Leaves do bow down at her feet;
A good hostess she is not,
For white fangs all her guests do meet.

Her mate stepped out of shadowed trees,
Moonlight shining on his mane;
A gentler beast this lion is,
Unlike the panther's love for bane.

And as they stood there in the trees,
Moonlight shining on them both;
Three cubs tumbled at their feet,
Preserving the feline's oath.

HanQi Zhai, Grade 7
F E Osborne School, AB

Nobody

I am walking forward
But not moving at all
I'm talking loudly
But no one hears me
I'm alive and breathing
But I'm dead to everyone
I'm right in front of their faces
But nobody can see me
I'm eating nothing but choking
I am a nobody
Because nobody cares.

I am lost in the dark
When it's light out
I'm walking on solid ground
But sinking in quicksand
I'm eating everything in sight
But still hungry
I'm breathing in fresh air
But taking in smoke
I am a nobody
Because nobody cares.

Gabrielle Dube, Grade 7
Kennedy Langbank School, SK

Skateboarding

I adore this sport
The sound of trucks grinding wood
Very inventive
The pure joy of landing tricks
My only great accomplishment

Joey Carreiro, Grade 7
Homelands Senior Public School, ON

On the Pond

Shimmering in the dull moonlight
Ripples in the pond
Swaying gently in the breeze
The swamp grass silently sighs
Pawprints gleaming near the shore
I sigh and throw a pedal in
I watch it serenely float about
Making ripples on the pond

Janelle Kraushaar, Grade 9
Grayson School, SK

War

War means death…
War means destruction…
War means fire…
War means bombing…
War means sorrow…
War means turmoil…
War means tears…
War means guns…
War means blood…
War means confusion…
War means mutilation…
War means sickness…
War means killing…
War means loss…
But after one side…
Or the other side…
Has finally had enough…
And lays down their arms
To surrender and give up…
War means peace!!!

Tyler Charbonneau, Grade 7
Vauxhall Jr/Sr High School, AB

My Best Friend

My best friend is someone cool,
walks the halls and makes boys drool
She could be with anyone
but hangs with me instead for fun
We do everything together
from taking hikes to checking weather,
Having sleepovers once a week,
when we're separated we can't sleep
We might not be in the same class,
but either way we both still pass
Even when she moves away
we'll still hang out every day
And while I'm writing this today
she's helping me not to stray
We make up songs and poems too
just like the one I'm showing you
So now you know about my friend
and we'll be together until the end!

Caitlin Verouden, Grade 7
Algonquin Public School, ON

7 Things I Love About My Life

Friends are like flowers
They get picked
And enrich your life.

Friends are like water
We take for granted
They are a necessity for life.

Friends are like the sun
They shine on you
And they brighten your life.

Friends can be a winter storm
They may ruin your day
But not your life.

Friends are like soil
It is a foundation to grow
To sustain life.

Friends are like autumn leaves
They may fall
But will grow back in the circle of life.

Friends are like hot cocoa
They warm you up when you're cold
And chocolate is my life.

Kristen Lazarou, Grade 8
St Joseph Separate School, ON

Time, Just Look

Take time to look, to actually see.
To experience,
The beautifulness, humbleness,
The peace.
Take time to look at the stars,
The moon, the flowers, the world.
Just take time and look
At what the world used to be.
Just take time to look at what
The nature of the world is.

Haylee Peterson, Grade 8
Hillside Jr/Sr High School, AB

Anger

A red ant biting people
A volcano about to explode
An ice cube melting in the sun
A hurricane erupting in Gustav
Pepper burning in your mouth
Fire burning in a backyard
A square ice cube that's melting
An old rough sweater
A cobra that's going to eat you for lunch

Kendall Kudryk, Grade 7
St Anne School, SK

Parents

My parents are a lot older than me and wiser
and they can cook very well.
They both like lots of blankets
because they don't like to be chilly.
My dad uses his gun a lot
and is very successful as a hunter.

Eric Fehr, Grade 9
Elm Creek School, MB

Life

There are going to be many people in your life
Family and friends, maybe a husband or wife
Friends may make you mad
Family can make you feel sad

You need to be honest to get through life
Or to you, life will be a knife
You need to make the right choices
Or in your head will be angry voices

A good life feels like a flower blossoming in your heart
Just like beautiful art
A good life looks like smiles all around
While you hear the whispering sound

You should always try your best
Or life will be like a very big test
Live your life how you want to
But know, how are you going to get through

Thofiq Hussain, Grade 7
Admiral Seymour Elementary School, BC

Beginning of a New Day

I lay my head back and look at the stars,
twinkling in the moonlight
They brighten the night
as if it were day
It's my most favorite sight.
My worries out of range.
The crackle of firewood lightly burning
is all that can be heard
I don't dare break the silence
that would be utterly absurd.
Soon dawn will completely be day
and this night will be lost.
Screams of children will fill the air
but at what cost?
You cannot put a price on joy
certainly you must see
Screams of laughter don't come in one,
but maybe two or three.
You clearly must see, one thing is key
Friendship is something you need
including you and me.

Natasha Simpson, Grade 8
Rutland Middle School, BC

To Make a World

A place where no one judges, so I remain as just me,
No one's there to put down my self-esteem.
Nothing's too real, nobody too fake,
Come out from the mask and let yourself be seen.
This is my world, and no one's in pain, nobody aches.

A place where we feel safe, no more of those cliques.
No more problems about your colour or ethnics.
Is such a place real? Or is this all fake?
Because they don't have to cry, that group needn't die,
I want this to be our world, so no reason to discriminate.

A place where we're one, everyone's equal,
Treat you and I the same, because people? They're people.
We're the ones to make it real, it doesn't need to be fake,
Everyone counts, we're all part of this puzzle.
So let's make it our world. Let's all start this change.

Flora Jung, Grade 8
Laurelwood Public School, ON

The Hunt

First the wolf pack starts ambushing their prey
Using a diversionary attack
They usually don't hunt in the day
They like hunting in the shadows of black

With a bright crescent moon over their heads
Leaving a brilliant yellow glow
With silvery mist covering their treads
The wolves in the pack get really low

The wolves lock their eyes on the deer's throat
And they attack the deer in a bound
The deer lets out a loud piercing note
Then all the blood starts staining the ground

As they gorge themselves some of them growl
When they are done they let out a howl

Tyler Hardisty-Levesque, Grade 9
Shevchenko School, MB

My Best Friend

You've been there for me
through the good times and bad
I know I can count on you
to be there when I'm sad.

All the laughs and memories we share together
I think of them and it makes me smile
Although we won't see each other for awhile
I know together our friendship will grow
and our friendship shall last forever.

Ashley Rowsell, Grade 8
Netagamiou School, QC

Cheer

I sit, on frigid bleachers
With screaming parents,
children
fans
We are the spectators. Watching the game go on
Watching the puck drift across the ice
hit sticks
get passed
fly into the stands
The goalie,
blocks shots
nudges players
protects the net
The players,
skate rapidly
check one another
give it their all
As the game nears conclusion we stand,
Brought to our feet by the intensity of the game
Only seconds left,
But all we can do, is cheer.

Roxanne Harrison, Grade 8
Kennedy Langbank School, SK

School

I am in school.
I feel so trapped.
I want to go and take a nap.
The teacher drives me to do more work.
But I won't last until after class.
That's when I get my break.
So then I can go and say how much I hate.
This big brown building the teachers appreciate.

Trevor Bobbitt, Grade 7
Netagamiou School, QC

Young Love*

Those who think love is unattainable
At an age where most things are not possible
Are those who have not experienced it,
True love in all its seriousness.

Because the connection that is sometimes shared
By two young people in love can compare
To anything adults might feel,
It could be just as meaningful, just as real.

Those who understand know how hard it is to describe
Those emotions you feel inside
Once you've found that one soul
Who makes you feel entire, complete and whole.

Anny Corrales, Grade 9
Laurier Sr High School, QC
*Dedicated to Kenny Laing Garcia.

Yellow Friend

I gazed up at the blazing sun
Giving off energy, forming life
Get near the radiant rays and you'll be done
The moon is like his mystical wife
The yellow fellow in the sky
Shining and showing off his happy smile
His cheerfulness will make you fly
You'll see him even from a mile
Showing up every day,
He gives you a dear friend
From morning to noon he will stay
Some light to you he will lend
Don't forget him
Without him, it will be dim.

Nosherwan Malik, Grade 9
Webber Academy, AB

B.C.

Bright red ball of fire
Coming from the east
Dark blue water in the foamy depths
Like a Root Beer Float dyed blue
Rocky, rough sea shore
Bright sea plants coming out of their dark sleep
The soft sound of my bed creaking
Red window panes knocking in the wind
The splash of water on the lifeless rocks
Brings life to them
The sound of birds awaking puts me to sleep
A wave of salty sea smell hits me like a train
It's the smell I like to get
Here is where it is, and here is where I want to stay

Bennett Schnurr, Grade 7
Linwood Public School, ON

Real Love Doesn't Need to Be Beautiful*

My love's eyes are dull and not very bright
Her lips are colourless even when made up
With skin that has no radiating light
And hair that looks like it has been cut up
Flowers smell pretty and sometimes are blue
But her odour is really horrible
And her face looks dead, with a lifeless hue
She's just a person who's real terrible
For some reason I love to hear her talk
Even though her vocals cause my headaches
No floating on clouds, but the ground she walks
So heavily in fact, that the ground shakes
But my love is true and fully complete
Truer than any fake poem or conceit.

Joe Walsh, Grade 9
Westcliffe Composite School, SK
*Based on Sonnet 130,
"My Mistress' Eyes Are Nothing Like the Sun"

Journey of the Words

The ink flows through my veins,
into the pen,
onto the paper.
Words form into sentences,
creating tale,
provoking thought.
Moving across the used-to-be clean page,
covering it with smudges of creativity.
Giving emotion the freedom to walk off the lines
into your mind,
and join you to the journey of the words
as they travel in literary form.
And whilst the flood of words starts to slow,
the tale unravels and reaches its end,
where the pen finally ceases
to spill its ink
upon the page.

Andrea Vulic, Grade 9
Michael Power/St Joseph High School, ON

Music Concoctions

They say that chicken soup is for the soul,
But the books are a fake.
What would you like instead?
Why, a juicy musical steak.

Why would I want dull old soup?
A soup that burns my throat.
Instead, have rice à la musique
guaranteed to make you gloat.

Why would I want soup with chicken?
A soup without a beat.
Instead, have bass and guitar,
A tasty musical treat.

So, instead of that lame old soup,
Have some cake of bass.
And the smell and look
Is something you cannot erase.

Brooke MacDonald-Talbot, Grade 7
Blind River Public School, ON

Coyote

Running through deep snow with a sly grin,
ears perked up and alert for food or predators,
grey-brown and orange the colour of its soft winter coat.
I can almost feel the cold, deep snow under its quick feet
or almost taste its curiousness.
About the size of a regular dog,
but in the night when you're lying in bed,
they can howl you to dreamy sleep.

Isaac Sherk Bauman, Grade 7
Linwood Public School, ON

Your Last Breath

If you could stand strong,
Maybe you'd belong,
You're doing it all wrong,
Like you have been all along,

Who are you?
You don't know what you're getting into,
If only I knew,
Why you feel so blue,

Your problems are not fixed by death,
Do you really want to breathe your last breath?
Your life has changed since you tried meth,
But that does not mean it's your time for death,

You now lay on your hospital bed,
Your death lays right ahead,
You're hanging in on your last thread,
The next part is what I dread,

I will always remember you,
As the girl I always knew,
But no matter what you do,
There are only few,
Who could be as strong as you.

Mélissa Godin, Grade 8
Mulgrave School, BC

Ripped

The world once possessed a golden hue
But now it's a haze a smoky blue
The sky is overcast with an unyielding cloud
A storm's on its way a big one no doubt
I arrive at a sapling deprived of its greens
Barely gripping on towards death, it leans
Nevertheless it'll have to do
A shield from the blizzard approaching on cue
Shards of glass cascading from up high
Slipping through my shield agony in my eyes
Like many thin swords silently slicing past
Red warmth escaping how long will I last?
Bit by bit I am ripped apart
Will I hold on or lose my heart?
But there is hope far, far away
Who is that character? I cannot say.

Cathy Wang, Grade 8
West Lynn/South Public School, ON

Too Fast to See!

Winding roads
Quick as lightning
Turning, swirling
If you take the wrong road you will be lost
Life!

Katie Leslie, Grade 8
St Mary's High School, ON

Are You Listening?

Someone bullies me I don't defend
to some people I don't blend
People make fun, I feel like a clown
when you pass by me, I seem to frown

Hours pass by in the daytime
hurtful words last a lifetime
People see me I always look down
when you pass by me, I seem to frown

I walked over to you and said, "hi"
you walked away and said, "goodbye"
Today I'm leaving out of town
when you pass by me, I seem to frown

Kathlene Peralta, Grade 7
St Patrick's Elementary School, BC

Brothers

Brothers
loud, noisy
annoying, boring, scrapping
reasons for a headache
siblings

Micheal Murray, Grade 7
Dorintosh Central School, SK

I Wish

I wish I were the sun
So I could help little buds bloom.
I wish I were a light
So I could help people see.
I wish I were a fire
So I could warm the hearts of others.
I wish I were a roof
So I could protect the vulnerable.
I wish I were an all-you-can-eat buffet
So I could feed the hungry.
I wish I were a key
So I could open people's minds
To the beautiful world around us.

Danika Kunimoto, Grade 7
McKernan School, AB

My Pain

My pain won't go away
I deal with it every day
One minute happy
The next minute sad
I wish this was a joke
I wish this pain was no more
So that life can be wonderful and fun
Can't my family just be one?
Pain, oh, pain hurts my soul
Will I be happy? Well I hope so!

Taylor Desbois, Grade 7
Macdonald High School, QC

Too Much at Once

Winter is almost over,
Spring is coming near,
In about 2 months summer will be here,
But I am not even ready for this weekend!
Coming from Toronto are my uncles and aunts,
Man, I haven't even put on my pants,
Too much pressure isn't good.
None of my work will be done,
Maybe a board game will keep them entertained for something fun.
I am so nervous,
I want to please them,
Hopefully all goes well and I live through it,
Golly, in a couple of months summer will be here.

Kayley Iacurci, Grade 8
St Mary's High School, ON

Benevolence

Parents save my world when I am blue
When worried they ask 'what's wrong,' as if on cue
I feel blessed when the righteousfully guide me along the way
I savour the feelings of warmth, which they give me every day

Their helpful hands reach out to catch me when I fall
They always come running when for their help I call
When sickness sweeps me from my health and no one else is around
They give a feeling of pure bliss without uttering a sound

When I'm in trouble and don't know what to do
They at times envelope and comfort me like loving parents true
When miserable moments settle deep into my heart
What we have joined together let no one ever part

Sarah Kleinsasser, Grade 8
Milford Colony School, AB

Perfect Ride

When I look down over the peak and smell the fresh mountain air
All I want to do is sit there for hours and stare.
It takes a while for me to get to my feet
But when I do the fresh air and I seem to meet.

Just as I stand there ready to go down the hill
A cold winter breeze moves by and I feel a chill.
Then I turn my board and the time begins to go by
As I move further, I feel like I can fly.

I carve into the beautiful white snow
It feels like the last time, it was like this was very long ago.
I see the trees swaying back and forth by my side,
But I get further and further away as I continue to glide.

When I begin to speed up, I leave it all behind,
The snow hits my face and leaves me feeling blind.
I reach the bottom and look down at my board
And as I approach the lift, I look back at the hill that I truly adored.

Breah Look, Grade 8
Hillside Jr/Sr High School, AB

5, 6, 7, 8

The music starts…
5 — are my toes pointed?
6 — posture held, pulled tight?
7 — running through the steps in my mind.
8 — I begin to dance.
Chasse, chasse, step tuck, chaine rock.
Are my feet parallel?
Arms straight?
Ball change step —
Am I ready?
Double pirouette, and with a perfect landing.
I go through the rest of the dance with ease,
The stress gone.
Finally I finish.
And as the music stops,
The crowd bursts into applause.

Kristen Mulder, Grade 8
Odessa Public School, ON

Grandpa

It's almost a year you've been away
It's coming close to that day
Where I have to grieve and mourn
Have to cope with my heart torn
Gotta cry myself to sleep
Try to make it through the day
Keep my head up and say I'm okay
Gotta sit there and try not to cry
I'll do my best, I'll try
I couldn't of asked for a better grandpa than you
Just one more time I'd love to say, "I love you."
Your laughing, teasing and grin
What a great grandpa you've been
You told us, "Do the best in everything you do"
It wasn't hard to love and cherish you.
You were our biggest fan
A lovable and unforgettable man
And because of that I'll never stop loving you.
Love you Grandpa!

Nina Desnomie, Grade 8
Grayson School, SK

Color of the Sun

Orange is…warm golden morning sunrise
gently illuminating our waking earth
vivid autumn leaves
swirling gracefully off majestic trees
a tiger dashing through the woods
its magnificent stripes blurring your vision
energetic midnight fireworks
their sparks decorating the gloomy dark sky
a deliciously juicy fruit
refreshing your endless thirst
a lovely, powerful color.

Anne-Sophie Beaudoin, Grade 7
McKernan School, AB

My Art, My Performance

that easy bliss
it's something we all miss
hard to realise that it all exists
and even on the days that I feel so low
I always look out and go put on that show

fake a smile and show them a good cry
showbiz is all about thinking up that great lullaby
be able to prove that cannot be shaken
making them believe that they were mistaken

as I watch and hear every sound
just thinking that I spin their head right round
just as I'm about to make a move
I start thinking look out!
Here comes the new and much improved!

Megan McGee, Grade 8
École secondaire Macdonald-Cartier, ON

My Rescue

An empty street, an empty heart
Left me memories with a mark
Makes me sick to my stomach
A start of uncontrollable panic
You came to my rescue because only someone like you
Knew that I couldn't do it alone
My heart feels like frozen snow
Without you I'd fall apart
And I need you to survive
Saving me was all I wanted, you were all I needed
Only spare knives, you meant the world to me
It wasn't that hard to see, because,
When you hold me this tight,
I feel safe throughout the night
Not worrying, or wondering what's happening
Blocking out the noise they were blasting
Knowing that what we had was everlasting
Even when we're hurting or crying
Only caring 'cause all I see is you
Only caring because this love was true

Sabrina Lau, Grade 8
École Secondaire Pierre-Brosseau, QC

Friends

Friends take your hand and show you the way.
Friends are the light added to your day.
Friends are the ones whose doors are always open.

Friends come and friends go.
It's like a never-ending show.
You're the beat that keeps me alive.
You're my friend till the day I die.

Iesha McIntyre, Grade 7
Macdonald High School, QC

Before I Go to the Land of Milk and Honey

Before I go to the land of roses, I want to have a car of my own
Have a driver's license win a million dollars
Have an airplane that's my own, some sweet day,
Have a pool in my house, have a house that does what you say
Find a hidden treasure, have a cell phone that has no bill, some sweet day,
Be a very good soccer player and be a very good football player too.
Save a person from a dangerous place and I would know what to do and it would be a fright
Go on a trip around the world, some sweet day,
Go to Disneyland and go to the Edmonton mall
See a real live hockey game, visit a war camp, some sweet day,
Be able to figure skate, be able to do karate
Have one foot on Canada and on USA, play a Violin, some sweet day,
Own my own laptop and computer, invent something useful
Catch a criminal that has been wanted for years
Last but not least I would like to experience the outside world, some sweet day.

Brigitta Wipf, Grade 8
Decker Colony School, MB

Midnight Dance

The days go on as like it never happened,
On the beach front the water crashes amongst the pier.
The waves ripple over the tiny wrecked shells that have washed up onto the beach.

Our hearts fly upon the ocean,
My reflection glows among the stars,
My footprints are engraved in the sand to where I lay,
From the day we have met it seems there is no point to rest until we meet again…
That feeling…that touch…nothing can replace our hearts for each other.

I dream we meet again and have the last midnight dance,
My heart lies with you until the day that I pass.
I say "I love you forever and always my love, you're the answers to my prayers, you're the gleaming, bright crystal in my heart."
I have always loved you right from the start.

For we have not finished our midnight dance, with the last glance of the breathtaking midnight, forbidden love…romance.

Jessica Shields, Grade 7
Pineland Public School, ON

Jonas' Escape*

Many different memories given to me, I just wish the other people could see.
My father, my mother they know nothing, about different things such as winter and spring.
So the Giver and I made a plot, at night I decided to give it a shot.
I left my family unit without regret, all the memories I would forget.

I brought Gabe who would have died, on my bicycle which was my ride.
After my last glance at the Giver's lair, I had no choice but to go Elsewhere.
I had to sleep at day and travel by night, until search planes came into sight.
I started panicking, and went insane, while Gabriel would call "Plane! Plane!"

The places I passed had rain and snow, and finally I saw some type of glow.
I knew Elsewhere was close by now, I went downhill and whispered "wow."
My whole life flashed before me, Asher and Fiona, I could see.
The wonderful tune that I heard, and then I couldn't speak a word.

Yuwei Xu, Grade 7
John Campbell Public School, ON
*Inspired by Lois Lowry's novel "The Giver."

It's Our Time to Shine

Every day, from morning to night,
I see beautiful birds take off into flight.
I see many plants, from flowers to trees,
And lots of insects, like butterflies and bees.

"The Earth is gorgeous," so you say,
It may not stay like this, to our dismay.
We need to take care of it every day of our lives,
And tell this to our family, such as our children and wives.

Global warming is not a pretty sight,
It scares most people, giving them a fright!
It will melt the ice and flood some towns,
It makes people sad, even glad clowns!

Take shorter showers, try 10 minutes or less,
Put ice cubes in your water; it will cause less stress!
Walk, carpool, take your bike or a bus
These simple things won't cause a big fuss.

If we work together, she will stay bright and pure,
And I am not lying that is for sure.
The Earth will stay a wonderful place,
And leave every child with a smile on their face!

Mikaela Domish, Grade 7
Chief Peguis Jr High School, MB

Procrastination

Procrastination, oh so fine
Helps us conveniently waste our time
Works just when you need it least
If it were living it would be a beast

Starts off by attacking you
As soon as it sees you've got homework to do
You finish a question and go onto the next
And soon as you know, you're playing K'nex

Homework forgotten, collecting dust
Since reading manga has become a must
Listening to music, eating snacks
Your homework's priority is now the last

It's due tomorrow and you totally care
But not enough to go over there
You say that you'll start up in a bit
Just not before you eat that and read this

The night has come and you're still not done
Procrastination, you'll blame that one
On the next assignment, you swear you'll beat it
Although you know you won't complete i-

Vicky Jiang, Grade 8
Homelands Senior Public School, ON

Between the Lines

To you, good friend
Who always watches
A silver figurine with remorseful conscience
Alas, your smile remains and so I remain
But constant stars atop the church with windows stained
A carved impression
Soon to die
Hidden beneath a mother's lullaby
Good mother hold me deep
Above the cloudy beggars' weep
Soon to fit between the lines
Of constant sea and constant time
Why do you leave so fast again
Between the hushed fox and the lying wren
Please I beg you to return
The widow's nest is now a fern
I lie here filled with sleep
For the friend that never weeps

Isabelle Thibault, Grade 9
Lower Canada College, QC

I Always Knew You Were the One

Like a flower you bloomed in my heart,
I could easily tell from the start,
I had a cut and just let it bleed,
You were my bandage in my time of need.
Your smile is brighter than the stars at night,
With you I've lost my sense of fright,
I'm hooked and can't be undone,
I always knew you were the one.

Kaitlyn Stewart, Grade 9
Sir John Franklin School, NT

Confidence

Where are you?
I NEED YOU!!!
I really, really NEED YOU!
You help me and others —
In such a big way,
You help me overcome my fears of school,
You give me a head start on every math test
that I write,
You nourish the courage inside me —
to loudly express my ideas to the world,
I know you are hiding! Where are you?
I've been trying to find you all my life!
Oh confidence, confidence, confidence!!!
Please don't hide inside me!!!!
Burst away from your hiding place!
Help me shine like a star!
Oh Confidence!!!!
Where are you?
Because I need you to help me
To succeed in life

Lillian Ying, Grade 9
Burnaby North Secondary School, BC

Beautiful

She wears a mask
Slapped on her face
By those around her
Their words
Clearly printed on it
Ugly!
Loser!
She tries to rip the mask off
To show the world
That she exists
And belongs
She screams
She can't get it off
If only the world could see
That she could be beautiful
If they would just
Let her try

Amanda Perkins, Grade 9
WP Sandin Composite High School, SK

Respect and Remember

Recall
offering lives
trusting men had valor
and now motionless, sacrifice
complete

Hannah Wipf, Grade 7
Milford Colony School, AB

A Poem Is a Feeling…

Surprise is like a crowd
Yelling in your ear
Excitement is all you can hear

Confusion is a question
You cannot figure out
So you wait for someone to yell it out

Tiredness is yawning
All through the day
Waiting to go home and hit the hay

Stephanie Hassen, Grade 7
St Anne School, SK

True Beauty

Beauty doesn't always show
True beauty is in your soul
It's the things you do
That make you, you
So you should know
Looks do matter
But not all the time
It's your personality
That makes you shine

Kathryn Guidry, Grade 7
Macdonald High School, QC

Dead Still

Dead still.
Everything and nothing within me at once
As my leaden heart opens and shuts, opens and shuts,
My chest screaming open and shut, open and shut,
And then it is dead still.

Dead still.
They run in, sense of urgency,
Fire roaring behind them like the tail of a comet or is it just me?
The rush of panic around me and through me and yet my heart is
Dead still.

Dead still.
Lightning bolts, striking, striking
There is no pain, only stillness as everything flashes and sparks a wild storm of fear
They try and try but the inside is
Dead still.

Dead still.
The room is silent as the mechanical grim reaper
Sings his song of triumph
A single note that goes on forever
Singing the end.

But I was not there to see it, for I was dead still.

Hayley Enta, Grade 8
St Andrew's Jr High School, ON

An Endless Spiral of Emotions

I walk through the front doors of school,
My friends are there, waiting to go to class,
And as we begin to turn the corner,
I glance to my right, and I see him.
My head begins to feel like it's spinning,
My ears hear a ringing-type noise,
My hearts feels as if it weighs a ton of weight,
And I feel as if I'm falling into a deep, dark black hole.
My brain is telling me to start running,
But my heart is telling me to stay,
It's a war between my emotions
And there I am, right in the middle.
My emotions are like fighting fish,
They disagree with each other constantly,
If only they were to agree on this,
Then maybe I could make a decision.
Then, I seem to clue in,
My head is an endless spiral of emotion,
And at that second, I knew exactly what I was to do,
I turn around, and hope that everything is about to fall into place.

Mackenzie Truman, Grade 9
Victoria High School, BC

Music of the Guitar

As you strum the strings
You think what a beautiful sound
Some people think what a horrible sound
But it does not matter
If you like the music of the guitar
As long as you follow your heart.

Ryan Bouchard, Grade 7
Macdonald High School, QC

Girls

Girls, girls, girls that's all we talk about as boys
Girls walking by, girls sitting around, girls skipping around
Is what catches our eyes
Girls in pink girls in yellow
It makes me feel like a lucky fellow.
For the girls all around makes my heart feel happy.

Girls, girls, girls. That's what we talk about us boys
Girls with their giggles, girls with their curls
Girls with their glasses and big eye lashes
That's what we talk about us boys.

One thing about girls, is that they are a wonderful thing
They make you cry, they make you smile
But most of all they make you feel on top of the world
When they say "hi" with a smile.

Attila Veszi, Grade 8
St Paul School, SK

In a Traveler's Domain

I have traveled so far,
Yet there is so much left to go,
My fate in this barren desert,
I do not know.

My camel trudges slowly,
I am sprawled across its back,
My stomach tightens and rumbles with thirst,
Yet I do not veer from my track.

I lift my head carefully,
And struggle to open my eyes,
The world swims and sways before me,
As I make out the sand and skies.

I see a pond of water,
And I stop the camel through dressage.
I stumble off my ride to quench my thirst,
And I realize that it is a mirage.

Such a perilous journey,
One of courage and pain,
Yet this is what is to be expected,
In a traveler's domain.

Farah Khan, Grade 8
Islamic Foundation School, ON

Teenagers

You see them in the streets, the park
They never leave before it's dark

They sit together their shoulders slouched
Treating the cities property like their couch

They look at themselves for way to long
So focused on image their ego grows strong

They're selfish, conceited and often not polite
Advertising themselves on the net they're at every site

The things they do are ridiculous
And if we are different they'll ridicule us

Somewhere in middle school things start to change
Their minds start to wonder and things get strange

They develop new talents, new interests and hobbies
Like lying and stealing and hanging out in lobbies

But there is hope for our generation to come
They will sort themselves out once puberty is done.

Amber Brown, Grade 8
Royal Orchard Middle School, ON

Freedom

Getting away from everything
Going as far as you let yourself
Your feet pounding on the never ending road
With the rain hitting the pavement like bullets
You just want to go faster
Getting away from everything
Forgetting everything, thinking of nothing

Kristina Finamore, Grade 8
Rutland Middle School, BC

Country Sunset

I'm sitting on a swing,
The cool wind rushing over me,
A fawn comes to sniff my face,
And a bunny's on the lawn

I'm sitting on a swing,
And I see the sunset's colors,
Of red, yellow and orange,
Blending all into one another

I'm sitting on a swing,
And dusk's starting to fall,
it's all so relaxing,
The black curtain's starting to envelope me.

Catherine Hoover, Grade 7
Linwood Public School, ON

Running Away

Walking alone
Dark, empty alleyways
Footsteps echo against pavement.

Wet asphalt
Raindrops cold on my skin
I'm not coming home this time.

The black sky
Has no stars to light my way tonight.

Am I crying?
Or is it just the rain
Streaming down my upturned face?

Is anyone looking for me?
Does anyone care that I'm gone?
Will anyone miss me?

The sky is too desolate.
My soul cries out for help.
But the world is empty

And no one hears me.

Kendra Hlynski, Grade 7
Westmount Charter School, AB

The Pet Store

The pet store
was crowded
people running
this way and that
Searching for a pet
A new friend
I headed for
the "small pets" section,
as I always do.
And there I saw
a wonderful being
with shining bright fur,
gleaming black eyes,
A hamster
How wondrous a hamster!
My new friend.

Victoria Cao, Grade 7
John Campbell Public School, ON

Remembered

Peaceful
Sacrificed lives
For people's protection
Humans live in peace free from war
Freedom

John D. Hofer, Grade 8
Milford Colony School, AB

Irrational

I may be quite naive
I'll share this anyway
I do not want to deceive
My friends, but someone needs to say
The troubles clouding round your lives
No answers actually needed
Happiness seems far right now
But your lives are not completed
Breathe in the air
Please stop complaining
There's worse out there
Much worse to come

Liah Wallace, Grade 7
Charles R. Beaudoin School, ON

Chocolate Kiss!

Seeds of melting chocolate,
a silver drop of glistening water,
like a drop of chocolate crystals,
Chocolate Kiss!
An ornament on a Christmas tree,
like a rose of baby teardrops,
and also a dimple of a cute child,
Chocolate Kiss!
A silver charm on a necklace,
like a cloud of melting chocolate,
and a silver gleam of exiting sunshine,
Chocolate Kiss!

Susie Martin, Grade 7
Linwood Public School, ON

My Daisy

As the wind blows,
My daisy sways with it
Back and forth, back and forth.
As the sun sets,
My daisy's petals glow
As white as the new fallen snow
Falling down, falling down.
As summer comes,
My daisy's middle shines.
As yellow as the sun,
Shining bright, shining bright.
As spring has made its way here,
Bees swarm around my daisy
Flying high, flying high.
As fall's leaves tumble to the ground
My daisies tumble too
Wilting, wilting.
As winter comes, my daisy dies.
But...soon summer will come again.
And my daisy will bloom
Growing and growing again.

Clarisa Cheesman, Grade 8
Hillside Jr/Sr High School, AB

Hutterites

H utterites are pleasant people
U nder strict laws and rules.
T hey go to the steeple
T o listen to God's word.
E verybody dresses the same.
R eaching out to help others
I n gentle and kind ways.
T eaching Children manners.
E veryone tries to share
S erving the Savior above.

Lisa Walter, Grade 8
Livingstone School, AB

Broken

Broken wings,
they no longer carry,
falling lifelessly to my side,
darkened by the sadness,
bloodied from the blades,
bruised from the hatred,
gray from the dread,
wet from the rain,
but also from the shame,
cold from the wind,
banished from my home lands,
nowhere to go,
forever to walk alone,
with broken wings at my side,
and rain to always fall,
never to see the sun,
never to have fun,
or feel love,
only forever to feel pain,
to feel afraid,
to be alone.

Athena Orbell, Grade 9
Spencer Middle School, BC

Memoirs

Stopping abruptly
The first flake falls
Memoir of long ago
Flashing and fluttering
Laughing and playing
My heart aches.
My chest cries.
My eyes start to swell
I CANNOT TAKE IT!!
The last memory flickers before me
I wipe away a tear
Then I scoff:
"It was just a memory.
Those days will never return."

Laura Gurnik, Grade 8
Heather Park Middle School, BC

Daddy's Little Girl

He walked down the driveway for one last time,
This was the day I said goodbye
He gave me a salute as I hugged him tight.
Grasping my arms to him so he couldn't leave.

Months went by and it was almost time.
I ran to the plane as a soldier walked by,
He handed me a letter.
I screamed and cried, "It's not his time."
It was too late, he was gone.
I'm still my daddy's little girl.

His name is carved in stone and his body, under dirt.
I visit him as he watches me.
I send some flowers, he sends back love.
I watch him below, he watches up above.

He was brave, he never lied.
Why is it that he died?
He loves me, I love him.
I'm still my daddy's little girl.

Shannen Burns, Grade 7
Macdonald High School, QC

Skies

The sky is so beautiful
And blissful.
Even though your storms will come,
They end and the beauty comes out.
The sun will set and you will sing,
As the stars twinkle over us.
And even though we don't fully understand you,
We know that you are a truly beautiful sight,
Both in the day and in the night!

Travis Shaw, Grade 8
Hillside Jr/Sr High School, AB

Dad's Love

My dad! My dad helps me with everything I do,
I take it for granted; sometimes I forget to thank him.
My dad! My dad drives me to places I need to go,
I tell him to go, stop, and when to make turns.
My dad! My dad supports me with everything I do,
When I play sports; either volleyball or basketball.
My dad! My dad gives me money when I need some,
No matter what it is for; useful or not.
My dad! My dad shows love to me and friends,
At times, it does not show, but I know it is there.
My dad! My dad left me, his family, and friends,
He left me memories and his belongings.
My dad! My dad is my coach, my friend, and my buddy.
He is my hero and admiration.

Ryan Dela Pena, Grade 9
Aurora Charter School, AB

Winter

Snow falls as the temperature drops.
Children dash to play,
In the fluffy pillows of snow.
Winter begins.

Families skating over shimmering ponds,
And sipping warm mugs,
Of hot chocolate.
Skidoos whisk through the fresh powder of snow.
Winter is in full bloom.

The temperature rises,
Snow begins to melt,
Children hop through puddles,
In squeaky rubber boots.
Winter is gone,

Until next year.

Brandon Munro, Grade 8
Kennedy Langbank School, SK

Tormented

I know that this could seem insane,
But even if telling you could be a shame,
Since the day that I first saw you,
I crave for you and I'll never get through
The torments and this endless nightmare,
Those are not anything to share.

Could I not think about something else
Than your visage that seems so appealing
And those endless qualities that make you unique.
The sparkling life has adorn thou
In such a way that you are like fine art,
Sculpted agilely by the angels' craftsman.

You attract the eyes like gold attracts humans
And worth more than all the world's diamonds.
The world stops spinning at your sight
Even the stars and the moon shines to thou.
Forsake to me by the distance
Never shall I be saved from your cast spell.

Philippe Paré-Langevin, Grade 9
Macdonald High School, QC

Dawn

Darkness
Like a crow flying in a pitch black night
Darkness
The night and day continue to fight
Darkness
The monster of nightmares, in the shadows
Darkness
Every day, the other to the gallows

Jake Stebner, Grade 8
St Paul School, SK

Mirror

The image in the mirror
Shows a reflection
Of yourself
In the glass
Bathrooms show
A reverse which is
The same as the opposite
Of me

Jason Moffat, Grade 9
Elm Creek School, MB

I'm Just a Kid

A new day to grasp
A fresh start
New adventures
I woke up it was seven

Thinking of what fun
Planning, preparing
Wasting the day away
Waited till eleven

Plans wasted
No friends, no fun
All alone…again
Just to figure out that no one would call

Alone…so bored
New adventures…by myself
New people to meet
I think I've got a lot of friends

Philip Nordstrom, Grade 7
Menno Simons Christian School, AB

I Hate Poetry

I hate poetry
It is the worst
But I still have to write
I think I've been cursed

I don't understand it
It makes absolutely no sense
I'd rather be painting
My grandmother's fence

Some find it inspiring
I think it's stupid
Especially the Valentine
Stuff about Cupid

So there you go
I wrote you a rhyme
I'm praying that it'll be
My very last time.

Emily Kennedy, Grade 8
St Paul School, SK

In a Bully's Eyes

In a bully's eyes I am weak.
In a bully's eyes I am nothing.
People walk and stare at me;
I am in pain as I walk.
Some try and help, but the bully scares them away.
In a bully's eyes, they take me apart starting with emotions.
In a bully's eyes, I am nothing but a victim and their target.

Time does not help my situation.
No matter how I avoid them they always come back for more.
I walk, but I do not walk alone — the bully trails behind hitting me with words.
They convince others to do the same.
In a bully's eyes I have no friends.
They say who would ever want to be my friend.
One day I did not look into the bully's eyes.
They tried to freeze me to the spot, so I couldn't move on my way,
But I said goodbye and I just walked away.

Megan Schumacher, Grade 8
Bessborough Drive Public School, ON

My Adventure

As I walked through the woods
I felt a chill run up my back,
I figured I was just feeling cold, when
The chill ran up my back again. There on the earth lay a snake.
I walked on and I heard the leaves rustle on the trees above me,
As I looked up I saw a flock of baby sparrows
Who had just awoken and wanted to explore their own world.
I still kept walking along when I heard my name being spoken,
I looked toward the sound and I saw something that made me cry,
I saw my old best friend, she was dead,
But the ghostly spirit of her spoke to me,
And when I got home, I told my new friend about…
All my adventures in the wild.

Wilma Waldner, Grade 8
Twilight Colony School, MB

Powers of Peace

I wish for peace on Earth
There would be no more sad mortified children
AIDS might end
Poverty would dismiss
That poor homeless
man would have
a smile as he sits
with his family to eat
dinner If I had
powers I would change
the world for the better society
would never be the same
If I had powers the world
would be all good I truly wish
the world's problems would resolve If I had
powers I would wish for peace on Earth

Jamie Quistberg, Grade 8
Laurelwood Public School, ON

Old Billy Bob

Down in a village sat Old Billy Bob
Chewing on his 94 year old corn on a cob,
When he died the corn was still not done,
So they gave it to his eldest son.

Lisa Lall, Grade 7
Homelands Senior Public School, ON

Night Demon

The creature, no, the devil, black as night,
A symbol of dracula,
Flying in circles and spirals.
It lives for the night,
Sleeping in the day, waiting, waiting, waiting,
For the world to fall into shadow.
The moon is its sun.
Though it is blind, its hearing makes it formidable, frightful.
It flies as silent as death,
Its spine — tingling screech
The only sound that breaks the silence of the night
As it locates its prey.
He swoops down and captures his prey,
The attack unexpected,
And sinks its dagger — like fangs into its meal.
Only blood, red as an apple, quenches its thirst,
And it drinks until it is satisfied.
Then the blood sucker spreads its leathery wings,
Its skin cold and hard as marble,
And takes off into the night. Swoosh,
No longer thirsty, its blood cold.

Alex Hildebrand, Grade 7
Linwood Public School, ON

Dots

Life, a grand, immense canvas,
One vision — to create,
Rows of colours,
Rainbows that have never touched the sky.
The tool, the paintbrush; us,
Caressed by the painter,
Carefully dabbing the white,
A little flower bud in the deep winter's snow.
Each speck seems insignificant,
But on the blank sheet begins to form,
Something not even we can grasp,
Until what was started; done.
Sometimes we struggle along the way,
The selected tint, unwanted.
Sometimes we allow the dots to form,
Each second to tick away.
We may look at each dot in abhorrence,
We may look at each dot in admiration.
But the only thing that is clear,
The painting will eventually cease,
And dots will be no more.

Tracy To, Grade 9
Markham District High School, ON

The Sun...

I look out my window and all I see —
Are the bright warm colors of serenity!

The sun is setting in the sky —
And I see birds flying by!

The sun is showing the last of its rays —
And then in my mind I silently praise!

Mirangi Patel, Grade 7
James S Woodsworth Senior Public School, ON

Metamorphosis

"I used to be...but now I am"

I used to be shy, but now I'm outgoing.
I don't know why
But that's the way I am.

I used to be messy, but now I'm neat.
I don't know why
But somehow I improved.

I used to be crazy, but now I'm not.
I don't know why
I guess I calmed down.

I used to be bad at school, but now I'm not so bad.
I don't know why
I guess I got better teachers.

I used to be lonely, but now I'm not.
I don't know why
But I guess I made friends.

Natasha Basnett, Grade 7
Worsley Central School, AB

A Leathery Silent Deer

Velvety like a soft kitten as I gently pat it
its eyes always ready to tell the dangers
its long slender legs can make any jump
as it darts away from his predators
    A Soft Silent Deer
Its multicoloured coat glistens in the sun
his ears pierced to hear the slightest sound,
and senses a human in a far away distance
its colour camouflages in the deep dark woods
    A Soft Silent Deer
Whoosh! like the wind as it makes a few twists and turns
he swiftly glides with his two fawns close behind
its soft whimper sounds like a coyote from far away
as it makes it back to its warm cozy thicket
    A Soft Silent Deer

Susannah Martin, Grade 7
Linwood Public School, ON

Counting Blessings

1. Biking along a country road, with wildflowers growing on the side, a baguette and lemonade in your front basket, stopping to lie down and make dandelion angels, looking at the turquoise sky and thinking that there's absolutely nowhere you would rather be on this beautiful summer day
2. Terracotta-red leather journals that feel nice when you rub your fingers on the cool, bumpy landscape of their covers
3. Finding a sentence in which the word 'nacreous' fits perfectly,
4. Running with your friends on a breezy September day, the sky a cold and crisp shade against the amber leaves, getting lost and not minding at all
5. Going to a book sale, and searching through boxes of cheap romances, the soap operas of literature, then unearthing a box full of Agatha Christie books all for $5.
6. Going outside on a winter afternoon to find that the wet, earthy smell of spring is in the air, and, you find the small pinpricks of growing bulbs poking through the melting snow.
7. Finding that I have too many blessings to fit this page.

Octavia Dancu, Grade 8
Emmanuel Christian School, QC

We Are the Guardians of the Planet

Every day, every moment, forests are being chopped, species lost, illegal hunting and melting ice caps
Something we all could have come together and stopped, so do you at least feel guilty, perhaps?

Take charge and provide your donation, because we will not be the ones who have to suffer
It is the poor animals and future generations, they are the ones who must go through tougher

Something as simple as walking to get around, installing solar panels, picking up litter
Or adopting a puppy from the local pound, would help make the world much less bitter

As a human being we all have a responsibility to care for not only ourselves
But for our planet and animals, to the best of our ability, so make it your choice to care for Earth more than yourself

Because our world is slowly dying each and every day, we must put a stop to this global insanity
Before our Earth slowly slips and fades away, to save our planet and all of humanity

We are the guardians of the planet, we must take control of the situation
If we work hard, we can eventually make it, because Earth is our only place to live and our only location

Patricia Liu, Grade 7
John Campbell Public School, ON

The Grizzly Bear Without Hair

There was once a grizzly bear without any hair. His friends made fun of him because he was bare.
Everybody hated him except Jonny Hare. The grizzly didn't think it was fair.

Grizzly went to the market at the town of Splox, to buy something to grow his brown locks.
But the store clerk hid in a box because outside there was a raging ox.

The ox destroyed the apple store. The ox ate up the roasted boar.
Then it counted 1, 2, 3, 4 and then it broke right through the door!

Grizzly turned his head to the east. Then he saw the mighty beast.
He found a bucket filled with grease. The bear poured it because he wanted peace.

The ox slipped on the grease and bonked his head, the store clerk shook him left and right and said,
"Oh my goodness I think he's dead!" Then his noggin started bleeding red.

The Bear is now a hero, instead of being a Zero.
Now he has a wife that's a Buffalo and he is now growing his hair-o!

Braeden Chambers, Grade 7
Barriere Elementary School, BC

Man's Best Friend
I sit outside crying.
Waiting for a miracle to come.
I never met my dad,
And got taken from my mom.

I am just a little pup,
Wanting a loving family.
Not an abusive owner,
Who hits and screams at me.

Across the street I see my friend,
Clawing at the door.
It opens and his owner yells,
"Get lost, I don't want you anymore!"

He kicked my friend and
Slammed the door. "BAM!" he starts to cry.
My friend is hurt, just like me
I start to wonder. Why?

I walk across the street to him.
Try to cheer him up.
"We have our whole life ahead of us.
We are only pups."

Kaelee Dyck, Grade 8
St Paul School, SK

World War I
You sit there in the murky water
It's like your grave without a flower
Your ears are deafened by the guns loud crack
You open your eyes and find you're still intact

Your friend assures that you'll be all right
you ponder the words and hope you last the night
The battle ceases and you see a bright yellow gas
You're frozen in terror as you reach for your mask

The gas gets in everywhere from head to toe
It burns your skin like hot water on snow
You wake up in the morning on a hospital bed
It's such a relief to find that you're not dead

It's one week's time and you're back on the front
Gaining inches by inches with no time to grunt.
You look at your friend, who gives you a smile
An explosion goes off and you cry like a child

You grasp your friend in utter dismay
Surely he didn't have to die that way
You feel a sharp pain, you clutch your chest
You fall to the ground just like the rest

Joseph Brockman, Grade 7
Our Lady of the Annunciation Catholic School, ON

Friendship
Friendship is something to treasure
It is something beyond measure

You do not have to have too many
Just enough to keep you company

They will stand and face the world with you
No matter what you have to go through

And the one who will stay with you till the end
Is your one and only special true friend

Dhriti Chakravarty, Grade 7
St Anne School, AB

It Takes All Kind
When I was born, nobody ever told me
What there was to come.
The hopes, the failures that I would succumb to.
The friends that I would be hanging onto,
The shape that has been made of this world
And I sometimes struggled, sometimes I succeeded.
I was told to be like water,
Don't let the ripples bother me,
To keep what I have, hold it tight, though it cannot be.
We were made to be humans, not water.
No matter now hard you try,
You are you, living, breathing, feeling.
You are you.
You touch the earth with every step you take,
You make, mold, shape your life.
The clay under fingers breaths.
Sometimes you don't know what you're making.
Sometimes it's perfect anyway.
What we make of this world will show as we age.
We may be strong, wise or unintelligent.
Either way, it takes all kinds to make a world.

Medina Durzi-Percy, Grade 8
Central Middle School, BC

Hills
Hills are for hiking
Hills are for climbing
Hills are for sliding in the winter
Hills are for good views
Hills are high
Hills are old
Hills are for environment
Hills are big
Hills are long
Hills are for trees
Hills are for houses on the hillside.
Hills are for making good pictures.
Hills are like very small mountains.
Hills are for animals like deer, crickets, birds, and insects.

Garrett Chelsea, Grade 7
Sxoxomic Community School, BC

Leaves

Leaves blow in the wind
They make circles in the sky.
Different colors
Of red, orange, green and yellow
They grow off of giant trees
Donnelle DiMarco, Grade 7
Homelands Senior Public School, ON

Darkness

As I went outside
Everything was dark.
The sky was pitch black
The stars lit through the dark sky.

The dark sky had dragged me
Through the darkness
I felt trapped.

It captured my eyes full of beauty
No one could see how beautiful it was.
Light lit the sky
Full of happiness.
Raine Empey, Grade 8
Hillside Jr/Sr High School, AB

Mad

Mad is a dark monster
Inside of you
That makes you
Hate everything and everyone
Montana Simon, Grade 9
Ratihente High School, QC

I Walk Alone

The trees guide me to the sea,
The stars tell me tales of the night.
The sea whispers to the sand,
The night sings my song.
The wind teaches me to dance.
Jeanne Yurris, Grade 9
Sir John Franklin School, NT

My Locket

My very best friend gave me a locket,
I always keep it in my pocket.

I'll treasure it forever,
we'll always be together.

All my other jewelry,
it's not the same can't you see.

I love my special locket,
which I still keep in my pocket.
Danielle Wong, Grade 8
Bessborough Drive Public School, ON

Blue

Blue is the ocean, it is glass on land. Blue sounds like wind
knocking against the fall leaves. Blue is smooth like silk.
Blue is the night, it is not dark or light. It is like bubble gum,
it starts off delicious until it fades to nothing but blue.
Marion Boddy, Grade 7
St Anne School, AB

Soccer

The ball bounces down the field.
Toward the goal laughing and giggling.
All of a sudden the balls stops dead in its tracks.
It's picked up and kicked all the way to the other end.
Number seven traps the ball and brings it down.
She dribbles the ball back to the other team's end.
She shoots she scores!!!
The ball jumps for joy in the back of the net,
Until it's sent to the center of the field to start again.
The referee blows the whistle to start the game,
There is ten seconds left in the game,
Number Seven has the ball.
She passes to number sixteen.
Who carries the ball to the net,
Number 22 on the other team tackles number 16 and the referee calls FOUL!
There is now five seconds left and the score is 2 all.
Number 16 takes the foul shot and kicks the ball
Who is enjoying all this attention
Toward number seven
She does a one timer into the net,
And the clock stops.
Nicole Saris, Grade 7
Westwind Elementary School, BC

Because You're a Jew

One night my grandpa told me,
About his adventures in World War Two,
I collapsed in bed with tears from his tales,
And drifted into a cold, misty view.
In the smoky skies I saw bombs dropping,
I heard the twisting planes and bloodcurdling screams of my peers,
In the misty air I heard soldiers' guns popping,
On my agonized beloved ones who were near.
In an effort to help my friends, I reached out my hand,
But before my eyes their precious blood was shed,
As numb as I was, from pain, grief and horror,
I thrust myself off the ground and ran up ahead.
I collapsed on my ratty clothes,
As I tripped over a sore, hollow body,
I turned to glance above and saw a man,
With a swastika sign that looked shoddy.
He reached through his jacket,
And pulled out a pistol that he pointed to my head,
In rage, panic and tears I yelled out "Why?"
And this is what he said,
"Because you're a Jew."
Yolanda Fil, Grade 8
St Raymond Elementary School, ON

Red Petals

The bloody red barbed cold fuzzies
It blooms just like an umbrella opening
It glows while the sun is out
Shining bright
It's pebbles drop one by one as the wind blows
The warm fingers gripping it securely
Handing it to his love

Alicia Lynn Pham, Grade 7
Blundell Elementary School, BC

Eyes of a Child

I see the pain in the girl's blind eyes
She is brave and strong, she never cries
But I can see the hollow; that gap left in her soul
"I'm fine," she whispers, but I see the empty hole
This girl's daddy, the soldier man, will never return home
Now her soul, poor and sad is left alone to roam.
Her mother, kind mother, died when she was young
I watched the poor girl, to Daddy's leg she clung
Now the feeble child is alone and lost
Kneels at a church, forehead, shoulders, heart all crossed
"Please, God, take care of my daddy for me.
My eyes are blind, I cannot see.
Mommy is not here, Daddy has gone away.
My world, I fear, is one unseen shade of gray."
"Amen," she says and stands, preparing herself to go.
I touch her arm, heartbroken, and see her green eyes glow.
Now, she sleeps softly, my tiny, newfound child
I took her in, that fateful day, where in the church, she smiled.
A smile meant only for me.

Bridget Melnyk, Grade 7
Westview School, AB

A Walk in a Forest

A walk in a forest
wind among the trees.
The grass is full of dew drops
shining like an emerald sea.
The sky is clear and cloudless
there's no snow or hail.
Melodious chirps fill the air
a song from the nightingales.
The pine trees yawn and stretch their branches,
it's a lovely weather.
I closed my eyes and breathe deep
in the sweet smell of the heathers.
A grey squirrel scurries up a tree
dropping an acorn on the ground.
A blue jay watches me with curious eyes
silently, with no sound.
A walk in a forest
feeling the summer breeze.
Nothing in the world
can make me feel more at ease.

Lily Han, Grade 7
F E Osborne School, AB

The Tree

Once there was a tree,
Not a tree but millions of them.
They grew, gave and danced,
With the soft breeze their leaves sang.
And still they stand for so many years,
Until the men appears.
They shape, cut and make,
And suddenly a city will take.
Gone is the beauty, the nature,
Who has been replaced for something we think better.
A large piece of destruction,
Killing the real meaning of Earth.

You might think it is only a tree,
But also a tree that gave us everything.
The real inspiration of nature,
Forever lives the tree.

Maude Vinette, Grade 8
Macdonald High School, QC

Keeping Up

Yes, the times may be rough
And, the times may be tough,
But there will someday be a better tomorrow,
Free from all of today's pain, misery and sorrow.

Keeping up the things that are important to you
From your head and heart to the laces of your shoe!

Somewhere in this god forsaken world someone has it worse,
So thank the good Lord and take it as a blessing…Not a curse!

So just keep keeping up the things that are important to you
From your head and heart to the laces of your shoe.

Louissa Barnes, Grade 9
Lorne Park Secondary School, ON

My Opportunity

I walk these streets with one thought
I should have dove for it
My life has been created for one purpose
Because if you had one chance or one opportunity
Would you grab it
Or would you let it slip away
Well my story is simple
I let my opportunity slip away
And that was the moment my life was taken from me
I should have reached but I let it slip away
And that was the second I realized my life is now over
All I have is these streets and one thought
I should have dove for it

Steven Papetti, Grade 8
St Mary Separate School, ON

Home

Home is the last true sanctuary.

Open the front door
and you're immersed into
another world.

Familiar comforts
provide a hideout from the
cruelness of the "real" world.

It welcomes you into
the caring arms of your family.

Home.

Where nothing can disturb
joy and security.

Kyle Loney, Grade 8
Rutland Middle School, BC

Life

I'm lying flat atop the cold floor.
It tilts to the right.
I try desperately to grip the surface.
I have no strength left.
I'm falling. I feel vertiginous.
My head is throbbing.
My eyes fatigued.
I open my mouth to scream.
No sound emanates.
My throat is dry.
My insides loose.
I can endure no more pain.
My feelings are paralyzed.
Impact rushes my body.
Gravity hadn't ceased.
My eyes are full of tears.
My heart is hammering.
I am powerless. Unable to move.
My bones are broken.
My spirit damaged.
Life is no longer mandatory. I've lived.

Danielle Hussain, Grade 7
Trafalgar School for Girls, QC

Special Sunset

Over the lake I can only see
Sunset,
Reaching down and
Glistening on the dark, blue water,
Sparkling and shining
With the dim light of the
Sun

Maria Boisvert, Grade 8
St Mary's High School, ON

I Remember

I remember
We first met

I remember
We first hung-out

I remember
Going to your house every day

I remember
Every text
Every MSN conversation

I remember
All the good and bad times

Don't hangout anymore
Don't talk either
Don't know why

Tylin Pigeon, Grade 8
Heather Park Middle School, BC

Behind Those Eyes

Those eyes,
That look down on me,
Is it disgust or pity?
That I see,
That I feel,
You make it seem easy,
Being flawless,
Like your life is perfect,
But that smile,
Doesn't quite reach your eyes,
Is there more to you?
Are you like us,
Maybe not so great?
Do those eyes cry?
When no one's around,
And no one knows,
Is there a real person
Or nothing more?
Behind those eyes.

Kirstin Pulles, Grade 7
Waverley Drive Public School, ON

Black and White

Black
Empty, void
Cold, black, infinite
End, death…life, begin
Large, heavenly, light
Positive, bright
White

Catharine Vangen, Grade 7
St Anne School, AB

The Mountain

Standing solid, true, bold
Flakes from Heaven —
Cover the jagged earth
No creatures, demons
To destroy this paradise
Yet…
Deserted, ancient, sacred
Leafy hands reach through
The white blankets
Grabbing at our legs
For warmth
As we ascend to the top
To justify our endeavors
What have we gained?

Charleen Grightmire, Grade 9
Delta Secondary School, ON

Polaris

Polaris
agile, swift
jumping, accelerating, trudging
machine, leisure, vehicle, speed
breaking, slowing, stalling
slow, clumsy
Yamaha

Jayden Gerhardt, Grade 9
Grayson School, SK

War — Human Nature

The crash of swords,
The gnash of hordes,
The clash of lords.

Death's deadly playground,
Woe all around,
Misery abound.

The rolling thunder,
The world asunder,
A horrible hunger.

The sound of boots,
Crunching down roots,
Carrying loots.

The screams of the dying,
The dead a' piling,
The living crying.

This is war,
It isn't pretty,
It sure isn't nice,
But it is human nature.

Justin Harvey, Grade 9
Sir John Franklin School, NT

What I Can Become

There are so many things I want to do
Before I hit the bucket I'll have to choose
This list of mine may change from time to time
And hopefully grow shorter from day to day

Before I go, I'd love to have a go at sky diving
Soaring in the sky into the heavens, oh so high

Before I go, I would love to try deep sea diving
Swimming in the deep blue water
Carelessly enjoying the peace

Before I go, I would even try my hand at mountain climbing
Climbing higher, higher into the thinning mountain air
For a single moment of success as I stand atop the summit

Before I go, I'd love to be part of the Olympic soccer team
Score a couple goals
Success, and win gold for Canada

Before I go…
I hope I get a chance to cross off all the things
On my list before I go.

Kristofer Waldner, Grade 7
Decker Colony School, MB

Midnight Massacre

The moon, ever so brilliant, hangs in velvet skies.
It illuminates the world amidst bloodcurdling cries.
Such cries break the ever calm silence,
Breaking the air in parades of violence.

Midnight it cries, one lone crow,
Singing songs full of horror and sorrow.
It's onyx eyes shine as it watches, intent and keen,
At the sight below, the crash of blades, it's silver gleam.

And so blade meets flesh, a guaranteed fight,
Of limbs bloody and broken, such brutal sights.
Of crying mothers holding their tender babes,
As they beg so fearful to not be slain.

And yet such pained cries fall upon deaf ears,
And so the sword comes down ending all fears.
Slicing slender throats silencing the screams,
The Massacre of the City, shattered the dreams.

And yet the moon, still ever so bright,
Still hangs amidst the sky, ever so high.
It illuminates the sky, yet such horrid cries,
Slice the silence and slowly die.

Linda Xuan, Grade 8
Homelands Senior Public School, ON

Pitch Black

pitch black but then there is light
a jagged line shoots through the sky, lighting
everything up for a second then, pitch black

hearing the roar of thunder, the waves crashing
against the rocks, the
breeze blowing through my hair, the smell of damp rocks
hitting the ocean

another jagged line goes through the sky lighting everything
up for a second then,

pitch black

Amanda Schuffels, Grade 8
Rutland Middle School, BC

Seven Days

As others are, I am not
My battle I could not have fought
For when the call came and rang my door
I knew not then what was in store
Long days and nights soon did arise
No longer will I see the skies
A week is all that can be said
T'ill comes the day we all dread.

Vanessa D'Amico, Grade 9
Villa Maria High School, QC

What's This?

What's this I feel? Disappointment, imperfection, hatred
The words on the page don't have a meaning to you
You don't see the way I live by
You see the way I live by a line

What's this I sense? Betrayal, secrets, fear
I had to find out by a member
You couldn't see how I felt
You weren't there when the suffering girl needed you the most

What's this I hear? Apologies, explanations, forgiveness
You say what you need to say and I'll say what I need to say
I'm done with the foolish child
We deserve better
I can't take this anymore

What's this I see? Broken, sadness, conclusion
You can continue with the world you live in
It won't make a difference with the world I live in
Don't worry I won't interfere with your new life

What's this I feel? Disappoint, imperfection, hatred
The words on the page don't have meaning to you
And never will you see the way I live by a line
Which stops now

Tayler Winstanley, Grade 8
St Joseph Separate School, ON

Ice

As I lay in the snow,
Frozen and stiff,
I can see the Ice Queen
Sending out sprays of frost over the land.
As she comes towards me,
I am numb with pain and terror.
Extending her icy blue arm,
She touches me and
Though I thought it not possible,
I become colder.
She lifts me up easily
And I find myself in a chariot
Made of ice and snowflakes,
Drawn by two white horses with wings.
In their eyes I see only black frost.
Flying away, the world fades,
And I know that I am gone.
Julianne Runne, Grade 9
Elm Creek School, MB

Life Without Music

Life without music is like
Minnie without Mickey

Life without music is like
Peanut butter without jelly

Life without music is like
Pooh without Tigger

Life without music is like
There's no world at all
Brielle Lalonde, Grade 8
Heather Park Middle School, BC

Winter

Snow falling
covering the grass like a blanket
winter is here
no time to waste
footprints in the snow
animals gone
snow falling like sugar
silence in the air
winter is here
to stay
Alithia McClair, Grade 8
Heather Park Middle School, BC

Friend

Friend
Cheerful, gleeful
Joking, singing, helping
A faithful angel, a shining star
Afrin Khan, Grade 7
Homelands Senior Public School, ON

Memories of Love

You were my little baby,
Who was always going crazy,
You were jumping here and there without getting exhausted,
And you were always happy and excited.
We used to have fun together,
We were best friends ever!

And now I saw you…and you were really sick,
You were not happy and excited, you were staying still like a stick.
I was scared that you'd die and it would be the end of it,
But I was always hoping that everything will be all right.
I was always staying near you with my First Aid Kit,
Ready to help you, while holding your paw really tight.

Few days later, I saw you dead,
Under the covers of your bed.
Even if it was hard and that I was crying, screaming and begging that you come back,
I will never forget you, while continuing on my track.
You will always have your own place for our memories and love in my heart,
And don't forget that wherever we are, we will never fall apart!
Andree-An Therrien, Grade 7
Macdonald High School, QC

Kiwi

On the outside you look like a meadow from the heavens above.
You feel like grass upon your sides, that make my day rise.
When I peel you, you sound like the push of a hand, on the surface of waves.
Inside you look like a beautiful green twilight, that shines so bright.
You feel like white sand, which gets stuck between my toes.
You smell like the night air, which smells quite fresh.
You taste like a midnight blue sea. Tell me why are you so addicting?
Nicole Jamie McMillan, Grade 7
St Anne School, AB

Peace, Love and Friends

No! Dear Heaven above,
Please tell me it is not so.
We can't handle this, you can't
You mustn't go.
They have already taken Father,
Why must they take you too?
Why now? Is it to make sure,
They killed our religion before it really grew?
We can't go through this alone,
Me and poor young Eliza.
Why must we live this out on our own?
You can't leave us! What? You aren't leaving?
Oh Mother that's great, you get to stay!
We have to go to the camp too?!?
Oh my must they take US away?
We are children, we have not done anything wrong!
What have we done for the Germans to hate anyone but other of them?
Why can't we have a world full of,
Peace, love and friends?
Alexandra Boyd, Grade 8
Macdonald High School, QC

Mouth Watering Anticipation

Because I haven't made myself lunch
yet
But no reason to
fret
I know what I will make
It will be great
Oh, how I love this food
Sometimes I eat and say,
'Oh, dude,'
It's even better than cake
This food is no fake
It's the food that I like to eat
But it needs to be cooked under much heat
This food is something you might not
expect
I don't know
But I think it's time to show
The great food I love,
RAMEN!

Simon Chen, Grade 9
Webber Academy, AB

Stay with Me

I never knew I was incomplete
I spent a lot of time staring at my feet
I was insecure when I found you
you led me to a cure
When you came along, you made my heart whole
and now I love you with all my heart and soul
When you are away
even just for a day
It really hurts a lot
So please never leave me
I would fall to my knees
And cry and beg you to stay
So just never leave me, okay?

Danae Hanna, Grade 8
Kalamalka Secondary School, BC

The Bond That Shall Unite Us

The sensation that can flow through everyone.
If only while others knew how.
Poverty would be a thing of the past,
Wars mythical.

Your destiny will smile upon you,
Therefore there is a fine line between destiny and faith,
The creation and continuity of this realm,
Will manifest itself in the wonders of human potential.

Where there is no longer a need for greed,
Many can be saved.
For we are all equal without barriers,
This is the bond that shall unite us all.

Gagandeep Singh, Grade 9
Beurling Academy, QC

Sprinkler

A bright, blue, blasting, sprinkler,
Thousands of glittering, silver raindrops,
Sprinkle, sprinkle, sprinkle,
Drizzling, splashing, wet and soaking,
A cold, fresh teardrop of joy as it goes down my throat,
Sprinkle, sprinkle, sprinkle,
Like pouring rain, rapidly, racing down from a puff of clouds,
The joyous taste that runs in rivers,
As clear as a shining crystal,
As natural and fresh as the ocean breeze,
Sprinkle, sprinkle, sprinkle,
Like a cold refreshing ice cream sundae,
As noisy as a water tap rushing into a sink,
Sprinkle, sprinkle, sprinkle.
A waterfall

Rachel Bauman, Grade 7
Linwood Public School, ON

Blue

Blue is like the color of the sky
Blue is what I see when I am at the water park
Blue is the color of my old friends eyes
Blue is like a calm pond at night
Blue is the color of the Toronto maple leafs jersey
Blue tastes like my favorite gum
Blue sounds like a wave on the ocean
Blue is a pair of comfortable jeans
Blue is the color of my old friend's eyes
Blue is color of my favorite car

Nicholas Dakin, Grade 7
St Anne School, AB

I Met Him on the Walk

I met him on the walk today,
A crumpled paper I threw his way.
He looked at it and said to me —
"Boy are you stupid, or is it just me?"
And I stood up from my deep bow,
Offended I was — I don't know how.
All I knew were his deep eyes,
The sincerest gray, to my surprise.
He looked at me, the pity vanished.
"You know," he said, "I could tutor you in Spanish."
One week later, I turn to him,
"Oh, it's you, how long it has been!"
"Too long," he says in a hoarse whisper,
Deep within, I now see his wisdom.
To think that this is how it happened,
A simple 'Fail' on my Spanish.
Now I have a brand new friend,
And yet this isn't all — the end!

Emiliya Ismayilova, Grade 7
EJ Sand Public School, ON

Why

Life is a puzzle that cannot be solved, from the day you are born to the day you are called.
Called to the heavens to be placed in a station, this place will become your final destination.
But do not worry and do not fret, your life was simple, you have no debt.
No debt to society 'cause you were good as good as you could be, though you should.
Accomplishments, achievements, many in your time, it's not all been easy you've shown me the sign.
I know it's hard to lie in that bed, one that will be you're last one instead.
It's hard to sit on this chair, and watch you die, watching you sleep as my heart cries.
Why is this happening to you? Why can't it be to someone that has nothing better to do?
I suppose everything in life has its place, all I want to know is why we are running this race.
Alone in that room, just you and me, nothing is said but I know you can see.
As that one single line has a harsh long beep, no ups no downs, not one small beat.
The cries from my heart rise up to my face, as if the floor was the end of the race.
I asked why again and again, but I know for certain this is not the end.

Aline Madian, Grade 8
Willowdale Middle School, ON

Remembrance Day

Remembrance day is a special day. We look back with joy and sorrow, upon the heroes that gave us freedom we have today. To many, it is a sad day. Family, friends, they are all gone because of war.

But what about the good things. Just as Jesus gave his life, these wonderful and brave people did, so that one day we may have peace. This country would not be the same today if these people did not die.

I guess we have two remembrance days, one in April and one in November, each with the symbol of the cross very much a part of them. Each with the memories of brave people that died so that we can have freedom.

So why do we do it? Why is there so much violence? Why should it be that people must give their lives so that others may be free? I don't think that will stop, but through Jesus Christ, it can definitely change.

Whitney Thomson, Grade 7
St Anne School, AB

Dear Environment

Dear Environment,
I'm sorry that you're rotting away, I'm sorry that you're not here to stay.
I'm also sorry that I haven't done anything to protect you from this catastrophe.

The Earth is slowly decaying, your land is slowly dying out.
I'm so sorry. I wish I could save you, I wish I could protect you, I wish that you will stay.

Next time I will try harder to protect you, I will try harder, harder and harder.
But, there won't be a next time.

After you're dead, you are dead.
I cannot bring you back, nor can anyone else.
You are precious. There is only one of you.
You can't keep up with us, and we ignorantly shun you when you are crying out for help.

I know there isn't a next time.
So I will try, try to protect you.
To give back to you what you have given back to us.
I'm going to take the initiative to save you.
Please wait for me, for I will fulfill my promise.
But for now, I will say to you, I'm sorry.

Adele Ka, Grade 8
Mulgrave School, BC

Reminiscence

Reminiscence, fog
orchestrated by
yesterday's Rock Royalty, soft swaying ballad
haunts, put a cover over my eyes
and I see green veracity:
pictures of piers over oceans; nurturing dead waves,
became memories of warmth, belonging.

Tall trees augment,
striving for layers of white sky, grayed with dancing wind
but they gave up, frozen in an escalating upward dive.
So stay unchallenged by peering eyes.

Inspired by unnatural philosophy,
half awake, half in reverie,
Aromas of mossy snow-sunken green seep,
Twilight captures versus outlines lost,
Twinges of melodies; legendary past.

I want to be imprinted by this raw fantasy
blink, pause, stay behind, wait —
twiddle forward
I'll be back,
pocketing time, remembering.

Kathy Wang, Grade 9
Semiahmoo Secondary School, BC

Math Is Fun

Math is always judged
Like a car that never budged.
Pattern, it's all about
So you don't have to pout.
When you solve the equation
It's like a family occasion.

You may get sad
But don't feel bad.
That's the point of math
It's a two way path.

It can be right — it can be wrong
It can be short — it can be long
That's why I love math
It's like a bath.
One minute you're belting out a song
The next minute you're sure it's wrong.

Math is a scary dream
But you don't have to scream.
Because math is really fun
Just like the rising sun.

Richard Tuong, Grade 7
Admiral Seymour Elementary School, BC

Forever

Forever is ever and ever and ever and ever.
It is a compound word made by for and ever.
There is no time, no date, and no limit of anything.
But it made anything sound as everything.

Forever is long and far,
Or even short and near.
It could be creative,
And it is imaginative.

It could be earth and space,
Or land and sky.
Orange?
Sure! Forever could be orange!

It could be whatever you like,
As long as it is endlessly,
It is For Ever,
And ever and ever and ever.

Debbie Pai, Grade 8
Mulgrave School, BC

Hatred

H ell is the metaphor
A ssault is its outcome
T error is its destiny
R eveals the dark side
E nd to peace
D estroys one's love

Muzakkir Navlakhi, Grade 7
James S Woodsworth Senior Public School, ON

Nature's Beauty

Beauty is riding
Your horse through the mountains.

Your horse moves
Through the mountains like
A stream through rocks.

The grass is tall,
Uncut and waving in the wind
Like your horse's mane.

Most things here have never heard a machine,
So the air is clean
And feels like it is cleansing your body
As it goes in and out
Of your lungs.

Then as you and your horse
Turn the corner and see the waterfall,
You know you have seen
One of nature's true "beauties."

Dusty Scribner, Grade 8
Hillside Jr/Sr High School, AB

Spelling

I nver did to gud in school
They always thught I wuzz a fool
I bawt a pc, jussst for spelchek you sea
But I can't turn it awn, oh how cruwel

Sarah LaPlante, Grade 7
New Horizons School, AB

Sadness

Mourning for others,
As tears drip from bloodshot eyes.
They form a puddle
As everyone else walks past.
You are alone in sadness.

Lily Wu, Grade 7
John Campbell Public School, ON

Shiny Reflection

As the orange
And the pink sky sets,
It reflects off the snow,
In the field across the highway.

It reflects
Like a mirror
As it glistens in the light.

The outline of the buildings
Towers over
Shiny puddles at dusk.

Marlee McGillis, Grade 8
Hillside Jr/Sr High School, AB

Calgary

Calgary is a
beautiful, wonderful
city.
Full of friendly
smiling people
everywhere you look.
A city full of
fun
with the Calgary
Stampede every
July for ten
days. Then in
winter the Calgary
Flames play in the
Pengrowth Saddledome,
along with
the Calgary Roughnecks
and Calgary Hitmen.
Calgary,
a city for everybody
to visit.

Jordan Hofer, Grade 7
Sunnysite Colony School, AB

Quiet

Quiet is like sitting in the room
blocking all those who make you mad or upset
and all you can do is lay there.
I am quiet, lying in the sun, waiting for everything to pass by.

Kristi Maurice, Grade 7
St Anne School, SK

Transitions

In the month of September hockey season starts
It's also the month where we put away the golf carts
The golf swing leaves as the slap shot arrives
Players start working to improve their strides
The golf shirts get hung up, shoes put away
The hockey stores start to sell out day after day
The equipment is broken in, ready to be used
Players toughen up, ready to be bruised
Me being the goalie, and so nice
I get to take the first cut, into the ice
It's such a different feeling, from walking around
As you glide along the frozen ground
From the puck drop, to your final stop
You work as hard as a horse
But it's not quite the same as a golf course
Then that final buzzer goes and the parents rise in their rows
They clap their hands in joy, as they celebrate with their boy
Before we knew it, it was March again and the playoffs were over
We didn't quite win the final cup
But we sure came close being the runner up

Jonathan Meakings, Grade 8
Mulgrave School, BC

Peer Pressure

The party, the people, the pressure, the drinks
After a few doses of those, your head will be hung low in the sinks
You know it's wrong, so why do it?
Don't make peer pressure get to your head
Kids tell you that it's right to do something
But the reality is, you're just being mislead
You shouldn't be pressured into everything your friends have to say
'Cause one day it may cost you your life
Now who's the one that will regret the day?
You are…you would have.
You could have stopped, but you didn't
You kept going and going and going until…
You were dead
So stop while you can, with this big future you have ahead
Think twice, be smart, make the right choice
Peer pressure is stupid
Help others recognize it too
Today, you could be pressured into drinking, tomorrow it could be drugs
Next, it could be taking your life
Please understand this and do what is right
Look at what you have in front of you, so many opportunities in sight.

Thalia Wright, Grade 8
Royal Orchard Middle School, ON

Students

I would like to make an announcement
to honour Our Lady Of The Annunciation school's best.

I think we would all have to agree
we rose above the rest.

Our most outstanding Artist was
Tyler Mcnight.
He's the one who painted all the desks white.

Our most outstanding Athlete is Bobby Bright
when he does a slam dunk it is amazing
to see him in flight.

The students that the teachers liked the
best was Mike Brash they liked him so much
they all gave him cash.

Congratulations winners.
Let's give them all a cheer
the Annunciation elementary students
of this present year.

Kyle Hurst, Grade 7
Our Lady of the Annunciation Catholic School, ON

Orange

orange is a flame burning away
orange sounds like thunder on a stormy night
orange is a sunset on the beach
orange is a rush of excitement
orange is life

Ryan Pretty, Grade 7
St Anne School, AB

stage call

notes, chords, riffs, solos
hanging in the air, like a bird against the sky.
music, bridging all gaps.
the strings still vibrating,
accompanied by the beating of your heart,
the roar of the crowd,
but a silence approaches.
behind the glare of the spotlight
lies the darkness of the void.
should i trust you with my back,
only for you to stab it in jealousy,
anger,
hate,
or despair?
if i could live on, untouched by the dust of the ages.
to stand here, in front of the crowd,
writing,
teaching,
inspiring all.

Brent Fallis, Grade 8
Odessa Public School, ON

Who Am I?

I am the wind in the trees,
The song in the breeze,
The earth sings my name,
But I don't bask in my fame,
Who am I?

Can you guess? Am I a bird, a tree, a pest?
Am I good or bad? Can you tell?
I believe what I do is right,
I would never surrender in a fight,
Who am I?

I am the Seeker of Truth, I wish to know,
I will find my answers before first snow.
Can you believe it? Is what I say true?
Well, you'll have to wait to find out,
But MY question is,
Who are you?

Rebecca du Plessis, Grade 9
Sir John Franklin School, NT

The Bone Chilling Cold

The gentle blowing of the wind
Brings me back to reality; back to the present.
Outside, the snow is falling
Making everything clean and pure
A winter's wonderland.
It takes all of my strength to arise from bed
To prepare myself for the bittersweet cold
I put on the amour for another battle
Against the elements of Mother Nature.
It's a day of survival
Another day of winter

Sandra Konji, Grade 9
St Peter Catholic High School, ON

Gray

Everyone around me is all the same.
This is our life and not a game.
You could not tell the difference between grass or hay.
The world I live in is only gray

There are no emotions nor are there feelings.
For this tragedy there is no healing.
Because we're all gray there is neither night nor day.
The world I live in is only gray.

What's the difference between you and me?
Absolutely nothing, can't you see.
In this world there is no bouquet.
The world I live in is only gray.

Bryan Blanco, Grade 7
St Patrick's Elementary School, BC

Cruel Kiss

the deadly
dreadful
cruel kiss
all honor lost
deliriously in the
gold coated moment
forever locked in
this state of
body and mind
one more romantic second
than all is gone
all is lost
with that…
one cruel kiss

Kelly Robertson, Grade 7
Menno Simons Christian School, AB

The Warm Glow Within

It's that feeling inside
That lights up your face,
Turns your mouth upwards
And makes frowns erase.

It's that warm glow within
That shimmers in your eyes,
Bubbles in your stomach
And comes out with surprise.

It could brighten one's day
That has not been too great,
And is certainly one thing
That never comes too late.

Whether it's a smile,
A giggle,
Or even a wink,
The possibilities are endless;
You need to just think.

Alina Poelzer, Grade 9
Webber Academy, AB

Life of a Cucumber

I'm cool like a cucumber
Left in the fridge

I'm in pain like a cucumber
Sliced into pieces

I'm crowded like a cucumber
Squished into subs

I'm sour like a cucumber
Pickled and left with the onions

Kevin Hong, Grade 7
Menno Simons Christian School, AB

Who Am I?

That girl in the mirror,
Is not me.
Tears streaming,
Makeup smearing,
What have I become?

Sadness overpowers,
My happiness
A frown,
Replaces my smile
What have I become?

A light shines,
My perspective changes
Bright blue eyes,
Smile upon my face
This is who I'll become.

Sydney Lough, Grade 8
Macdonald High School, QC

The Arrival of Disaster

Birds swim through the air,
silently in defiance.
Fish fly through the reef,
chanting their sad song in fright.
Global warming has started.

Sandy Wong, Grade 7
John Campbell Public School, ON

Fish

The smooth surface,
Of the water was broken,
By the splash!!! of a rainbow trout
In the sunshine and the water,
That sprinkled down with the trout.

SPLASH — SPLISH — SPLASH!!
SPLASH — SPLISH — SPLASH!!

It was fighting through the white water,
Looked like a streamlined train,
In top speed speeding along the track.

FLIP — FLOP — FLIP
It went as it landed on
The bank.

And it was a flash of sunshine,
In the water.
SPLASH — SPLISH it jumped,
up into the air.
SPLASH — SPLISH — SPLASH!!
SPLASH — SPLISH — SPLASH!!

Jacob Bauman, Grade 7
Linwood Public School, ON

Summer

The cool summer breeze
Lying in the green meadow
No worries or frights
Lay there looking at the sky.
In the sky are soft white clouds.

Chris Aultman, Grade 7
Homelands Senior Public School, ON

You Know Me

I sit and wait
here.
You know me,
my name —
Burned.
I have waited long
and then your hands
take me.
They almost destroy me.
You did drop me
and tore up my insides.
Yes you —
You did.
Sad,
it does end
and then I have
to watch you pick out a new one.
It hurts to see,
but I wait and you'll see.
Somebody else will
read me.

Jaime Silva, Grade 8
OV Jewitt Community School, MB

The Day I Was Waiting For

The flowers are blooming
Winter has gone home again
The bells are ringing
Spring has finally arrived
I was waiting for this day.

Anisa Abdirahman, Grade 7
Homelands Senior Public School, ON

The Unknown Children

The unknown children live in a fog
They are in desire of spray paint
Because they love
Graffiti.
They do not have a house
If they do, it is unknown
They breathe air
You never know when they
Strike!
Always sleep with your eyes open!

Patrick Labun, Grade 7
Menno Simons Christian School, AB

Life

As the morning sun makes its appearance
The world goes into life
The morning birds sing
To tell there is light.

People emerge from their caves and rush about
As daybreak appears
Gathering gold to feed their kin
As the sun sits high above

Life goes on and on; the circle never ends
Every day's the same
Appear, emerge, rush, return
Until the end of their days.

When the dust has settled
And the sun sinks low
The people return home
To their own families.

Kneeling, sheltered by the warm glow
Praying; thanking Him for shelter, warmth, and care
For His love and compassion
Then snuggle up in bed.

Susie Waldner, Grade 8
Twilight Colony School, MB

Loveless Games

You have to quit playing games
It doesn't quite work that way
You disappear and reappear
How do I know if this time it's true?
That I can believe and trust you

How do I know that you're genuine,
Or faking again this time?
I shouldn't let you get in close
I already know that I'm weak
You've already had me once before

Getting over you was one of
The worst things I had to do
It's not fair that you can come back
And make me suffer again
I don't know what to do about you

I'm like putty in your hands
You can mold me, control me
I'm dying when you leave me
And alive when you come back
It's so dangerous for me

Émilie St-Cyr, Grade 8
École secondaire catholique de Casselman, ON

Drew Barrymore

Drew Barrymore is truly beautiful!
She's in movies, commercials, and magazines.
I guess being a superstar isn't so painful!

Julie Garcia, Grade 7
Homelands Senior Public School, ON

Giant Snow Globes

Massive lakes and a sunset's glow
as far as the eye can see
no set climate no set time,
blankets upon blankets of snow covering falls untouched trees.
Car crashes as thick as flies,
yet somehow you are calmed by the wind's easing flow.
Mountains towering over your problems,
making them insignificant knowing they WILL!
Stand through the ages.

Lars Sonmor, Grade 9
Westcliffe Composite School, SK

Reflection

When I look in the mirror
It's someone else I see
I stare into the eyes of a girl who isn't me.
She boldly stares back
With her head up high
I just gaze away, letting out a sigh.
She seems so content
No sign of a tear
But deep inside she too has a fear.
When I look in the mirror
I don't know why she's there
Where am I? I must be somewhere.
I stare at the reflection
Expecting the odd child
And what surprises me is she looks back and she smiles.
I thought this girl was vile
'Cause she had her head up high
But who am I to judge? Ponder, wonder why?
We judge to hide
The feeling we cover
But deep inside, someone new we may discover.

Sana Abuleil, Grade 8
Laurelwood Public School, ON

The Rose

My love for you is like a red rose,
It started as a seed but it's grown and grown.
Its roots reach deep down inside of my chest,
And it grows even more with each passing breath.
The delicate petals lay beautiful and pure,
For all the thorns that this proud rose bears,
They are all softened by the thought of your care.
Soon the rose grows old, withers and dies,
But the love that helped grow it will last for all time.

Danika Gibson, Grade 8
Macdonald High School, QC

Monochrome

What if life was a Rubik's cube
A few memorized turns
And the piece is as it should be
Problem easily solved
Unchangeable.

What if life was the colour black
Ketchup is spilled but not seen
Sticky fingers smear invisible lies
Limp cloth in age-old laundry basket
Concealed.

What if life was a game of solitaire
Chaos is aligned
Each card an easy decision
Black and red are the only colours
Simple.

What if life was that boring
Oatmeal would be poetry
Walls would be white
The mountain would be flat
Monotone monochrome.

Stephanie Yip, Grade 8
Don Valley Jr High School, ON

Storm Dancers

The sky is dark
The clouds are black
A storm is brewing
In the midst of nothing
Slowly but steadily, the rain pours down
A crack and a boom mark the beginning
Of a long and loud night
Suddenly a flash
And eventually another
Show that the Storm Dancers
Are emerging
The Storm Dancers are lightning
And the lightning zigs
Sparkling and shimmering
And the lightning zags
Twinkling and shining
And the Storm Dancers
Dance all night.

Jade Bedesky, Grade 8
Ecole L'Heritage, ON

Flowers

I adore flowers
Flowers have glamorous leaves
I love purple ones
I plant them in my garden
And their stems are very green.

Layla Radovic, Grade 7
Homelands Senior Public School, ON

My Angel

You watch me day and night;
It seems I am always in your sight
The miles cannot spread us apart
Because no matter where you are,
You will always be dear to my heart
Once upon a time when there was you and me,
I was your angel, and you were my nanny
Now you are my angel there is no doubt about that,
But I wish we could go back to once upon a time when no one was sad
My angel, I miss you.

Alannah Mulcahy, Grade 8
Villa Maria High School, QC

The Unknown

All the time and passion you put in this sport,
Every day you worked harder and harder.
You put every bit of effort and enthusiasm into everything you do.
Whether it be passing, shooting, or thinking.
This is a sport of teamwork.
If you give up, you might as well give the team up.
If you think too much you're not good enough,
If you don't think at all you get yelled at,
You have to be smart on what you have to do.
Even when the crowd is cheering and there is a lot of pressure,
You can't focus on them you have to focus on what you have to do.
If you make one wrong move you could cause the game.
If you make the right move you'll know at the end how it feels to win.
I play this sport because you need team work and to be passionate,
That's why I play the sport of basketball.

Colten Neufeld, Grade 8
St Mary Separate School, ON

These Hearts

The sun may not always shine upon us
Or be there to lift our torn souls. But don't let this get you down
For, you know, I will always be there for you to hold.
The angered skies will not always yield to our pleadings
For them to keep the rain hidden beyond our fears
But, close your eyes and know…That I will always be here, right here.
These angry winds and cyclones that repeatedly shake the earth
Will surely destroy what took years to build
And in these vacant spaces…We will feel ourselves succumb to the reeling darkness
And collapse at the powerful force of our guilt.
The thunder will shake and split these hearts in two
And we will frantically, in the empty silence,
Search for a solace that we've never before found. But in this endless darkness…
We are caught in a moment that has never burned so profoundly.
Light will penetrate through this unyielding confusion
Shatter these walls that swarm between us
And evaporate these destructive emotions
In this long, convoluted moment, we must find,
Given time and strength…A little peace of mind.
Empty and alone on these many endless nights
These hearts…though weak and ready to break, will unite.

Rachelle Wollman, Grade 9
Twilight Colony School, MB

Spider

O great spider
So magnificent
Can climb on a tree without hardness

O fast spider
Jumps fast
Making a web for their prey

O powerful spider
Kills their prey without a snap
They bite an animal so bad

O brave spider
Defend its loved one to the death
A loving spider I wish my life was a spider

Sean Rembulat, Grade 7
Westwind Elementary School, BC

There Is

Open your eyes, there is so much to see
Open your ears, there is so much to hear
Open your mouth, there is so much to say
Open your mind, there is so much to learn
And open your heart because, there is so much to love.

Bryanne Lacombe-Gobeil, Grade 8
Macdonald High School, QC

Goodbye

You left without saying goodbye,
I wish I could have another chance to say "hi."
I was halfway around the world when you left me,
I remember when I would sit on your lap to drink tea,
I miss you,
I love you.
I promise one day I will meet you up there,
I wish I could be there
Just to be with you.
I thought I would never get through.
In me I felt pain,
When you left, my life became plain.
When you gave me that stuffed animal when I was six,
It was like a big fix.
One day,
I will see that passing away,
Isn't the end but a new beginning.
I love you my dearest grandmother.

Chloe Beaini, Grade 7
École secondaire Sainte-Famille, ON

Saadia Khatoon

There was a girl named Saadia Khatoon
She really wanted to go to the moon
Once she snuck into a rocket
But got caught when her phone started to ring in her pocket.

Shumail Irshad, Grade 7
Homelands Senior Public School, ON

Friends

Here I am all alone
Lots on my head
But mainly how I made my friend
One cold rainy day

Voices on the playground
No wait! In the crowd
I see someone
Never seen this person

I confront him
Tears on his face
Lots of blood on his leg
Don't know what to say

It just took one simple word
To be his friend
I help him up
And say don't worry it'll be okay

Here I am all alone
Lots on my head
But mainly how I made my friend

Francisco Berrazueta, Grade 7
Admiral Seymour Elementary School, BC

Sunrise

The sun awakens over the majestic peaks
Into the valleys and fields it flows
This is a scene that is truly unique.

The snow-white mountains sparkle at the beak
Above the tree-line, where nothing grows
The sun awakens over the majestic peaks.

In every crevasse, the sunlight seeks
In the gentle, bright rays, the mountain glows
This is a scene that is truly unique.

The alpine meadows, as white as a sheet
The dazzling sunshine puts on a show
The sun awakens over the majestic peaks

Flowing through the mountains is a shimmering creek
The crest is high; the valleys low
This is a scene that is truly unique.

The whispering wind of the valley speaks
A language of mystery, a lonely ode
The sun awakens over the majestic peaks
This is a scene that is truly unique.

Liam Wicken, Grade 7
St Patrick's Elementary School, BC

Yellow

Yellow is calm and collected, it is peaceful and happy,
It is a banana or a sunflower it is a bumblebee buzzing busily as it collects pollen.
It is when you look up at the sky and feel happy, calm and relaxed.

Jillian Janes, Grade 7
St Anne School, AB

The Porcelain Heart

Under the rainbow, after the rain, a porcelain heart lay unbegotten
The glass was shattered, the pieces were scattered
The heart was silent and forgotten
Walking passersby took no notice of such an object worth no focus
Sad and lonely was the heart, the reason why it broke apart
And then a child of cheerful folly came up upon it for her dolly
Picking it up with gentle care, she smiled at it with a loving air
Warming comfort was her touch, the porcelain toy revived in a rush
Taken home to smiling faces, shown around to many places
And the porcelain heart was loved again
The years passed by with a gentle flow, but time alas was its deadly foe
The girl had grown up, and up with ease, the heart was dusty and sad without need
Her touch not lingered for moments no longer, the childish love spent, now meant for another
The heart was taken out for a final walk, and placed beside a cuckoo clock
Was pushed aside and fallen down, and landed on the roads of town
The girl-turned woman remembered with pain, the happiness of which she long threw astray
The innocent laughter rang in her mind, as she gazed on obstructed by the barrier of time
The childish heart then now fond memories past, a fancy diddle, not meant to last

Under the rainbow, after the rain
A porcelain heart lay unbegotten

Allan Song, Grade 8
Homelands Senior Public School, ON

A Generation's Obituary of Sadness

You have gone away today. It is a beautiful sunny day, not a cloud in sight, not a trace of gloom in the wings.
All is calm and peaceful on this day, and you are gone. You have left us, and for this we can no longer weep.
You left holes in our hearts that can now be filled once more.
You were always there, throughout our whole lives.
You never gave up a chance to follow us, through the good times, and the bad.
You were waiting around every corner, ready to take us by surprise.
But today, dear deceased, we mourn not for our loss.
You were one of those burdens that we can make do without.
You were one of those dreaded emotions that kept coming back, even when we asked you to stay away.
We are joyful now Sadness, that you have finally passed.
Our time has come, and yours has ended. We will rise up and you will fall.
We will triumph, and you will not be there to bring us down.
Your absence will bring joy into our hearts freely, without the threat of being smothered.
We are no longer afraid to be happy, because you, Sadness, cannot take away our uplifted spirits.
We have inspiration and faith. You no longer rule us.
Our generation will raise the bar; make the changes we were meant to make.
Sadness, you will no longer stand in our way.
You and your wicked ways of fear, discouragement and sorrow will no longer hold us down.
Our new way; happiness, courage, strength and hope rises up to help us through.
Today is a new day. There is no sadness in sight.
You are gone, you have left us. And for this, we can no longer weep.

Sara Lejour, Grade 9
Centennial Regional High School, QC

Living in Sameness: Jonas's Perspective*

Dreams at morning, feelings at night,
Watched all the time; never out of sight.
Everything was the same, never any fun,
But when I met the Giver, the realization begun.

As the new Receiver, I learned a lot of things.
Like what snow is, and that birds have wings.
Memory by memory, I learned of the world,
But the bitterness of pain also unfurled.

It was unbearable, feeling that pain.
It brought on emotions I just couldn't restrain.
And when I learned what release meant,
Out the door my old life went.

Taking Gabriel with me, I went on the search,
The search for the Elsewhere somewhere on Earth.
Hoping that my leaving would bring about change,
I crossed the bridge feeling a little bit strange.

As the days pressed on, survival became hard,
Until we finally reached a hill in a yard.
As we shot down, on a red sleigh,
I finally felt Sameness giving way.

Chen Chang, Grade 7
John Campbell Public School, ON
*Inspired by the Lois Lowry novel "The Giver."

Father's Worth

God is our wonderful Father
Who gave us an incredible father.
When I think of all the material things
in his lifetime he might have had
if he hadn't chosen to be
such a loving, caring dad!

He shares his time, wealth and talents
with those closer to him than life,
with his children,
and their loving mother, his wife.

To them he gives and gives and gives
and never calculates the price.
To make his family happy
to him is gain and not loss.

What is a father's value?
No estimate can be made.
A compassionate father is priceless,
for him no charge can be paid.

Bhakti Bhatt, Grade 7
James S Woodsworth Senior Public School, ON

A Perfect Cloud

Fluffy cotton candy shaped for the mind
covering the bright yellow sun, giving the
sky some personality to live, moved by
wind calmly following the eye of a person,
hovering above the town, city, wherever
you live, stretched far across anywhere you
could imagine but its always in the great
blue sky, clouds are not just used to block
the sun but to enjoy and to use your imagination.

Justin Bhatia, Grade 7
Blundell Elementary School, BC

Young, Gifted and Black

Many inspirations
So many to follow.
From Martin Luther King to Barack Obama.
Intelligence.
Confidence.
The list goes on,
From music to public speaking.
Amazing actors and singers.
From our inventions to our insights.
From our struggles to our accomplishments.
As African American people, we have made it a long way.
Not even slavery could keep us down.
As Malcolm X once said, "By any means necessary."
With those words,
I can do anything.
The time has come,
For I too will make a difference.
Because I am young, gifted and black.

Kayla Sinclair, Grade 8
Macdonald High School, QC

A Passion in My Heart

Basketball is heard,
At the break of dawn.
Everyone is tired,
But tiredness will soon be gone.

Basketball can be seen,
As a game with lots of rules.
And in the end,
A trophy with lots of jewels.

Only real players know,
That basketball comes with a heart full of passion.
Win or lose,
It does not matter.

Basketball is a drink of refreshing water,
It makes my tense body relax.
After a day of hard work,
I know that basketball is the way to go.

Tammy Ho, Grade 7
Admiral Seymour Elementary School, BC

Roses

The little rose bud
Flourishing, so beautiful
In those gorgeous shrubs
Florescent colours so red
The fragrance is alluring

Angela Nguyen, Grade 7
Homelands Senior Public School, ON

Over the Sea

Optimistic fantasy turned into a low.
Spun into love then outta control.
Hate filled, loving tears.
She'd too often run from all her fears.
All confirmed.
She'll pull it together just for him.
His hands, his touch, his cheesy grin
So easy to give
Too hard to let go
His caring side is all she will ever know
The blaze betraying all her lies
Pain undenying in her eyes
Never seeing him again
Only chatting with her lover, her friend
With their lives in different motion,
She will still keep him in her heart
Even when he's across the ocean
That's as good as it will ever be
And no matter what she will love him
Sea to shining sea.

Sonia Lagrandeur, Grade 7
École secondaire Macdonald-Cartier, ON

An Ode to My Friend Lily (Wu)

She sits near me
quiet and neat
She drinks tea
and likes to tap her feet

Her name is Lily
like the one in a pond
She's quite silly
we have a special bond

She's always been there
through the good times and bad
She always shares
and never gets mad

A hand she will lend
when I am in need
She is a great friend
Doing a great deed

Angela Cheam, Grade 7
John Campbell Public School, ON

Baby Blue Jay

I get called upon to witness each new conquered feast.
I've now discovered I have hands, and toes upon my feet.
I'm an energetic bundle, to hold me makes someone's day.
My grandpa fondly nicknamed me his "Little Blue Jay."

Jay Wasylciw, Grade 8
Worsley Central School, AB

Flowers

Red, red roses so very brilliant,
Their colours like red delicious apples
Their are other colour roses too,
Pink cotton candy, yellow lemons, and white
Glittering snow,
Violets so brilliant, bright, blue as an ocean
Peacefully rumbling
Drip, drip, drip the rain fall, helping the
Colourful creative flowers grow,
Purple lilacs in fragrant bunches
Lilies and Trilliums so white as wooly so
Wooly sheep, and yellow marigolds that sweet,
Blue forget-me-nots so lovely in a pleasant row
Oh the colourful pansies looking so happy in
The azure sky, drip, drip, drip the gentle showers coming downward,
The sweet-scented lemon drops so very attractive,
And the peaceful, perfect petunias in so many blooms,
Flowers big to small, colourful to white,
Living could not go on without these beautiful flowers,
Drip, drip, drip it can flood the flowers down
Colourful, brilliant, fragrant flowers all around the world!

Magdalena Martin, Grade 7
Linwood Public School, ON

Love

Love begins with two
It can start with me or you

Love is a bond, no one can see
And makes a special world for you and me

Love is a feeling where your world is filled with delight
And make everything in your world feel so right

Compassion can show love in so many ways
Compassion makes the blaze in your heart and the sun start raise

Compassion is showed when caring for someone you know
And the compassion you show will start to show

But when war has come between the touch of love
It feels like a dove has fallen from above

If war will stop, we will be together
Like a chain firmly stuck forever

Natesh Kukerja, Grade 7
Fairwind Senior School, ON

Life's Journey

We enter this world with good reason,
Slowly we blossom,
Like flowers in spring season,
We learn of life's values,
We learn of its morals,
We learn to endure its joys and its sorrows,
We start to grow,
We start to mature,
Life's ups and downs we must now endure,
We begin to live,
We begin to love,
We are then set free to fly like a dove,
It's time to get settled,
It's time to find,
The special someone with whom we will bind,
As we get older,
Many illnesses we endure,
May our life end peacefully,
'Tis all we wish for.

Akhil Khurana, Grade 8
Great Lakes Public School, ON

Valentine's Day Two

I hope you enjoy Valentine's Day
for the feeling it brings is as warm as May
it brings back memories, old and new
when we were little and to us this day was ew!
Isn't Valentine's such a sight?
Doesn't it make life seem so bright?

Maybe it didn't for you were so small,
but now it should for you are big and tall
Valentine's Day makes us feel the joy
it's like we were little and we just got a new toy
So now you see how wonderful it is
except for the part when people kiss!

Paiker Jaffery, Grade 7
James S Woodsworth Senior Public School, ON

The Day After Tomorrow

The Day after tomorrow where will we be?
Will I be with you?
Will we still be happy?

My mind shutters with unthinkable thoughts.
I want to be free,
get rid of these knots.

I think of the way things are in my life.
It gives me great sorrow,
Please give me that knife.

I want to know why this happened to me.
The day after tomorrow will be better you'll see.

Carrie Tarnopolski, Grade 9
Selkirk Jr High School, MB

Summer

Beautiful like a flower bed in full bloom,
and gentle as a newborn lamb.
Ripe, yellow wheat fields,
an ocean of sweet, fresh, clean smelling hay,
lots and lots of farms as far as the eye can see.
Splash and I dive into the cool water,
a soft breeze touches my sun tanned face.
Buzz, buzz a bee goes buzzing by,
swish, a tiny twister goes by in the sand.
Sweat is trickling down my face,
I hear the loud noise of a threshing machine nearby,
this is what summer means to me.

Menno Sherk, Grade 7
Linwood Public School, ON

Dolphin

As I look out to the horizon, in the distance
I see a creature jump as if claiming its existence,
As it hits the water again once more
It slowly makes its way closer to the shore.

Then it begins to put on a show
In and out of the water below.
As it moves through the water without a care
It again does a flip through the air.

Soon the creature begins to play
And I wish I could sit there and watch it all day,
But soon I have to go in
And as I look back, it seems to be flashing me a grin.

Just like many creatures of the sea
This one is as beautiful as can be,
And just as it does one more spin
I turn away, away from the dolphin.

Kendra Look, Grade 8
Hillside Jr/Sr High School, AB

Stinky Feet

Sweaty feet can really stink
Like a dirty dishrag in the sink.
Be careful when the shoes come off
The smell can make you choke and cough
From those stinky feet.

We can fix this smelly woe
By washing the jam off your toe.
Just take a bath
There will be no wrath
From those stinky feet.

Dallas Houston, Grade 7
Community Bible Fellowship Christian School, MB

Heartbreak Romeo

Life isn't a fairy tale,
so don't be surprised if you fail.
You'll always have me as a friend,
But this is the way the story really ends.

He broke your heart,
tore it apart.
I know it sounds corny,
but that's the end of the story.
It feels so real,
but sadly it's not what he would feel.
He's a wannabe, got to go,
Heartbreak Romeo.

Amanda McLeod, Grade 8
St Mary's High School, ON

Monsters

There are monsters under my bed.
I can hear them when I sleep:
Giggling, gurgling, groaning.
It gets kind of annoying
But I've gotten used to it.

Actually, they've become my friends.
They all have their own tastes.
I gave them names:
Melvin, Petunia, Ted.

Every night they come out to play.
We have to be very quiet.
We play lots of games:
Grounders, tag, dress up.

They won't always be there.
Eventually, they will leave.
And go to cooler places:
Spain, Japan, Tahiti.

But even then, we'll be best friends
Forever and ever.

Emily Shields, Grade 8
Mulgrave School, BC

Eyes

Blue as the sea,
in the half light of the moon.
Round as the earth in space,
so perfect and true.
It is a portal to the soul,
of every thing and being.
It is a looking glass,
for you,
and for me.

Destiny Fox, Grade 7
Barriere Elementary School, BC

Blue Sky

Blue sky, Blue sky
Where do you go?
When the clouds
come in
do you go out slow,
do you go out fast
Blue sky, Blue sky
one thing I know,
You always come back
When the clouds go.

Emma Thomson, Grade 7
Pacific Christian School, BC

Not Living Sneaks

Walking through the woods,
Creeping up on me is a creature.
Bam!! It hits me.
Covered in snow,
Who knew trees could be
So, so sneaky.

Hanna Peterson, Grade 8
Hillside Jr/Sr High School, AB

Breeze

The wind is breezy
Just like a small butterfly
With really big wings
Swirling around joyfully
Landing on fields of flowers.

Jessica Wong, Grade 7
Homelands Senior Public School, ON

The Lonesome Forest

Everyone's alone
they're calling but no one hears
the end of no return
scary and dark

They're calling but no one hears
trees so big so small
scary and dark
waiting and waiting…

Trees so big so small
screaming shouting
waiting and waiting…
Help!

Screaming and shouting
the end of no return
Help!
everyone's alone.

Elysa Kotylak, Grade 7
Menno Simons Christian School, AB

The Day

After the sun began to show
the soldiers came to seek
the one who must be shown
the good and the bad
the right and the wrong
but what they didn't know
is that he would save our souls

After the day was done
they rolled a rock into place
but when the woman came
the man was not there.

Brittlyn Wintringham, Grade 7
St Paul School, SK

Awesome

Cars
Sleek, aerodynamic
Fast, exotic, turbo fire
Blazing, European, Japanese, nitrous
Customization, horsepower, turbo
Ferrari, Lambos, Hondas
Head turning
Cars

Raza Qadri, Grade 8
New Horizons School, AB

Just Banana Bread?

Dear banana bread
As I eat you bit by bit
I wonder how it must feel
To be sliced up into a dozen

Dear banana bread
Is this torture to you?
Though I see you only as food
Have you not the same rights?

Dear banana bread
I am like a cat and you are like a mouse
When it comes to the likes of you
I have learned to eat

Dear banana bread
I have stopped consuming you
But I feel that it is just too late
So much of you has already disappeared

Dear banana bread
I can't believe you're going to forgive me
Even after everything
I did to you.

Pia Leung, Grade 8
Laurelwood Public School, ON

Little Dreams

Little dreams they come so fast
They are the things we cannot grasp.

We try so hard to succeed,
But when we get there we fall to our knees.

The feeling in your inner core
The pounding of it at your door.

You try to open but no one's there
On your face an empty stare.

You look about in the shadows
So lost, so confused, so alone.

You see an image bathed in light,
Your running forward…but then you stop.

You look into a moonlit mirror,
At the image in its face,

But all you see is what was holding you back
It was just your fears.

Emily Robb, Grade 9
Senator Patrick Burns School, AB

Graduation

Remember?
The way we cheered for each other.
The many risks we took
For the sake of friends
We vowed to keep forever.
Wounds we have reopened,
And healed over time
With friends that'll say goodbye one day
Yet still live in our memories.

Remember?
How the leaves changed colour
When we first met each other?
All the hurtful words that were flung and
The same old classrooms where once again laughter resided?

Remember?
The days we spent together,
And the promises we made to each other.
So shoulders back, heads held high,
Again we shall wipe tears from each other's eyes
Because it is finally time
To say goodbye.

Ker Lee Yap, Grade 8
J N Burnett Secondary School, BC

Life Gets Better as You Like Yourself

No matter how you are,
You have to like yourself first,
We are all unique like a twinkly star,

Never call it a bad day when luck won't be pursued,
Remember everything happens for a reason,
First comes the worst,

Tears in your eyes aren't worth to cry
Deny the sky,
Hold it high,
There will be the happy sigh,
Defy as the sun rises for the true ally,

Think for yourself not the words others think,
Some can be right or wrong,
Allow — follow the gods like Apollo,
Smile through your tears,
As the years fly,
Be aware! Feel the flares of delight and the rhythms that blare,
Lies may die,
Be you, your dreams will come soon like a surprise.

Arminta Thurairajah, Grade 9
Pierrefonds Comprehensive High School, QC

Erik

Erik is a cool guy
With brown hair and brown eyes
He plays sports to get some exercise
He is happy most of the time
He feels excited when playoffs come around
He eats spaghetti before each game
His friends are cool, loyal
He is grateful to be healthy, and happy

Erik Climenhaga, Grade 7
St Paul School, SK

Summer's Day*

You do remind me of a summer's day,
But you are more lovely and much more fair.
For some days are bitter and others gay,
But summers are too short and much too rare.
Sometimes it is too hot and we do burn,
Others are cloudy and not warm enough.
Nothing stays the same like we all do yearn,
But the course of nature's change is quite rough.
You are the eternal summer that lasts,
That keeps the possession of perfection.
Death does not bring the end after you've passed,
You live in this poem of affection.
If men continue to live and to see,
This poem lives on and your soul be free.

Josh Bond, Grade 9
Westcliffe Composite School, SK
*Inspired by "Shall I Compare Thee to a Summer's Day"
by William Shakespeare

Purple

Smelly
Fruity
Over powering
Acidic
Strong

Taste
Cool
Sweet
Strong
Sugary

Sound
Bubbles
Splash
Waves
Tapping

Feel
Relaxed
Mellow
Calm
Warm

Hanna Huys, Grade 7
St Anne School, AB

Autumn Is Here

Leaves fly through the skies,
The cold air blows through the trees
Autumn is coming.
Liam Deery, Grade 8
St Mary's High School, ON

The Phone Call

I got a phone call last night
I hung up with a fright
My dad's not coming home
And now I'm all alone
I trudged the stairs that felt like towers
I sat in my room and cried for hours
I prayed to God that night
Then I lay staring at my ceiling light
I call my mom with sorrow
She said she'll be home tomorrow
When my tears hit the floor
I missed him much, much more
My dad was a great man
I was definitely a fan
He was in a world known fight
But I knew that he'd be all right
Now I know how others feel
But I don't know if my heart will heal
Those last words he said to me
I love you and you love me
Quynlan Mracovcic, Grade 7
Westside Academy, BC

You're Not Alone

When a child is born everyone is blessed
And people still today believe we are born alone
Not so we are born with the countless people around
Not to mention the blessing of the room when you are born
And cannot truly be defined, it can be felt
As a feeling of warmth and happiness but to witness such blessing
Dany Ménard-Martin, Grade 7
Macdonald High School, QC

A Moment in Memories

A walk to remember, the thoughts that I had I never saw you like that
Your beautiful smile, your heavenly eyes
All that we shared slowly faded
I tried to hold on but the strings slowly snapped
Knowing you was like saying, I held hands with an angel
We took a walk we all will take
Why you walked that path, the question will hang
So I held your hand, until we reached the gates
I held you so close you drift so far
I'll never forget who you are
Your wings turned to gold, your face was so cold
But I know you're now happy where you now sleep
Your memories buried in my heart down so deep
So now even though it's time to say goodbye
I promise we will be together again soon
So I'm begging please don't cry
You touched my face as you spoke these words
Wiped my tears and kissed my cheek, slowly our king took your hand
You walked on the clouds, shone like the stars
You already know but I'll say it again I love you...
Cali Fairway, Grade 8
St Mary Separate School, ON

Broken Soul

I'm an orphan not yet nine
Each day and night under starry sky cheeks shining with tears alight
I travel, alone, a lone wolf lest I be caught by the urchin train,
Yearning for a place to stay a place to call my home
People who love me like I love them
I sleep on the pitted ground, a dream burning in my heart,
Day and night I walk alone
At day the scorching sun beats down on me, at night the stars twinkle their tune,
A million fireworks frozen in space watching the world below,
I pass by towns and cities, lights a giant fiery blaze
Laughter alight on peoples lips, children dance and sing their joy
A world unlike my own,
People avoid my waking self, they sense my empty soul, my vacant eyes
And my lifeless heart that beats forsaken of hope,
A void-less person, unforgiving of fate, dying every day a little more
Dawn blends into dusk, my breaths slow down,
A gentle breeze caresses my face as I walk the path set out for me since birth
A rose in a lily patch wild and untamed,
Hope dies out, flame of life burns away, pulse everlasting slow
World behold my beauty gone, thy eyes will never know.
Caitlin Roberts, Grade 9
St Thomas More School, AB

Have You Ever Wished You Could Fly?

Have you ever wished you could fly?
Feeling the cool breeze while you are soaring.
Zooming through the world, up in the sky.
Have you ever wished you could fly?
How can we? I wonder why.
Passing by crowds as they are roaring.
Have you ever wished you could fly?
Feeling the cool breeze while you are soaring.

Xandro Ren Acuña, Grade 7
St Patrick's Elementary School, BC

The One

He is graceful, yet powerful
Commanding, yet just
Invisible, yet there
Listening, yet there are millions of prayers

He is the wind whispering through the grass
The sun shining rays through the clouds
Rain washing away our thoughts
A grain of sand forgotten in the ocean

When I am hungry, He feeds me
When I am thirsty, He gives me a drink
When I am in darkness, He lights my path
And when I am sad, He is always a shoulder to cry on

He is the creator of life
Everyone's Father
The Holy Spirit

Michelle Babak, Grade 7
St Joseph Separate School, ON

Passionate Discovery

With passionate contemplation comes self-discovery,
The young one used this to attempt recovery.
Defying the laws of pride,
She lengthened her stride —
Providing respect,
One that others would not detect.

Howbeit,
T'was not long before her light bulb lit.
Despite how often the struggle recurred,
Of one thing she was always assured:
It is finer to bear outstanding skirts,
Than to clone the pattern of others' shirts.

With a fresher take on old ways,
She gradually realized her traits' pays.
Life became a constant rhyme,
It no longer felt like she was just passing time.
She has overcome the fear of being inferior,
But the intellect at heart matches not the exterior.

Kelly Lee, Grade 9
Laurier Sr High School, QC

A Diamond

A diamond is like a star
glistening on a clear dark night,
in the middle of nowhere.

A diamond is like a raindrop
falling from the sky on a bright sunny day,
shining as it falls to the ground.

A diamond is like water
flowing slowly through the rivers,
sitting still in the huge ocean,
rushing down a waterfall hitting the bottom.

Karly Rachey, Grade 7
St Anne School, SK

Flowers

Gazing at flowers makes me warm inside.
Looking at the beautiful colors
they make everything look prettier
all around the yard.
The yellow flowers gleam in the sun.
In the warm summer breeze
I scan through the beautiful yard.
There stood a colorful, single flower
begging for some raindrops.

Joanne Hofer, Grade 8
Sunnysite Colony School, AB

Desert Cowboy

When darkness departs by dawn's early light,
The golden sun glows pushing back the long night.

I saddle my pony for another days ride,
I'm happy just knowing my friend's by my side.

Old Red's my companion, he's all that I need,
You'd have to search far for a trustier steed.

I pull on my boots, shake the dust from my hat,
Pack up our belongings and give Red a pat.

Through hot desert sand and cactus we go,
The day's wearing long, where we'll stop we don't know.

Tired and thirsty we rest making camp on the trail,
We'll drift off to sleep to the song of the quail.

Tomorrow may bring us yet closer to home,
But we're happy together where ever we roam.

Allyson Furman, Grade 8
Hillmond Central School, SK

Where Land and Sea Meet

One last gulp of humid sea air
before I dive into the ocean blue
beneath me a rainbow of colours parade,
dance.

They are puzzled by my foreignness
as I theirs,
they watch me carefully,
timidly
I watch dazzled and amazed
as the sunlight shines from above
making them shimmer like diamonds.

Everything here is so different from one another
but it all meshes together seamlessly.
Creating a breathtaking place
full of endless surprise and discovery.

But my journey must now end
I wish to stay longer
but that's what makes it so beautiful.

Kristen Ponte, Grade 8
Rutland Middle School, BC

Magic

It sounds like the thunder before the storm.
It feels like the earth after
the first rain drop hits the ground.
It smells like red roses.
It tastes like Florida sweet strawberries.
You see it everywhere.

Mackenzie Heck, Grade 7
St Anne School, AB

Life

L ife is seen
I n the world
F orever in the rushing water
E ven in a poet's writing

L ife is heard
I n the voice
F amilies laughing
E agle's crying

L ife exists
I n the mind
F or life to exist
E ternally

L ife needs appreciation
I n the thoughts
F or the
E nthusiasm to endure

Alyssa Hui, Grade 7
Admiral Seymour Elementary School, BC

Spring

Worst time of the year
Floods, wet clothes, slipping, sliding
Rotten smells
Smelly, wet shoes fill your nostrils
Snow melts
Beautiful white sights
Turn to dirty, ugly browns.

Worst of all
Bugs bustle back home
Tiny flying insects
Sip at your blood
Through your veins
Like needles
Leaving you bruised, disgusted, sickened.

Annoying, unforgettable
Reality of nature
Hoping for winter wonderland to reappear
Killing the critters off
Hoping for sweet summertime to arrive
Loving the blooming flowers
But you have to wait.

Seth Lowry, Grade 8
Heather Park Middle School, BC

Dear Mr. Thompson*

I am writing you to say
I fully regret my decision that day
To us it seemed like just a sign
I wanted Morgan to be mine
When I went outside that night
I trusted him without a fright
That was the night we had our first kiss
The entire evening was filled with bliss
I was right where I was supposed to be
Me beside him and him beside me
We thought we were making the right decision
We sawed and chopped the signs with precision
First we took THICKLY SETTLED
We know now we shouldn't have meddled
Getting caught was a chance to take
Little did we know the problems we'd make
Then we snatched MORGAN ROAD
My love for him finally showed
CHERRY STREET was just for pride
I am so sorry your wife died.
From Remy

Brianne Kroeker, Grade 9
Elm Creek School, MB
*Inspired by "Driver's Ed Project" by Caroline B. Cooney

Don't Go

I spent every waking moment with you,
And every sleeping moment thinking about you.
I can't live a day without being here,
And I can't live a moment without you near.

You showed me your world and I showed you mine,
It was all fun until we ran out of time.
You told me you loved me and you told me goodbye,
It all happened so fast all I could do was cry.

Don't go please don't leave
You are the one I want,
The one I need.
Don't go.

I can't do anything anymore,
Because you left and my heart was torn.
Without you holding me I feel so alone,
And I continue waiting for you to come home.

I spend every sleeping moment with you,
And every waking moment thinking about you.
I live the rest of my days sitting right here,
In our very spot, where I know you'll always be near.

Candice Braithwaite, Grade 8
Homelands Senior Public School, ON

You're Only a Blank Wall

Encompassed, surrounded by bleakness
Overtaken.
Trapped between misconceptions and cryptic memories
Hidden.
Plastered behind layers of apprehension, and dishonesty
Enough to squeeze your soul, shallow breaths.
Gasped. Choked.
Yet, serene, as if forgotten.
Like the appearance.
Mistreated. Abused.
Scarred with retching secrets as a billowing cloud of stone,
Constantly changing, yet the same.
New stories unable to be spoken,
Whispered. Concealed.
Appearance is misleading.
A shaded white.
A floral time warp.
A baby pink with new beginnings followed by white.
Brilliant white.
Blank and fresh, covered up.
Ignored.

Karley Skaret, Grade 9
Webber Academy, AB

Lego

I may be small but
I have a plastic heart
I may be in pieces
I may be a phenomenal object
But most of all I can be anything
I may be a choking hazard
I may be as colorful as a painting
Or maybe a lonely piece of Lego
I am a lonely fish in a fishless lake or maybe
In the corner of the tallest tower
In the deepest cave to the highest mountain
I am the atoms of your imagination
You can imagine the biggest ideas
I can be that
That makes me special
I can be the knives in your feet in the middle of the night
Big or small, brilliant or sad that's me the lonely piece of Lego.

Jordan Balogh-Callow, Grade 7
Westwind Elementary School, BC

Kissed

I don't know how it happened,
I guess it's cuz of your smile,
but every time you're not here,
it's as if you were away for miles.

What is it about you
that I cannot resist.
Is it cuz when you talk to me,
I feel my whole world is being covered in mist
Covering all the people whoever laughed at me,
Made fun of you,
and treated us like crap.
Covering all those memories,
I know won't ever last.

I don't know how it happened.
Oh how am I so shy?
What I do know is that
I love you
no matter how and why.

Raquel Centeno, Grade 7
St Anne School, AB

I Love You Mommy!

You yelled at her when she kissed you in public,
You ignored here when she asked for help,
You've never thanked her for anything she's done.
Now as she lay still and people are crying,
You wonder why you did all of those things.
Now you want to yell at the heavens
To bring her back so you can tell her you love her.
But all you can do is lean over her, kiss her goodbye,
And tell her you love her with all your heart.

Emily LaFortune, Grade 7
Macdonald High School, QC

Happy Flappy
Happiness is the feeling that explodes inside your head
Jumping up and down and all around with a smile on your face
Feeling with joy, love and excitement, we hope you will calm down soon

Isabella Gut, Grade 7
St Anne School, AB

Everyone Hates This Part of Life
The sun is smiling down on us
But the tears are still streaming down on their faces
Some say he'll go to heaven
Some say hell
But today it doesn't matter if it's heaven or hell
Today is a special day
A day that some may remember and others will forget
But most will remember the good times and bad times
And this is why they are sad today
A loss of someone you love is tough
Death is natural, there's nothing to fear
Because everyone dies one way or another
Everyone will witness a loss too
And some may have witnessed two
Death is like a mystery
An empty, black box
No one knows how it is
People are most likely to fear "After life"
They think: "What will happen to me when I die?"
Others may think: "Before I was born, I didn't exist, when I die it will be the same."
But deep down in these people's hearts, they hope there will be a happy ending to everything.

Kiana McFadden-Houle, Grade 7
École secondaire Macdonald-Cartier, ON

Ode to the Guardians of Our Planet
Thank the ones whose love and care makes a difference for you and me
Who do their best to share clean air and make us all feel free
Who reduce, who reuse, who recycle who know how to reduce pollution —
By always using their bicycle! To destroy pollution and create a solution!

Who realize the importance of keeping the Earth a safe and clean haven for all
Who who know what this Earth is worth and know we'll never let it fall.
We've got one world, one chance, one hope
And without it, we won't survive so let's not mope.

Let's change the future for generations to come
'Cause if we don't change for the better what will we become?
I've got a hunch we'll make it through I know we can if we try
Without our planet, what will we do? We'll all probably just die.

So go home and think — what can I do? I'm sure you'll find some way to avail
To make our world feel like new and so we'll never fail
Never fail on making sure that our world makes it through
And we'll never be unsure that us loving our world could be untrue.
We are the guardians of our planet we have to make a change
Instead of lying around, pretending nothing's wrong 'cause our world cannot be exchanged.

Stephanie Liu, Grade 7
John Campbell Public School, ON

Satin Ivory

I sit upon a silken throne
Overlooking a meadow of satin ivory,
Between the stream,
And the stage of my grand orchestra.

The toads are my choir; the old willow, my conductor.
The jay sings the lead, and I lean back to rest.
They play not for approval, but for everlasting joy.

I am the ambassador and I ready myself for morn,
To represent a heaven such as this,
To those who need no guide.

Seannah Rose, Grade 8
Hillside Jr/Sr High School, AB

Me

I am Alice, future looking bright
I am a push over when someone needs help
I am a leader when someone needs to follow
I am dramatic when people are in trouble
I am outspoken when I do not agree
I am a reader of all sorts of things
I am a cat when I sneak around
I am a voice that stands out in a crowd
I am Bella when I trip and fall
I am Renesme cute and small
I am Edward protective in every way
I am Jane, vicious and mean
I am rain when I pour out my soul
I am living waters, the place I call home
I am myself and I like it that way

Joy-Ann Tucker, Grade 8
WP Sandin Composite High School, SK

I Am…

I am,
a portal to another dimension
the place where anything can happen
words flow out and wrap around
making the scene full of knights, heroes or creatures
sometimes I'm a mystery or maybe a romance
we're all great reads of action and chance
stories of people and places,
captured in our pages of paper and ink
I'm easy to carry and I tell fantasies of knights,
heroes and super advanced technology
I can reach out and grab the lives of people
and etch it into myself
I'm popular if I'm interesting and new and
I'm valuable if I'm old and rare
I give knowledge to young and stories for old
with unlimited titles for all ages young and old
In the night I an read aloud and I am a knight
fighting for children till they sleep.

Eric Lee, Grade 7
Westwind Elementary School, BC

Letting Go

I was scared
Remember my parents separating
Heard them fighting
Saw my mom crying
Worried that I would have to live with one or the other
Thought I was headed to a foster home
But, I want to change.

I am strong
There's a good path
Need to find it
Try to stay strong
Feel upset
Forgive my parents
Now, I can change.

I will be strong and brave
Choose to never cry
Dream my parents back together
Hope they get along
Predict they'll work it out (I hope)
Know that I will even if they don't
I will change.

Nikki Sieben, Grade 8
Heather Park Middle School, BC

Love Is a Beautiful Lie

You ask me what love is,
And I reply
Love is nothing but a beautiful lie.
On the outside it may seem great,
But only darkness and despair is inside.
My heart weighs heavy with pain,
And I always find myself calling his name.
I loved him with a flame eternal that even now it burns,
Even if nothing is there to keep the flame burning.
And after my days of grieving and pain,
My yearning for you is gone.
I know in my mind, my heart and soul will belong to you,
On and on, my love for you will always stay the same.
So now we've gone our separate ways,
During these long, harsh days,
It was your name that crossed my mind.
Of every minute, of every day.

So now do you see why I say;
Love is nothing but a beautiful lie.
And just like flowers,
Our love for one another dies.

Marlena Muir, Grade 8
Selkirk Jr High School, MB

A Dream

A dream can be soft,
like an angel's wings.
A dream can be hard,
like a gray rock in a cave.

A dream is a fading picture,
of your life beyond reality.
A dream is your soul escaping,
to distant and foreign places.

A dream is an unconscious thought,
who knows where it could take you.
Indigo Johnson, Grade 7
Barriere Elementary School, BC

The End

The energy draining day is near the end,
Calmly sitting, on a log on the beach.
Then I look up, to see the golden sun,
Setting to the west.
It's our little star looking for a friend.
Drip, drop, drip, drop
Goes the running water peacefully,
As a lone boat glides across.
It seems that the warmth
From the sun is seeping,
Through my skin,
To warm my heart.
As perfect as nature itself.
Nick McKee, Grade 7
Linwood Public School, ON

Summer

The sun is shining
Pretty flowers are growing
Ya! Summer is here
Let's go put the sprinklers on
I was waiting for this day.
Javeriya Zia, Grade 7
Homelands Senior Public School, ON

My Melody

Won't someone stop this song,
So I won't sing along?
I'm becoming addicted to the beat,
I wonder who put it on repeat.
If only I had took the chance
When I could have put it in advance,
Or perhaps I should try to rewind
But that would be just a waste of time.
The more I listen, the more I see
The better this song is coming to be.
The lyrics and rhythm, I absorb it all.
Maybe this song isn't so bad after all.
Christina Waye, Grade 8
Netagamiou School, QC

Perfection

We all strive for perfection — it's what we want to be.
It helps us live our lives in peace and harmony.
It puts a smile upon your face and makes you shine with glee.
Be all that you can be and you'll have perfection indeed.
Madelyn Whittaker, Grade 8
Bessborough Drive Public School, ON

Moments Like These

For a moment, I sit here motionless
The clicking of my clip echoes in my head
So silent around me, I can almost feel its soundwaves
Beginning to ring in my ears and screams for an end
But my fingers keep reopening and closing my hairclip
On the beat, it remains, while the blurred faces of old friends speed by
With their slurred quotes and signature physicalities
Our memories carved in my mind
The silence between me and pure nothingness
It's deafening, I want it to end
Rage is gaining up on me, I've lost control of my mind
It's me against my outer shell
Remembering how it used to be
Movie nights, immaturity, inside jokes
And now, now everyone's changed
Claiming that they're merely living their teenage lives
When in reality they may be losing them
This moment of silence is purely a wake up call
A realization that your life may be swerving downhill
But you need to help others, so that they might, just might,
Have moments like these.

Kristen Vanderwee, Grade 8
Macdonald High School, QC

Daddy*

Dear Daddy,
I only knew you for three and a half years.
And I wish you could have stayed longer.
But you didn't and I guess that's life,
There are so many things I wish I would have done with you.
And I am going to tell you that wherever I go,
You are not far behind,
Only because I truly love you.
Even though you are gone, I still look up to you,
And tell you in a way, "You are still and *always* will be my role model."

I know that I am your daughter,
Because I have your hair.
It curls like you wouldn't believe,
And it gets annoying sometimes.
For now that is all I want to tell you,
But really for real,
I just really, really, miss you!!!!

Roxane Navert, Grade 8
Macdonald High School, QC
*Dedicated to my father Gilles Navert who passed away on April 29, 1998.

A Sweet Surprise

Halloween is the night to be spooky and scary,
Or even dress up like a beautiful fairy,
So, here I am, an extinct dinosaur,
Going around and knocking on every door,
Waiting to munch on everything that's sweet,
Ignoring what the dentist told me not to eat,
Walking down the streets for hours and hours,
Yelling trick or treat for sweets and sours,
Why are these people screaming so loud?
And calling me the loser of this crowd,
It's getting dark, I'm getting a scare,
How many more miles do I have to bear,
I wonder why people are still staring at me,
Could it be my bag, just could it be,
Hey! No! Where's all of my candy,
I feel so foolish, so distracted,
This is not the way I should have acted,
I should have looked, I should have checked,
Now this Halloween is surely recked,
I might as well knock my head on that pole,
Ah! Why did my bag have to have such a big hole?

Taskeen Ahluwalia, Grade 8
The Valleys Senior Public School, ON

That Is Who I Am

I am like the sun, keeping very bright
with my light shining today.
I am unique, just like every snowflake
I watch go down the lake.

You can say that I am like an open door
I never close it when someone is feeling poor.
I am like a baby bird,
I will never give up till I get my freedom.

Just like a book,
I am always looking for adventures and finding new ways.
I am like a lock,
tell me a secret and it will always be safe with me.

I am like a big wave in the ocean,
strong and powerful, nothing can stop me from being me.
I can be as silent as a mouse,
but I am also outgoing like the dancing colours in the sky.

I am like a photo album,
all I keep is nothing but good memories.
Just like music notes, I like to go with the flow.
I am who I am, I am me.

Julie LeClair, Grade 7
École Séparée Lorrain, ON

A Rushing Snowplow

Roar, screech, rumble,
its advancing like a blasting jet,
ROAR, like a thunderstorm approaching,
A scary monster promising along.
Roar, screech, rumble,
Like a giant rough rock,
Appearing to devour the glittering snow,
Crushing millions of glittering snowflakes.
Roar, screech, rumble,
Snowflakes fling around,
Coming to settle.
But — roar, screech, rumble,
Here it appears,
The huge, rough, booming
        Snowplow

Angie Brubacher, Grade 7
Linwood Public School, ON

My Generation

My generation will always change,
It will never be the same.
The next generation will create new stuff,
To make life less tough.
Like flying cars,
Or moving to mars.
The older generations will not be pleased,
Wait until they get ceased.
My generation has created lots of new things,
But by 2015 we kids will be kings.
I hope other people are like me,
Always being happy and full of glee.

This is my generation and it will always change.

Darian Elliott, Grade 8
Dewberry School, AB

Question?

Wind blows fast
Take your time 'cause the moment won't last
I don't care but I think I should
You won't talk to me but I wish you would
I try to hold back
I try not to let it show
But everywhere I go, I see you
You're like an ongoing show
Express
Compel
Given, might as well
It's no longer about me
It's no longer about you
I know we have our problems
But, if we don't talk…

What am I to do?

Jamilah Dei-Sharpe, Grade 8
Fairwind Senior School, ON

You're My Everything
You're my everything,
Everything to me.
I'm your nothing,
Nothing to see.

You walk past me,
In the hall.
You don't look,
I'm ready to fall.

You're my all,
You're my everything.
And for you,
I'll do anything.

I won't disappear,
I won't go away.
You may think that,
But it won't come, that day.

You love me,
I love you.
But with every day,
We don't know what to do.
Dylan Maddocks, Grade 8
Westview School, AB

Flames
Oh sad flames
So tiny and dull
Leaving me in darkness
How can I make it all right?

Oh hungry flames
Gulping up the wood
Then asking me for more
How can I do it all in one night?

Oh angry flames
Sometimes puny, often giant
So different so unsteady
What can I do without a fight?

Oh happy flames
Dancing in the dark
Lighting up my room
Much to my delight!

Though every flame is different
Sad, hungry or even happy
Deep, deep down in every flame
Is still a bit of light.
Nathalie Janssen, Grade 7
Westwind Elementary School, BC

War
We are now at war
Weapons of mass destruction
Planes flying above
Dropping bombs down to the ground
Will I make it home again
Joel Bruce, Grade 8
Kennedy Langbank School, SK

Wash Away
I don't get why,
You catch my eye,
My heart swims,
Growing wings for it to fly,
To soar clearly upon blue caress,
Suddenly thirst attacks me,
The rainfall seemed to have defeated,
The overpowering burn,
Sunshine break cloud,
Overtaking the gray sky,
It calls your name!
It asks you why?
Arising to the way I feel for you,
So lost,
So in love,
with you once again.
Keighlan Gustus, Grade 8
Vanier Catholic Secondary School, YT

What If…
What if books were all movies
And we never had to read
Would our brains go to mush
Or would they be as small as a seed

What if horses wore hats
To keep away the sun
And what if cows wore slippers
And thought they were lots of fun

What if the world were square
And not round
Would we fall off the edge
Or would we just not make a sound
Jacey Tarr, Grade 8
Kennedy Langbank School, SK

The Boys of Months
There is a boy named December
Who was related to November
Who wished he was July
So he could say bye-bye
Then he was actually September
Cody Dan, Grade 7
Sxoxomic Community School, BC

Dear Judges,
I wrote so many poems,
I was unable to decide,
Which one I should send you,
So go ahead and cry.

I'm an awesome poet,
Everyone agrees!
But it's so *very* sad,
You won't get a rhyme from me.

I wrote on so many wonders,
Socks, trees, and flies!
Everything you could imagine,
Rocks, knees and skies!

So here is my apology,
It was a good contest.
But out of all my poems
I didn't know which was best!

Ring up your secretary,
I know this news must hurt.
Tell her you didn't receive a poem,
From Miss Mary-Joy Schellert.
Mary-Joy Schellert, Grade 8
Bella Coola Adventist Academy, BC

Fall
Leaves fall
like a light blanket.
Animals hide
School opens
Summer fades
Wind blows
Bugs die
Hunters hunt
Temperature drops
Lakes freeze
Snow falls
like a heavy quilt.
Alana Legeard, Grade 8
Heather Park Middle School, BC

Soccer
Running down the field,
Using my body as a shield,
To protect the soccer ball,
As I'm running I trip and fall,
My check takes a shot,
But the goalie already had it caught,
The final score was 2-3,
We had won thanks to the goalie.
Jason Deol, Grade 7
Eugene Reimer Middle School, BC

Blue Summer

A clear blue sky in the summer of May
Filled with clouds and rare blue jay

A wave like no other splashes the shore
Rises from the depths of the blue ocean floor

Searching for blue seashells that shined
But sadly there's not one I could find

Riya George, Grade 7
James S Woodsworth Senior Public School, ON

Something Inside

Is there another being locked deep inside of me?
Waiting in my deepest depths for me to set them free?
Am I the only one who sees the stars, widespread?
The only one who sees the things I see inside my head?

Or is there a greater glory out there waiting just for me?
Is there another part of my inner being?
Reading my story, page by page?
Watching, waiting, silently backstage?

Have they yet read my last chapter?
Is it left yet to be seen?
The time is now, to change my story, to be the main actor,
To change what has not yet been.

Amanda Sylvester, Grade 9
Bert Church High School, AB

Be Fair

To have lots of friends, you must be fair
You must be kind and just
You have to give them a chance and care about them
Admit when you're wrong, you must

You must be an honourable person
You must be someone everyone knows they can trust
You can't cheat at games or copy someone's work
Be truthful and honest, you must

You have to help out your friends
And never ever be unjust
Treat everyone the same
Think of everyone as equal, you must

You should give everyone the benefit of the doubt
Don't get angry for no reason or combust
Give everyone a fair chance
Don't judge anyone harshly, you must

You have to be a good person
And not someone your friends mistrust
And then you will know that you're doing well
Be a good person and be fair, you must

Rachel Bromberg, Grade 8
Pleasantville Public School, ON

Space

I walk underneath the sky so bright,
To me, this is a gorgeous night.
I wish you were here to catch a glimpse of Mars,
Even though I know you're in amongst the stars.

Shelby Kaczur, Grade 8
Macdonald School, SK

Dream

I'm standing here in the pouring rain,
I can't see what's in front of my face,
The rain is so thick

I'm trying to walk,
But my mind is blank,
I'm trying to find what I'm looking for,
But can't find anything,
I'm seeking so hard,
But nothing is happening

I walk a little further,
And there's a light,
The light is so bright,
I think it's what I'm looking for,
But I'm wrong

It's just my dad opening the curtains,
Saying wake up,
So I wake up just to find out it was only a dream.

Jamie Gagnier, Grade 7
Our Lady of the Annunciation Catholic School, ON

The Untouched Pie

I said yes
To cleaning up the mess
That he left behind again
I have to mend
The holes he left
I told him no more theft
He wasn't allowed to take my heart
So I tore apart
Even though it left him staring at his pie
With silent tears tumbling down onto his tie
And I started weeping
So I ran away
That was the last time
I'd ever seen such dazzling eyes
But that's all in the past
Now I'm standing here staring up at the sky
And wondering if he ever touched his pie.

Celine Grimard, Grade 8
Holy Cross School, SK

Leaves Budding

Leaves budding
trees waking
rivers flooding
ice breaking

Winter is gone
spring here to stay
light out at dawn
how beautiful is May

Flowers opening
caterpillars crawling
apples growing
summer is calling

Mud squelching
children playing
birds singing
willows swaying

Leaves budding
trees waking
rivers flooding
ice breaking

Julia Sieben, Grade 7
New Horizons School, AB

Fall

Falling leaves
Frost, cooler, flurries
Thanksgiving, Halloween, birds
Easter, newness, rain
Growth, beauty
Spring

Philip Dunphy, Grade 7
St Anne School, AB

Love

Love is a powerful thing
That doesn't always happen
But when it does,
You must cherish it forever

Love is so beautiful
That sometimes it's hard to see
You must open your eyes
And realize
That love is so unique

Love is unforgettable
That will stay with you forever
No matter who you're with,
No matter what you do
Love will always find you

Katheryn Morrissette, Grade 7
Macdonald High School, QC

Would You Love Me

Would you
Love me if I had the great riches of El Dorado?
Would you
Love me if I were as poor as the bum I see walking by my house?
Would you
Love me if I had the greatest personality in the world?
Would you
Love me if I had the best looks in the world?
Would you
Love me if I had all the stuff that you ever wanted?
Would you
Love me if I were just myself?

Brandon Prance, Grade 7
OV Jewitt Community School, MB

Voyage

You arrive on earth, escaping your prison.
Surrounded by demons in white.
Right after you're born, your class is in session,
Your roller coaster ride begins and you enter a maze, evading the exit.
When born, a four-legged creature, consuming from a gentle baby bottle.
As you mature, the coaster will go up and down.
You'll approach dead ends within your maze, and will learn new lessons every day.
Time begins to slip away, and before you know it, you'll be lying on your deathbed.
Scanning through your experiences, with your frail, exhausted mind.
As your time winds down, you've realized, the ride has expired,
You've been dismissed from class, and you've reached the exit of the maze,
The exit you stalled to confront, once the lights reach out to you,
Bid farewell to Earth, and greet hello to heaven…Or hell.

Ricky Guan, Grade 7
Blundell Elementary School, BC

Cold Day in Canada

A deep breath
Sharp cold air fills my lungs
Everything seems so peaceful
A little bird is curled up
Upon the delicate frost patterned branches that gradate from white to grey
A deep breath
Clearing my mind…The cold wraps itself around my contour
My cheeks, my nose, my fingers, my thighs
All tingle with the cold
My eyelashes stick together sometimes
A reminder of the temperature
Deep breath
The insides of my nose freeze as the fresh chilled air is inhaled
I look down
A few snowflakes float down from my hair at this small movement
The snow sparkles like millions of microscopic crystals
Each of them unique
I close my eyes and inhale
A deep breath
I sigh…so content
To be in this beautiful winter wonderland we call our home.

Noelle Wilmering, Grade 8
Laurelwood Public School, ON

Wish

I wished upon a star
that you would come
but you were far

You said you loved me
and off you went

Someone sent me flowers
I saw them when I came out of the shower
on the flower there was a note
saying you were gone

As tears ran down my face
my heart went at a fast pace
I burst out crying
I wish they were lying

But you were gone
and I wished upon a star
that you would come
but you are too far.

Sydney Legare, Grade 7
Macdonald High School, QC

The Palm Tree Sways

The palm tree sways in the air,
Side to side without a care,
Gently whispering in your ear,
"You are at peace when you are here."

The palm tree dances gentle and slow,
Passive and patient, with nowhere to go,
Gently moving with the gusts,
The simple palm tree has no lusts.

The palm tree waits for you all day,
When you come it has naught to say,
Gently waving when you pass,
Its leaves, sun-stroked, calm and green as grass.

The palm tree tickles you as you go by,
Its simple way of saying "Hi,"
Gently saying hello and good bye,
Passive and patient, without a sigh.

The palm tree sways in the air,
Side to side without a care,
Gently whispering in your ear,
"You are at peace when you are here."

Kate Ward, Grade 7
Westwind Elementary School, BC

He Likes to Run

My horse likes to run
He is a young stud colt
The color of chestnuts
He likes to run.

Jumps and bucks over rocks
Respects the fence
Smart as a whip
He likes to run.

Eats hay and oats
Carrots and apples are treats
No sugar for him
He likes to run.

Likes to socialize with other horses
A nose rub is appreciated
Willing to be rode
He likes to run.
He likes to run.

Ross Taylor, Grade 7
Community Bible Fellowship Christian School, MB

A Forever Lastin' Friendship

My friend Alexia, can it really be
That we've been best friends since four years ago?
I swear you do mean everything to me,
And when I see your face my smile glows.

As best friends, we were meant to spend our life,
Having so much fun, we knew we'd last
Losing you would be like getting stabbed by a knife,
Every moment spent together was always a blast.

Getting in a fight with you would be rare,
Our busy lives, known both smooth and rough;
Without each other, we could never bare,
Our friendship kept us strong when things got tough.

To me you're a beautiful golden feather,
I love you Alexia, always and forever.

Serena Trignano, Grade 8
LaSalle Catholic Comp High School, QC

Tropical Beach

Have you ever been to a tropical beach?
Where the sand is smooth and so white.
And ate a delicious, juicy, peach.
Have you ever been to a tropical beach?
And the ocean seemed out of your reach?
But, enjoying the sun so hot and bright.
Have you ever been to a tropical beach?
Where the sand is smooth and so white.

Sinthuja Selvakumaran, Grade 7
St Patrick's Elementary School, BC

The Killers

They were kids with an ambition in life.
They wanted to become rock stars and have the time of their lives.
Rock and roll music brought in so much effect.
They practiced and practiced until everything was perfect.
They knew that they were able to achieve their goals, if they tried.
They wrote songs together about truth and pride.
They finally got a record deal when they were recognized.
By Island Records, who knew that this is the best band that they could find.
They wrote more songs and recorded an album or two.
Their name is The Killers and they are the best band since 2002!

Janna Katsouros, Grade 8
Macdonald High School, QC

This Room

There's this room,
With decks of cards, and light bulbs strung.
With wracks of old things, lost or forgotten.
There's this room,
Far off in a basement, where old walls cannot suffocate,
The screaming sirens of police, fighting dingy crimes.
There's this room,
Where players stick to their seats, in thin shirts, hairy chests revealed.
Their eyes shift, men not to be double-crossed.
There's this room,
Where sweaty, dirty adults go to play a dangerous game.
Where fate lies on the faces of the cards, and in the hands of the addicts.
There's this room,
That destroys lives.
Where families are lost, because daddies and brothers gamble away everything.
There's this room,
And in it, monsters are made.

Jenna Gould, Grade 9
Frontenac Secondary School, ON

Longing

The stars scrunched too close together in the midnight sky, like too much confetti on a game show's season finale.
But I could hardly complain.
The jagged, unearthly mountains closed around the innocence of our tiny, warm-looking town;
protecting us, holding us.
Gentle, whispy clouds drifted easily across the darkened sky,
eerily, yet beautifully illuminated by the titanic moon.
Like a cookie cutter, the mountains halfway covered the shining sphere,
their silhouette making it appear as if someone had taken a bite out of it.
The crisp, fall air seemed too cold to accommodate the crickets and their persistent chirping,
yet there it was.
As annoying but peaceful as ever, their cries echoed across the valley,
sending a comforting sense of belonging to the fortunate soul's ears it reached.
While I sat, pensively and comfortably, the towering, distant rocks called to me,
promising discovery and adventure beyond the dangerous peaks in view.
But I knew I couldn't listen.
As much as it pained me, I had already accepted the fact I wasn't prepared for the task.
I would wait…for now at least.

Kiara Robillard, Grade 8
Westview School, AB

Long Endless Road

Long, straight, narrow, abandon road,
I drive.
I been driving on this road for far too long.
I've been trying to get me back home.
I been traveling on this road for far too long.
Long endless road.

Chelsea Thorsell, Grade 8
Rutland Middle School, BC

Miami

The blazing, scorching sun above me,
Burns me up like I'm its enemy.
The basketball players, Miami Heat,
I love this place it's extremely sweet.

The people around are truly kind,
"I wanna' live here mom!" I whined.
The C.S.I. people I want to meet,
I love this place it's extremely sweet.

The beaches were filled with white sand,
It burned my eyes and feet as I stepped on the land.
I went in the water, took a dip with my feet,
I love this place it's extremely sweet.

My cousin bought me a gold Miami shirt,
People's eyes around me started to hurt!
We had fun it was a very nice treat,
I love this place it's extremely sweet.

Carlota Reyes, Grade 7
St Patrick's Elementary School, BC

You

Wrap yourself in a word.
It's you.
It's what you think defines you.
Wrap yourself in a world.
It's your home.
It's where you think you belong.
Wrap yourself in an object.
It's your obsession.
It's what you think you'll always need.
Wrap yourself in a person.
They're your safety.
They block the bad things.
You are oblivious to your surroundings.
And when a storm clouds over,
You find a loose string.
So you pull on it.
And not knowing yourself,
You must search your limits.
Your "safety" blanket comes undone.
And you find that you wrapped yourself away from you.

Brunna Ribeiro, Grade 8
Laurelwood Public School, ON

Dark Shadows

The trees sway back and forth.
The rustling sounds leave shivers up my spine,
Blowing cool air against my hair,
Tickling my flesh, chilling me to the bone.
The howling uproar captures my attention,
Relying on me to search for my own shadow.
Glistening lights of the streets shimmer.
They dance around me silently,
Creating an unseen wall,
Between the darkness and light.
My shadow is a cold quiet mouse.
It copies whatever I do,
Even with all the distractions, it perseveres.
My shadow is an invisible being,
It creates large black creatures that haunt,
Dark figures that walk by,
The colors drain from their faces,
Revealing the hesitation of many.
My shadow is a spooky ghost.
It disappears at night, but appear, once again,
As the morning approaches us.

Deborah Peng, Grade 7
Westwind Elementary School, BC

I Will

Snow… I remember that
It's beautiful right?
It's white… and really bright
I don't see it anymore
Well it's over now, the doctors say I can't

I look at the mountains
I walk out in the sun
Life is different, it's not fun
People always stare and I really do care
Well it's over now the people say I can't

School is hard
I know people tease me
They act as if I'm a flea
When they approach me
Well it's over now my friends say I can't

The time is here, it's time to fight, I can make it, I just might
We can do it together, it will be a fright
But knowing you're there, I think I'll be all right
There are two words I keep hearing from time to time
I can't, I can't, I can't
But this one time, *I will*

Noojan Mazaheri, Grade 8
Mulgrave School, BC

King of the Court

Smudge doesn't have a crown,
Nor a throne on which to sit down.
He's a kingly, furry beast.
Upon the cowering mouse he'll feast.
A towering, black, massive beast
With sharp, pointed, shark teeth,
Softened by a white cloudy patch
With crooked ears and paws that match.
He wanders through his court at night.
Other cats bow down in his sight.
He fights and prances, and often sneezes,
And every night, does what he pleases.

Joshua McMuldrock, Grade 7
Westwind Elementary School, BC

Spring

Spring is here
I'm happy to say
The birds and bunnies
Have come to play
The snow is melting
The puddles are forming
The sun is shining
I hope it's here to stay.

Nicole Klassen, Grade 7
St Paul School, SK

My Little Kitty

Fluffy and cute
Happy and playful
Grey
Two white spots
Small
Four paws
Two little ears
Smell and eyesight
Are very keen
My little kitty is a cuddling machine

Mark Mosure, Grade 8
Heather Park Middle School, BC

Our Horse

Our horse, strong and full of muscle
Golden as the sun,
Its body, smooth under my hand,
Four white feet race like the wind
On an autumn day,
The hooves stamp on the road
Like thundering typhoons.
It whinnies, galloping jumping
over the creek in our field.
Young and powerful it pulls our wagon
without much effort at all.
Our horse is a wonderful animal.

Anson Martin, Grade 7
Linwood Public School, ON

Age

Shall I compare thee to the wilting beauty of our sky
Its streams of light glazed all things you have not touched
You who let things pass
You who have stood by while the world turned to ashes
You who helped the old man die
You whose fixed stare melts possessions
You who all beings fear
You who goes on eternally
Never stopping
You are ageless
For you are age

Nicholas Marriott, Grade 8
Vancouver Waldorf School, BC

Before I Hit the Bucket

In a day or two I'll butcher chickens for the first time, with my bare hands
you see, I got this list of things I'd like to do 'Before I Hit the Bucket'
so maybe someday they'll be machines to butcher the chickens for me
and maybe I'll fly to Hamiota in a plane all by myself for a doctor's checkup
I'd love to drive somewhere far and wide on a small green or red flying car
or maybe ride on an elephant and then hop onto the giraffe's back
I'd feel quite thrilled when all is done then I'll ride on a roller coaster
that sweeps underground and curves in a ball and flies through the air
then I'd go skydiving with a friend and faaaaaaaaaaaaaall through thin air
from there I'd go scuba diving with the whales, sharks and the fish
and be in the newspaper oh the fame, what a thrill
I'd have a jet all on my own and invite friends for a ride
and have tea, in a house made of glass what a swell time I want to have
before I hit the bucket come along with me, and join the fun.

Estelle Wollman, Grade 9
Decker Colony School, MB

The Years I Don't Remember

I don't remember seeing the soldiers fighting for their lives.
I don't remember seeing the poppies growing in the fields.
I don't remember hearing the sounds of guns going through my ears.
I don't remember the feeling of losing a loved one or a friend.
I don't remember feeling the mud on my face.
I don't remember hearing the cries for help.
I don't remember the feeling of losing a leg, arm, or my sight.

But I do remember the sounds of cries for joy.
I do remember hearing the sounds of birds singing in the morning.
I do remember waking up in the morning with the feeling I'm safe.
I do remember seeing soldiers handing out poppies on Remembrance Day.
I do remember sounds of joy and not sorrow.
I do remember feeling thankful for what they gave us.
I do remember the peace and freedom we have today.

I hope I will still hear the birds singing and the kids laughing next morning.
I hope life will be safe for the next day, year or millennium.
I wish the fight will just stop and the peace will begin.
I believe we can change the world if we quit the fighting.
I think about this wish every day and hope soon it will come true.

Waris Ismail, Grade 7
Blundell Elementary School, BC

The Showcase

Her eyes (she lies) are crystal clear,
to loath his piece of art;
for cracks are here, and pieces lack there,
to form what seems to be abstract.
Yet, a showcase down reveals a frame
of marble and pure gold.

"Ooo's" and "Ahh's" fill the room
to whom it's only fair. The frame.
When suddenly, to all's surprise, a voice calls out,
"I am standing here, my eye's crystal clear,
and all I see is an empty frame."

Confused faces turn from the boy to the frame
and stare in disbelief. Just an empty frame.
The boy then walks a showcase down,
only to be followed by a discouraged crowd.

Once again the boy calls out, "I am standing here,
my eyes crystal clear, and I can't help but stare at
this magnificent piece of art. There are cracks here,
and it's lacking pieces there, but yet it is full of beauty."

"Ooo's" and "Ahh's" then fill the room,
to whom it's only fair. She blinks.

Tunchai Redvers, Grade 9
Sir John Franklin School, NT

Way Up There

Hey you say, love is on its way,
It's closer every day, as I think how you'll pay.
You're so sweet,
I can feel my heart beat,
But you cheat,
As I got weak.
You're like a dove,
So up above,
But you can't love,
'Cause you're the only one you think of.
I thought we were going to last,
But that was in the past,
Our relationship sure ended fast,
It looked like you had a blast.
I told myself you were so bad.
I could feel the pressure build as I got mad.
You could tell by the look in my eyes that I was sad.
I said in my head if only he had.
Said one little word that meant so much
We could have meant so much more.

Ashley Rudiger, Grade 8
École Séparée Lorrain, ON

The Question

Receiving hugs and giving kisses,
Don't forget to tell the Misses,
Love fills the air,
The night sky is almost as lovely as her hair.
You look into her adoring eyes,
And feel just like you're hypnotized.
You wonder if she feels it too,
The questions just pops out of the blue.
"Will you marry me Jess?"
"Oh Alan, yes!"
You get down on one knee and show her the ring,
She feels like she could fly, like she's going to sing.

Brianna Foss, Grade 8
St Mary's High School, ON

Where Will I Be

I saw you guys and what you went through
I looked at myself in the mirror and saw all of you
You look at me as if I'm a hero
I look at you as if you were a zero
You've done nothing with your lives so why should I
I'm flesh and blood and look at me so far
And you always tell me that I will go far
I don't believe you so I won't try
You take me and shake me and tell me don't cry
I guess it's true and I can't deny
I will become something and you will cry for me
The tears of joy
But no matter what
I'm still a Ward Boy

Kolten Ward, Grade 9
Selkirk Jr High School, MB

My Last Adventure!

Slowly drifting down…down…down
Bubbles rising all around,
Seaweed tickling at my toes,
The crisp sea water pinches my nose.

I swim forward just to see,
A giant octopus right beneath me!

There's a reef ahead with tropical fish,
Not one of their colours you could miss.

I round a bend and come into view,
Of a wide open space coloured with blue.

A whale of imposing size has spotted me,
So I hide behind this rock to wait and see.

Oh me! Oh my! I cannot see in this dark,
The rock that I've found is really a SHAR…

Tyanna Dixon, Grade 8
Bella Coola Adventist Academy, BC

Life

From your first step
To your last breath
From childhood
To death

There are so many things
That one can achieve
Throughout their life
If they believe

To save the environment
To help others in need
To fulfill your goals
Or to do a good deed

Live life to its fullest
For it is very short
Do whatever you can
And give yourself support

So as life passes by
Do things in a variety
For the question is:
What are you doing for your society?

Joey Thompson, Grade 8
Mulgrave School, BC

Natural Fire

How can you expect to find,
Something fresh and new,
When you cannot even find,
What's in front of you.

How can you expect to see,
What is hidden from your eyes,
When you cannot even see,
Where the truth really lies.

How can you expect to smell,
All the scents you knew,
When you cannot even smell,
The ones the wind gives to you.

How can you expect to hear,
What everyone has said,
When you cannot even hear,
The voice inside your head.

How can you expect to feel,
Your minds every desire,
When you cannot even feel,
Your heart's natural fire.

Kayla Brick, Grade 8
JA Cuddy Elementary School, MB

Mice

The mice want a big block of cheese
Running around
Smells the cheese
Runs forward

Running around
Snap a trap
Runs forward
Waiting until they find the cheese

Snap a trap
They found it
Waiting until they find the cheese
Then it's gone

They found it
Smells the cheese
Then it's gone
The mice want a big block of cheese

Angelica Lai, Grade 7
Menno Simons Christian School, AB

The Snowman

We built a snowman,
Built him out of snow;
Should have seen how fine he was,
All white from top to toe.

Poured some water over him,
To freeze his legs and ears;
When we went indoors to bed,
We thought he'd last for years.

But, in the night a warmer kind
Of wind began to blow;
Jack Frost cried and ran away,
With him went the snow.

Devin Logan, Grade 8
Heather Park Middle School, BC

Nature

Darkness fills the air,
The moon pierce through the night,
Glowing brightly in the sky.

A cherry blossom,
That's forgotten its' color,
It's now a snowflake

A red moon,
Surrounded by a red light,
Shining through darkness

Timothy Yeung, Grade 7
Blundell Elementary School, BC

A Ride with My Dad

I feel the wind in my hair
I can see road everywhere
As I ride on my dad's gold wing
I feel that I can sing
As I smell the clean fresh air
This time with my dad is very rare
I don't like to hike
I'd rather ride the bike
I will never get sad
If I ride with my dad

Laura Spyker, Grade 7
Westside Academy, BC

Imitation of Beauty

The faint glow of a morning sun,
that is what you imitate
when your light filters through

so subtly that it may be a mirage.
I can't really tell
if you are real

or if you simply pretend to be real.
If so I will let you know,
it's working.

Amy Hinz, Grade 9
Muenster School, SK

Other Girls

Some girls are so original,
Different,
Weird
And so obscene.

Others are so tiny,
Beautiful,
Snobby
And so clean.

Some girls are so athletic
Courteous,
Kind
And smart.

But thinking about all of this
Gives me a heavy heart...
God knows that I'm not
Perfect;
I know that I'm not
Small.
But I always need to stop and think
Of what I wish to be at all.

Jane Steward, Grade 9
Mount Prevost Middle School, BC

Love…Is It?

This word doesn't say it all…love…is it?
Now let us not love in word, rather truth.
Now look at us, in love is that just it?
We say that's all but we always hide truth,
Truth of fear, of death, of separation.
We say it's true love that's just a thought.
So, say what may it be? An illusion.
You see this true love, it cannot be bought.
Not sold at the market, not bought by stock.
It's only found deep, deep down in ones heart.
We had good times when we would walk and talk.
But these words had never come from ones heart.
We live these lies that we are constantly told.
We will stay together, 'till we get old.

Nourhan Nasrallah, Grade 9
Hon W C Kennedy Collegiate Institute, ON

Twilight

You sit all alone
In the darkness of twilight.
Thinking of your way of life,
And how it, in ways, has been wasted away.
Gazing at everything fly by, soon it's the end
Of the year.
You're waiting for your name to be called,
Because it's your graduating year.
After the grad video,
You say to all your friends, goodbye.
Forgetting that you'll see all of them again
During the exquisite summer
Sleepovers and birthday parties,
Not inviting certain people.
Leaving them to wander around in the darkness
Of Twilight.

Mariah Elyse Mirzayan, Grade 7
Blundell Elementary School, BC

Beautiful

As I look into your eyes,
They sparkled,
Like stars in the sky.

I was breathless,
Heart taken,
And speechless.

There were many words I could have said,
But I didn't know how to say them.
They were all misspelled in my head.

You were as beautiful as a dove
Flying in the sky,
But I didn't know how to express my love.

Carley Brett, Grade 7
Dewberry School, AB

I Miss You

I really miss the days we walked
And all the times we laughed and talked.
I really wish that you were here
I just can't help but shed a tear.
There's pictures of us on my wall
Smiling under the trees so tall.
I loved your cute, sweet, friendly hugs
I can't ignore the pain that tugs.
There's things I truly wish to say
But I just can't…another day!

So hopefully you'll know for sure
That I am just a bit demure.
I really do hope that someday
You'll know in your heart what I wanted to say.

Natalie Penner, Grade 8
Community Bible Fellowship Christian School, MB

I Just Want You Back

Life is anomalous; it's not cut out for me
I just don't fit in, while you fit perfectly
I wish I was stronger, intellectual and courageous
To be striking and exquisite, exultant and audacious
Take me away, because I feel like I'm falling
My very existence is what I'm forestalling
To live in a world that's problem-free
To be the person you want me to be
You left me there disheartened and wrecked
I lost your love and your respect
Being without you is like a heart attack
Darling, I just want you back

Samantha Deeley, Grade 8
Macdonald High School, QC

Very Bad Day

The weather is raining
sh — sh — sh — sh

My umbrella bounces the rain
pop — pop — pop — pop

Sliding on water
p-wow — p-wow

My umbrella flies away
hoo-weeeeee

After midnight, I am home, my mom shouts
aa — akk!!

David Park, Grade 7
Menno Simons Christian School, AB

A Friend

A friend stays forever
Not because he's clever
It's because he cares about you
He would never try to harm you
He will be at your side all the time
Even when you climb
No matter what happens
You will always be forgiven
A friend is like a brother
We just don't look like each other.

Yousef Sheteiwy, Grade 8
Pineland Public School, ON

Lone Soul

Is it wrong to be different,
Or to have different pain?
I'm not retarded,
But I might just be insane.
Sometimes I'm just unnoticed,
Sometimes broken down
With reasons unexplained
And actions that confound.

Nobody's perfect,
Yet I'm the one to blame
For other people's mishaps
And for others' vexing shame.
I am a lone soul
And I am exiled
I walk alone now
Like a convicted child.

So now I walk alone
But I do not mind
I'd rather be alone
Than with those stereotypical kind.

Joel Krause, Grade 9
Webber Academy, AB

Central Park

A peaceful garden
Lights the flat city landscape
A cotton pillow
Of bright colorful fabrics
Paradise in a dark world

Lilly Gates, Grade 7
John Campbell Public School, ON

Illusions

Illusions
Awesome, distorted
Grasping your attention
Collapsing images with potential
Optical-obstacles

Hanna Sweet, Grade 8
Odessa Public School, ON

Finally Home to Stay

As his life flashed before his eyes I felt as if time stood still,
He didn't make a sound but tears were running down his cheeks.
I wish he didn't feel this way,
No one deserves to feel this way.
He looked tortured and wounded and he had a defeated look in his eyes.
As I held his cold body in my shaking arms I wanted to yell you're too young to go,
But I didn't I just couldn't.
I loved you for so long and the thought of it all being over in just one night,
Makes me want to bawl!
I sobbed in spite of myself,
But when I looked down at your pale helpless face,
I sobbed harder, but in spite of you.
I listened to your heartbeat slowly stopping,
I tried to capture the sound for the very last time,
I knew it wouldn't be much longer until your little heart would never beat again.
His heart got slower and slower until it finally stopped.
There you lay motionless in my arms,
And I couldn't help but thinking,
You took the long way around,
But, you're finally home to stay.

Abby White, Grade 8
St Mary Separate School, ON

I Can't Be Without You…

A part of me went missing yesterday, and I didn't know why I felt that way;
But once I realized, I remember the lies;

The way I felt, when I looked in your eyes;
The missing part of me, is now clear to see…

Your heart is cold, you're hard to hold;
You broke my heart, now we're apart;

You left me in despair, like you didn't care;
All those lies, you couldn't hide;

All those memories, and now we're enemies;
You felt no pain, I couldn't say the same;

Once you were gone, my heart became strong;
I know it's true, but that can't keep me away from you.

Samantha Martin, Grade 8
Macdonald High School, QC

Imagine

Imagine swiping your toes across a crystal floor
the rhythm of the music taking your body and swaying it back and forth
spinning across the floor like a wild tornado taking over the countryside
your stomach tossing and turning as you take over the firm stage
your heart starts racing
as you hear the first beat of the music
ringing in your ears

Abby Warren, Grade 9
Leo Hayes High School, NB

Dreaming

It has been a long, hard day
And I'm finally going to bed
No, I'm not excited for the rest
I'm getting out of my head

I'm in a very distant land
Where no one's quiet or sullen
Where I can ride a dragon, or be on TV
Or even meet Edward Cullen

Harry Potter is totally real
And humans can actually fly
Animals can talk, and trees can dance
And the Grand Canyon is filled with pie

In this place, the world is perfect
There's no traffic or pollution
The ozone here is completely intact
And each problem has a solution

Oh, how I wish this strange and wonderful land
Were how every person could be living
But sadly, this can never be
So I guess I'll just keep dreaming

Sarah Hollywood, Grade 9
Bowmanville High School, ON

Octomom Hypocrisy

Octomom
Run out of tentacles
Struggling 14 kids
With only 8 arms
Her defensive suckers
Won't let them get her

Drilling holes with her radula
To get what she wants
Looking like Angie Jolie
Won't help her bizarre behavior

Though she has octopus intelligence
It won't get her far
With many worries on her gills
She's addicted to feeling superior

Real tragedy,
National Scandal.
But what has happened?
We created Octomom

Ayat Nizam, Grade 9
Hon W C Kennedy Collegiate Institute, ON

Hope

I have Hope
That I will grow stronger
I have Hope
That I will be a better person
I have Hope
That I'll succeed
I have Hope
That if I fall I will get up again and again
I have Hope
That we will find a cure for cancer
I have Hope
That we can make our world a better place to live
I have Hope
That I will live happily
I have Hope

Shawn Hendren, Grade 8
Royal Orchard Middle School, ON

I Love You

I love you
But do you love me?
This has been my ongoing question for years
As hard as I look and as hard as I try
I am still left empty inside
You have abandoned me and left me on my own
Therefore my love for you sometimes escapes me
I ask myself why do I love you and keep coming home
My life would be much less complex without you
But the deeper I search, I discover that I love you
Because you are my mother

And I will do whatever it takes to be by your side
Through the good and the bad and the inevitable

Lauren Gardner, Grade 7
Macdonald High School, QC

The Monster I Have Become

They are surrounding me,
the negative thoughts,
they really shouldn't be there,
the ones I love have turned me into a monster,
transformed me into a clone,
but I love it so much,
seeing the look of devastation,
but it's so wrong,
I try to stop but the acceptance overwhelms the conscience,
maybe one day they will forgive and forget,
but hurting tons of people for just a few you love,
it happens every day,
what a shame,
it's uncontrollable,
the envy,
the power.

Victoria McCaughan, Grade 7
Waverley Drive Public School, ON

Wisdom Imparted

These hands have held
A lifetime's worth of
Baby sparrows and steely hammers
I have much to tell

These eyes have seen
30,000 days of life,
Of sunsets and of sunrises
I have much to divulge

These ears have heard
More secrets than walls,
More hymns than gods
I have much to confess

This heart has wept
Too many days
For joy, for love and for sorrow
I have too much to impart

What you know
A mere inkling
Of what is soon to come
I have nothing left to tell.
Pamela Austin, Grade 9
Webber Academy, AB

Ice Bear

The wind ripples
His thick fur coat,
It tugs at his hide,
But he can take it.

The snow stings
His furry paws,
It whips into his face
But he can take it.

The ice disappears,
What was once vast
Hunting grounds is now
Just barren, cold sea.
But he cannot take it.
Nyssa Jacobsen, Grade 8
Hillside Jr/Sr High School, AB

Summer

Summer's on its way
The snow is melting away
The ground is now damp
The hot sun is beating down
At last! Summer is now here
Tarone Gnaneskanthan, Grade 7
Homelands Senior Public School, ON

Spider's Web

The spider spins the web of lies,
As the luck inside you dies;
And lets the sleeper stir,
Time hasn't left you as you were.
A guardian must stand alone,
Protecting his ancient home,
The guardian protects the doors,
As the ancient temple lures.
Most will try to go inside,
But the brightest stay back and hide.
Only those that have known,
Let the guardian stand alone.
Jonathan Dyck, Grade 9
Elm Creek School, MB

Poems

P eople from the circus
O n crazy
E lephants doing super
M agic tricks
S urprising the audience
Ryan Gillings, Grade 8
Macdonald High School, QC

Run

Want to run
Get away
Leave
Salvage the pieces
Move on

Want to hide
Don't try to find me

Want to read
Briefly leave the world behind
The mingling of paper and ink

Want to write
Let my feelings run
Into the page

Let me run
Kailey Young, Grade 8
Heather Park Middle School, BC

Dark Knight

The Dark Knight is here
Criminal's run with terror
He hides in the dark
He sneaks upon criminal's
And he saves the day again.
Qais Sahel, Grade 7
Homelands Senior Public School, ON

Take the Stage

Time will be time,
Family will be family,
Dreams will stay dreams,
Until they become a reality.
No one can doubt
Your path or your choice.
Life is short,
Move along now.

Enter, Stage left,
Exit, Stage right.

Move forward slowly
Then take flight.
Off to new places
Full of old welcoming faces.

Enter, Stage left,
Exit, Stage right.
Sally Ferrari, Grade 7
McKernan School, AB

She Tried

Gasping for breath.
Straining her arms.
She managed to crawl onto safe land.
Her face wet with water and tears.
Her eyes filled with sorrow.
Her voice was too weak.
Too weak to talk or cry for help.
She lay tired.
Screaming for air.
Her chest was rising fast.
Too fast.
But it quickly slowed down.
Then it stopped.
No movement. No air.
No pulse.
She tried God, why didn't you save her?
Why did you let her go?
There are reasons.
but we will never know.
She tried.
Avani Patel, Grade 7
Westview School, AB

The Rare Soul

Humans can swell up
They like to be mystical
Some of them are graceful
Sometimes they burn with rage
Some people like to sleep a lot
Christina Cox, Grade 7
Menno Simons Christian School, AB

Bittersweet Farewell

As the sun reaches the edge of the world
and shadows become snakes of reality,
the red-orange sky drowns the sea
in the blood of the death of one day.

Joanna Ritson, Grade 9
Webber Academy, AB

The Graceful Beast

The graceful beast prances about,
Dancing on the meadow floor,
As a hunter nears,
Its eye on the beast,
And the graceful beast runs.
The chase has begun,
The beast runs and runs,
Faster and faster,
Then he comes to the end of the wood,
A field he had entered.
So open and undisclosed,
But still the beast runs,
Until suddenly...
BANG!!!
The running has stopped,
The beast now lies in agonizing pain,
For what has the beast done to deserve this,
The worst pain to suffer?
The beast lies in the field, surrounded by blood stained flowers.
Dead.

Tyson Morgan, Grade 8
Worsley Central School, AB

Grades 4-5-6

Note: The Top Ten poems were finalized through an online voting system. Creative Communication's judges first picked out the top poems. These poems were then posted online. The final step involved thousands of students and teachers who registered as online judges and voted for the Top Ten poems. We hope you enjoy these selections.

Top Poem Grades 4-5-6

Sunset

I sat, oblivious to any distraction.
in awe, at the colors the sky had to show.
as if, tonight was its last chance to shine.
gleaming, a round ball of fire sank slowly down
to touch, the calm, shining water below.
and around, the sky shone, giving me a mix of feelings.
colours, from the palest gold to the richest purple.
and then, colours faded into a velvety night.
such stars, as I had never seen before
so bright, and twinkling they were.
that when, as I got up to leave,
I paused, and thought one unanswerable question.
How does the sky do this every night?

Heidi DeWitte, Grade 5
Charles Beaudoin Public School, ON

Top Poem Grades 4-5-6

Puppy Love

They say puppy love is a most powerful thing,
Me and my pup are like a finger to a ring.
I don't know what I would do without him,
As if he's my lifeguard when I swim.
We stick together, forever.
Through good times and bad.
He comforts me when I'm sad.

We're close like family,
We'll live together happily.
I watch him grow every day,
From the moment he came, to stay.
Every morning I scream out loud,
"Elvis, I love you," I say it proud.

Now our joy must come to an end,
I will lose a dog, and a friend.
I knew this could not last,
Those years just went by too fast.

He's in a better place, his soul goes above,
But he's always in my heart, where I love.
In my heart we will always be together,
Elvis I love you, now and forever.

Jessica Jagiello, Grade 6
Ecole Ste-Jeanne-d'Arc, ON

Top Poem Grades 4-5-6

Fire

A fire blazes brightly through the forest.
It is a black hole consuming every thing it touches.
This blazing hot inferno furnace burns and devours everything.
A mass of destruction flickers and dances hypnotically.
But do not underestimate its appearance,
For it leaps from tree to tree, branch to branch swallowing leaves and spitting ashes.
Fire takes anything it wants, because nothing can stop it.
He rages through the countryside wearing a bright coat of scarlet with a soft inner indigo.
He knew that neither his cousin acid nor his brother lava could create such chaos.
Plants withered and stones split,
but to fire,
this was all just a day's work.

Bill Jiang, Grade 6
Blundell Elementary School, BC

Top Poem Grades 4-5-6

Nature Awakening

The grass rustles around
As if it's shouting with glee
The day is just starting
And the sun is as ready as can be

The wind rushes through
As the birds fly in the sky
The bugs crawl around
And the treetops tower high

Then suddenly the clouds turn dark
As the sun runs away
The lightning strikes
And the storm kills the day

Maira Khan Afridi, Grade 6
Harry Balfour School, AB

Top Poem Grades 4-5-6

Creatures of the Night

An owl flies through the night.
Clothed in silence, strength and might.
Flying through until it's light.
Creatures of the night.
A lost wolf howls alone.
Walks away and gnaws a bone.
Sleeps through the morning light.
Creatures of the night.
A raccoon raids a little nest.
Where six tiny chicks do rest.
Pleased from its midnight meal.
Not caring what the mom might feel.
Goes in a hole to block the light.
Creatures of the night.
Slowly, slowly light comes in.
So another day begins.
Sleeping through the day's light.
Creatures of the night.

Tiana Klippenstein, Grade 4
St Alphonsus School, MB

Top Poem Grades 4-5-6

Just Smile

If you couldn't see or hear me
Things would be quite changed.
You wouldn't know if I was fast or slow
Young or very aged.
Having glasses wouldn't matter,
Braces, not a thing.
You might know my taste in music,
But not if I could sing.
You'd ignore my accent
And that hole in the knee of my pants.
My crooked tooth would disappear.
We'd both be good at dance.
So try to ignore the small things.
Your mood will grow by about a mile,
And since you have no choice to see or hear me —
Just flash me a smile.

McKenna Ogg, Grade 6
East Selkirk Middle School, MB

Top Poem Grades 4-5-6

Too Many

We walk by the graves as the ground turns to frost,
The wind calls the names of all who we lost.
Crosses to remember those who have died,
To see each of their faces, we would have cried.
So many poppies as we stand by the tree,
For the sons and the daughters that fought to be free.

The great war had begun, he thought how neat,
To go to the Germans and hand them defeat.
Little David from Regina was stationed in Nice,
A tour through Europe to bring them some peace.
Letters and candies arrived in a basket,
Their little son David was brought home in a casket.

Beth the teacher thought it would be cool,
Off to Afghanistan to help build a school.
One day teaching English with all of her calm,
Disguised as a book was a powerful bomb.
Helping little boys and girls with all her talks,
Beth the daughter and mother brought home in a box.

We may not march on forever,
But we shall always stand tall.

Joshua Schwalb, Grade 5
St Mark Separate School, ON

Top Poem Grades 4-5-6

Remembrance Day

Remember
Everyone who died
Missing their loved ones
Everybody's loved
Moments be gone
Rows of poppies
Always nestling in the wind
Celebrate for those who lived
Everybody wants to be home
Dying for freedom
Assistance is needed
Yesterday was the war
But now it is over.

Brady Tattrie, Grade 5
Pat Hardy Elementary School, AB

Top Poem Grades 4-5-6

They Fought for Us

Soldiers lived and died
They fought for us
And many tears were cried.

These brave young men
They volunteered, for peace
And to restore amends.

Many died as we live today
Because of these young men
We can live freely on our way.

As others still fight
And others are very sad
All we can do is pray for their might.

Christopher Van Hagen, Grade 6
St Mary Choir and Orchestra Program, ON

Top Poem Grades 4-5-6

Tree of Seasons

Treading through the snow and rain,
Breaking through the sun and heat,
Standing through the fear and pain,
Living wisdom old and strong.

Roots surrounding like a mane,
Leaves fallen forming a sheet,
On a tree, a snowflake lain,
Surviving winter, cold and long.

Experiencing winter pain,
Waiting for spring's warm greet,
Trunk still and silent like monster slain,
Standing and waiting for spring's song.

Elegant and poised as a crane,
Blooming flowers in mild heat,
Robins chirping in the rain,
In the wind, very strong,
Is the birds' return song.

Beatrix Wang, Grade 6
Waverly Drive Public School, ON

My Year in Grade 4...
Was exciting and fun,
For all the work I had done.

You go outside for recess
In the morning glow,
And in science class
The bowl was going to overflow!

In gym we played a funny game and
Our math class was so insane.

Art was cool we made a tree,
School is over yippy!
Dillon Pratt, Grade 4
Tisdale Elementary School, SK

Clouds
clouds are so soft,
white and grey
they're beautiful when the
rainbow dives through.
Emily Dunlap, Grade 5
Chiganois Elementary School, NS

Freedom Won
Remember the soldiers who
sacrificed their lives for our freedom

They had to smell
The stench of dead bodies.
So we could smell the sweet
fragrance of flowers.
They felt the pain of gunshot wounds.
So we could feel freedom.
They saw people die
right in front of them.
So we could see the birds
flying south for the winter.
They heard the explosions of bombs.
So we could hear the birds singing.
They tasted dirt as they hit the ground
So we could taste delicious food.
Some soldiers died and
some veterans survived.
The veterans enjoy the freedoms
they fought to preserve.
We are thankful.
Aran Thiessen, Grade 5
Mornington Central School, ON

Garfield
Goofy, funny
Best comic book in the world
Rude to Odie dogs
Joshua Scott, Grade 4
St Alphonsus School, MB

When a Friend Comes Around
There is nothing much to do in this town
But when a friend comes around it is something to be cherished
You laugh, play and talk all day because they are all you have
There is nothing much to do in this town
But when a friend comes around it is something to be cherished
You play with them at school each day and share your secrets
There is nothing much to do in this town
But when a friend comes around it is something to be cherished
You share your emotions with each other when you want to cry
Or when you feel a little down
A friend will be there
There is nothing much to do in this town
But when a friend comes around it is something to be cherished
You help each other with going through life and overcoming obstacles
There is nothing much to do in this town
Especially when a friend moves away
Then you are sad and have nothing to do again
But be happy that the friend came your way
And hey you might meet another friend one day
So be patient and you will see making friends is easy
Jake Forsyth, Grade 6
Eric Langton Elementary School, BC

The Best Week Ever
On Sunday I bought a Kx 140 Kawasaki with a bored out engine!
On Monday I went to the Motocross finals in Edmonton and got free goggles!
On Tuesday I found a tame tarantula in Australia!
On Wednesday I found a tame iguana in Mexico!
On Thursday I bought a Lamborghini Murcielago at Edmonton!
On Saturday I got all the systems and games in the world!
All in all it was the best week ever.
Kaden Barsi, Grade 4
David Ovans Elementary School, AB

Pink
Pink is a pig splashing in the mud.
Pink is a marker so colorful and bright.
Pink is a car with purple rims.
Pink is a cook book with a hundred pages.
Pink is a dress with many colors.
Pink is a girl so pretty and bright.
Pink is a crystal that must be found.
Pink is my hair so fresh and so clean.
Pink is the brightest colorist greatest prettiest pinkest colour of all!!
Tony Klassen, Grade 6
Mornington Central School, ON

The Rain Forest
It is raining in the rain forest again, drip-drop.
The grass is blowing in the wind, whoosh-whoosh.
You can hear the wind whistling through the vines, whistle-whistle.
You can even hear the snakes hissing, sss-ssss.
You can hear the rain fall down, drip-drop.
But most of all you can hear the animals sleeping, zzz-zzz.
Shiann Sianna Alexandrea Collins, Grade 4
Margaret Wooding School, AB

World War #1!

Most deadly war
Cold, muddy!
600,000 Canadians and Newfoundlanders
60,000 of them died!
40,000 died protecting peace and freedom!
Triumphant
Canada's 100 days
90th anniversary
First World War
The war to end all wars
But sadly it did not!
Barely 20 years later
DANGER AND DEATH!
Snipers, machine-gun fire and artillery!
Will it happen again? Or not?

Andrew Mandziuk, Grade 6
East Selkirk Middle School, MB

Birds

Birds are like an airplane flying to random places.
The bird flies to catch a prey.
It glides down to the river to catch a fish.
Goes back to home and gives the kids a fish.
The kids eat the fish at the speed of light?
The kids are growing.
They now have their own kids.
It's winter now the birds have to fly to a warm place.
They come back when that place is cold.
They go back to their old nest.
Next day! It starts raining.
Tons of worms are on the floor.
Thousands of birds eat them all.

Samuel Wong, Grade 5
St Mark Separate School, ON

I Used to…/But Now I…

I used to hate eating horrid veggies
But now I don't really care what I eat
I used to really like the amazing color of blue
But now I like the color flaming red
I used to hate my sister's hitting
But now I just hate her loud arguing
I used to hate reading nonfiction
But now I like to read about huge structures
I used to feel queasy in vehicles
But now I don't feel sick in cars anymore
I used to think I go missing in Vancouver
But now I don't because my parents stay close to me
I used to think history is dumb
But now I think it is good to learn about history of wars
I used to not be able to ride a bike
But now I can ride like a pro
I used to be a hockey player
But now I am an amazing hockey goalie

Trey Spanier, Grade 6
Silver Star Elementary School, BC

Bosco

Bosco is cute and he likes *The Wiggles.*
When he hears *The Wiggles* he likes to jiggle and giggle.
Bosco and me like to play.
We play the whole day.

Ronny Ly, Grade 4
Calico Public School, ON

terry fox

terry was born in '58
and trying hard was his trait
he loved all sports
and played on courts
when a teen
at age eighteen
cancer came
and was hard to tame
terry amputated his right leg
and in its place was a plastic peg
with it he ran from coast to coast
to help the people who were diagnosed
with the syndrome, he had known
but halfway through his marathon
he was withdrawn
because his cancer had spread
and led him to his sickbed
in 1981
terry was done
and though he may be gone
he is alive in every stride for his marathon

Soyeon Hwangbo, Grade 5
Our Lady of Perpetual Help, BC

My First Medal

Today, today today is the day
I'll make my mom and dad proud today

I might get a medal today yes today
I cannot stop talking I have too much to say

My swimming competition is today
and I will not stand weak like yesterday

oh but I'm too nervous and scared
I might fall and wreck my swim wear

But my team will cheer and I'm not scared
if other teams laugh I won't care

Then I got it I got it a gold medal
it's antic it's antic it's not normal

Hurray Hurray
I got my first medal today
Today!

Lena Sobze, Grade 4
Good Shepherd School, AB

Spring
Oh spring, oh spring,
What a wonderful thing.
I can smell the daisies
and I can eat the berries.
Oh spring, oh spring,
I am on your side,
So I won't lie.
I can play in the hay.
If I can say I like to play,
Almost all the sports,
of some sort.
Goodbye all my friends,
I'll see you at the end.
Krystal Rader, Grade 6
Ecole Ste-Jeanne-d'Arc, ON

Ice Cream Extreme
The ice cream man's siren rings
I jump up and down with glee
Oh how I love ice cream
It's the best thing in the world to me.

Skipping cheerfully I go
Dashing over to the ice cream man
I ask him for a vanilla scoop
And then off again I ran.

Off I go through the paved streets
With my ice cream in my hand
Coming to a sudden screech
My ice cream fell to land.

Standing in shock
As if I were a ghost
I picked the soggy cone up.
Oh how I wanted it most!
Nikki Bosch, Grade 6
Harry Balfour School, AB

The Great Game
Hockey oh hockey
Why are you so great?
Every time I go on the ice
My feet start to skate.

I grab the puck
And go for the net
I look for my partner
Then I give her a set.

We went 2 on 1
And then she scored
So we went to celebrate
While the whole crowd roared!
Corbin Welsh, Grade 6
Harry Balfour School, AB

Play
Come and play
Today in May
We could go to the mall
Or play ball
In our stacks of hay
In the middle of May
Let's play hide and go seek
I bet I could hide for a week
Please come over and play
Hope you say O.K.
We can play
In our bay
We can swim
while we watch the sun dim
We can play on our swing
While we sing
We could walk a mile
And not take a while
What do you say
Will you come and play?
Shawn Brady, Grade 6
St. Francis School, ON

Waterfall
Waterfall
big, fast
splashing, thundering, crippling
death trap for fish
water-tumbler
Trevor Clost, Grade 6
John T Tuck Public School, ON

Spring
The snow melts away
On this warm and sunny day
At Park West School, yay!
Lauren Cotie, Grade 4
Park West School, NS

Nature
Tan is for sand at the beach.
Yellow is for the sunshine.
Brown is for grizzly bear
sleeping on a nice leaf bed.
Green is for green grass.
Red is for Canadian leaf.
Blue is for the sky.
Melissa Coulson, Grade 4
David Ovans Elementary School, AB

Titanic
The unsinkable
Well not quite unsinkable
Why would you think that?
Alandra Kreshewski, Grade 6
Linden Lanes School, MB

Orange
Orange is the juice
You drink in the morning
Orange is the shirt
When somebody is boring
Orange is the fruit
You eat with lunch
Pumpkins are orange
And come in a bunch
Orange is the color
You see on a bird
Orange is the ribbon
When you come in third
Orange is the carrot
That rhymes with my name Jarrett
Orange is the boy
Who has the ferret
Orange is the paper when you tear it
Orange is the color you wrote with
When you made up the word zarrett
Orange is my favorite color
I can hardly bear it
Jarrett Patenaude, Grade 6
Mornington Central School, ON

A Way Through the Day
As I make my way through the day,
In the beauty of Taipei,
There I stand,
With all unplanned,
In the night,
I spot a light,
There stands the moon,
Followed by a tune,
What I hear,
Is a premier of what will appear.
Alex Rasiga, Grade 6
Ecole Ste-Jeanne-d'Arc, ON

Life
Life has its ups and downs,
Its happy smiles and frightening frowns,
Overall its a happy place,
To learn to love,
To praise God with Grace,
Don't waste time being sad,
life is a peaceful place,
Not for you to be mad.
Jenna Cross, Grade 4
St Alphonsus School, MB

Flower and Sunshine
Flowers start to grow,
Sunshine gave them energy
They are so pretty
Alta Gong, Grade 4
Park West School, NS

Spring

The flowers,
pop up as if a jack has just sprung from its box.
The meadows sprout up,
the ice melts,
and the frogs jump up into the daylight.
So fast it comes and goes.
We pollute it every day,
make it shorter.
Let's Stop!!!

Ryland Dembek-Blair, Grade 6
Central Public School, ON

Teachers

Teachers are totally awesome.
Teachers are very smart.
Teachers are as sweet as blossoms.
Teachers use a shopping cart.

Teachers can be totally wild.
Teachers give you a great big smile.
Teachers are sometimes mild.
A teacher's kindness can be felt from miles.

Tyanna Care, Grade 4
St Alphonsus School, MB

The World

The world of ours is green and blue
But of course there's other colors too
There's people
There's happiness and all
It's beautiful to tell you the truth
Just think of the positive
It's all up to you
Think of the forests
Think of spring
Think of everything that makes you sing
The world is nice, it's true
You just have to believe in you

Martha Stanley, Grade 6
École élémentaire catholique Georges-Étienne-Cartier, ON

Colours of Spring

Blue is the sky
Pink is the butterfly.
Gold is the crops
Silver is the newly hatched minnows that go flip, flop.
Green is the leaf buds on the trees
Black and yellow are the bumble bees.
Red is the rose
Clear is the spring cool wind that blows.
Violet is the sunset
Orange is the sun who's light reflects off raindrops
And then over the rushing river and over the tree tops
There stood the first rainbow of spring.

Tiara Meier, Grade 4
David Ovans Elementary School, AB

They Remember

They saw their friends fall to the ground,
so we can see flowers grow from town to town.
They smelled the stench of death,
so we could smell the sweet fragrance of flowers.
They felt the pain of shooting guns,
so we could taste fresh baked buns.
And that is why we should remember,
the forgotten soldiers.

Graham DeLong, Grade 6
Mornington Central School, ON

Courage

With the clock clicking down tied one to one
And my friend screaming loud this is really fun.
With the other team rushing down the ice
I remembered I had a pocket full of courage,
I told myself not to cheat
Then one old hockey team cannot be beat.
And I took the puck away from their team
I skated fast and got a breakaway
And as the puck went going down
With me beside it with the goalie starting to frown.
I took a really hard shot that went down the ice
And their team surrounded it like pairs of mice,
My friends laid down, shook hands and begged
And the puck went in right through their legs.
With my friends picking me up
Yelling we won the giant playing cup,

Jacob Ferdinand, Grade 5
Chiganois Elementary School, NS

Sun

The sun is in the sky so high it hurts just to look at it
The sun is my life and destiny
The sun makes me glow.

William McDonald, Grade 6
Anola School, MB

New York City

A population of 8 million people.
New York City a place that I call the Big Easy.
Times Square, Broadway, Wall Street are famous.
New Amsterdam used to be it's name in 1664.
It has the largest and most successful bank, Citicorp.
Home to a famous magazine, The New York Times.
Home to the Statue of Liberty from 1886.
It is a very very diverse city.
Had a very interesting history.
Home to Brooklyn Bridge.
Tragedy struck this place once.
A very humid city in the east.
Named after the state the city is in.
Is a excellent educational center.
It is a place to wonder.

Gurpreet Singh Chopra, Grade 5
Khalsa School - Old Yale Road Campus, BC

Drew
There once was a boy named Drew
On candy he'd chomp and he'd chew
To brush he forgot
His teeth started to rot
And now he just has a few
Keaton Noble, Grade 6
Barriere Elementary School, BC

The Dominican Beach…
The Dominican beach,
Turquoise clear water,
White hot sand,
Coral reef with jazzy colored fish,
Palm trees swaying with the wind,
Waves hitting the shore,
The Dominican beach.
Emil Michael Klos, Grade 6
St Maria Goretti Elementary School, ON

My Brother
My brother is oh such a pain
he will clearly drive me insane
I see him come home
and let out a groan
please send him away on a plane.
Austin Dergousoff, Grade 6
Walnut Road Elementary School, BC

Stanly — My Bearded Dragon
Stan the man, from Tennessee,
Love to cook with only me.
He baked soufflé and cricket pies,
And everything that I despise.
Then he looked at me, with despair,
That achy quaky little stare —
I'd like to cook alone please,
Then he walked away from me.
And that my friends, is all he said,
Until he finally went to bed,
When he said, "by the way, Ashly"
"Some crickets got away from me."
Ashly Baptista, Grade 4
Trelawny Public School, ON

Dog
My dog ate my homework,
I don't know what to do.
My dog ate my homework
Then he ate my shoe.

I went to go outside,
My feet got soaking wet.
I went to play ball,
But my dog ate my bat.
Abbey Franklin, Grade 4
Deloraine School, MB

My Special Place
This is a place where my thoughts run free.
And where there's open land to run in
and where it's just me and the echo of
my voice bouncing off the beautiful green trees
and where I can go when things go wrong
where your secrets are trusted and sink deep beneath the ground
where there's nothing but nature
where you can walk field to field without stopping once
where you know you're not alone because you know there are
animals hidden behind every rock, every tree, every bush
where the air smells so alive
where the rain is so pure that you can almost see right through it
and where the sky is so blue you can almost see the stars
ready to burst out into the night sky
and there is only one place like that and that is my grandparents' farm
a place I will always take with me!
Courtney Orser, Grade 6
Sir Isaac Brock Public School, ON

Remember Always
On a cold November Day
A lone veteran stands alone
Thinking of many years ago when he was young
He remembers the sounds and sees the sights of war.

He saw the blood of the dead
So we could see the colors of the rainbow.

He heard the cries and moans of the injured
So we could hear the sound of joy.

He tasted the stale food and the sour stench of dirt
So we could taste yummy fruits and vegetables.

He smelled the horrendous smell of fire and death
So we could smell the candied blossoms of flowers.

He felt the pain of the cries of the wounded
So we could feel the safety of our families.

Now we have freedom of speech
Now we have freedom to worship
Now we have freedom of choice
Thanks for the soldiers who sacrificed their lives for our freedom!
Edna Hoover, Grade 5
Mornington Central School, ON

Pencils
They can be smooth or sharp
After sharpening them the length shortens
Erasers stand out at the end
Wooden centers are covered by plain or decorative ideas
They can be new or old but the results never change
For years they write down your thoughts and for me in this poem
Melanie Lanthier, Grade 5
Forest Hill School – Senior Campus, QC

Nature

watching desert dunes
the light sand blowing away
hot, thirsty and light

Kanin Wilson, Grade 5
Howard De Beck Elementary School, BC

Autumn Leaves

When you hear autumn leaves you think of the season
When I hear autumn leaves I see my best friend

My best friend who would do anything to keep me safe
My best friend who sees me crying is there for me
Next to me…
She is not just a dog she is my best friend…
Autumn Leaves

Madison Murray, Grade 5
Chiganois Elementary School, NS

Powerful Peace

Peace in our world,
Peace in our life,
Powerful peace.

Peace is such a powerful gift.
It's the feeling of waking up in a safe home,
Or the special feeling of when you sing "Oh Canada."

Peace in our world,
Peace in our life,
Powerful peace.

Think of all those giving veterans who fought for us,
They saved our lives,
They brought peace, and hope to us and our country.
Be thankful for peace and be a peace maker.

Peace in our world,
Peace in our life,
Powerful peace.

Kate Moran, Grade 6
St Mary Choir and Orchestra Program, ON

I

Hamid
tall, smart, and creative
brother of David
lover of chocolate, video games, and sports
who feels happy at school
who needs a mom, a dad, and a brother
who gives gifts to his brother
who fears war, bugs, and swimming in cold water
who would like to be on a ship
resident of Toronto
Johangiry

Hamid Johangiry, Grade 4
Calico Public School, ON

Bobbie

Running, jumping that's not my horse
She is a pretty laid back type of horse
Very nice
Smooth canter
When I ride her she is…The best horse ever!
I love the wind in my hair when I canter around
The ring.
Especially when it is a hot summers day.
The thing I love most about her is…
I can't pick she is such a great horse
She is a very special horse to me and my family.
I love her very much!

Emily Nelson, Grade 5
Chiganois Elementary School, NS

Death*

You will start to cry,
Death is a tragic thing.
You won't hear the bell,
But then in heaven, a bell will ring.

But everyone eventually will hear that bell ring,
You will start to cry.
They will go away,
But then think they don't really die.

Jillian Crowe, Grade 4
Deloraine School, MB
*In memory of my Great Grandma Stroud.

Things That Go Bump in the Night

When you are settling down to go to sleep
Do you ever think of things that crawl and creep?
Slithering, sliding, scratching, clawing
Hissing, moaning, cackling, cawing

Hiding deep under your bed
Leaving you awake, shaking with dread
Meanwhile, hidden from your eyes
A ghost wakes up and moans and cries

You lie petrified in your bed
So scared you've almost turned to lead
Glass shatters, banshees weep
Like terrorists invading your sleep

Demons are waking: shadows do the corpse jig
Something's tapping your window; it's an innocent twig
Skeletons party: an undead orchestra band
Ribs as xylophones, their trumpets are hands

But then the moon rises, and you hear the werewolf call
A monstrous beast; three men tall…
…Despite what I've told you, and all I've just said
I know where they're hiding; they're hiding in your head

Laura Brennan, Grade 5
Elboya Elementary and Jr High School, AB

Leah Harry
L ucky
E at
A ristocratic
H appy

H umble
A rt
R eliable
R omantic
Y ell
Leah Harry, Grade 4
Sxoxomic Community School, BC

Virtues
Assertiveness,
Cleanliness,
Consideration,
What are they?
Virtues!
Cooperation
Courage
Determination
These are the gifts of character
Known as virtues
The world would be boring
Because people would be the same
So here are some more
Diligence
Enthusiasm
Flexibility
But to me the most important ones are
Generosity
Honesty
And last but not least loyalty to friends
Austin Bennett, Grade 5
Chiganois Elementary School, NS

The Boy Martyr
The cold night was full of fear
His death was getting very near

He chose to listen to God's voice
Now he would suffer for this choice

They told him not to read God's word
But the Master's kind voice he heard

"Be a revolutionary"
"My cross is what you will carry"
"This is not the end of your life!
Your future lies in heaven with Christ"

The flames began to lick his feet
"Lord it's you I come to meet."
Brooke Tower, Grade 5
Westside Academy, BC

Casey
C ake
A pple
S oda
E asy
Y oyo
Kassandra Robbins, Grade 4
Sxoxomic Community School, BC

Sports
Football
Intense, rough
Running, tackling, dodging
Defense, offense, face-off, goal
Pounding, crunching, tripping
Official, winning
Hockey
Noah Poitras, Grade 5
Bernard Elementary School, BC

Love
Love is like the colour pink on
Valentines Day
Love tastes like a
Tasty and sweet candy
Love smells like the
Sweet scent of a
Rose in the spring time
Love looks like a
Sunset over the
Glistening lake
Love sounds like the
Summer breeze blowing
Gently
Love feels like your heart
Overflowing with joy!
Jacki Brubacher, Grade 6
Mornington Central School, ON

Easter Eggs
The good Easter eggs,
Taste super, good and yummy!
I hope it will stay.
Easter, Easter Day I love!
The Easter Bunny will come!
Tonight I will sleep.
While there is some candy,
For me tomorrow!!
Elizabeth Green, Grade 5
Pat Hardy Elementary School, AB

Colors
The sky's color now
At sunset tonight at dusk
Such a nice color
Nick VanBuskirk, Grade 4
Park West School, NS

My Cat Stu
Eyes of green
Claws of bronze
King of licorice
Sleeper of dawn

Little brown nose
Long spiked claws
Lover of milk
Tiny little paws

Tail of stripes
Tummy of ox
Fur of silk
Smarter than fox

"M" on forehead
Jumps like tiger
Fatter than tree trunk
Not a liar

Eyes of green
Claws of bronze
King of licorice
Sleeper of dawn
Arden Jones, Grade 6
Sir Isaac Brock Public School, ON

TKD Tournaments
Broken boards
Old popcorn.
People yelling
"KIIIIYYAAA!"
Pain from sparring.
Listen to your
Instructor!!
Jacob Code, Grade 6
Ormsby School, AB

Presents
P repare to shop.
R unning to look for gifts.
E veryone franticly shopping.
S natching up some toys.
E cstatic about all the presents.
N ot able to wait for Christmas.
T oys unwrapped on Christmas morning.
S o much fun!
Michael McCrady, Grade 6
Mother Teresa Catholic School, ON

Spring Weather
The snow melts away
Leaving behind bright green grass
Summer is so soon!
Kristin Peters, Grade 4
Park West School, NS

My Family

My dad is fun but he wishes he had a son,
My mom is cool but she said we will never have a pool.
My sister is funny and my mom calls her honey.
I like to go shopping but I don't have much money.
My family doesn't have a pool, but my family is still cool.

Haley Irving, Grade 4
Colby Village Elementary School, NS

Thank You Lord for Everything

Thank You for my pet.
Thank You for my vet.
Thank You for my family.
Thank You for the talents God gave me.
Thank You for the mammals.
Thank You for the animals.
Thank You for the farmers.
Thank You for the barbers.
Thank You for my friends till the end.
Thank You for the teachers.
Thank You for the preachers.
Thank You for the trips I've been on.
Thank You for the people that have gone.
Thank You for school.
Thank You for the air that is cool.
Thank You for the books.
Thank You for my looks.
Thank You for letting me see.
Thank You for me.

Brandon Weir, Grade 6
St Mary Choir and Orchestra Program, ON

Earth

Earth appears to be like a dazzling disco ball,
Crystal clear water,
Flowing rivers, lakes, and seas,
Tasteless but yet refreshing

Earth has a surface like a solid rock
It has lush green land,
Green grass, and beautiful trees
Dry soil covers our land

Earth is on an axis and spins once in
Twenty-four hours
Day is between sunrise and sunset,
Giving light
Night is between sunset and sunrise,
Giving darkness

Earth is about humans, animals and plants
Those live in our Earth's atmosphere
Being alive,
Just breathing clean air
Staying healthy, just to stay alive!!

Lucas Lalonde, Grade 6
East Selkirk Middle School, MB

Orange

Orange is the colour of joy
Orange tastes like soft squishy taffy
Orange smells like juicy spring flowers
Orange sounds like a crispy carrot being eaten in spring
Orange feels like soft waving grass
Orange looks like an excited dog in the water
Orange makes me feel fantastic, joyful, loving
Orange is my favorite colour

Richard Marchese, Grade 6
John T Tuck Public School, ON

Visions

Yesterday in the middle of the night,
I discovered something that gave me a fright.
A great vision descended upon me,
My Lord, God had come to meet me.
I am humbled in his presence,
He has left me with a change of mind and heart,
That now I need to make a brand new start.
I regret my sins and intend to renew,
All the things that I have done to others and you,
My faith has changed,
I feel new,
My Lord God has changed my life,
And now all that I need to do,
Is to make a new change in you.

Shayne Oberhoffner, Grade 6
St James Catholic School, BC

Forever Friends

The one and only word;
friend
someone who is there for you,
till the very end

The world is so big, the population is huge,
so everyone is unique;
so be nice and show respect,
and they'll be your *friends* till you're antique

In my opinion, *friends* are there for you always
they may not be in sight, or lengthwise apart,
but they'll always be there,
down there in your heart

They don't need to be exactly like you
it's nearly impossible to find,
but show respect and show you care
for your *friend* may even be blind

The one and only word;
friend
someone who is there for you,
till the very end

Natalie C. Auersperg, Grade 6
Eric Langton Elementary School, BC

Morning Dew

Drip of morning dew
I pluck the little petal
Dancing to the ground.

Fatuma Abdullahi, Grade 6
Ormsby School, AB

Pain

Feel me, give me, see me,
I am everywhere
I'm your nemesis,
Until I help you
I'm your buddy,
Until I hurt you
I scream at you,
Then you scream back
I am eager to do my job,
Though it is no easy task
I am a messenger,
An agonizing reminder
I destroy, hurt, kill people,
Yet I hunger for more
Send me, stop me,
The second one's hard
Mentally, physically,
I do what I do
Feel me, give me, see me,
I am pain.

Greg Warren, Grade 6
Westwind Elementary School, BC

Raining Cats and Dogs

It's raining cats and dogs,
It's also raining bull frogs,
Meowing and barking,
And croaking a lot, loudly too,
My, what are we going to do?!

Jacob Gascoyne, Grade 6
Bella Coola Adventist Academy, BC

I Wish...

I wish I were an owl
flying through the night sky
soaring above the trees
as silent as the wind

Joscelyn Bruggeman, Grade 5
Bernard Elementary School, BC

If I Were a Hamster

If I were a hamster,
I could travel through walls,
I would be an awesome one,
I could also be famous,
I could see everything from down low,
I could meet mice and rats.

Danielle MacDonald, Grade 4
Colby Village Elementary School, NS

The Forest

The forest is a jumbo place.
You could see the huge tarantula climbing the mighty tree from the top of the waterfall.
You could hear the damp waterfall collapse from the cliff.
As the bold eagle swiftly glides for its prey,
You will feel the moist rain drop from above.
Snakes will slither around as the charming rabbit bounds through the forest.
Rivers are slim and smooth.
You will see it flow through the forest.
There are rocks, old and solid.
You will see all of the forest.

Trey Wyatt, Grade 4
Margaret Wooding School, AB

Home Alone and on Your Own Safety

When your parents have gone to the store,
Don't ever open the door for you may be sorry,
And have to tell your parents, a really long story.

You're on your way home from school,
A stranger drives up and says
"I'm to take you to the pool."
Ask him "Just why would you
Like to do that? Why" he replies "Your father
Sent me, that's why; he also said to say hi."
Ask him "What's my father's name, and what is our family code?"
He answers "Your code is 1122, and your father's name is Drew."

If he is right, jump right in, and have some fun,
But if he's wrong, tell an adult you know is safe, and then run away.

Mom and Dad have gone shopping,
Your big sister is upstairs, the floor she is mopping.
The phone rings — you answer, the caller wants
To speak to your mother or father
Please don't say "They are away"
Instead say "They are really busy right now, may I take a message?"
Then hang up and tell your mopping sister Lizzy, and later on, also tell your parents.
Use these safety tips and prevent yourself from getting harmed.

Maria Wall, Grade 6
Mornington Central School, ON

Sports

Sports are fun.
Sports keep you active.
Sports can also keep you healthy.
I play sports with your friends too.
I play a lot of sports like basketball, baseball and hockey. Sometimes soccer too.
Sports are something most people like to play.
Or use to play.
Lazy people that don't like to play sports can just sit there and be bored.
I like to play basketball with my friends.
Plus hockey and baseball too.
I like to play sports with my friends and family.
Do you like to play sports?

Prabhdeep Singh Athwal, Grade 5
Khalsa School - Old Yale Road Campus, BC

In Room 114*

In the room of 114 a party's always happening.
We love to go, we hate to leave
In the room of 114.

In the room of 114 there's turtles, fish and starfish too
Come step in you'll love it too.

The best part of the day is being in homeroom
where we'll play and learn fractions and write poems like these.
In the room of 114.

Paige Collins, Grade 4
Kingswood Dr Public School, ON
*Based on the class of room 114

The Ocean...

The ocean is very
peaceful and relaxing
to listen to.

The ocean is like a
silent butterfly
gliding through the sky.

The ocean makes tall
waves like a giraffe
reaching for the sky.

As the ocean leaves the shore
a trail of beautiful sea shells
can be found for all to enjoy!

Taylor Fogliato, Grade 5
Queen of All Saints Elementary School, BC

The Beast

I was in my room one night,
When I heard a noise that gave me a fright.
The thing I saw at my bedroom door,
Was a beast that was frightening and nothing more.
It had a vicious and deadly stare,
Survivors from it were very rare.
It had teeth that could chew through steel,
And a stomach that could digest any meal.
It got ready to lunge for my head,
Then I knew that I was dead.
The situation was very bad,
For there's no beast more frightening than my dad!

Ben Liu, Grade 5
Charles Beaudoin Public School, ON

Origami

With origami you can make anything.
Make it out of paper or even dollar bills (ka-ching)
Show it to your friends, mom or dad.
The only reason not to show it is if you're really bad!

Dustin Lloy, Grade 4
Colby Village Elementary School, NS

Do You Remember?

I thank you God for peace,
Peace is what we know.
If we had war in Canada,
Then we would have to go.

In our nation's vision,
The veterans fought for peace.
They tried to stop the war,
But a lot were deceased.

But still some survived,
Went home to their family.
Their wives and children smiled,
They were as happy as can be.

We go to Flanders Field,
See rows and rows of crosses.
The people buried there,
Gave us peace through their losses.

Michael Fisher, Grade 6
St Mary Choir and Orchestra Program, ON

Rose

R ed like a firetruck on the run
O n special occasions we give it to our loved ones
S pecial to me and you
E njoyable for all!

Varuni Visagan, Grade 4
Kingswood Dr Public School, ON

'Twas the Night Before Christmas in Heaven

'Twas the night before Christmas up in Heaven.
Not a person was stirring, not even angel Kevin.

The angels were singing up there with care.
Hoping Jesus the Saviour, soon would be there.

Mary and Joseph were snuggling, for a good rest.
And they were hoping for, the very best.

When all of a sudden, they heard a great clatter.
Mary and Joseph, were in a great matter!

They were looking for a good place to rest
Mary came across an inn, for the very best.

The inn that they chose to stay in was full.
The only place to sleep was with the cow and the bull.

The baby was born inside the manger
Hoping to be safe from all great danger

Now God sent Jesus to us all.
And it began in a humble stall.

Emma Loveridge, Grade 4
First Lutheran Christian School, BC

A Wish...

I wish I were an eagle
soaring in the open sky
hunting for smaller birds
quietly

Dawson Fraser, Grade 5
Bernard Elementary School, BC

Moon

The moon is a speaker
Talking to the world
He talks of the future
And the good that's in store
He shows us we're better than we think
We raised civilization
And he watched us all the way
He shines with what was before us
And darkness with what went wrong
The moon is a teacher
Teaching us life
A light bulb
Telling us we're right
His counsel has given us hope
Still we take it for granted
Sadly, it's morning
Slowly, he fades

Quinn Toyoda, Grade 6
Westwind Elementary School, BC

Cool

C at
O liver
O livia
L eah

Jaclyn Sargent, Grade 4
Sxoxomic Community School, BC

If You Find a Rock

If you find a
Rock that
Shines very bright
Then you found a traveling
Rock. Hold it in your hand
And imagine the
Places you can go

Luis Hernandez, Grade 4
Calico Public School, ON

Colors

C oral
O live
L ily
O rchid
R oyal
S moke

Isabelle Goupil, Grade 4
Colby Village Elementary School, NS

The Seagull

white and grey
light as feather
mean as hawk
hates bad weather

eyes of fury
likes to squawk
has sharp beak
it always mocks

flies up high
likes to steal
chomps and chews
for its meal

white and grey
light as feather
mean as hawk
hates bad weather

Jenna Drager, Grade 6
Sir Isaac Brock Public School, ON

Antelope

Black, white and brown speed.
An antelope running free.
Going to the wild.

EJ Raiche-Tanner, Grade 4
Colby Village Elementary School, NS

In the Night

Darkness runs alone now
The stars shaking in the wind
Along the sky's edge

Kiernan McNeil, Grade 6
Harry Balfour School, AB

Spring Break

I had spring break.
We went to the lake.
It was a sunny day.
I went out to play.
I had a lot of fun.
Out in the sun.
Now I am going back to school.
I hope I have enough tools.

Sabrina Simmonds, Grade 4
St Alphonsus School, MB

Fall

The leaves change colour
The puddles fill with water
The wind blows stronger
Trees look bare and very tall
Prepare for winter cold.

Gino Cross, Grade 6
Bernard Elementary School, BC

Cans of Soda

In Canada we drink cans of soda.
In America we drink cans of soda.
In Africa we drink cans of soda.
In Asia we drink cans of soda.
In Oceania we drink cans of soda.

Charli Richaud, Grade 4
École Renaissance, ON

I Am

I help you make the big
Decisions you can never make
I say what is good and
Say what is bad
Sometimes you like me
Sometimes you hate me
Sometimes you never want me there
Some people let me in
Some people don't
But you are the one who chooses
To let me in or not
Will you choose to?
I am your conscience.

Nick Barrett, Grade 4
St Martin De Porres School, AB

Green Is...

seaweed of the sea
mint chocolate chip ice cream
the lily pad of a frog
plants
frogs
peacock feathers
sweater of kids
the folder of a student
a care bear
a sticker for effort.

Cross Harrison, Grade 6
Bernard Elementary School, BC

Magical Snowflakes

The most magical thing I've ever seen
was drizzling snowflakes
preparing a gentle
and peaceful
white blanket on the ground
for all who come to play

Jenna May Clune, Grade 6
Mother Teresa Catholic School, ON

Dogs

Jump, up and down
Waiting to get their bone
They do puppy eyes and we laugh
Hooray!

Maggie Nendsa, Grade 5
Pat Hardy Elementary School, AB

My Griffin

Grips, Grops, Grypes, Greeps
Patiently the Griffin sleeps
Until morning he is quite a snoring
When he awakes then off he takes,
To come and get me,
Then I hop on
And we make our bond,
And then we're gone to where I'm headed.
In the sky and over the trees.
Through the valleys on the breeze,
We have so much fun sailing in the sun,
I'm sorry to say our day is done,
Maybe tomorrow we'll have more fun.
Grips, Grops, Grypes, Greeps

Nicole Vanderwolf, Grade 4
David Ovans Elementary School, AB

In the Jungle…

In the jungle I saw a Brut bruit
eating a Goory fruit,
I also saw Joogley-fish
snapping on a Sooy-gish!
In the jungle I saw two Zox,
who really, really love to box!
In the jungle, I saw a lagoon,
filled with Zonalanos, Giolos and plenty, plenty of Ribanoos!
In the jungle, I saw Mr. Bruess,
sketching a Igyluess!
In the jungle I saw a moosaloem,
but unfortunately, this is the end of my poem!

Ali Rhayel, Grade 5
École Renaissance, ON

In the Dark

In the dark I can hear
Things creeping here and there
Something in my closet
And in the kitchen faucet
In the dark I can hear
Things creeping here and there

In the dark I can see
Things right in front of me
I see the clock ticking
And fingernails clicking
In the dark I can see
Things right in front of me

In the dark I can smell
A monster maybe I just can't tell
Something boiling in a pot
Oh, I just wish it would stop
In the dark I can smell
A monster maybe I just can't tell!

Alexandra Blinston, Grade 6
Our Lady of the Annunciation Catholic School, ON

Dreams

My skates have not touched the Canadian
Women's home ice,
but it's my dream.

I have not been in the Canadian
Women's home dressing room,
but it's my dream.

My eyes haven't seen the Canadian
Women's hockey team in real life,
but it's my dream.

I haven't worn the Canadian
Women's hockey jerseys,
but it's my dream.

And the only thing I can say now is someday
maybe my dream might come true.
My skates may touch the
Canadian Women's ice.

Kenzie M. Robinson, Grade 5
Hamiota Elementary School, MB

Old/Young

Wrinkles, sleep
Talking, wobbling, yawning
Before old they're young
Teasing, bullying, annoying
Joyful, playful
Young

Richelle Desjardins-Desrochers, Grade 6
École Renaissance, ON

Black

Black is the colour
of the sky at night
Black is the colour
of your shadow
Black is the colour of the
most poisonous scorpion
Black is the colour of
the snow pants you use to play
Black is the hoot of
The owl that whoos at night
Black is the colour of the
wrecking ball that tears a building in two
Black is the colour of
the fire coals that keeps you warm
Black is the colour of
your pencil crayons and markers
Black is the colour of
the glasses that help you see
Black is yours and my favorite colour
No other colour could beat my colour Black

Isaac Dyck, Grade 5
Mornington Central School, ON

Winter Fun

Winter is coming and it's coming fast. I can't wait until the winter fun begins. When the children wake up snow will fall so hard. The children will rush so hard down the stairs. And by the time they get done outside there will be so much on the ground. They jump up and down.

Dominic Raikes, Grade 4
Deloraine School, MB

Service of the Country

Canadians, Aboriginal and Newfoundlanders alike, died in service for their country for peace today.

Those who saw action fought as scouts, snipers and reconnaissance in trenches.
They were among the best and managed to survive gun fire, snipers and artillery bombardment and still managed to help fight.

Now they rest in peace because they died for their country.

Blake Carter, Grade 6
East Selkirk Middle School, MB

A Strange Power

How, sir? I'm asking you, how?
How could something so simple, be so powerful?
How to describe it? Well, I really don't know.
How to describe its powers, its greatness, when I see it, my brain slows.
I think of wind, strung powerfully across a deep pit of nothing, of nowhere,
it's a strong, thick, but simply small head, mounted upon a long, wide, thick, straight, barred and dotted neck.
A neck, that digs deep into a strong, and a hollow body of sorrow, happiness and sound.
And right where the stomach should and would be on you, sir, or me,
is a big, round, gaping hole, with thick strings of iron stretching over its wide expanse of dark,
and continuing back up the long, wide, thick, straight, barred and dotted neck, until they finally rest on small, steel pegs,
and string through the small black holes, and spin round and round, until the right sound comes out.
And, with this strange, beautiful, triangular, bendy device,
I can strum these thick iron strings, and produce amazing sorrows, happiness and sounds, beautiful sounds,
from this great gaping hole!
What's that you ask of me? What do I call it? Well, I don't know!
It should be a simple, but powerful name,
how about,
guitar?

Dale Diamond-Burchuk, Grade 6
Brock-Corydon School, MB

Water

A vast blue ocean as big as the world.
The musky scent of animals dwelling in the swamp is like a dead fish slowly floating to the top of the sea.
The sea splashing against the rocks on shore is like a mighty giant.
The push and pull of the ocean as I swim through is like the waves at a waterpark.
The salt of the sea.
I wish I was a waterbender.

Denver Cameron, Grade 6
Ormsby School, AB

Paradise

The beauty of the golden sunset coming down magically, seeing the silhouette of a boat on the glittering water makes you feel like there's only peace on earth. The sunset has gone down and all you see is mystical bright lights from the city. The sun has come down once more and the trees look quite unique and swamp like. You see bursting lights flashing and cracking in front of the Disney castle. The sunset along the ocean while fishing on the dock is an amazing thing to look at. A setting sun shines over grey flowing water. Wow, this sure is gorgeous.

Amanda Johnstone, Grade 6
Linden Lanes School, MB

Questions of Fairy Tales

Why must I wander,
Unaware of the perils
Into the great woods?

A cute little house,
Chairs big or small, hard or soft,
Which bed shall I choose?

Up, up, up I climb,
What's at the top waiting for,
English men like me?

Small men around me,
An evil witch chasing me,
What is there to do?

One is made of straw,
The others of brick and wood,
The big bad wolf, waits?

Stuck in the water,
Where is he, that prince of mine?
Wish he was with me…

Guess the fairy tale,
From each one of the verses
Get a prize…or not!

Ghislaine Sinclair, Grade 6
Willingdon School, QC

Clear Like a Window

It is in the morning
My blinds are open
Revealing life
I show you the light
I can be the beginning of the end
Or the end of the beginning
I could just sit there and watch the wind blow
Or watch the sky snow
I'm like a door to unworldly emotions that have been
Locked up for years and years to come
I can show you beauty
I can show you fright
I am a window as powerful as the dark night

Brendan Woodley, Grade 6
Westwind Elementary School, BC

Spring

Wet green grass,
Children leaping with joy,
Like a volcano of flowers erupted above me,
Insects darting into the back of my throat,
Rubber boots splashing in muddy puddles,
Spring is finally here!

Allicya Mitchell-Barore, Grade 6
Ormsby School, AB

Bullying

Bullying is painful.
It feels like a fast ball in the gut,
Or in the head.
They take your lunch money,
Your feelings and more.
They make you feel down, dumb, and
Lonely and too scared to talk
Ever to your friends parents even teachers.
If you get bullied don't be scared,
Stand up!

Gabrielle Hamilton, Grade 5
Chiganois Elementary School, NS

Summer

Hot windy breeze all summer long,
laughing and singing a fun summer song.
I watch the birds high in the sky,
And count them as they fly by.
I lay beside my backyard pool,
And feel glad I'm not in school.
I spend hours in the summer heat,
and laugh when the cold ocean water hits my feet.
I run with my kite in the beautiful bay,
And count another fantastic day.
Summer is here to stay for a while,
and that is why I have a permanent smile.

Stephanie Pezzutto-Levac, Grade 6
Ecole Ste-Jeanne-d'Arc, ON

While Water Rushes To and Fro

The burning sun stops its flow,
while water rushes to and fro.
The crops blossom with no complaints,
as people flourish with no restraints.
The animals smile,
for a while.
The humans come,
while humming some,
and take what they need,
a meal that will feed.
A year goes by,
and crops fly.
All while water rushes to and fro.

Nicholas LeBel, Grade 6
Our Lady of the Annunciation Catholic School, ON

Man's Best Friend

Man's best friend is by your side.
it is a strong animal that shall never hide.
When you call its name it shows up right there.
To help you with your time to spare.
A trusting animal that will help guide your way.
So please just say…
It's a Man's Best Friend!

Nicholas Seidel, Grade 4
St Alphonsus School, MB

Water

Water,
splashy, yet fun to play in,
deep, cold, waves whistling,
in the water fishies swimming around,
swimming in the
deep, dark, ocean.
Carlos Monette, Grade 6
Bernard Elementary School, BC

My Dog, My Mickey

My best friend,
Since I was a baby.
My dog, my Mickey.

With a black shimmery coat.
And fangs that were always a smile!

Side by side all the time.
Until 11 years later...

He had to go away forever.
Only in my thoughts.

Every night I think of my Mickey.
Waiting for someone just like him!
Samantha Daria Calleja, Grade 6
St Maria Goretti Elementary School, ON

Dega

I have a dog named Dega,
He is humongous and oh so mega.
Because he's so cool,
He has to drool,
So huge, is big dog Dega
Skylar Whaley, Grade 4
Deloraine School, MB

Star

A star isn't up there for show
It's up there for light
It's there to remind you of
All the wonderful and bright
Moments you have had
It's there to guide you in the
Right direction
It's there to give you hope
To tell you to never give up
It's there to give you a
Wish which will hopefully
Come true someday
But the most important
Thing of all is that
You can look at it when
You're feeling lonely
Dylan Tomiuk, Grade 6
Mornington Central School, ON

Out the Window

When I look out my window I see a...
Circus with no spectators,
Wizards practicing spells on Godzilla!
Blue and red orangutans climbing a giraffe's spotted neck
Scientists spying through telescopes as they study the sky and planets
A laughing unicorn awaits a princess
As a black rhinoceros lavishes himself in mud.
Off in the distance the sun starts to rise
I know it's going to be a good day!
Sheridan Ramsay, Grade 6
St Maria Goretti Elementary School, ON

These Hands of Mine

These are the hands
That touched my first chocolate.
And the hands that caught my first football.
These are the hands that helped me get balanced on my first step.
These are the hands that touched my clarinet today.
These are the hands that touched my little baby sister.
These are the hands that hugged my mother and father when I was sick.
These are the hands that will help me get a job as a football player.
These are the hands that will carry my son and daughter
THESE HANDS OF MINE!
Jacob Martin, Grade 5
Forest Hill School – Senior Campus, QC

Maya

My sister Maya makes marvelous machines every morning.
Maya also makes munchies like marshmallows, macaroni and mustard.
Many come munching on Maya's meat.

Maya's friend Meaghan makes musical instruments like maracas.
Meaghan met Maya at Minneapolis.
Meaghan Lavack, Grade 4
St Alphonsus School, MB

Storm on the Beach

The wind is like a cat,
    strong and powerful, clawing at your heels with the bitter cold.
The waves are like mighty stallions,
    roaring and galloping to a steady beat, crashing on the shore.
The ocean spray is like sand,
    stirred up by the biting wind and blown into your face.
The sky is like smoke,
    thick and hazy like the smog above a battlefield after gunfire.

The rain is like the stars,
    scattered here and there, creating a hazy mist.
The sand is like autumn leaves,
    scooped up easily by the wind and carried in the winds strong grip.
The air is like ice,
    frigid and wintry, freezing and damp against your skin.
The storm is like a volcano,
    pleasant and delightful until the anger is unleashed from within.
Katie Best, Grade 5
Carnarvon Community School, BC

Aria

Once gray like the clouds on a gloomy day
with lightning down her back.
Fur soft as cotton
eyes of bright topaz.
But now,
nothing more than dust,
a stone above her head
flowers waving sadly from her breast.

Meara Patterson, Grade 6
Aurora Elementary School, AB

The Planets

There are eleven planets all together,
Venus and Pluto have very bad weather,
Mars is red and Neptune is blue,
Ceres and Eris are very new,

Earth can have people because it has air,
Jupiter can't, that's no fair,
Mercury is right next to the Sun,
It's kind of small and it has no fun,

Saturn and Uranus have really big rings,
They're beside each other and they think that they're kings,
There could be other planets way out there,
Up in space in their galaxies somewhere!

Reid Senga, Grade 6
East Selkirk Middle School, MB

Spring

The whispering wind, the sunny sky,
For this is a sign of spring,
The wet dew on the grass, the birds chirping in the trees,
With these lovely things I know that spring is on its way,
The flowers coming up out of the fresh soil,
The grass is no longer yellow,
I say to myself that surely
This is spring.

Hope Smylie, Grade 6
J Douglas Hogarth Public School, ON

A Polar Bear and Her Cub

I wake up floating on an ice flow.
The ocean is shaking us as if it wants us to go.
Come on little one, time for a swim.
Trust me it won't be grim.
You jump in, I jump in.
Then I snap at an arctic char's fin.
I miss but it's all right,
because I won't give up this fight.
Let's swim back up.
The hunters are close, but do not fear
we will find somewhere to hide,
somewhere very near.

Tristan Lebrun, Grade 6
Morin Heights Elementary School, QC

Terry Fox

There was a brave man in Canada's history
His name was Terry Fox
He ran to fight cancer
Even though a leg of his was lost.
He and his best friend teamed up
After months of determination and hard work
The Marathon of Hope started from St. John's, Newfoundland
One to run and one to drive
That really shows teamwork.
The Marathon of Hope
A long run indeed
About 5000 kilometers
Not at all he dallied.
When he was almost 23
Which is still very young
On June 28th in Thunder Bay
The cancer spread to his lungs.
He was driven to the hospital
When a pain in his chest occurred
Terry died in 1981
Cancer, he almost conquered

Evelyn Tran, Grade 5
Our Lady of Perpetual Help, BC

Once Upon a Memory

Pins and needles through and through,
If you now hate me
How can I still love you?
Whenever I looked into your eyes
I always felt a sparkle inside me.

You were always there for me
I always felt safe beside you.
You were like candy
That I always craved for.

Although when you left
I felt a thousand swords stabbing through my heart
But I still looked at you as my once upon a memory

Claire Wu, Grade 5
Spul'u'kwuks Elementary School, BC

Through the Night

I sit in my bed wondering what it would be like
If I could see through the light
All through the night
For someone to hold me tight
In my pj's
On my carpet
Flying away
in the distance
on the moon
all night
tonight

Soleil Carroll, Grade 5
Kingswood Dr Public School, ON

Cats and Dogs
Cats
Cute, Small
Adoring, loving, scratching
Cats and dogs fight
Amusing, sniffing, barking
Fun, active
dogs
Gabriela Goyo-D'alessandro, Grade 4
École Renaissance, ON

Some Days
Flap your wings and
Soar away and remember
Tomorrow will be a new day
Don't get mad
At the littlest things
Because once in a while
Everyone has a bad day
So go ahead and soar away
And tomorrow make the best
Of your new day!
Jazmyn Shepit, Grade 6
Lincoln School, MB

I Wish…
I wish I were a bird
flying through the sky
watching kids play
freely
Olivia Schroeder, Grade 5
Bernard Elementary School, BC

Marc-Antoine
M ath lover
A rtist
R ight handed
C alm

A ctive
N ice
T ry one's best
O lder
I ntelligent
N ative French
E xcellent
Marc-Antoine Gagnon, Grade 5
École Renaissance, ON

Giant
Giant
Head in the clouds
How did you grow so tall?
It would hurt if you were to fall.
Huge man.
Jenkins McKim, Grade 6
Harry Balfour School, AB

Racism/Acceptance
Racism
Prejudice, fearful
Discriminating, segregating, stereotyping
Injustice, unfairness, justice, equality
Enjoying, liberating, succeeding
Happiness, joyful
Acceptance
Lindsey Smith, Grade 6
Ecole Akiva, QC

Riding!
I love riding.
It's so fun!

I love riding.
The wind speeding by!

I love riding.
It's so smooth!

I love riding.
My horse Cody!
Kayleigh Lyne, Grade 5
Mornington Central School, ON

Camping
Camping is so wonderful
Camping is so calm
With the wind swaying through the trees
Back and forth, back and forth
And just lie there in the cold puffy grass
Breathe the fresh air
In and out
While you lie
You can hear the warm fire cackling
In the distance
With cold river calmly flowing by
And that is truly like…
Kyle Dudley, Grade 6
J Douglas Hogarth Public School, ON

The Awesome Ocean
The soft golden sand,
Blows in the cold morning wind.
When sand dollars start to disappear.
The rocks were dark.
The water was cold.
The fish floppy and slippery.
The dolphins were dancing.
The whales were powerful and grey.
The seagulls were swooping.
The boat was creaking.
The seashells were sparkling.
I love the awesome ocean.
Dailyn Larose, Grade 4
Margaret Wooding School, AB

Bear/Teddy
Bear
Ferocious, savage
Growling, hibernating, eating
Cave, forest, bed, home
Cuddling, snuggling, dressing
Adorable, lovable
Teddy
Emma Freistadt, Grade 5
Bernard Elementary School, BC

Food
Spaghetti, lasagna, perogies
They're all my favourite foods,
And every night I wonder
Am I in the mood.

Carrots, celery, apples
My hamster likes them all,
If she eats too much though
She might turn into a ball.

Salad, meat, cookies
So tasty and so good,
If my mom would only give me more,
I wish she really would.

Soups, desserts, popcorn
They're really fun to eat,
We have them at sleepovers,
And what a tasty treat!
Stephanie Sachvie, Grade 6
Lincoln School, MB

The Tree
The tree,
That grew with glee.

It sang a song,
When it heard the clock gong.

When the leaves fell,
Down to the well.

It was sad,
And not glad.

For he knew he would get cold,
When the sun wouldn't shine like gold.

But when summer came,
He thought it was a game.

And when it got warm,
He did not mourn.
David Ratcliff, Grade 5
Bella Coola Adventist Academy, BC

Snowflakes

Snowflakes are falling to the ground
Swirling and circling all around
Before it snows there is a breeze
Then the snow begins to freeze
Snowflakes are drooping without a sound

Tayler Martine, Grade 6
Silver Star Elementary School, BC

Best Day

The lemon yellow sun
is going for another day.
The grass sways in
the whispering wind.
Crickets sound for another night as
frogs croak by the nearby pond.
Just to think of this made me smile,
as I lay in bed after the best day of my life.

Katelyn Drader, Grade 6
Aurora Elementary School, AB

The Kindergarten Room!

I walk in to the Kindergarten room
Sit down and observe
Looking, moving, breathing
Asking myself "I wonder what they're thinking"
Sitting there on a tiny chair
That's hard like a rock
Feeling so large
Watching kids running around
Smashing each others blocks
Getting frustrated, yelling, stomping
This class was like a jungle
There were kids all over
Some frustrated, some sad
And even the odd one happy
I turn my head nothing exciting
I turn again
There right in front of me I see…
A sand fight
These kids were mad
Throwing sand like it was spoiled spaghetti
Screaming, laughing, and much more!

Caitlin Sawka, Grade 6
Anola School, MB

Spring Is…

Snow melting and rainy too.
You hear little droppings and wonder who.
You listen to the rain.
But it does not bring pain to nature.
It actually helps nature to grow.
So soon you can row your boat.
Gently down the stream.
Just like in some kids' dreams.

Amanda Armstrong, Grade 4
Tisdale Elementary School, SK

My Pets

I have two dogs named Yogi and Tyson
And when we go to eat,
They always go eat their food
And then come back and drool on my friend's feet.

Crunch, crunch, chomp, chomp
Squeak, squeak, squeak,
There goes the sound
Of my little hamster's feet.

Jump, jump, shake, shake
Chirp, chirp, snap, snap,
There goes the sound
Of Lizzy on my brother's lap.

Stomp, stomp, chomp, chomp
There goes Tyson playing in the rain,
On his own chain with a ball
With someone's cane.

Ashley Jackson, Grade 6
Lincoln School, MB

My Skates Have Not Skated

My skates have not skated on an N.H.L. ice surface
My hockey sticks have not shot a goal into an N.H.L. net
My shoulder pads have not hit the boards of an N.H.L. arena
My helmet has not hit the ice of an N.H.L. ice surface
My hockey bag has not been in an N.H.L. dressing room
But yet someday, I hope to play in N.H.L.

Brody Smith, Grade 5
Hamiota Elementary School, MB

Eternal Darkness

I couldn't feel anything,
I couldn't be bad or sad or glad
I was lonely,
As if I was invisible.
All emotions were gone,
I was nothing.
I was lost in a world of hate and unhappiness
But I couldn't feel anything,
I was lost in a darkened world with nothing
I could leave or even see,
I was blinded.
Enraged, starvation, depression
I wanted to feel all of them but I couldn't.
I was locked up in eternal darkness
Lost forever,
I was trying to feel fear,
But I couldn't
I wanted to scream, love, hate, yell,
But I still couldn't feel anything.
Without my emotion I would be nothing,
And that's what I am.

Tyler Radke, Grade 4
St Martin De Porres School, AB

Fractions

Fractions are like a pizza,
Everyone needs to have their share,
But when one doesn't get an equal share,
He'll give you a mean glare.

I want no part of fractions
They only bring me grief.
Half the time on the quarter quiz,
I can't explain what one eighth is.

It took many students to decide,
That we'll divide them side-by-side.
They say it works, I don't know why
You turn the page over and multiply.

Many students find it so amusing
That learning fractions is confusing.
Why, we could learn this stuff real fine,
If they'd take out that silly line.

Rodrigo Villalobos, Grade 5
St Mark Separate School, ON

The Pyramid

The desert
Where am I?
Camels all around
No one else.
A massive pyramid in front of me
It's dark.
Nothing's here but sand and sky
I am alone
The warm winds blow
Silence.
A hand grabs my shoulder
I turn
The desert is a mystery.

Patrick Phillips, Grade 6
St Maria Goretti Elementary School, ON

Sunlight

Rising slowly
Beams of light
Across the horizon
In my sight.

Glowing strongly
With delight
Bright and beautiful
Cause no fright.

In my face
Is the light
I always adore
The bright sunlight.

Sara Catingan, Grade 6
Waverley Drive Public School, ON

I Am

Jordan
fun, creative, fantastic
brother of Brian and Shirley
lover of candy, video games, and coffee
who feels happy to be alive
who needs vacation, Wii games and DS games downloaded on my Ry card
who gives good ideas to people
who fears heights, trouble, and getting eaten alive
who would like to travel more
resident of Toronto
Carrillo

Jordan Carrillo, Grade 4
Calico Public School, ON

The Invasion

While lying on my back to make an angel in the snow,
I saw a greenish light appear, a giant U F O!
They unloaded in terrifying sizes and shapes,
with their weapons they destroyed the landscape.
I tried to run I tried to hide I tried to look for cover,
but I was caught and brought aboard their ship with the evil hover.
In terror I saw them pillage the land,
our armies could not withstand.
The odds are a million to one,
the invasion has just begun.

Dorian Andres, Grade 6
Ecole Ste-Jeanne-d'Arc, ON

I Meant to Clean My Room

I meant to clean my room today,
But a swarm of bee's came flying into my room
When I was opening the window for some fresh air,
And then I tried to fight them off with a spoon
Which I found behind my computer desk,
Well they just got even madder.
And when our fierce battle ended it was time for me to go to bed,
You know I get in serious trouble if I don't go to bed on time.
I meant to clean my untidy messy room today,
But the angry black and yellow tornado got in the way.

Teagan Flett, Grade 6
Linden Lanes School, MB

About Me

This is what you should know about me
I am someone who is intrigued by many things in the world
I need a hard working maid to clean my room, full time
I want my mom to stop babbling to me about my unclean room
I will try my hardest to achieve my goals in life
I hope that more people will care more about our environment
I dream that someday I will graduate from grade twelve
I like when I camp I see dozens of frogs jump gracefully on the sandy beach
I feel powerless against bullies
I will one day protest about the making of cigarettes
I wonder if all the wars will ever end.

Lillian Law, Grade 6
Bernard Elementary School, BC

Sisters

My sister is so annoying
and she is so boring
all she does is eat and sleep
and sometimes she makes me smell her feet
sometime she will awake
but then I will never get my break
there is nothing else to do
because it is all about you
but you can't make a rhyme
but I will teach you sometime
you whine mostly every day
when it's always time to play
and you do it in your way
and I will always love you
and I bet you love me too.

Cassandra Costa, Grade 4
St Alphonsus School, MB

Love

L ove is sort of odd
    even though it comes from God

O n Valentine's Day people send their love
    the love that comes from above

V alentines are fun to send
    sometimes you need to lend

E verybody enjoys the love
    that comes from above

Whitney Anderson, Grade 4
Westside Academy, BC

The Camping Blues

I went on a camp and it was really damp.
I stayed in the tent till the rain went.
I didn't have anything to eat and I wanted a treat.
I wanted a pancake and a swim in the lake.

Jarrett Rodrigues, Grade 4
Colby Village Elementary School, NS

Awesome

When you train at skiing, does steam blow?
Do your nails in the toolbox ever grow?
Does the fan on the roof cheer you along?
Can the belt on your pants scream out a song?
When the Canucks tie a game is it a knot?
Does your fly buzz around when it's hot?
When you duck from a punch do you quack?
Can the eye of a needle look back?
Can the bark of a tree scare the neighborhood cat?
Does the sole of your shoe swim around your front mat?
Does your hot dog have a big furry tail?
Can the foot of a mountain kick a pail?

Cooper Yates, Grade 6
Westwind Elementary School, BC

Lemons and Melons

Being a lemon is not an easy thing
But being a melon is a sure thing.
I had a lemon for breakfast and lunch
and melons on Monday for brunch.
I got sick that day "poor thing" my mom said,
"Are you sick?" "Oh here, have a lemon stick."

Ashwak Rhayel, Grade 6
École Renaissance, ON

Bully

When I went to school.
There was a bully.
He was so rude.
His name was Ollie.
But I told my teacher.
She said, "Ignore it."
I ignored it but it didn't work.
Not even one bit.
He got 5 tiks from the teacher.
And he had to do some lines.
Then he got a D.T.
Then he made some signs.
But he learned not to bully.
Then he stopped and wanted to be my friend.
This is the power of one.
And that is the end!

Alexis Edwards, Grade 6
Harry Balfour School, AB

My Day Shopping

It was the best and worst of days.
SHOPPING!
Looking at shoes.
HORROR!
Heading towards E.B. Games.
HOPE!
Turned and going to American eagle.
AGONY!
Getting popcorn from kernals.
DELICIOUS!
Accidentally dropped the popcorn.
HUNGER!
Driving home.
RELIEF!
I survived until next time
it was the best and worst of days mostly worst

Aidan Wilson, Grade 5
Charles Beaudoin Public School, ON

Emerald

Frogs leaping from lily pad to lily pad
Leaves soaring through the air
Grass waving when wind blows
Green

Emma Cheetham, Grade 5
Forest Hill School – Senior Campus, QC

The Beach

As we walk across the sparkling sand.
We found an entertaining crab.
We found a crawling lobster.
The birds were flying happily in the sky.
The shells are beautiful and shiny.
Water is so clear.
You can see the colorful fish.
Dolphins jumping in the water.
Whales swimming happily in the sea.
The beach is a beautiful place to be!

Jasmine Danielle Kirkness, Grade 4
Margaret Wooding School, AB

Bully

Oh all of the lies,
All the fighting,
And helplessness,
And so much crying,
They never leave,
They bring others down,
To feel good about themselves,
When they do don't frown,
Instead stand up to them,
No more lies and fights,
You won't feel helpless,
No more crying,
They will leave you alone.

Rachel Ward, Grade 6
Vincent Massey Public School, ON

We Remember

On a cold November's day
A soldier stands alone
With still the thoughts and
Sounds of war
Running through his bones
Brave men fought
And many died
While their families cried and cried

Now many of those
Brave strong men
Are out in Flanders Fields
Among the dead

All the poppies that
Are bought
Are in remembrance
Of those who fought
So just remember on this day
Of all the people far away
Who lost their loved ones
In the war that brings us sorrow
More and more

Mackenzie Smith, Grade 5
Mornington Central School, ON

The World

The world has many places
and lots of happy faces.
The world is very bright
and beautiful at night.
In places it could be winter
In cities it could be spring
In countries it could be summer
or it could be everything.
In the world there are places
that are very nice.
In the world there are places
as cold as ice.
Our world can get dirty or it
can be clean
Our world can be nice or it
can be mean.
The sky is so beautiful when you
look up above
But the world is something I will
always love.

Montana Ward, Grade 5
Chiganois Elementary School, NS

Reading

This soothes me
I can read for ages and ages
My mind can run free
And I am all to myself
I can think my own thoughts and dream.
My own dreams
But why is this
Is this me?
Why yes, yes it is
Reading is me

Jessica Kehoe, Grade 6
Falmouth District School, NS

My Dream

In my dream I could fly
Up into the sky
I could sail the wide ocean
For as long as I want
In my dreams,
I'm free to do whatever I want!

Alycia Buller, Grade 5
École Renaissance, ON

Hockey

H itting is so much fun
O h! You gotta penalty!
C heck him! Check him!
K athryn you're benched
E at your dust
Y ay we won!!!!!

Kathryn Rosa, Grade 5
École Renaissance, ON

In Fall

All the leaves fall
The temperature falls
The gourd gets crisp,
And starts to freeze
The fall

Caleb Matheson, Grade 6
Falmouth District School, NS

Purple

Purple streaks in my blonde hair
Purple swirls in a tornado
Purple slugs squashing under my boots
Purple sounds like rain,
Flowers blooming in spring,
And a leaf falling off trees
Purple tastes like sweet grapes
A violet from New Brunswick
And sweet sap from a maple tree
Purple feels like squishy play dough,
Soft cold wind on my face
And squishy mud in my toes
Purple can change your mood
Purple.

Madison Russell, Grade 4
J Douglas Hogarth Public School, ON

Someday

I say
Someday
I shall fly
Across the land
Near the bridges and
The mountains
By the light of the bridges

Feeling the dancing wind
On my face
To see the beautiful lights
In my eyes
Near the bridges and the
Mountains
By the lights of the bridges.

Kailyn Ng, Grade 5
Spul'u'kwuks Elementary School, BC

Shine

Shine on the snow
shine on me
shine on the dog
shine on the tree
shine on the house
shine so fair
shine on the book
shine everywhere

Alyssa Rol, Grade 4
J Douglas Hogarth Public School, ON

Halloween

On Halloween night,
I saw an eerie sight.
Maybe a ghost, a ghoul
or an angry malamuel.
I crept along the path
moving left and right
searching for the fright.
I jumped, I hopped, I leaped
over lumps, bumps, and stumps.
A ghost slithered by through a bump!
As I shivered my way along I ran over a ghoul
or was it that malamuel?
But in my doubts I didn't know the routes
and I ran into that angry malamuel.

Kandace Law-Quon, Grade 6
East Selkirk Middle School, MB

Butterfly

Mom's sick with five kids that try to help out,
she's like a rag torn and worn-out.
Stuck, tired in bed, and old like a piece of thread.
Mom's sick with five kids that try to help out.
As I lay in bed I pray,
that she will be better on Sunday.
Mom's sick with five kids that try to help out,
she's like a rag torn and worn-out.

Kayla Taylor, Grade 6
Ecole Ste-Jeanne-d'Arc, ON

I Love to Dance

Before you read what I have to say,
Get a comfy blanket and lay.
Everyone has a different story
some are great and some are gory.

Well this story is mine,
and I think it's just fine.
Some people like dance, just like me.
I'll tell you when I started just wait and see.

I started dancing at one and a half,
and now watching me that young makes me laugh.
When I dance, I feel so good.
And when I do hip-hop I wear a hood.

When I was young I did ballet and tap.
Now I do acro and jazz and clap.
My favourite move is a front walk-over into the splits,
and that dance move just naturally fits.

Now that is the end of my story.
I hope you didn't find it boring or gory.
Dancing is great exercise, it's my hobby too.
Everybody can do it, how about you?

Elizabeth Simzer, Grade 4
Jack Miner Public School, ON

War

War is a sad thing
A conflict between two countries
A decision of life or death
A battle for glory featuring brave countries
Families in solemnness
Waiting for that good or terrifying call
War is scary

Harry Leach, Grade 4
FW Gilbert School, MB

My Secret Place

When I go to my
Secret place I feel
Special and excited.
I go to my secret
When I am sad or
Just need to think.
I like my secret place
Because it's like
A bright day
Even when it's not.
My secret place
Makes me feel
Like jumping
For joy I would
Tell you where
My secret place is,
But then it would
It would not
Be so secret.

Olivia Antongiovanni, Grade 5
Queen of All Saints Elementary School, BC

Mountain Climbing

gazing at the top
goal is to climb the mountain
my lungs are on fire

Maggy Li, Grade 4
Howard De Beck Elementary School, BC

Poppy Fields

Poppy fields,
Row on row.
Flowers on graves,
Wrapped in a bow.
Families worrying at home
Of the lands where their sons roam.
Soldiers sent to fight,
But some don't make it through the night.
Fields stained blood red
From the lives that are lost
Or left for dead.
But some memories are not so bad.
Some are happy, although we are sad.

Liam Hood, Grade 6
Central Middle School, BC

I Had a Snowman

I had a little snowman
It was big and round
When I went down a hill
It rolled right down
I asked my mom to keep it
She said oh no
So my friendly little snowman
Stayed outside until one day
I went outside and it wasn't there
So I told my mom it ran away
But no one really knows
So I guess I just have to wait
Until next year.

Faith Billiaert, Grade 4
Deloraine School, MB

Foam Ball

Now I'm not talking
about any
foam ball —
This one I mean —
That's small
And easy to roll,
That's an amazing color of blue
like the deep ocean,
That has the funniest smell
Like raw steak.
The ball says "Bonk"
As it hits the table.
This ball is one
Of a kind.

Kyle Feschuk, Grade 5
Hamiota Elementary School, MB

Shadow

Doesn't have colour
Cannot hit
It follows you
Can't abandon it

When it's sunny
And you step out
It's already there
Cannot shout

Replica of you
Has no detail
Gets bigger or smaller
Even for a whale

Doesn't have colour
Cannot hit
It follows you
Can't abandon it

Judy Hong, Grade 6
Sir Isaac Brock Public School, ON

These Hands of Mine

These are the hands that hold the handle bars of my bike.
The ones that feel through darkness when I can't see.
The ones that hug my parents when I get sad.
My hands freeze when I don't wear mittens.

These hands hold the play station controller when I sit in front of the television.
The hands that relax when I am lazy.
My hands hold the pencil while I do a test.
The hands that press the buttons on the key board.

The hands that clutch the steering wheel of my dad's car.
The ones that write the exam when I'm in college.
These hands of mine shall hold the football ready to toss it to my son.
These hands will rest in peace.

Branden Desormeau, Grade 5
Forest Hill School – Senior Campus, QC

How About a Dog

A day in bright summer, in a tone very pleasant
I asked my parents if I could get a dog.
One more try, I thought; maybe I wouldn't get outfought
I said all the benefits, how happy we would be
If I came home everyday and he would come to greet me
With a lick on my face and a very pleased bark, my eyes would gain a spark
That would lead me through the day and it would be better than okay
If I were to get a dog.
Stop! Stop! Stop! I heard them say
I sighed and realized, this would not be like breeze in midday
My parents continued their speech of worry
For who would clean up after him? It's not going to be easy!
What about the shedding and everyday walks?
And how will he remember where we live, and in which block?
It could be east, it could be west
How would he know? He might just walk into a bird's nest!
We would need to train him, and where would the time come from?
And let me tell you, I'm about to explode like a bomb!
I turned my head in sadness, as I slowly walked away
Maybe I could ask about this on a much nicer sunny day.

Armand Deghati, Grade 6
Webber Academy, AB

Picture Day

Today is picture day at my school.
I get in line and everyone looks so cool!
I have to wait awhile,
but soon it's my turn and the photographer says "Smile."
I sit up straight and show off my white teeth,
and hope this picture is one to keep.

The next week I get my picture. Lisa says "Wow, look at hers."
I love my picture — everything is just right —
my clothes, my expression and even the light.
I'm so happy, I don't know what to say,
but I manage to squeak out "I can't wait for the next picture day."

Catherine Goncalves, Grade 5
Guardian Angels School, ON

The Little Monkey

The monkey was the cutest thing I had ever seen. Big brown eyes, shaggy brown fur. Sweet monkey laugh. Eating bananas then throwing the peels on the ground. Swinging through the trees. I laugh at him he laughs at me. His little belly button, cute as a button. Then a zoo keeper came along and took him away. My eyes filled with water, tears streaking down my cheeks. Then it hit me like an arrow in my chest. I was never going to see that little monkey again...the next heartfelt day I went back to the zoo and looked for that cute little monkey swinging in the trees, but he was not there. He was not there the next day, or the next. Then one day I went back to the zoo and found the little monkey swinging in the trees and yelled so loud the people in China heard. And from then on the adorable little monkey never left.

Sylvia Lamothe, Grade 5
Charles Beaudoin Public School, ON

Computers

Computers run the Internet and keep us connected,
And they also do things too dangerous for humans to do at all.
They are the things that keep us updated,
But we still can't confuse the devices that connect us from the moments that keep us together.
The things we do on computers can be very useful at times,
But the Internet has its downsides likes viruses and trackers.
You really need to look out for these few things,
For if you don't absorb this mural, you will pay.
The way the computer works is really marvelous,
And they help our productivity quite a lot.
But really please understand the COMPUTERS DON'T SOLVE EVERYTHING (yet!)!
Now then do we all understand?
The Internet can lie, and people can spy.
The world is now unsafe, unprotected,
And all our information can leak worldwide.
So just be careful, and I can't stress this enough:
THE INTERNET'S NOT SAFE ANYMORE; IT'S YOUR RESPONSIBILITY TO STAY SAFE!!!

Kevin Yue, Grade 6
St Mark Separate School, ON

What Is Truth?

The wind blows on mountains high as I stare at the valley below. I seek the truth of the world, as unseen as the air that flows. I shall keep on my quest until I turn to dust and then will I declare myself done. I shall look under every rock, even if it takes me all eternity to find what I should have and is rightfully mine.

Anelya Miriam Fridland, Grade 6
Westside Preparatory High School, BC

Winter Wonderland

On a diamond sparkling Christmas Eve, our heart warming family enjoying this fine time.
The sight of lovely stockings and glimmering,
white snow and tightly wrapped presents makes me feel excited about Christmas!
Smelling the nice scent of pine needles and feasts magically makes everyone feel warm, cozy and happy.
I can't wait to touch the nice, hardcover books and awesome toys people bring me.
The taste of roasted turkey and other yummy foods makes my mouth water like crazy!
Hearing melodious caroling outside brings joy to all of the families.

Ben Mueller, Grade 4
David Ovans Elementary School, AB

To My Father

So many memories we made together it's so sad you're gone forever as the days go by I try not to cry. I can't help but think, are you watching over me? I know you were sick with a terrible disease and now I feel the disease has been passed on to me. The disease of grieving the disease of not receiving not receiving your love and care not receiving your hugs and kisses but I know somehow you will always be there.

Jessica St. Jules, Grade 6
John T Tuck Public School, ON

Mother Kangaroo

A leaping kangaroo aggressively
Feeds joey
While being
A shelter
And
Bed.
She also notices
A lion tiredly
Glance towards
Her baby.
She
Leaps away protectively.
Kirsten Brown, Grade 6
Linden Lanes School, MB

Silence

Minute of silence
Birds chirping, flying, singing
Two nests in a large tree
Will Bullard, Grade 6
Silver Star Elementary School, BC

Bananas

Bananas
slippy, squishy
falling, peeling, eating
monkeys love to eat
Amazing!
Andrew Court, Grade 6
John T Tuck Public School, ON

The Championship

my very first,
actually the slippery seconds
just melting away
we are down by five
still 70 more yards to go
although it felt like a million
the ball is snapped
slapped straight into my hands
I could feel the poor pigs skin,
warm in my hands
the receiver rush down the field
as if on fire
running out of time
the ticking, as if taunting
desperate as far as desperate can go
I throw the ball
It soars gracefully through the air
The receiver leaps
grabs the ball against his helmet
into the end zone
the crowd goes ballistic
we have won the Super Bowl.
Dylan Johannesson, Grade 6
Aurora Elementary School, AB

Cherry Blossoms

The sun setting on
A blossoming cherry tree
So yummy and sweet
Samantha Jee, Grade 4
Park West School, NS

Sonic/Shadow

Sonic
Fast, funny
Running, dashing, spinning
Character, hero, villain, darkness
Hovering, hitting, shoving
Evil, sneaky
Shadow
Connor Ferguson, Grade 5
Bernard Elementary School, BC

Snow

It is beautiful.
It's like shiny, white crystals
I'm sure it is snow
Francisca Annan, Grade 4
Park West School, NS

Raven

When I hear
A raven's call
My breath stops
My heart falls

The reason why
The sky is blue
Is because the raven
Hasn't found you

But you will see
The grass turns black
As the sky starts to dim

"The raven's here!"
The children fear
They will never see
That blue sky again.
Erin O'Leary, Grade 6
Falmouth District School, NS

Winter Summer

Winter
Cold, white
Skating, freezing, drinking
Dark, fun, light, water
Swimming, running, playing
Hot, fun
Summer
Johnathan Carvalho, Grade 6
St James Catholic School, BC

Kung Fu Panda

There once was a panda named Po,
Who could not bend very low,
He knew kung fu well,
But he almost fell,
So down went that panda named Po.
Isabelle Van Dinter, Grade 5
Westside Academy, BC

Sports

Hockey
Cold, energetic,
Skating, deking, scoring,
Defense, forwards, midfields, goalies,
Dribbling, shooting, slide tackling,
Fun, skillful,
Soccer
Michael Lizzi, Grade 5
St Mark Catholic School, ON

The Willow Tree

The willow tree sways
back and forth, back and forth
While the leaves fall.
Zoe Granger, Grade 6
Bernard Elementary School, BC

My Fish

My fish splish-splash in their tank all day.
When I get home from school,
I like to watch them play.
Chris MacLellan, Grade 4
Colby Village Elementary School, NS

Tate

There once was a boy named Tate
Who sat on the edge of the gate
He watched the cows eat
All the green hay and wheat
Next thing he knew it was eight
Ashton Bell, Grade 4
Deloraine School, MB

Field of Peace

Flanders Field, poppies sway,
in the muddy fields, day by day.
We now lie in a field of moss,
resting under each cross.
Lives were lost in Flanders Field,
peace was brought in Flanders Field.
We soldiers fought for peace
but some of us lost our lives.
As we die, dark fills the sky.
We try to stand our ground,
but now we lie in it too.
Marc Shewchuk, Grade 4
FW Gilbert School, MB

Do Your Part

Peace, not a gun or a bomb,
Peace, but a kind word or sharing,
Peace, it's not that hard.
Peace, from the wisest scholar
Peace, to the youngest child.
Peace, we can all make a difference.
Peace, as Tenzin Gyasto once said,
"If you wish to experience peace,
Provide peace for another."
These are words we could live by.
Peace, if we all made even a little effort,
Peace, we can make a big difference.
Peace, do your part,
Make peace
Peace

Bridget Heeman, Grade 6
St Mary Choir and Orchestra Program, ON

Fall

The leaves crunch when you jump on them
Like the sound
Of someone biting into a crisp apple.
The orange colored leaves
Are slowly falling off the trees
As delicate as feathers floating
Down when you drop them.
Running into class
On the first day of school.
And me dreaming about my summer.

Megan Meredith, Grade 5
Queen of All Saints Elementary School, BC

Spring

G reen grass growing on a lawn.
R ed fire burning in the fireplace.
O range sun glowing in the bright blue sky.
W icked brown swirling in the misty air.
T eal blending with the nature's grocery
H ot, humid spring day.

Albert Wipf, Grade 5
Milford Colony School, AB

Pink...

is a tasty gum ball
is the feel of a solid marker
is the scent of a batch of roses
is the sight of a piece of paper
is the noise of liquid nail polish moving around
is the feel of a balloon with red stripes
is the inside of a juicy watermelon
is a big bowl of ice cream
is the colour of your house
is the look of a Care Bear.

Therren Alberta, Grade 6
Bernard Elementary School, BC

The Cold Fun...

It's white, it's fluffy coming from the sky,
Don't look and stand there or watch it go by.
Jump up and down and catch it too,
Or twirl and let it fall on you!

It's cold and freezing that's what they say
But don't stop now just go and play!
The colorful snow suits red, green and pink,
Soon you'll take it off and have a hot drink.

Mom sees you out there having lots of fun.
You roll then jump and now you run!
You run to the ice rink and get on your skates
And there are your friends Mark, Bob and Kate.

As you look up in the sky above,
You think of all the things you love.
The winter snow is what she brings
That soon they will melt into spring.

As you're thinking while you skate,
It starts to get a bit too late.
You see an open door of light
As you walk in you say good night.

Alexandra Carroll, Grade 6
École élémentaire catholique Georges-Étienne-Cartier, ON

I Remember

I remember coming to the hospital each day
I remember all the sorrow filling days
I remember the tears in your eyes
I remember your humble apple pie
I remember when I saw you cry
I remember the day you faded to dust
I remember your cross in the grave
I remember the flowers that laid on your bed
I remember all the things you gave to cherish my
heart each and every day
I will remember you forever

Jaiden Boscher, Grade 6
Aurora Elementary School, AB

Beyond the Orbit

Beyond the orbit is a beautiful place called "SPACE,"
It has planets and stars, and trust me they're very far,
Along with the moon and the big giant spoon
That most people call the Big Dipper.

So let's have some fun
We'll name the planets in order closest to the Sun,
There's Mercury, Venus, Earth, Mars, Ceres, Jupiter, Saturn,
Uranus, Neptune, Pluto and Eris.
Beyond the orbit there's lots of neat things including
Saturn's beautiful rings.

Kaleb Dickson, Grade 6
East Selkirk Middle School, MB

Hamsters

The hamsters in the
Sink are learning how to surf
Using bars of soap.
Danielle Sabean, Grade 6
Falmouth District School, NS

Hawk's Eyes

Eyes looking straight at me,
Dark eyes looking down at me,
Scary looking hawk.
Kate Daoey, Grade 6
Ormsby School, AB

End of the World

The sky is falling
My mom is calling
I don't know what to do
It is getting out of control
And I am losing my soul
The earth is exploding
The birds are not flying
I want to know why
But I think I would cry
My mother said
I lost my head
And I agreed
'Cause I'm the lead
In...*The biggest liar*
Ashley Stopay, Grade 5
École Renaissance, ON

Earth

Earth
So beautiful
Grassy fields
Cool breezes
Tall trees
Earth is a miracle
Open your eyes
See how perfectly formed
Everything is
Don't take it for granted

We are part of Earth
If we lose it we lose ourselves
We will no longer be alive
Don't take it for granted

Because
If we do
We will soon lose
Our Earth
So...
Don't take it for granted.
Logan Ferguson, Grade 6
St James Catholic School, BC

The Best of Friends

The best of friends will turn a frown into a smile when you're feeling down.
The best of friends will always care and have something great to share.
The best of friends will believe in you even if there is only two.
The best of friends will always be nice more than twice.
The best of friends will be great and there will be no hate.
If you find the best of friends you will find they are quite a treasure
If you use your mind.
Mckenzie Kruger, Grade 4
J Douglas Hogarth Public School, ON

The Time Has Come...

The time has come...For men to die.
For flak to burst for paratroopers to rain from planes in the sky.
The time has come...
For mines to go off. For buildings to burn.
For screams to be heard.
For men to die on the death filled beaches of Normandy.
The time has come...
For canons to roar. For ships to sink.
For men to fight to the bitter end.
For the blood to stain your memory.
The time has come...
For our air force...
For our navy...
For our ground forces...
For our people...
To Be Free.
Jacob Rich, Grade 6
Mornington Central School, ON

Spring

Spring is like a baby who grows in summer, winter, and fall,
Like us, it grows bigger, but of course it starts off small.

It's the beginning season, when plants begin to sprout,
We've seen our first plants this year, let's all scream and shout.

All the spring flowers shall colourfully bloom,
They'll brighten our gardens and colour our rooms.

Now the spring showers will help them grow,
And our lilies and daisies will sprout up from below.

Spring clothes have now stocked our stores, barely any winter ones remain,
This is also time to switch our closets and put our spring clothes in again.

The snow has now melted and gone all away,
So now instead of snowsuits, we'll be wearing vests to play.

We've waited three whole seasons, and finally it's here,
Everything in Spring is terrific, and this poem makes that clear.

Once this spring is over, we'll have a while to wait,
So let's make the best of this one, and hope the next doesn't come late.
Sarah Alnemer, Grade 6
Academie Marie Laurier, QC

The Empty Place in Your Heart
The empty place in your heart
Is the loneliness of all mankind,
Feeling left out in the world.
The empty place in your heart
Is having no one to talk to;
Not even one or two.
The empty place in your heart
Is the loneliness of all mankind.

Hans-Corneille Ntumba-Kanyinda Tshikangu, Grade 6
Ecole Ste-Jeanne-d'Arc, ON

Bonita
Wise, black, sleepy.
Her beautiful brown eyes catching the sunlight show
a look of wisdom as her black body drifts to sleep.

Royal, proud, content.
The flamboyant queen struts along the sidewalk
as regular bystanders gasp in amazement.

Cute, hungry, curious.
Her cute face whining at the sight of her
silver dinner bowl makes me want to give her
second helpings.

Furry, fast, joyful.
Her furry body is a blur as she races towards the ball,
tail furiously wagging.

Lovable, appealing, friendly to all.
As the neighbours stroll around the block,
She bounds up to them and they
share beaming smiles.

My own canine companion is my very best friend.

Ian Leighton, Grade 5
Surrey Connect School, BC

Snowflakes
Go inside a snowflake
Ride it to your house.
Drift on air and
Sway to the
Kitchen floor.

A snowflake is
White like a fresh cloud.
It slowly and calmly
Floats to the ground.

It feels like a feather pillow
And it's joyful
Like me
Building a snowman.

Nicholas Eng, Grade 5
Queen of All Saints Elementary School, BC

My Life and His
When I was 8 days old, I had a briss.
When he was 8 days old, he got a spanking.

When I was 2, my mom put a suss in my mouth.
When he was 2, a Nazi put dirt in his mouth.

When I was 3, I learned how to skate.
When he was 3, he learned how to pick up bricks.

When I was 4, I ate a doughnut.
When he was 4, he ate a piece of stale bread.

When I was 5, I got a hockey stick.
When he was 5, he got a grenade.

When I was 6, I hit a homerun.
When he was 6, he was hit by a Nazi.

When I was 7, I got an XBox 360.
When he was 7, he got shot.

Ryan Kalisky, Grade 5
Ecole Akiva, QC

Why?
Michael Phelps,
My hero,
My role model…
When I heard about him smoking marijuana,
I felt sad.
Disappointed,
and I wondered…
Why would he use this substance to darken his future?
To disappoint fans…
Why would he put over 400 chemicals
in himself?
Why?
Why?
Why?
Maybe because of…
peer pressure,
he thought it was cool,
But now,
now he is sorry…

Janice Chok, Grade 5
Spul'u'kwuks Elementary School, BC

Monkeys
Monkeys are big and they are small.
They play with balls all day long!
They nibble on bananas and do not know when to stop.
They have those ears and that freakishly long tail.
That smile that will not go away.
That is why monkeys are so silly.

Karlie Hartman, Grade 4
Tisdale Elementary School, SK

Colour My World

Red is fire,
Cherry and tomato,
And also tomato cerise.
Fire burning in the night,
And music, even fire crackers.
Apples, soft silk ribbons,
Markers too.
Red.

Scott Harrison, Grade 4
J Douglas Hogarth Public School, ON

Sun

I like the warm sun
when she shines like a light
it makes me feel wonderful
when she is right

With her warm hand
she tries to hug me
I like her warm touch
she's a good friend I see

I like it when she's happy
The plants are small
when she gives them sunshine
then they grow tall

She shines down on everyone
like a beautiful light
we dance around and smile at her
when she shines so bright

Tabea Hofer, Grade 4
Sunnysite Colony School, AB

Spring Is…

Rain falling from the sky
Birds come back from South
Snow melting all around
Lots of puddles everywhere
It is wonderful
It is very beautiful
And the flowers start to bloom
There is lots of flowers!

Miranda Mann, Grade 4
Tisdale Elementary School, SK

A Funny Joy

I had this funny feeling
It felt very appealing
I bounced all around
I went round and round
It felt like joy
Better than a toy
Us people call it happiness

Allison Smith, Grade 4
St Martin De Porres School, AB

Dogs

Dogs are fun,
There my #1.
Dogs are so cute,
They could wear a suit.
They're so cool,
They have their own school.
Dogs are sometimes worth lots of money,
Sometimes they act kind of funny.

Danika Holliday, Grade 4
St Alphonsus School, MB

Day/Night

Day
Sunny, bright
Playing, working, exercising
School, friends, dinner, stars
Reading, sleeping, dreaming
Dark, peaceful
Night

Chase Johnson, Grade 5
Bernard Elementary School, BC

Spring

The snow melts away
and it's the first day of spring
blooming flowers start.

Mariam Wurie, Grade 4
Park West School, NS

The Detective Club

In this Detective Club,
There are problems to solve,
Fingerprints to rub,
While ideas evolve.

We can read palms,
Spy in a tree,
As long as we're calm,
We can avoid that bee.

There is a new mystery,
No time for school work,
I'll catch up in history,
Before I go berserk.

I'm having trouble,
To guess the culprit.
The one who has a bubble,
Well, just a little bit.

Tonight there's a meeting,
For the Detective Club,
And we'll be eating,
A roasted shrub.

Helena Turgeon, Grade 6
École Renaissance, ON

Feelings and Emotions

When you're happy
You smile
When you're sad
You frown
You have feelings
And emotions
That go up and down.
You cry, you bawl
You get pushed
Then you fall
You get right back up
Your feelings and emotions
Are getting messed up.

Sarah Murphy, Grade 6
Falmouth District School, NS

Competition

I can do the splits
I can do high kicks
I can do pliés
As good as chassé
I pick up a hoop
And do a loop
My competition was great
And I did not make a mistake

Abby Edginton, Grade 4
St Alphonsus School, MB

A Tree

A tree with branches so long,
To carry out nature's mellow song,
With long branches inter-winding
Twigs and leaves inter-binding,
When the cold air starts a-coming,
So all the children start a-runnin',
For I cannot bear,
The frosty cold air.

Patricia Rondeau, Grade 6
George Bonner Middle School, BC

Trigger

Evil, calm
Growling, napping, barking
Trigger does not like me.
A Dog

Jordana Morrison, Grade 4
Good Shepherd School, AB

Love

Grass may be green
Water may be blue
Birds may be singing
As fast as my heart beats
For you

Dawson Braun, Grade 4
St Alphonsus School, MB

My Big Race

I feel the snow brushing on my face.
The sound of the horn.
I'm speeding down the hill
Dodging the flags not worrying
about whether I win or not.
Just worrying about finishing on time.
I look behind me at all those flags.
My poles by my side.
I hear all the people cheering me on.
Ice all down my jacket.
My face is frozen.
My goggles are all fogged up.
I can barely see, but I still see the flags.
Shivers all down my back
my hands freezing as ice.
I can barely hold on to my poles.
My skis covered in snow.
It's snowing like mad.
It's really hard to see.
Wait I see it, the finish line,
I WON!!!

Sarah Simpson, Grade 5
Forest Hill School – Senior Campus, QC

Mother Nature

I change the seasons as I go
From the blooming of everything and the rain
To the shining sun and the bright blue sky
That will soon fade into the windier days
And the reddish golden change in the leaves
Then I will make one more change
Before I go and do it all over again
That change is the white and the snowflakes fall
Who am I
I am Mother Nature

Jessica Hein, Grade 6
Aurora Elementary School, AB

Racing

Cars race on the track
racing around tight corners
going very fast
stopping at pit stops for gas
burning rubber as they leave

Piers Waldie, Grade 5
Forest Hill School – Senior Campus, QC

Solitary

Bare trees
like big bare bones
nothing covering them.
Stripped naked by winter's dark wrath.
Lonely

Nikol Grishin, Grade 5
Howard De Beck Elementary School, BC

These Hands of Mine

These hands helped me paint.
I used my hands to play with my toys.
My hands helped me to swim.
My hands helped me to learn to count.

My hands help me to catch the football.
My hands help me to balance.
I use my hands when I am a soccer goalie.
I use my hands to say hi to my friends.

My hands will help me plant trees for the environment.
My hands will hold my soccer trophy.
My hands will help me drive.
My hands will help me do my job.

Nicholas Petrakos, Grade 5
Forest Hill School – Senior Campus, QC

Holocaust

The Holocaust was an ugly thing
People who voted for him got a sting

And you ask who is this him I speak of
His name is Hitler and he lost his love

He lost his love for human kind
His parents died, he said he didn't mind

But it is true that he did lie
Which might have led to his deny

That the Jews could not have the same rights
But in the end, they won their fights

The Holocaust was an ugly thing
Sorrow and blood is all that it did bring

Alisha Mann, Grade 6
Westside Academy, BC

Loud!

Loud is black
Like an exploding bomb.
Loud is like a traffic jam
That annoys grown-ups on
Their way home from work.
Loud is like a nerf gun
Firing and blasting someone.
Loud is like two cars smashing together.
Loud is the sound of cheering fans
At a Canucks game.
Loud is powerful like an elephant
Making a hole in the ground
When it stomps around.
Loud makes me feel startled
Like an unexpected gunfire.

Anthony Maljevac, Grade 5
Queen of All Saints Elementary School, BC

Aqua

Aqua is fish swimming gracefully, feet jumping in cool puddles, and boats sailing freely in the ocean.
Aqua is the taste of saltwater splashing.
Aqua smells like the chlorine of an indoor pool, and your hair after swimming.
Aqua makes me feel calm and relaxed.
Aqua is the sound of waves crashing against the rocks, and the whooshing sound of a waterfall.
Aqua is bubbles floating, a surfboard gliding across the open sea, and raindrops falling in the night.
Aqua is water.
Aqua is Earth.

Paige Leedale, Grade 6
John T Tuck Public School, ON

Light Cotton Candy Blue

Light cotton candy blue is the colour of the sky swelling with billowing cumulus clouds inviting me to contemplate upon it, thinking of an image for each and every cloud, on a lambent summer's day.

The decadent light cotton candy blue colour of the cotton candy tempts the hungry children as it winks at them in the fluorescent lights from behind the movie theater snack bay.

The light cotton candy blue of the incandescent lake is radiating as kids swarm around it in their vibrant bathing suits, ready to jump in it, with the sun's luminous, powerful rays beating on their sunburnt backs.

Adorable light cotton candy blue clothing adorns the walls of "Paddington's Baby Store" enticing new mothers and their bouncing baby boys to come in to explore the multitudes of racks.

Light cotton candy blue evokes a distant memory of Granddad's steely blue eyes gazing inquisitively at me, as he reacquaints himself with his Canadian granddaughter.

Light cotton candy blue is the colour of the cascading waterfall that washes over the amateur canoeists struggling to remain upright in the rapidly surging waters.

Celeste Catena, Grade 4
First Lutheran Christian School, BC

Yellow

Yellow is a daffodil blooming in the spring, a bee buzzing in the air, a dandelion in the field.
Yellow is the taste of a banana.
Yellow smells like vanilla and liveliness.
Yellow makes me feel joyful.
Yellow is the sound of chirping birds flying though the air.
Yellow is the burning hot sun, flowers blooming in the garden, and is the peaceful sound of music.
Yellow is me.

Taylor Alderdice, Grade 6
John T Tuck Public School, ON

Sometimes

Sometimes you are like an ocean caught in an angry storm.
And then you rock us all like the little boats dotted on the Pacific.
Sometimes it is like a lullaby. Sometimes not.
Sometimes you are calming and soothing and carry the same scent as spring after a long winter.
That is a nice scent. Perhaps that is the nicest.
Sometimes you are like a fountain.
You cry so much that I have to remind you that I am the child, you are the grown-up.
Not the other way around.
But always, you carry around who you will always be.
Whether it is on the outside or hidden in the inside, you will always be my mother.

Eva Rodrigues, Grade 4
Laura Secord School, MB

My Boots Have Not Been Set

My boots have not been set
in the shiny and glimmering stirrups.

My legs have not sat
in my fresh and clean jodhpurs.

My fingers have not been
in the gripped coal black gloves.

My fingers have not touched
the beautifully braided reins.

My eyes have not met
the back of my winning horse's neck.

My hair has not been placed
in a tight bun underneath my velvety helmet.
But
These are my dreams that are yet to be told.
These are my dreams so let them unfold.

Sarah Gauld, Grade 6
Sir Isaac Brock Public School, ON

Sheep

Under a tree's
Leafy ivy crown, encrusted with dainty ruby jewels,
Gleaming in the sunlight,
Lays a cottony cloud-like bundle,
Swaying to the calm lullaby of the murmuring wind.
His slender face is huddled and buried in a coat
Of heavenly diamond fluff,
Wrapping around his tight snowy skin.
His soft umber eyes shimmer
Like a multicolored disco ball.
A stub of a tail curls behind his bony knobby legs.
A young copper bell jingles from a vermilion ribbon,
Draped around his neck.
Chewing daintily at several strands of emerald grass,
He cowers under the towering sapphire sky,
Stretching as far as the eye can see.

Peace.
Silence.

Zen…

Mira Refvik, Grade 6
Brock-Corydon School, MB

Ants

line of
ants is like a
line of soldiers marching
onto a boat to go to war
thump thump

Kevin Robertson, Grade 5
Howard De Beck Elementary School, BC

Thanksgiving

T is for thanks that we say each year.
H is for the happy people on Thanksgiving.
A is for the place where Albertans celebrate.
N is for the nice people who settled in Canada.
K is for the kindness that the First Nation gave.
S is for the settlers who helped create Thanksgiving.

Jason Ng, Grade 4
David Ovans Elementary School, AB

Night

The sun
Was slowly
Falling down
And finally
It was night.

Then the
Bright moon
Was shining
In the
Black sky.

The stars
Were twinkling
Like shimmering
Diamonds.

I slowly
Shut my curtains
While staring
At the beauty.
Then I quietly
Tiptoed
Into bed.

Margherita Venetsanos, Grade 5
Queen of All Saints Elementary School, BC

Vampire

Ice cold hands pale white feet this Vampire cannot be beat.
Italic eyes that change at night.
No wings but it does take flight.

It was built to soar.
It was built to fight.
To take down its prey it must use its might.

Feeds on blood.
Fangs of fire.
Never trust it because it's a liar.

Sparkles in the light.
Show it's true.
Watch your back it's coming for you.

Megyn Cordner, Grade 4
St Alphonsus School, MB

Ontario

Ontario
Rocks, trees
Swimming, boating, hunting
Helmet, toque, hat, hood
Skiing, skating, sledding
Prairie, wheat
Manitoba

Jordan Lajeunesse, Grade 6
Linden Lanes School, MB

The Forest

I walked the hard dry sand.
Under the bright yellow sun.
Among the majestic tall trees.
Above were colorful birds.
I walked below the fluffy clouds.
I feel the magic atmosphere of the forest.
And dream of fantasies lost in time.

Brook MacKenzie, Grade 4
Margaret Wooding School, AB

Hockey

Is the best sport
He shoots and scores a goal
What a goal top shelf, what a goal
Hockey

Peter MacDougall, Grade 6
Falmouth District School, NS

Words

Some words you say
Some words you pray
Some words you write
Some words you sight

Some words are bright
Some words are polite
Some words are sad
Some words are bad

Some make you glad
Some make you grand
Some make you high
Some make you sigh

Some give you a smile
Some give you style
Some give you a flight
Some give you delight

Some words are great
Some words are fate
Some words are glide
Some words are pride

Hassan Khan, Grade 4
Islamic Foundation School, ON

A Soundless Harmony

An orchestra blaring notes in my ears.
However, I hear crickets chirping in silence.
The people are yelling,
The kids are screaming, they sound like whispering melodies.
The earsplitting booms of military artillery are just the beats of the drums.
Music playing is soundless like I'm deaf.
Jet roars down the runway,
But sounds like a squeak of a mouse.
Animals yawning are the sound of snowflakes hailing down on
Everyone and everything.
Fires burning, oceans swaying are just a soundless song.
Kids laughing, and babies crying are full of silence.
Everything in my life is just a soundless harmony.

Matthew A. Cheung, Grade 6
Blundell Elementary School, BC

The Dress Was Pretty

The dress was pretty.
She looked fabulous in the dress, a beautiful shade of purple.
The decorative pearls shined and sparkled.
Sequins caught peoples eyes when she walked by.
The bottom of the dress was ruffled in a beautiful silky purple.
Everyone stared when she walked by.
It matched perfectly with her hair and shoes.
She was perfect in the dress.
A shy nobody like her could have a chance to shine and stand out.
The dress was pretty, the dress was *beautiful*

Juliette Krausewitz, Grade 5
Charles Beaudoin Public School, ON

I'm Lucky

When I think of peace, I think of the soldiers and God,
they're almost like two peas in a pod.
Just think. They all sacrificed their lives for us.
Imagine if it was you.
Shooting, bombing and dead bodies everywhere.
You must be silent, if you were hiding there.
I don't believe in that kind of peace.
When the choir sings, and the orchestra plays
and all the misty beautiful bays.
The rain pouring and the snow falling,
I can almost still hear the doves calling
and I'm lucky, I can hear the Canadian geese.
These are the things that come to my mind when I hear the word
PEACE!

Lindsay McVittie, Grade 6
St Mary Choir and Orchestra Program, ON

Flowing Water

Spring is like water, nothing is softer then water, yet it can over come rock
Blossoming flowers wildly pink and shockingly blue.
The newborn howl of a pack of wolves that are rid of winter.
A flowing creek as slow as a turtle and as soft as a newly softened sheet
I want this spring to stay.

Michael Code, Grade 5
Ormsby School, AB

Friendship

Friendship,
should last to the end.
Friendship,
is what you share with a friend,
and it should never be pretend.

It's hard to find someone you trust,
because you're not always sure
when sometimes that person will leave you in the dust.
You think your friendship is pure,
and then it's gone, and there's no cure.

One day they're your friend and the next they're not,
then that's surely not friendship.
Even though you've known them since you were a tot,
friendship is something special that everyone's surely got,
but to know that it's true your friend has to care for you a lot.

Emma McNorgan, Grade 6
Ecole Ste-Jeanne-d'Arc, ON

All Four Seasons

Winter — winter is cold winter is white
though the sun's farther away it's still shining bright.
Summer — summer is hot, not cold not cool,
in the summer there is thankfully NO school!
Spring — Spring is warm but not as hot
as the summer that flashed away in a dot.
Fall — fall is chilly with the leaves blowing around.
After fall the leaves will all be found on the ground.

Kristen Adams, Grade 5
Colby Village Elementary School, NS

If School Would End

I wonder what things would be like
If there was no school,
What would the children do?
Would they run around all day,
Or would they jog with all their might,
Or would they fly a kite.
I wonder if the teachers would be glad,
Or if they would miss school and be very sad.

Ben Wipf, Grade 5
Milford Colony School, AB

Books

Have you ever read a book
One you couldn't put down
One about fantasy or one about the world?
Have you ever read a book
One that is incredibly long
That took over two months to finish?
Have you ever read a book
One you couldn't put down?

Alexa Stouffer, Grade 6
Linden Lanes School, MB

Tonto

Tonto is my best friend,
He is short from end to end.
His breath smells bad,
And he sometimes looks sad,
When I pet him or play with him
His sadness turns to gladness.
He is the king of his bed,
He loves being fed.
He loves his soft mat,
He is spoiled and fat.
Even though he is as stinky as a skunk,
As fat as a walrus,
As slow as a slug,
And as sharp as a marble,
He is my dog and I love him just the way he is.

Quaid Parel, Grade 6
Aurora Elementary School, AB

Water Lilies

The sight of graceful water lilies lying on the water restfully.
The sound of small ripples dancing joyfully.
The feel of wet water hugging gently.
The taste of salty water being sipped slowly.
The smell of the fresh outdoors, the wind moving rapidly.
The astounding artist Claude Monet.

Jacob Krane-Paul, Grade 6
Ecole Akiva, QC

Donna/Philip

Donna
Cute, smiley
Playing, crawling, crying
Rice cereal, jump-a-roo, potatoes, video games
Yelling, bike riding, jumping
Happy, friendly
Philip

Susan Williams-Smith, Grade 5
Bernard Elementary School, BC

Elliot

His black shiny coat
Luminescent light green eyes
His cracked dry paws
His very loud roaring purr
His huge bottomless stomach

Olivia Sledge, Grade 5
Forest Hill School – Senior Campus, QC

Spring

I listen while the soft,
Gentle music hovers in the spring air
And the spring foals play in the sweet morning dew,
As the soft tweet, tweet of the song bird
Joins in the melody's slurring lullaby.

Bailey M. Wilson, Grade 5
Hamiota Elementary School, MB

Bullying Hurts
Bullying hurts
They steal your lunch money
They hit and punch
They hit you in the guts
Give you wedgies
And steal your veggies
Make you feel sad, stupid and angry
They make you feel out numbered
With the gang.
Rachel MacDougall, Grade 5
Chiganois Elementary School, NS

Rain
Drops on my window
Pounding on the big green trees
Sparkles in the sky
Grace Evans, Grade 4
Park West School, NS

Pine Trees
A snow covered road
Snowflakes gently falling from the sky
Snowflakes draped over the pine trees.
The branches forced to the ground
Down, down they go
Brushing the top of the pure white snow.
Alina Giblin, Grade 6
Mother Teresa Catholic School, ON

Remembrance Day
Poppies are red
we wear them to remember
the soldiers who died
in the war.
The soldiers were brave
and now, we have peace!
Kathleen Shewtchenko, Grade 4
FW Gilbert School, MB

Stanley Cup
The Stanley Cup in your hand.
The crowd chanting for you.
Your teammates cheering for you.
Important to your team.
You would taste victory.
Jordan Wolff, Grade 6
Ormsby School, AB

A Day at the Fair
The gate is open
People of all shapes and sizes
Gasp at what they see
Fun rides and the rollercoaster
Having the time of their lives.
Ryan Brown, Grade 6
St James Catholic School, BC

Fight/Talk
Hit, abuse
Yelling, kicking, punching
Talking is better than fighting
Resolving, thinking, helping
Nice, respect
Talk
Zachary Plumb, Grade 6
École Renaissance, ON

Trees
Trees are nature's prize
They appear before your eyes
Arching over creeks
Climbing over peaks
Their roots dig down deep
They hop and leap
Over rocks and stones
Yet they stand there all alone
Just being nature's beauty
Some have leaves
But they are all still trees
Start small and grow, grow, grow
They get whipped and blown
Yet they stand still
Get cut and put in a mill
It's all for us
They must be nature's beauty,
They must be trees.
Andrew Ardell, Grade 6
Westside Academy, BC

My Rainbow Life
Blue sky
Up where birds fly so high,
Waterfalls so ravishing
As I watch the water rush down.

Green grass,
Softly swishing along
With the rhythm of the wind,
Gardens growing so high,
Because of the hot summer sun.

Orange sunsets waving goodbye,
Purple flowers blooming.

Spring, colorful, amazing joy.
Joanne Wipf, Grade 5
Milford Colony School, AB

The Secrets of Spring
playing together
beautiful flowers blooming
sitting by the sea
Kayla Scott, Grade 4
Park West School, NS

The Perfect World
The world will stay green
The grass will keep on growing
Trees will always grow
David Kirkwood, Grade 6
John T Tuck Public School, ON

Under My Bed
Something is under my bed,
and I don't think it wants to come out.
I'm not afraid but I think it is,
it doesn't want me to run about.

I don't know what its name is,
or even how it got here.
I didn't see my door open,
now I'm building up some fear.

I'm getting out of bed now,
I hope that I'll be fine.
I just want to get out of here,
before mom thinks he's mine.

The thing is making weird noises,
like do, dang, doy, dang, doy.
At first it seemed quite scary,
but now I know it's just my toy!
Liam Smolenaars, Grade 5
Charles Beaudoin Public School, ON

A Wish
I wish I were a snowflake
falling from the clouds outside
blocking up the roads
joyfully
Rayn Merkley, Grade 5
Bernard Elementary School, BC

A Walk in the Storm
A cold wind whistling
and whooshing wildly.
Snow falling furiously
from the foggy sky.
Shimmering snowflakes
spraying in my face.
Fluffy flaky flurries
falling fast.
The cold air crawling
up my crisp coat
The storm sweeping silently
down the slippery streets.
So cold and cruel yet
white and wonderful.
As I walk warily in
the white winter storm.
Frank-Edward Nemeth, Grade 6
St Raymond Elementary School, ON

My Seven Days of Happiness

I found my way to like to run skillfully hitchhiking Sheep Cliffs.
I trained wild horses and flew with them.
I loved when I was an amazing artist in the mountains.
I loved when I lived in the mountains and jogged every day.
I adored when I was like a mother of two children.
We always played tennis.
I swam speedily off the boat to snorkel in the sea.

Meagan Christman, Grade 4
David Ovans Elementary School, AB

Plants

Plants are big
Plants are small
They are different from each other
They help us a lot
Plants decorate our garden
They make our garden beautiful
We can buy them from the stores and grow them at home
Plants grow some good foods
We can use the things that grow on plants to grow new plants
Most plants have leaves
Most plants have stems
We can grow plants inside or outside
Some plants grow flowers and some grow fruits and vegetables
Plants have lived as long as dinosaurs have
Many plants grow in the dirt

Prabhjot K. Bajwa, Grade 5
Khalsa School - Old Yale Road Campus, BC

The Earth's Crust

sight seeing the rocks
big huge holes in the Earth's crust
I want to jump in

William Lam, Grade 5
Howard De Beck Elementary School, BC

Summer Day

It is a beautiful day,
And the sun is glowing
Like a bright new light bulb.
The tide is way out in the
Deep blue ocean.
As I walk through the sand
And collect white shells,
Reminds me of the time
I went on a hike and I was
Collecting rocks.
It is a beautiful sight
Watching the sun fade,
And go down between the
Rocky mountains.

And me, remembering my
Favorite summer day!

Cossette Epplette, Grade 5
Queen of All Saints Elementary School, BC

Red...

is the taste of a yummy candy cane
is the big Canada flag flapping in the wind
is a pretty poinsettia
are berries in a pie
the taste of mouthwatering watermelon
is crisp apple on a big green tree
the smell of the gorgeous bouquet of red roses
as yummy as ripe juicy strawberries
is as hot as a blazing fire
is a poppy growing in Flanders Fields
is a cherry on a cake
is a spicy hot chili
is a little lady bug on a leaf
is a shiny little ruby.

Allysha Savoie, Grade 6
Bernard Elementary School, BC

The Hiking Trip

T'was the best and worst of hiking trips
Mountains,
Cold, tired, lost
Exhausted!
Trees, animals, nature
Wild!
Cuts, scars, bumps and bruises
Pain!
Exploring, seeing new things
Unique!
Frostbitten, famished, uncomfortable
Distressing!
No school, no work.
Nothing but each other and the forces of nature.
It was the best of hiking trips,
It was the worst of hiking trips.

Saige Mukherjee, Grade 5
Charles Beaudoin Public School, ON

Cheetahs

Watching cheetahs hug
snuggling with warmth together
inhaling the love.

Vandy Liu, Grade 4
Howard De Beck Elementary School, BC

The Earth

The water flows in my mind like an eagle in the sky.
The rocks talk to me, and the birds sing.
The water flows so very fast it hurts so much.
The grass swings back and forth, trying to tell me something.
The wolves are coming running away as fast as I can.
The wolves chase me, bush after bush, running.
They run past me, they search and search and search.
I run and search for anybody that is here in the forest.

Tyler Herbert, Grade 6
Westwind Elementary School, BC

'Twas the Night Before Christmas…
'Twas the night before Christmas
And down at the rink,
No hockey players there…
Only their stink.

The Zamboni is finished
Cleaning the ice.
And the doors are closed
To keep out the mice.

The uniforms hang
In the lockers so neat,
Waiting for the players
And the next team to beat.

It's quiet just now,
But not for long.
'Cause Christmas Day means,
A party with song.

The arena will open
For all to enjoy,
A free Christmas skate
For each girl and boy.
Kevin Kentel, Grade 4
First Lutheran Christian School, BC

Thunderstorm
Thunderstorm a power so immense,
It keeps you in suspense.
As fast as the speed of light,
So bright in the night.

Despite, it's as nice as the starlight,
It might give you a fright.
An action so captivating,
It's as if you were dreaming.
It has such a passion,
That represents compassion.
Siyobana Buzamlak, Grade 6
Ecole Ste-Jeanne-d'Arc, ON

The End of the World
Today is the end of the world.
You won't see any more squirrels,
The birds won't chirp,
They are lying in the dirt.
It is from the smoke and the smog,
There are no trees just logs,
Some begged to differ,
That there was no litter,
But now it is too late,
Today is the date,
For the end of the world.
Brandon Archibald, Grade 5
Chiganois Elementary School, NS

A Whole Lot of Excitement
On Tuesday I surfed wildly across the Beaufort Sea.
On Wednesday I won eighty million dollars!
On Thursday I drove a jet restlessly around the wide open world.
On Friday I saved the earth from global warming.
On Saturday I walked a whole marathon,
while I saved a thousand animals form a giant waterfall.
On Sunday I discovered the secret of time travel.
On Monday I dug out a pirates buried treasure!
Ruby Odell, Grade 4
David Ovans Elementary School, AB

Spring
Spring is the best season of all; it's even better than fall.
Spring is the season of flowers and much, much more!
Birds and squirrels come, to play on a sunny day.
Everything goes green and the Earth is full of colour.
All the birds come out of their nests chirping and chattering everywhere.
Out of hibernation all the creatures come to play out in the sun.
Fruits grow all around, red and green all around you.
Flowers can be red, blue, green, and yellow all colours of spring.
Kids play with the flowers all day and night.
Once it's sunny kids go outside and enjoy the sunlight.
Parents and kids all love spring because it's sunny and warm.
People walking around the streets enjoying spring.
Games, activities, and lot of fun, enjoying things to do.
Hope you enjoy the spring times, and remember that spring is the best season of all!
Banreet Kaur Johal, Grade 5
Khalsa School - Old Yale Road Campus, BC

Dark vs Light
The brightness of the stars,
Reflect the lives of ours,
Spelling mankind's memoirs.
To you what shines brighter, the stars or the scars?

You stand in the dark, an endless night,
It's a brutal fight,
Between dark and light.

No matter how many times light tries to flourish,
It can never nourish,
The dark will never relinquish.

Because dark thoughts and poisoned hearts have won the battle,
We've given up all hope, we've fled the saddle.

All because we only look where we want to see,
We only hear what we want to know,
Because we are mortally scared of the unknown.

Where is our Saviour, the warmth, the light, the sun?
This isn't his fight, He's done.
This is our fight. Our fight to face the truth, the unknown.
To face the evil, to face ourselves.
Sean O'Byrne, Grade 6
Ecole Ste-Jeanne-d'Arc, ON

I Have a Dream at 11

As I looked out the window
I saw the most beautiful thing ever.
It was a BIG BIG stadium!
I wondered what it looked like, from the inside.

I closed my eyes and I could see inside.
Rows and rows of seats,
Filled with 60,000-70,000 fans shouting!!!
Around the stadium I read the names of the Greats
    #81 Randy Moss
    #12 Tom Brady
    #54 Tedy Bruschi
    #10 Javen Amyotte

Oh wow that's me!
That's my name.
Even though I am only 11,
I have a DREAM!

Javen Amyotte, Grade 6
St Maria Goretti Elementary School, ON

Crystals

Crystals are powerful
Crystals are valuable
Crystals can be red, pink, or blue
Crystals on the stairs
Crystals on the floor
Crystals can be all over you
You can find them in the store
You can find them in a market
But whatever you do, don't break them
Crystals matter, they really do
They tell you if you're sad or happy
Even though you don't have a clue
Crystals are good to have
They don't make you cry
Don't just have one, have many

Pranita Prasad, Grade 5
Khalsa School - Old Yale Road Campus, BC

Skating

It was a cold night
With snowflakes falling on my face.
The only sounds are of my blades
Scraping the ice on the frozen pond.
I see miles of open space covered with white
My blades make pretty patterns on the ice.
I glide back and forth on the ice slowly enjoying the ride
I lean forward to gain more speed
My cheeks are turning red and I feel the snow
On my cheeks more heavily now.
I take one last look at this winter wonderland
And start walking slowly back to realization.

Emma Lauren Sheehan, Grade 5
Forest Hill School – Senior Campus, QC

The Ocean

The waves in the ocean, lapping and gentle.
The rocks sparkling and huge.
The water is salty and blue.
The shells in the sand, small and colorful.
The dolphins friendly and playing.
The coral is flowered and beautiful.
The whales are reeling and diving.

Tyra Cross Child, Grade 4
Margaret Wooding School, AB

My Friend

My friend
    Picks strawberries
        In the summer months
           Up in the hills
             She likes picking the berries

Olivia Johnson, Grade 6
Sxoxomic Community School, BC

Magical Rainbow

Red, orange, yellow, green, blue, indigo, purple, like a rainbow,
The moist air left after the rain, like a shower,
Water speeding down the sidewalk, whoosh,
The damp dew leftover from the rain,
Water from the rain,
It's a rainbow.

Stephen Votary, Grade 6
Ormsby School, AB

The Beach

The sun shines on a hot summer's day
couples walking down the bay
waves are crashing along the shore
at the beach nobody's bored.

Sand is as smooth as a baby's skin
children make sand castles out of buckets and bins
people swimming all day long
and some are playing ping pong.

Lots of couples get married at the beach
while others decide to preach
sometimes the beach is really cold
then the sun turns to the colour gold.

The sky is a beautiful baby blue
it is as blue as my favourite glitter glue
shells are everywhere from water to shore
when I see seagulls they're usually in groups of four.

Now I've said this before
waves are crashing along the shore
it's the end of the day
there's no one walking down the bay.

Taryn Howe, Grade 6
Barriere Elementary School, BC

I Got a New Hen

I got a new hen
I named him Ben
He was so small
Not fat, not tall
I raised him until he was ten
I keep him in a big dirty pen
In his pen we have loads of fun
Playing with friends in the sun
One friend is Steve the big purple dog
Tony the smelly enormous green hog
They play all day
I play and we play
"Quite a mess we make," I say
Rolling around in all that hay
Now it's time to go to bed
and lay down my tired head
Good night I say to my small hen
Until tomorrow's playtime in the pen.
Jordan-Quinn Mitchell, Grade 4
St Alphonsus School, MB

Pebbles

If you find
a group of small rocks,
you'll know they're pebbles
the way they slither through your fingers,
like sand, so rough but still so soft.
Polina Kamaev, Grade 4
Calico Public School, ON

Math

Fractions are like synonyms
They both have equivalents,
Bottle and a jar, two quarters and a half.

Fractions are like students,
They always follow rules,
The only difference is,
They do not go to schools!

Fractions are like my homework,
They are always incomplete,
But if you don't finish it,
Your grade will greatly decrease!

Multiplying is like money,
They both can increase and decrease,
But if you lose your money,
It is not very funny.

Multiplying is a mind map,
They can both extend greatly,
It will only stop,
When you get mathematician's block.
Adnan Machado, Grade 6
St Mark Separate School, ON

Sun Set

Sun sets overhead
The waves crash the sandy shore
Gulls screeching above.
Lindsay Hauser, Grade 5
Ormsby School, AB

The Great Blue Shark

The great blue is swift.
It has glass diamond sharp teeth.
It is humongous.
Patrick Nelson, Grade 4
Colby Village Elementary School, NS

Oceans

Beautiful oceans
Waves all over, white and blue
On a nice cool day
Arash Ghasemi, Grade 4
Park West School, NS

Beach Time

At the sunny beach
I go and jump in water.
It is loads of fun
Gagandeep Singh, Grade 4
Park West School, NS

The Forest

I was walking in the forest.
I saw some damp and sparkling leaves.
Interesting gigantic trees.
Growing in fascinating valuable soil.
Green tall grass.
I heard some slippery slimy snakes.
I walked into a mucky, dirty marsh
with huge thick trunks.
Wet cold rain.
I walked into a big open place.
That had colorful beautiful butterflies.
Some charming glad birds
there were lovely, pretty flowers,
amazing, squirmy ferns.
To top it off,
a shiny peaceful waterfall.
Dylan Whittaker, Grade 4
Margaret Wooding School, AB

Mentos

I meant to bring your mentos today,
But I swear I had an appointment,
And I wrote mentos on my hand,
And even in a red pen,
I meant to bring them,
But my mouth kind of got in the way.
Kennedy Bell, Grade 6
Linden Lanes School, MB

Red Is…

the colour of tulips in the garden
the taste of a juicy ripe apple
the touch of the ruby on my mom's hand
the sight of Elmo standing alone
the sound of the Canadian flag waving
the feeling of my soft pillow
the first aid kit in my class
the colour of Team Canada's jersey
a pair of soft silk jeans
the smell of love.
Brooke Larson, Grade 6
Bernard Elementary School, BC

The Sea

Surrounding the Earth
Day by day it comes to play
It brought life one day.
Thomas Francis, Grade 6
Bernard Elementary School, BC

Frenemy

Friend
Kind, thoughtful
Playing, talking, sharing
Buddy, games, hate, lies
Bullying, hurting, humiliating
Mean, cruel
Enemy
Alyssa Hildebrandt, Grade 5
Bernard Elementary School, BC

You Are My Happy Ending

If I were a puppet you'd be my director,
If I were a boat you'd be my sailor.

If I were a fish you'd be my sea,
If I were a flower you'd be the bee.

If I were a student you'd be my teacher,
And since I am me, you are my master!
Sammy Mulyk, Grade 6
Sacred Heart Academy, AB

Smells

Christmas is coming
I can smell the…
Chestnuts roasting on a fire
Fresh poinsettias
Christmas trees too
And the smell of gingerbread men,
Coming out of the oven.
And when they all come together
IT'S CHRISTMAS!!!
Sean Ragnauth, Grade 6
St Maria Goretti Elementary School, ON

The Goalie

Here I am sitting in the crease,
Hoping I get through the game in one piece.
The other team shoots the puck
Man, that stick save was pure luck.
Now it's over time and as I sit in my net
My mother begins to fret.
The score remains zero to zero
The game still looking for a hero
Into a shootout we go.
The puck moving to and fro.
My stomach is in a knot
As they take the final shot.
But once I steer the last shot away
The fans erupt into cheers of "Hooray!"
For the goalie.

Bailey Ferguson, Grade 5
Chiganois Elementary School, NS

Our Humanity

What happened to our humanity?
We wanted a world without boundary,
but yet we are so afraid,
just to walk to the arcade.
Where euthanasia exists,
and people throw their fists.

Why can't we just have a world with peace
and wars to cease?
Where animals have rights,
where people are free to walk in twilight.

So I ask again,
to the women as well as the men
and I hope they will answer honestly.
What happened to our humanity?

Marie C. Leunissen, Grade 6
Ecole Ste-Jeanne-d'Arc, ON

Sports

Sports are awesome
Sports are crazy
Sports are cool
They give you exercise whenever you want
Soccer, hockey, basketball, football, tennis, golf, are all sports
Sports are fun
They keep you active and healthy
The most famous sport is soccer
In hockey you put the puck in the net
In soccer you put the soccer ball in the net
In golf you put the golf ball in the hole
That is why sports are good to your life
We join sports to be active
Sports also keep you away from violence
I love all the sports in the world!

Balpreet Chohan, Grade 5
Khalsa School - Old Yale Road Campus, BC

I-poem

Andy
Nice, smart, patient
Son of Lan Tran, Tu Tran
Lover of basketball, cat, computer games.
Who feels respected by children and adults
Who needs food, love and clothes
Who gives funny jokes, and stuff.
Who fears dogs, stage fright, high buildings
Who would like to ride a go-kart
Resident of Vietnam
Tran

Andy Tran, Grade 4
Calico Public School, ON

World War

Courageous troops
Away from home
Deal with day-to-day stress
Loved ones have to worry

Deadly crisis
Death and danger
Trenches are cold and muddy with rats and fleas
Never stop attacking

Fought their enemies
Challenges of *saving lives*
Honored with medals
Making the free and peaceful country
we have today

Jaydi Overwater, Grade 6
East Selkirk Middle School, MB

My Rock

Now I'm not about talking
About any rock —
This one I mean —
That's smooth and rough at the same time
That is oval shaped,
That I can throw up and down
And catch in my hand,
This rock smells like the outdoors,
And tastes like grass
Because that's where I found it,
Still and silent, motionless.

Riley Madsen, Grade 5
Hamiota Elementary School, MB

After Rain

A cool smell of clouds along with the spicy scent of autumn.
A crimson carpet of summer's old skin.
The wind whispering secrets in your ears like a best friend
And the clouds across the sky reflecting in the puddles.

Kate Reeve, Grade 5
Corpus Christi School, ON

Rain

Rain is disturbing
it ruins your day
but in April it's ok
because in May
it all pays off
the grass is green
and flowers are bright
so rain just might...
be ok.

Sam Currie, Grade 5
Chiganois Elementary School, NS

My Teacher

M emories
Y ou're funny

T eaching us
E xcellent
A mazing skills
C urious about us
H ealthy person
E asy work
R esponsible

Owen Bratton, Grade 4
J Douglas Hogarth Public School, ON

Soccer

Soccer — lots of fun
You can shoot the ball and score
Score! All people cheer
The soccer team wins the game
You have to run fast playing

Jason Sharp, Grade 6
St James Catholic School, BC

Autumn

Autumn is the season
When leaves fall from trees
Autumn is the season
When geese fly south
Autumn is the season
When there are colourful leaves
Autumn is the season
When we start plowing
Autumn is the season
When we rake leaves
Autumn is the season
When cold temperatures begin
Autumn is the season
When I like jumping in leaf piles
Autumn is the season
When we collect pumpkins
Autumn is definitely
The best season of all!

Rachel Martin, Grade 5
Mornington Central School, ON

Sarah: The World's Greatest Sister

Several times I do recall a laughing, smiling face.
It brings joy into my heart to see her waiting at the door.
Smiling wide her gap-toothed grin for all of us to see,
never in my life have I seen such a blissful face before.

After school weary and worn, I glance upon our street.
I see her walking home like a princess of the ancient lore.
Her manner is that of Camelot's queen her step is just as dainty,
if she were to rule she'd give service to both rich and poor.

Ranking in the highest when it comes to little sisters,
in the 7 years she's been alive she's never been a bore.
Though at times she can be more than just a bit annoying,
never in my life have I seen such a blissful face before.

A favourite of the teachers and a favourite of my own,
she becomes a favourite beggar when we take her into stores.
Yet she still withholds her judgment and listens to her heart,
because in her heart and in her brain is goodness to the core.

Had you ever met her, had she charmed your heart,
you'd be on the boat to heaven, and she would be your oar.
Her face is sweet and friendly, you'd know it anywhere,
because never in the world has there been such a blissful face before.

Kirsten Kinchlea, Grade 6
Waverley Drive Public School, ON

What True Happiness Could Mean

If the earth could be so great...

Could we end all fights and wars,
Shall everyone be rich and no one poor?

Can no one be hungry and everyone enough to eat,
No one will ever again be getting beats.

Will people learn to deal with being angry and stressed?
Or not ever having to feel sad and depressed.

Everyone deserves a lot of friends and family that love you,
But your health too, is a very big value.

Is it possible for everyone to have food, shelter, good health and friends?
If you think my list of happiness is done, I'll tell you it has just begun.

Eugenia Liang, Grade 5
Sir James Douglas Elementary School, BC

Fall

Gold, burgundy and brown leaves piling kilometers high.
Fresh air dancing all around
Flying birds, tired bears and chipmunks harvesting for the months ahead.
Rough, crunchy leaves falling on my face.
Hot apple cider rushing and scorching down my throat.
I should have brought a sweater.

Kyla Dahl, Grade 6
Ormsby School, AB

On That Blue Sunny Day

On that blue sunny day we went to town
and my dog Maggie was in her cage outside
and somehow she got out and ran away
before we came back and she never did come back
my dad said she ran away because she
didn't want us to see her die
but I don't know why.

Courtney Cummer, Grade 5
Chiganois Elementary School, NS

'Twas the Night Before Christmas in Dreamland

'Twas the night before Christmas in Dreamland,
My cute little polly sitting cuddled in my hand.
As I dream about Angel, the best dancer in town,
She can dance very daintily, looking up or looking down.

Tonight is the show in which she will be dancing,
I think about horses, all of them prancing.
She does pirouettes, 29 in a row,
Believe me, I counted, while wearing a bow.

I will be dancing in that same show,
My dad said I smiled, looking cute in my bow.
The next day we went to a little antique store.
I peered in the window, then opened the door.

Guess what I saw, so prettily made.
Ten glass ballerinas, all smelling like sage.
So my dad had to buy me one little one,
After all that, I had lots of fun.

I don't really want to,
I'm not very keen.
I really don't want to,
Get up from my dream!

Lydia Swart, Grade 4
First Lutheran Christian School, BC

Thank You Veterans

I hope there are no more wars.
The guns, grenades, and bombs put away.
Tanks, submarines and fighter planes are quiet,
Peace all over the world one day.

Not all of the soldiers survived,
Most of them never got found.
Families lost their brothers and friends,
Crosses mark their place on the ground.

We will never ever forget,
What they unselfishly gave.
For loving peace over hateful war,
Thank you veterans for being so brave.

Christopher Molnar, Grade 6
St Mary Choir and Orchestra Program, ON

Hunters*

Little Anne is really smart,
but you might call her a runt.
Even though she is small,
she's always in the hunt.

Old Dan's got lots of brawn,
he's usually found in a fight.
Whenever a coon sees him,
he will get a fright.

Billy's got the brawn,
he's got the brains.
You can mostly find him,
on hunting lanes.

When Billy saw that ad,
he had a dream.
Now that dream has come true,
he's got a hunting team!

Christopher Janowski, Grade 5
St Mark Separate School, ON
*Based on "Where the Red Fern Grows" by Wilson Rawls

The Dangerous War

Imagine being a Canadian
Soldier in the Korean War
With *Dangerous* troops in their
Barbed wire and mine fields

Soldiers
Soldiers living in the *cold* and *muddy* trenches
With rats and fleas

Far away from homes,
Friends, family
Canadian heroes *Remember*
Soldiers and end all wars

Jeanine Smith, Grade 6
East Selkirk Middle School, MB

A Masterpiece of the Evening

Bright colours
Dance their way across the sky,
Surrounding the sun.
The wisps of clouds, the paintbrushes,
The colours, the paint.
Soon a picture has been finished.
Such beauty
A camera could never truly capture.
The sun gives one last sigh,
And disappears behind the dense mountains.
Velvet colours linger,
Then blend into the night.
Another day has passed.

Leah Brodovsky, Grade 6
Central Public School, ON

Mars

Aliens, Martians, extraterrestrials
People thought they lived here
Space creatures
Like monsters
In movies.

The planet is red
Made from rocks
Hot, close to the sun
Like an orange red marble
Spinning.

The rivers dried up like snow
In the summer
Leaving red rocks
To dry

Greek, warrior, brave
Mars was named after the God of War
Like a general in the army
Charge!
Jordy Middleton, Grade 6
East Selkirk Middle School, MB

Moon Flower

My mind lets go a thousand things.
The birth of a king,
the death of a queen,
the rise of the sun and yet to bring.
The very first hour it began to bloom,
that pretty rose flower to be my doom.
Into a vase that flower did go,
until its power began to grow.
My mind lets go a thousand things.
Was it the date of a war,
or the death of a king?
Those things that I recall
are gone forever every one so small.
Bethany Van Hierden, Grade 6
School of Hope, AB

Tiny

weird and black
biting, squirming and whining
she is my best friend.
a dog
Myra Mines, Grade 4
Good Shepherd School, AB

Darkness

Darkness floods the sky
Bright stars twinkle the deep sea
Waves rush up on shore
Spencer Diederich, Grade 6
Harry Balfour School, AB

Spring

Flowers are blooming
Children are playing outside
When snow melts away
Jeonggyun Lee, Grade 4
Park West School, NS

Grey Wolf

Eyes like a cinder;
Ears shaped like a pizza;
Claws like slashing knives;
When he hunts everything hides.

Legs as strong as trees;
Paws like thunder;
Speed like lightning;
When he growls everything shakes.

Colour like clouds on a rainy day;
Head shaped like a pineapple;
He sharpens his claws on bark;
When he fights no one survives.
Grey Wolf
Lena Martin, Grade 5
Mornington Central School, ON

Hearts

God gave us two eyes
Two ears
Two arms
And two legs
But why only one heart?
Because the other one
Was left for us to find
Brandt Eldridge, Grade 6
Falmouth District School, NS

Rivers

Waves wash away sand
Flowing gently waters run
Swimming in rivers
Esmée Hotson, Grade 4
J Douglas Hogarth Public School, ON

Taya

Taya Taya
You're so beautiful and sweet
so when you cry
my arms and heart and ears
will be open for
your tearful words
sorrowful problems
I am so so so sad for my
beautiful step sister.
Devyn Fox, Grade 4
Good Shepherd School, AB

The Kite

Goes flying through
The air like a balloon
Lightly drifting upward through the
Blue sky!
Breanna Kehoe, Grade 6
Falmouth District School, NS

Underwater

The oceans and seas
The homes of coral and fish
A place to explore
Wildlife under the water
An extreme environment.
Chantalle Hernandez, Grade 6
St James Catholic School, BC

Streaming Colors

Blue, the deep feeling of depression,
Shoulders in a slump,
Sadness weighing you down,
Weeping crowds the coffin,
Death, the saddest feeling of blue.
Green, smooth and tasteful,
Wonder and hope,
Rolls silently,
Lines cast shadows,
Shadows across beautiful shades of olive.
Yellow, a large golden sunset,
Streaming colors across the sky,
Light over the rippling water,
Sun fish into the maple trees,
I wish…
Brooke Andreae, Grade 6
WP Sandin Composite High School, SK

Spray Bottle

Sitting, seemingly docile
Waiting to be
Summoned, by
It's human warrior.

When it is brought
Down upon us it
Gets ready to strike.

Then, it leaps at
The larger creature and
Strikes it.

Filling it with a
Watery poison, then it
Pulls back its plastic
Head, and rests.
Dale McTavish, Grade 5
Hamiota Elementary School, MB

The Worst Lunch

The worst lunch I ever ate
had blue mushrooms which I hate.

I'm getting tired of cheese strings
And I would much rather have some candy rings.

Once in my lunch I had a piece of cake.
The problem was it tasted rubbery and fake.

I also had some tuna on a bun.
My lunch was not much FUN!

Justin Beaulieu, Grade 4
J Douglas Hogarth Public School, ON

Life

In life there are tears,
In life there are smiles.
In life there are fears,
in life there are styles.
In life there is happiness,
in life there is pain.
In life there is me.
In life there are dreams,
nightmares as well.
Life is a word which has a lot
of meanings.
Terrible, great, miserable,
bad, good, depressing.
But life if life so
make it memorable for
your own good before it's too late!

Manroop Kaur Sahota, Grade 5
Khalsa School - Old Yale Road Campus, BC

Water

Our well is caving in.
It's put our family in a spin
We don't know what to do
It has made us all quite blue.

When we turn our faucet on
The water is not drawn.
The pump is full of gunk
The water cannot be drunk.

It is very hard to shower
With no water power.
When our water is not clean
It requires a filter screen.

A new well must be dug
The casing must be snug.
It has to go down deep
And clean water we will reap.

Dylan Liske, Grade 5
Community Bible Fellowship Christian School, MB

Racism

We're not the same skin color,
Does that mean we have to hate each other?
If you hate people they're form a different race,
You should call yourself a disgrace.
There's a beautiful world we can create,
If we cooperate.
And it's not that hard,
Think of it as a reward,
To be able to live in peace with one another.

Leeya Tesfamichael, Grade 6
Ecole Ste-Jeanne-d'Arc, ON

Have You Ever...

Have you ever been on a holiday
That you absolutely hated
Because your parents embarrassed you?
Have you ever been on a holiday
Where your dad just had to know a million people
Because he is very popular around town?
Have you ever been on a holiday
That you absolutely hated?

Kristen Nerbas, Grade 6
Linden Lanes School, MB

Emerald

Emerald, like shiny grass;
When the sun shines down in spring
Emerald like the seaweed,
Deep beneath the sea
Constantly waving goodbye
Emerald like the leaves on trees,
Swaying in the hot summer breeze
Emerald like certain cocoons,
Until a butterfly escapes,
It's long emerald wings fall like drapes
Emerald like some of my clothes
Or the plants that I own
Emerald like the twinkling Christmas lights
That surround my tree
On Christmas eve
Emerald is never weary,
In fact, it is quite merry!
Emerald is beautiful,
'Cause when it comes to colors,
Emerald is the nicest thing,
Reminds me of spring flowers!

Laura Escueta, Grade 6
Eric Langton Elementary School, BC

Global Warming

Big machinery in the forest cutting down the Cedar trees.
Polluting on the Pacific Coast just to make money.
No wonder we're having global warming in Antarctica.

Frankie McCamley, Grade 6
Walnut Road Elementary School, BC

The First World War
Canadians bravely away from home
Fighting to restore *peace*
Miserable freezing cold soldiers
In the trenches

Put their lives on the line
Being in the First World War
Enemy *sniper* with machine guns

Danger and death
Worry at home
Soldiers are *NOT* forgotten
Connor Spratt, Grade 6
East Selkirk Middle School, MB

Sing with the Angels
It seemed too sad to be true
Why'd she leave us so soon
To travel up, to high heavens
And sing with the angels

She left all of us to our pain
Trying not to break down
She went to the heavens above
To sing with the angels

She suddenly left in the spring
We thought she was quite well
She left for heaven that day
To sing with the angels

We cried all day, all night
The grief was unbearable
She went to heaven that day
To sing with the angels

We'll love that dear girl forever
Love her 'till this world ends
She wants to go to heaven
And sing with the angels
Melissa Byer, Grade 6
Waverley Drive Public School, ON

My Dog at the Beach
At a sunny beach
Every time my dog lays down
instead of playing.
Kyla Dalley, Grade 4
Park West School, NS

Beach Time
At the beach soft sand
warm under my cold bare feet
go swim and cool off.
Andrew Clarke, Grade 4
Park West School, NS

The Seeker
A dark murky water like a foggy night.
This ferocious creature murks through the water.
As it goes slowly through the water seeking its prey.
Here comes a fan boat scaring it away.
As it moves on it gets deeper and deeper going through the murky water bay.
As it gets darker it gets lucky with its prey.
Scott Nelson, Grade 6
Barriere Elementary School, BC

My Youth and Hers
READER: When I was one, I found a friend.
ASSEMBLY: When she was one, she wished her friends were still alive.

READER: When I was one, my mom cried of joy.
ASSEMBLY: When she was one, her mom cried of pain.

READER: For my first birthday, I made my first wish.
ASSEMBLY: For her first birthday, she had nothing to wish for;
she knew it wouldn't come true.

READER: When I was one, I said my first word.
ASSEMBLY: When she was one, she had to be silent.

READER: When I turned two, I went to camp.
ASSEMBLY: When she turned two, she went to a concentration camp.

READER: When I was two, my new sister was born.
ASSEMBLY: When she was two, her sister was buried.

READER: When I turned two, I decided my favorite number was 2.
ASSEMBLY: When she turned two, she got a number she didn't like at all.
Adina Gazith, Grade 5
Ecole Akiva, QC

Marathon of Hope
In the hospital Terry had a dream,
He would run with his friend, Doug as a team.
Doug would drive in a van
As Terry ran, and ran, and ran.

When Terry ran he was filled with hope,
The pain in his leg, he learned to cope.
A disease so gigantic, he had to conquer,
Inspiring speeches he became quite the talker.

After 18 miles he felt pain in his chest
He knew he had to rest, but he kept trying his best.
People watching, clapping and cheering,
Hopping down the highway, his goal nearing.

The cancer spread, Terry Fox died,
$23.4 million was raised and memories of Terry became worldwide.
A Canadian hero so strong and brave,
The Marathon of Hope, with his heart he gave.
Paige Graffos, Grade 5
Our Lady of Perpetual Help, BC

What Is White

White is freedom for those who suffer
White is a cloud that flies so high
White is a dove, the sign of peace
White is a flag or surrender
White tastes sweet like vanilla
White sounds like an avalanche
White smells like white chocolate
White looks like snowfall
White makes me happy
White is freedom for those who suffer

Albert Tsan, Grade 6
Admiral Seymour Elementary School, BC

Hopeful People

They lived in war
They lived in trenches
They lived in a huddle for their lives

As days passed by
Their wives would cry
Desperately hoping their husbands would not die

In 1914 and 1939 our soldiers fought for us
They fought in world wars
Now we try to gain their everlasting trust

When we sleep at night,
their lives are in fear of bombing
When we hug our family,
their hearts are in a painful longing

Now we show our veterans that we still care
Isn't it sad how war has never been fair

Tina Flaherty, Grade 6
St Mary Choir and Orchestra Program, ON

Hills

Hills are for babies.
Hills are for kids.
Hills are for teenagers.
Hills are for adults.
Hills are for birthday parties.
Hills are for fun.
Hills are for everyone.
Hills are for rolling down.
Hills are for picnics.
Hills at home are for sliding down and having fun.
Hills make a perfect picture to paint.
Hills make a perfect place for kittens and other animals.
Hills make a very good view.
Hills are a perfect place to rest.
Hills are for rolling down and going up.
Hills are perfect for me and you.

Ses Jack, Grade 5
Sxoxomic Community School, BC

The Girl with the Watering Can

The sight of the sun rays shining brightly.
The scent of flowers dancing harmoniously.
The feel of freedom running breathlessly.
The taste of the green grass and the wind laughing joyfully.
The sound of nature smiling at the girl gleefully.
The passionate artist Pierre Auguste Renoir.

Jennifer Ben-Menashe, Grade 6
Ecole Akiva, QC

The Bully Bob

Have you heard of the bully Bob?
The guy who can pick up logs?
Well, he was transferred to our school today,
It filled our class with dismay.
He isn't smart, his grades are low.
He named his pencil Mr. Poe.
But recess is the worst part,
He bullies us like he's got no heart.
He has an eight pack and muscles as big as the mall.
But did I mention he is only two feet tall?

Brendan Kravik, Grade 5
Queen of All Saints Elementary School, BC

Believe

Do you know what it feels like,
To be stood up,
To not be part of the popular group?
Well, I do.
You feel unwanted,
Like you're invisible.
You can see in my eyes,
How much I am hurting inside,
Who would want such pain?
I'm not the only one who feels this way.
Stand by me and everyone else,
Together we can stop this.
There shouldn't be a popular group,
We should all just be friends and not treat each other badly.
Believe in yourself and things can change!

Elizabeth Tamas, Grade 6
Strathcona-Tweedsmuir School, AB

The Stars

They're natural light,
they are also fairly bright.

They come out with the moon,
it's 7:00 they're going to come out soon.

In it, you can see the milky way,
but not during the day.

They watch down on us,
even when we cause a fuss

Tori Sveda, Grade 4
Good Shepherd School, AB

Blue Is...

Blue is a pool on a hot summer morning waiting to be jumped in
Blue sounds like a waterfall coming down and exploding into a still pond
Blue tastes like a succulent freezie on a humid summer day at record high temperatures
Blue makes me feel cool and laid back
Blue is a clear sky on a beautiful day at the dawn of summer
Blue feels like soft velvet on a child's stuffed animal
Blue is relaxed

Matt Blois, Grade 6
John T Tuck Public School, ON

Facts About Wars

The First World War was fought from 1914 to 1918. It was the largest and most deadly war up to that time. Living in the trenches was a miserable experience. Danger and death were ever-present, due to enemy snipers, machine-gun fire and artillery bombardments. Aboriginal Canadian soldiers brought special skills to the army in the 1st World War.

In 2008, our country is taking the opportunity to honor these Canadians in ceremonies commemorating the 90th anniversary of the end of the 1st World War. 90 years is a long time and the world has changed in many ways, but the contributions and sacrifices they made played an important roll in Canada's development into the free and peaceful country we have today.

Josh Thompson, Grade 6
East Selkirk Middle School, MB

Nova Scotia

N ova Scotia is a province in Canada.
" **O** ne defends and the other conquers," is the motto of Nova Scotia.
V ery high tides are found in Nova Scotia.
A pples and blueberries grow in the Annapolis Valley.

S callops, crabs, clams, pollock, herring, salmon, and haddock are all in Nova Scotia.
C ape Breton island and a mainland are the two parts of Nova Scotia.
O sprey is Nova Scotia's bird.
T here is an ocean around Nova Scotia.
I n Nova Scotia, they have a pulp and paper industry.
A tlantic Ocean is the ocean around Nova Scotia.

Meg Wall, Grade 4
FW Gilbert School, MB

My Long Journey

The wind whistled in the air it twirled and weaved through my hair
As I started the longest journey in my life a journey of much adventure and strife
It started at a castle as black as the night the hallways were lit with an eerie candle light
All of a sudden I saw two eyes beaming like lasers, but little in size
It was a wolf, but not overly scary. It seemed young, but it was hairy.
Then it ran tingled in fright. Right then I saw a terrible sight
There stood strong and tall, two armed guards with daggers and all.
I put up a fight I did quite well, unfortunately I stumbled and fell.
They took me away and put me on chains. I felt the adrenaline running through my veins.
As around the corner a shadow crept, as the guard behind me gently slept.
It was the wolf and he had the key, he came up and dropped it for me.
As I unlocked the cell and dropped the chains, I picked out a path using certain lanes.
When I saw the face of the dark king, I had a flashback of the terrible things,
He killed my parents I say he's mean. He's the darkest man I've ever seen.
So I shot an arrow I found on the ground. It killed the king with blood all around.
Finally I worry no more, for I am free to explore.
And that was my story of adventure and strife. It was quite the journey in my life.

Mykaelah Dixon, Grade 4
Jack Miner Public School, ON

The Forest

As I walk through the forest
I see the strong brown trees.
Twisting in the gusting wind
Tree by tree,
The wet sparkling leaves fall to branch from branch.
While the monkeys leap and play.
The tigers roar.
The panther stalks.
As I swing on green long vines,
I fall on the padded soil.
I pick myself up.
When I pick myself up.
I look up.
What do I see a coral snake.
Slithering by the trees.
As I walk home I think of a Wonderful place.

Aaron Tichler, Grade 4
Margaret Wooding School, AB

Eternal Flame

There is a flame that goes on and on,
and keeps on burning without a flaw.
The people call it without any shame,
for this is called the eternal flame.
This flame is not a big bonfire,
but it is the one that holds your desires.
Try, try, and try some more,
and you might just get what you were looking for.
But never blow this flame away,
because it just might take your life away.

Shifa Garewal, Grade 6
Dixon Grove Jr Middle School, ON

Pink

Pink is the colour of love,
Pink tastes like candy hearts on Valentines day,
Pink smells like roses, fresh and sweet,
Pink sounds like soft music, playing quietly,
Pink feels like fluffy teddy bears from someone special,
Pink looks like sparkly jewelry hung on my neck,
Pink is my favourite colour.

Kate Garland, Grade 6
John T Tuck Public School, ON

Sunset

The ocean shore laps the land,
Between my toes as I feel the sand.
The sky is blue,
Like the waves,
The sun is bright,
Like a fireball floating in the sky,
Its rays hit the clouds like rainbows above,
The day is almost done,
And another day is soon to come.

Krista King, Grade 5
Queen of All Saints Elementary School, BC

Remember

R emembering the brave soldiers that fought for freedom.
E very faithful soldier that sacrificed themselves in war.
M en and women who helped the feared soldiers.
E very one of the soldiers' braveness inside and out.
M any of the loved soldiers' fear and pride.
B ringing peace to poor and foreign countries.
E ach risk in dying in this cruel war.
R ed glowing poppies that grew around the
many crosses of the silent dead.

Shawn Lallier, Grade 4
David Ovans Elementary School, AB

Tubing

I am going tubing,
On a very cold day,
I am on the chair lift,
I look at the sky
I feel the snow on my face
As I slide down the hill,
I feel the chilly snow going
Along my back, I take off
My boots and there is snow
In my socks! I start screaming
It was so cold!!!

Stephanie Graham, Grade 5
Forest Hill School – Senior Campus, QC

Soccer

I love Soccer,
Yes I do,
I play defense,
And that is true,
I like to run,
And block the shots,
If I mess up I'll have bad thoughts,
At the end of each game,
We always end up winning,
But we tell everyone that
Is just the beginning.

Ashley Mukhti, Grade 5
Nativity of Our Lord Catholic School, ON

Cheetah

The cheetah is like a race car
That goes 100 miles per hour
It goes swoosh, it roars and it is as fast as lightning

It catches its prey like going on a scavenger hunt

It is gold
And it is really bold

When the cheetah is done with it's fun it goes home for lunch

Jasmine Narayan, Grade 4
Kingswood Dr Public School, ON

Frustration
Frustration is
dark orange.

It sounds like
a deep sigh.

It smells like
an overused outhouse.

It tastes like
a moldy
piece of cake.

It looks like
blurred vision.

Frustration feels like
a treat that you can't quite
reach.
Mason Lindley, Grade 4
Heritage Christian Online School, BC

Beautiful Art
Stickers
Sticky, decorative
Beautifying, shining, glowing
Cards, envelopes, crayons, markers
Sketching, colouring, erasing
Creative, artistic
Drawings
Jewel Hand, Grade 5
Bernard Elementary School, BC

My Dog, Macy
My dog is so funny
With her orange curly hair
Everybody loves her,
She makes friends everywhere

When we go for walks,
She prances so proudly
But when she is outside alone,
She barks so loudly

She loves to get
A belly rub
But she hates
Having a bath in the tub

I guess what I
Am trying to say
Is that my dog
Is here to stay
Jamie Fournier, Grade 6
École Renaissance, ON

The Sun
The sun is shining o so bright
Giving off a massive light
Although we see the sun so big
To other stars it is a twig

Our sun is part of many stars
Many stars that travel far
Even though the sun is yellow
It is not hot, it is very mellow

To make people feel relief
I will sum this up in brief
The sun as we know it is big but small
The sun as we know it is short but tall
Kyle Zacharkiw, Grade 6
East Selkirk Middle School, MB

One Young Canadian
Imagine
One young Canadian
Had a huge impact on Canada
Living outdoors on the front line
Enemy snipers,
Artillery bombardments
Exchanging gunfire instead of gifts

The Germans were shelling one morning
A shell burst and killed two Canadians
A miserable experience
Death and destruction
Danger was ever-present
Great courage during
The battle

One young Canadian
In a maze of trenches
Died in service to their country
Important in Canada's development
Restored peace
The world has changed
Jorja Ferguson, Grade 6
East Selkirk Middle School, MB

Apples Are…
Apples are crunchy and,
they are munchie.
They taste delicious,
and they are nutritious.
Sometimes they're green,
and other colours too.
I like to eat them, do you?

Apples are awesome!
Carter Sawatzky, Grade 4
Tisdale Elementary School, SK

Rose
R uby red
O pen
S mooth
E ver so sweet!
Dylan Holman, Grade 5
Pat Hardy Elementary School, AB

Seed
A seed is planted and thus a flower
And like a child both blossom and grow
The wild bird sings as the flower grows
Soon he will be on his way
But know he is my seed
Gabrielle Torrealba, Grade 4
Colby Village Elementary School, NS

Snowmobiling
In the middle of nowhere
miles and miles of open land
nobody else except the machine and you
snow everywhere
Fields of snow as far as the eye can see
nothing except snow and tracks
That is what you leave
after a day of snowmobiling you and
your machine are tired
Austin Bierkos, Grade 6
Aurora Elementary School, AB

What Am I?
I am bright
I am hot
I don't come out at night
I give off lots of light
I am the Earth's closest star
I am a friend with the moon
All the planets orbit around me
I am the Sun!!!
Nicole Schmid, Grade 6
East Selkirk Middle School, MB

My Dad
He likes to hunt
My dad likes to hunt bucks
He is good at shooting his bow
My Dad!
Mattie McCarthy, Grade 6
Falmouth District School, NS

Summer
Laying in the sun
Just chillin' on the treetops
Summer is so fun
Ashley Card, Grade 6
Falmouth District School, NS

Moonlight

The shine of the moonlight
An owl hoots
The flutter of wings
Then quiet

An owl hoots
It lands on a branch
Then quiet
The silent darkness presses in

It lands on a branch
The shadows loom in the moonlight
The silent darkness presses in
Another hoot

The shadows loom in the moonlight
Dawn has yet to come
Another hoot
The night stays for now

Dawn has yet to come
The flutter of wings
The night stays for now
The shine of the moonlight

Daniel Liu, Grade 5
Elboya Elementary and Jr High School, AB

Glowing Planet

Named after the goddess of love and beauty
We bathe in her blistering light
The star, the star of feminine right

Covered in lava,
A fiery blaze
Her flowing, fiery locks
Of gold and red
Come as a welcome shock

So dry so hot
No moisture no moons
She is alone, you can hear her cry
In the voice of the elegant loon

As order of birth she is older
And must protect the Earth
She took the blow and from below came a thank you
Came she now blazes bright as is her right

She, the heroine be the
One to save her younger sister
E
Her name is Venus
And she is gorgeous

Sanisha Taylor, Grade 6
East Selkirk Middle School, MB

A Tornado

A tornado is
Like a roller
Coaster rolling
Around a turn.

It sounds like
Two grey cars
Crashing.

It looks like
Water slowly
Swirling down
The drain.

And me
In the middle
Of the storm.

Michael Glover, Grade 5
Queen of All Saints Elementary School, BC

Cowboys

There was a cowboy who rode from the west.
But when his horse got shot, from the right.
He drifted out into the beautiful sunset.
He was never seen again.

Kristopher Bzdel, Grade 4
Tisdale Elementary School, SK

Off

A light in the distance flickers slowly on and off.
But the light inside of me has already switched off.
I no longer have hope, hope to call my own.
Inside I am empty; been left all alone.
No one to come to my rescue, to watch through the night.
No one is there to hold me
No one can hear my cry.

Germaine Konji, Grade 5
St Clare Catholic School, ON

Dear Mr. President

Dear Mr. President
I hear about soldiers dying
I almost hear their cries
I don't want war
I don't want hatred
I just want love and peace
I almost hear the shells exploding
I hear their screams of pain
I hear a mine exploding and a dozen screams
I see the fields covered with white crosses
Each one covers a brave, brave man
I write this letter right to you
I hope I've done enough to tell you
WAR is very wrong!

Donovan Gerber, Grade 5
Mornington Central School, ON

Sun

Shining
Right in my eyes
Sun rays warm everything
Golden streams rushing from the sky
Sunshine.

Miranda Walsh, Grade 6
Falmouth District School, NS

April Rain

Shimmer, shimmer goes the rain.
Yippee! The Spring is here again!
I run across the lane,
to see a beautiful, shining rainbow.

I love to smell the fresh raindrops,
resting lightly on flower pedal tops.
I love the sweet scent in the air
of the April rain.

I love to run through puddles fast,
that sit there quiet, like shining glass.
I love the feeling of the wet, dewy grass
under my feet.

I'm glad that Spring is here at last!

Emma Runquist, Grade 4
Westwind Alternate School, AB

Cats

C ool creatures
A ll different colors
T oo fun
S uper nice pets

Cole Fatels, Grade 4
Linsford Park School, AB

The Dream

I was watching a movie
I feel asleep
I had a dream
It was Halloween night
I got dressed up in my costume
I went trick-or-treating
I saw a man with a knife
He started chasing me
Faster and faster I got
Running out of breath
I ran to my house
I locked the door
I woke up
The doorbell rang
It was him
The guy with the knife
That was a Halloween night to remember

Ashley Jay, Grade 5
Hamiota Elementary School, MB

My Morning and Hers

Reader: When I woke up, I growled, "10 more minutes."
Assembly: When she woke up, she was proud to live another day.
Reader: For my breakfast, I ate eggs and pancakes.
Assembly: For her breakfast, she ate a crumb of bread.
Reader: On my way to school, I listened to CDs in the car.
Assembly: On her way to work, she listened to gun shots coming from the sky.
Reader: When I enter class, I greet my friends with a hug.
Assembly: When she entered work she was greeted with a slap.
Reader: In class we learn that people are homeless
Assembly: In her life she was homeless.
Reader: When I don't finish my work, I get homework.
Assembly: When she finishes her work, she gets sent to heaven

Kiki Cooper, Grade 5
Ecole Akiva, QC

Green

Green is like a frog jumping up and down nonstop
Green tastes like a sweet candy bursting with flavor in your mouth
Green feels as bright as a warm summer day
Green sounds like birds chirping and dogs barking
Green looks like a horse running gracefully and freely in the wind
Green smells like rows of sweet smelling flowers
Green is the brightest, sunniest color in the world

Carissa Marshall, Grade 6
Mornington Central School, ON

Pictures

They are a painting of your past
They bring back the memories you might or might not want to remember
They can be used for a person's career or might just be taken for fun
With a click of a shutter, an impression is formed
They might be blurry or sharp and clear.
They are the ones that will capture
the memories that will last for a lifetime.

Pictures

Kira-Marie Lazda, Grade 5
Forest Hill School – Senior Campus, QC

Thinking

As I sit in the light of the stunning sunset and stare at the
glistening ocean I think about what I must do to make my life
worthwhile, without the man I truly long for.

It is like a mystery unsolved and I just can't figure it out.

My life is like a spinning spiral; it spins up and then down again.

It has take me so much time to think about how I will possibly
make things right, if only I could relive my life from the time that
things went wrong to the time they were fixed.

I would be overjoyed to stop my depression. But here I am, still
thinking.

Vanessa Lohr, Grade 6
St James Catholic School, BC

My Tricycle

My tricycle is fast.
My tricycle is slow.
My tricycle is red and white.
This is my beautiful bike.
Some people call it a trike.
My tricycle is the best!
My tricycle's wheels are black and rubber.
My tricycle is sometimes a pest.

Caitlyn Edmunds, Grade 4
Tisdale Elementary School, SK

Math

Math is fun.
My learning has just begun.
My pencil is ready,
And my hand is steady.

Adding is easy.
Using a calculator is cheesy.
Subtracting gives us less.
But can sometimes make a mess.

Multiplying is tricky,
And my teacher is picky.
I have to get it right,
Or my teacher might bite.

I use my red pen,
To make corrections again.
My teacher doesn't like mistakes,
Too many, means no recess breaks.

Matthew Hartwig, Grade 5
Community Bible Fellowship Christian School, MB

Colors in the Sky

If you want to see a rainbow
Just check out the sky
You'll see seven colors stacked up high
Colors sparkling and shining
As clouds go by.

R ed is like the cherries growing in the trees
O range is for the pumpkins at Halloween
Y ellow is like the sun shining in the sky
G reen is for the grasses growing on the hills up high
B lue is like the deeply dyed oceans
I ndigo is for the noisy little blue jays
V iolet's for the saskatoons that make my tummy smile.

Mother Nature uses these beautiful colors to paint
A rainbow just for you
So follow its path
And you just might find a pot of gold waiting
For you at the end of the rainbow.

Stephen Schadeck, Grade 6
Aurora Elementary School, AB

What Is Blue?

Blue is the tears that
Run out of your eyes
Blue is a soft blanket
That was once washed
Blue is the water
That people drink
Blue is the sky on
A very nice day
Blue tastes like
Mountain water
Blue smells like
Blueberry pie
Blue sounds like
The calm ocean waves
Blue feels like
Icy-cold water
Blue looks like a
Sapphire ring
Blue makes me
Want to go swimming

Kevin Tran, Grade 5
Admiral Seymour Elementary School, BC

Nature

Walking down the path
with the cold trees over me
speechless but so calm

Arshdeep Jagdeo, Grade 5
Howard De Beck Elementary School, BC

Music

A smooth, colourful, wonderful thing.
This is surely what we call music.
A part of life that's just for amusement,
Or maybe not.
Piano, voice, violin, kazoo.
You can make music with almost anything.

Red, blue, green, pink,
C, D, F, G.
A certain colour with a certain key.
Each tone has a colour.

Not everybody understands music.
Not everybody gets rhythm.
Not everybody can sing.
Not everybody has an inspiration.

You can hear it.
You can see it.
You can feel it.
You may not taste it,
But it is definitely music.

Theodora Peirson, Grade 6
Central Public School, ON

A Small Rock
There once was a small rock,
who looked like a piece of chalk.
He declared he was not
what people thought.
Too bad he could not talk!
Jake Popovich, Grade 6
Harry Balfour School, AB

The Beach
I love going to the beach.
Sparkling golden sand.
Roaring waves dazzling my eyes.
Fragile white sand dollars.
Wet shells,
Right out of the ocean.
Slender tall palm trees.
Horrible snapping crabs.
Colorful shells and slow turtles.
Hungry gliding seagulls.
Old and rusty boats.
Beautiful blue sky.
Now you see,
Why I love the beach!
Justice Summers-Denman, Grade 4
Margaret Wooding School, AB

Rabbits
I love rabbits
They're really cute
Their colour is black and white
They're little
Their tails are white
And they're amazing
Jana Oueidat, Grade 4
École Renaissance, ON

Chantelle
C atches your smile.
H and in hand, friends forever.
A nimal-lover.
N ever crushed your smile.
T ries hard at school.
E specially nice.
L ends a helping hand.
L oves music.
E nergy and enthusiasm.
Chantelle Karockai, Grade 6
Harry Balfour School, AB

A Bit of Nature
Small prairie farmland
Snowy mountainous background
Cool moist fresh spring air
Jason Reich, Grade 6
Silver Star Elementary School, BC

Spring
The sun comes out now
When the flowers are sprouting
They sprout very tall
Marcellus Cogswell-Wright, Grade 4
Park West School, NS

My Wish for the World...
There is food for everyone,
Poor people will have a home,
No one will fight,
Everyone will get along,
That no one will bully in schools,
Or in the world.
Karina Muench, Grade 4
Tisdale Elementary School, SK

Frogs
Frogs are green,
A bug eating machine
They're slimy n' all
As they jump in the fall

They squat on a pad
Driving flies mad
Silently stalking
Not even talking
Until...BAM!
Dinner is served.

Slurp...
Burp.
Tony Parker, Grade 6
Bella Coola Adventist Academy, BC

Candy
Candy is very good
You can eat them in the woods

Sometimes it's colourful
Sometimes it is beautiful

I like licorice and gum
Every time I eat it I say *yum!*

So much sugar and so sweet
You can eat it whole wheat
I prefer it all week

If you don't like candy
It won't be friendly

I like it so much
I eat it at lunch
Zoe Plumb, Grade 5
École Renaissance, ON

Spring
When all the snow melts
All the children start to play
On a nice spring day
Alfred Neil Ortile, Grade 4
Park West School, NS

My Cleats Have Not Walked
My cleats have not walked in
the Rogers Centre in Toronto.

My glove has not catched a ball
in the Rogers Centre.

My equipment bag has not been
hung in the Blue Jays locker room.

My hand has not felt a professional
baseball glove.

My eyes have not beheld the crowd
cheering for their team.

My head has not been adorned
with a Blue Jays baseball cap

Yet
I still hope one day
all these dreams will come true.
Fernando Garcia, Grade 6
Sir Isaac Brock Public School, ON

Timber
T alented
I s smart
M uscular
B ig and strong
E nergetic
R eleases love.
Christian Basaraba, Grade 5
Pat Hardy Elementary School, AB

Movie Night
M ovie night
O n the roll
V oices are nice
I n the theatre
E nd of the movie was nice

N ice movie
I t was awesome
G reat movie
H appy ending
T heatre
Nathan Decker, Grade 4
Colby Village Elementary School, NS

The Dream

I flew, I flew,
I got the flu.
I ate, I ate
the number eight.
I waited, I waited
to weigh my fat cat.
But in the end, I got a big fat hat.
I went back home,
dreamed of Rome,
Woke up, and went to pick up my cat,
but then everything went all black!
And there I was back with my cat!
But my cat was wearing my hat!
And within my reach,
I saw a beach!
And on the beach, I saw a man!
Oh! Wait! I realized I have a fever of 110!
The beach and the man on the beach were just me, being silly!!!

Rachel Christopher, Grade 5
École Renaissance, ON

Snowflakes

Snowflakes, snowflakes all around.
Snowflakes, snowflakes how you fly?
I wonder, I wonder I really do.
Snowflakes, snowflakes, why are you white?
Snowflakes, snowflakes, talk to me.
Snowflakes, snowflakes, how do you do?
Snowflakes, snowflakes, snowflakes.

Mason Leier, Grade 4
Tisdale Elementary School, SK

The Woolly Mammoth

The Woolly Mammoth, a spectacular beast.
It's a famous creature, to say the least.
It grew to a huge size, about 15 feet tall.
And when it stood, it towered over all.

It was a vegetarian, which means it ate grass.
Its weight, well, it had a huge mass.
When the Ice Age came of freezing snow,
it would migrate to where the valleys were low.

The Colombian Mammoth, a different one,
was 16 feet tall and lived in the sun.
The Woolly Mammoth was smaller than it,
and differed just a little bit.

Humans used to hunt this big beast
and when they killed one, my what a feast.
The mammoth is extinct in all of life's zones,
but we know what it looked like by its fossils and bones.

Nicholas Santamaura, Grade 4
Jack Miner Public School, ON

Shoes

Flats, converse and high heels too
I love my shoes way more than you
I wear them everywhere I go
some practical, some just for show

Shoes, a cushion for your feet
keep them clean, tidy and neat
shoes keep your feet nice and snug
in their place, all five toes lined up

shoes get old but still are treasured
holding memories that can't be measured
ready to be shared with a friend who
loves shoes, as much as you

red, yellow, white and green
shoes are nice, never mean
my shoes will make you drool
but that's ok because all shoes are cool

Rangana Talpe, Grade 6
Central Public School, ON

It's Your Bed

It's soft,
It's comfy,
It's cold when you get in it at night,
It has something to put your head on at night.
It's a place where you dream,
When you were little you might have had an accident in it,
It's a place where you forget the whole world.

Talissa Krilick, Grade 5
Forest Hill School – Senior Campus, QC

Orange

Orange is the color of autumn the best season ever.
Orange tastes like creamy, delicious pumpkin pie.
Orange smells soothing like a nice massage.
Orange sounds like crinkly leaves in a big pile.
Orange feels like Halloween.
Orange looks like kids trick or treating on a cool dark night.
Orange makes me feel calm.
Orange is my favorite color.

Cameron Hart, Grade 6
John T Tuck Public School, ON

Blue

Blue is the colour of water
Blue tastes like a slushy
Blue smells like blueberries
Blue sounds like the wind on a cool summer's day
Blue feels like I'm free
Blue looks like a bowl of jelly
Blue relaxes me
Blue is my favorite colour

Curtis Bambury, Grade 6
John T Tuck Public School, ON

Summer and Winter

Summer is great
But winter can make you late
Because of the bad weather
My best friends name is Heather

My friend has a few pugs
in winter there are no bugs
all the bugs are dead
But now I have to go to bed

Emily Lorincz, Grade 4
Good Shepherd School, AB

A Wish

I wish I were a dog
running through the house
trying to find my food
happily

Brendan Hunt, Grade 5
Bernard Elementary School, BC

Useless Things

An apple without seeds
A garden without weeds
A pong without a ping
A harp without a string

A table without legs
A chicken without its eggs
A basketball without a net
A pet store without a pet

Candles without a fire
TVs without a wire
Sewing machines without clothes
A foot without toes

A tap without water
Players without a cap
A storm without drops
A farm without crops

Athan Georgallidis, Grade 6
Sir Isaac Brock Public School, ON

The Zoo

Do you know what I see in a zoo?
I see cages large and bright.
Flowers fabulous and colorful.
There are rhinos, snotty and angry.
There are giraffes tall and fat.
Monkeys, hyper and amusing.
Striped zebras running fast.
Lions loud and sneaky.

I love seeing the zoo!!!
Randyn Boyko, Grade 4
Margaret Wooding School, AB

If I Were in Charge of the World*

If I were in charge of the world
I would make sure everyone was fantastically nice
There would be no more bullies
People wouldn't kill each other
There would be no more miserable tsunamis
There would be no more solemn wars
People wouldn't have to die in villainous pain
There would be no more horrid homeless people
Terry Fox would still be alive and found a cure for terrible cancer
Hitler didn't kill all those unlucky people
People could eat as much as they want and still stay incredibly skinny
People didn't have to pay nasty bills
There was no more sinful tax
No one was kicked out of their happy little house
There was no more evil malevolent government
The world was faithfully peaceful
There was no more wicked unhealthy food
There whole world loved super veggies
There was more helpful school
Everyone was super duper active
Aliens lived on Earth

Juliana Cleland, Grade 6
Silver Star Elementary School, BC
*Patterned after "If I Were in Charge of the World" by Judith Viorst.

The Race*

I was racing down the road,
Trying to beat the other man to the finish line,
As I came zooming down Eagle road,
There was a sign I did not see,
Perhaps because I was going to fast,
Then I saw a boy and a dog playing on the road,
I tried to honk my horn but they did not hear me,
I was going too fast to hit the brakes,
I tried anyways but it was useless,
The boy was saved but I hit the dog with a thud,
There was blood on my car,
There was blood on the road,
I was about to stop and to say that I am sorry,
Until I saw the car that I was racing make a sharp turn,
So I didn't stop to say sorry or apologize,
I just continued my on race,
Then I thought that the sign up ahead said look out for children,
I still feel terribly sad about that one day that I,
Did not even stop just to say one word,
SORRY.

Harleen Maan, Grade 6
DM Eagle Public School, ON
*Inspired by Sharon Creech's "Love That Dog"

A Stormy Day

Fierce, sharp waves crashing on edgy rocks with fearsome roaring rage.
Thunder clapping are sudden flashes with a tremendous boom.
Cloudy gray skies show no sign of revealing the blue behind it.

Celine Wang, Grade 6
Walnut Road Elementary School, BC

I Am

I am a kid with an interest in the scientific arts and a concern for the world
I wonder if new Renaissance is coming and if it will come in time
I hear the announcement of a breakthrough, no matter how small
I see one of the few people that are like me
I want to play a part in the coming revolution
I am a kid with an interest in the scientific arts and a concern for the world

I imagine that there is no
such thing as imaginary — if we want it to be true
I feel the diligence of those working for a better tomorrow
I touch the earth: our home, our life, our neglected responsibility
I worry that man will never learn right from wrong
I cry that 6,000,500,000 people took this long to finally make a difference
I am a kid with an interest in the scientific arts and a concern for the world

I understand there is still time to undo the tangled web we weaved
I say that behind the wall you put around yourself, everything's O.K. — In reality, it's not
I dream that man will wake up before they have nothing to wake up to
I try to spread the news about scientific advances
I hope no more will suffer for our ignorance
I am a kid with an interest in the scientific arts and a concern for the world

Andrew Cunningham, Grade 5
Torquay Elementary School, BC

When It's Spring

You'll know when it's spring when the birds start to sing and the flowers bloom.
And the children play delightfully in the woods behind your house.
You'll know when it's spring when you take your morning stroll,
and find dew in the grass and when you look out your window, you see only pure blue sky, and cotton in the sun.
And your mom and your sister are out almost every day, sunbathing.
You'll know when it's spring when the little sparrow you've been nursing will take off on new wings,
and you find morning glories smiling at the sun.
And your new best friend leaps through the grass, making daffodil necklaces.
You'll know when it's spring when the little cocoon breaks to give way to a beautiful coloured fairy,
and new caterpillars are housed in your bedroom window.
And when your mom asks you to thank Mother Nature for the sun.
You'll know when it's spring when your mom can't find use for indoor plazas anymore, and your dad shifts his garage outside.
And when you camp outside on starry nights, dreaming about the magic spring brings!

Eman Zahid, Grade 6
Islamic Foundation School, ON

We Will Remember

I had a very strange dream last night,
it was about destruction, but also all that is bright.
The world was at its darkest hour.
There was no more peace or poppy flowers.
We had forgotten what veterans did long ago,
when they went to Europe to face the foe.
I suddenly remembered the one war doctor, brave and strong.
Surely his message would show them all, why we remember the wars that lasted so long.
I used the soldier's message of peace and love,
to set an example for even people who thought they were too good to receive the message from above.
I touched their hearts and softened their souls,
so that we may remember until the poppies in Flanders Field no longer grow.

Jeff Liebusch, Grade 6
St Mary Choir and Orchestra Program, ON

My Bubbles

I once blew a bubble
It turned into a double
My bubbles are very shiny
But they did not have a hinny

My bubbles met a bird
The bird was not a nerd
The bird's name was Kim
She lives where it's dim

My bubbles kept on floating
But they did not keep gloating
Because they met a monkey
And he was very funky

They never stopped
They never popped
They kept on going
Smiles were showing
Kate Richards, Grade 4
Westside Academy, BC

A Wish for Someone I Love

If I could grant a wish for you,
I would get a thrill or two

Let your money buy a house,
make sure it doesn't have a mouse

May you always be healthy,
instead of being wealthy

May all your children be successful,
and for them to be respectful

May you discover a destination,
or instead the whole wide nation

If I could grant a wish for you,
I would get a thrill or two
Kylie Dowden, Grade 6
Sir Isaac Brock Public School, ON

The Beach

Fragile colorful seashells.
Sand that is golden and soft.
Rocks sturdy and strong.
Dolphins sometimes playing.
They are friendly!
Fish can be speedy and swift.
Octopi are leggy,
Sometimes squirting at you.
The water can be gentle and calm.
Sarah Brown, Grade 4
Margaret Wooding School, AB

Wheels

Wheels, wheels go round and round.
They all run along the ground.
Wheels can make vehicles very, very tall.
Wheels can be big or small.
Vehicles can go very, very fast.
You cannot even see the wheels go past.
Sometimes cars go very, very slow.
Then you can see the wheels really go.
Austin Dagg, Grade 4
Tisdale Elementary School, SK

Wishing Stars

If only…
If only wishes could fly
Then the grass will finally turn green
And the stars will finally twinkle.

It was long ago I made this wish,
yet it never disappeared.

If only wishes could fly
Then frowns will turn to smiles
And writing will turn to art.

It was long ago that sadness followed,
Yet it never disappeared.

If only wishes could fly
Then poems will turn to songs
And you would finally come back…

But if only wishes came true.
Tiffany Sham, Grade 5
Spul'u'kwuks Elementary School, BC

Vampires

Deep gold eyes, ruby red lips.
Pale, cold skin, body hard as bricks.

Beautiful creature. Beautiful indeed.
It will eat you, if you bleed.

It will suck you, suck you dry.
You're a snack, through their eyes.

Straight white teeth, coated with venom.
If it bites you, you'll be one of them.

To transform, it'll take days,
You'll scream and shout, from the pain.

Deep gold eyes, ruby red lips.
Pale, cold skin, body as hard as bricks.
Rezhneh Behruz, Grade 6
Sir Isaac Brock Public School, ON

Water/Land

Water
Clear, wet
Foaming, freezing, fast-moving
Fish, ponds, islands, trees
Growing, living, unmoving
Green, dry
Land
Cassandra Reber, Grade 5
Bernard Elementary School, BC

Fire Belly Toads

They rule
They are so cute
Are fun to take care of
Like to hop around in their cage
So fun!
Mikhail Koscielny, Grade 5
Pat Hardy Elementary School, AB

Green Is…

green is the smell of evergreen trees
the taste of chocolate mint ice cream
the texture of soft moss
the sight of puny pine needles
the sound of whistling trees in the forest
the feeling of peacefulness
the taste of green jelly beans
the sight of big ferns
the texture of soft evergreens
the taste of sour limes.
Richard Palmer, Grade 6
Bernard Elementary School, BC

Eagle

Spread its wings
has large beak
black and white
does not speak

Hunts for food
has no teeth
fast as lightning
what a beast

Lives in mountains
has sharp claws
glides in clouds
has small jaws

Spreads its wings
has large beak
black and white
does not speak
Elee Zammar, Grade 6
Sir Isaac Brock Public School, ON

If I Were in Charge of the World*

If I were in charge of the world
There could be opportunities for excellent education
There would be way better work hours
People would get to have the jobs they wanted
Everyone would have enough money

If I were in charge of the world
Factories would run on water
There wouldn't be any more global warming
Horses would replace all the cars

If I were in charge of the world
There would be absolutely no such thing as guns
Cures would be found for all the deadly sicknesses
Animals wouldn't be slaughtered

If I were in charge of the world
Snow would look like little tiny crystals
Everything would be made flowering vegetation
If only I were in charge of the world

Katelynn Cook, Grade 6
Silver Star Elementary School, BC
*Patterned after "If I Were in Charge of the World"
by Judith Viorst.

Endless

Olive wars bring fight to countries,
Gray smoke charges from huge guns,
Red blood oozes from weak, torn-apart soldier's bodies,
Orange fires erupt from ear-shattering bombs,
Black darkness blinds leaders' vision,
Will the terrible scene ever end?

Judy Kleinsasser, Grade 6
Milford Colony School, AB

An Exciting Week

On Sunday I won a fast KTM 300
On Monday I made it into the finals in motocross
On Tuesday I bought a Monster Energy biking outfit
On Wednesday I started a cross country race
On Thursday I took a fast jet to Mexico
On Friday I went skiing on a nice hill in Jasper
On Saturday I finished my cross country race
All in all, it was a very exciting week!

Erika Toker, Grade 4
David Ovans Elementary School, AB

Grandmother

My grandmother could play the drum with her heart.
She could dance with the earth and melt with the snow.
She could slurp spaghetti up like a tornado.
She could run like a wild coyote.
She may be as strange as an alien
But she is my lovable, huggable, teddy bear.

Laura Flett, Grade 6
Aurora Elementary School, AB

Clever Snow Ghost

A chilly ghost goes through my skin,
Needles whip at my face,
The strong scent of wet snow all over,
Clever, evil snow plotting,
Giving an undefeatable, strong message,
Saying that, I should never come out again!

Astrid Caceres, Grade 5
Ormsby School, AB

Fire

Friendship is a fire,
It warms you and you admire
Its beauty, strong and bright
But then the flame becomes white

And the fire dies down
And you want to drown
Because you feel as if the core,
Has lost the warmth it once held before.

The fire no longer crackles,
You feel as if you're in shackles,
Until the fire can ignite
And you feel as if there is light,

That once again it can warm you
And you know in your heart it is true,
That you and the fire
No matter how dire

Can survive the winds of hate,
No matter what your fate.

Paul Chen, Grade 6
Elboya Elementary and Jr High School, AB

My School

I go to Khalsa School,
it makes everyone drool.
My school is very new,
there's new people too.
My old friends are there,
and also new ones too.
It has a big field,
and a big gym too.
It has a big parking lot,
and a playground too.
We got the old buses,
but we're the new school.
I sleep in classes,
while my friends wear glasses.
I have religion classes,
and I don't need glasses.

Sukhmanpreet Kaur Gill, Grade 5
Khalsa School - Old Yale Road Campus, BC

Animal Sounds Can Hurt

Animal sounds can hurt people's feelings
like saying "moo"
to someone that's bigger than you
like saying "oink"
to someone who likes to eat a lot.

Aaron Little, Grade 5
Chiganois Elementary School, NS

Winter Has Come

There's a chill in the air
I wish I could hibernate
Like a big brown bear

Sam Friesen, Grade 4
Deloraine School, MB

Boy/Girl

Boy,
strong, tall,
video games, fights, sports,
running, jumping, skipping, shopping,
clothes, shoes, make up,
smart, pretty,
Girl

Stephanie Nelson, Grade 6
Bernard Elementary School, BC

My Mom

Caring, loving
You'll see
Calls names
Cooks well
Kind, cool
Sometimes embarrassing
Does chores
Unlike Dad
Love her
She is
The best!

Zambrine Saeed, Grade 6
The Valleys Senior Public School, ON

Apples

Apples grow on great big trees,
Worms like them and so do bees.
They all have different colours and size,
Some are made into yummy pies.
They are a teacher's crunchy treat,
They are healthy, red, and sweet.
They are round and make you smart,
They are seeds before they start.
They need water to help them grow,
They can't sprout in frost or snow.
Apples grow on great big trees,
Worms like them and so do bees.

Cheyanna Kidd, Grade 4
Tisdale Elementary School, SK

Summer Day

Blue is the colour of the sky on a July morning
Blue tastes like salt water from the ocean
Blue looks like a waterfall in the summer
Blue feels like pool water rushing through my hands in the hot sun
Blue makes me feel joyful
Blue is my favourite colour

Andrew Miles, Grade 6
John T Tuck Public School, ON

If I Were in Charge of the World*

If I were in charge of the world
I would have all the prejudiced people banned
There would be no more throbbing and excruciating pain from needles
No one would die unless they wanted to
All dreadful wars would have water guns instead of real guns

If I were in charge of the world
There would be fashion police around every corner
Instead of icy cold snow there would be delicious cotton candy
Students would teach the teachers
Adults could get any job they wanted

If I were in charge of the world
I would make a new animal that could handle global warming
Instead of smokes there would be Popeye sticks
If you cut down a tree you would have to plant a new one
If only I were in charge of the world

Jensen Toews, Grade 6
Silver Star Elementary School, BC
*Patterned after "If I Were in Charge of the World" by Judith Viorst.

Lucky

My cat; kitty, her nickname is LuLu.
Calico: gray, orange and white.
Big-hearted, fast and shy; scared of strangers.
Petite, her manx tail bobs along,
Comfortable around me.
Soft, cuddly, melting in my lap.
She smells like vanilla.
Her eyes are gold on the outside and brown close to the middle, like mine.
Meow…tick, tick, tick as she walks across the hardwood floor.

Rebecca Chatham, Grade 4
Bella Coola Adventist Academy, BC

The Last the Very Last

I wish I was a butterfly I could go wherever I want
Now I have to listen to people telling me what to do
Now it's all black and sad and dark everywhere you look
I wish I was a dove and there would be peace and bright yellow

If only I had control I would make the world full of hearts and love
Every time I look around I see people ill and sick with tears coming out of their eyes
If I was a star I could wish whatever I wanted and all my wishes would come true
Now I am stuck inside this creepy place not knowing what will happen next

Ariella Meltzer, Grade 5
Ecole Akiva, QC

Go Inside
Go inside an iPod
And see a bunch of songs.

With this little entertainment system
Surely you can't go wrong.

Use it to listen to music,
Watch videos or play a game.

After using this system once,
You'll never be the same.

It comes in many colors
Like pink, silver, and green.

This little mini jukebox is
The best you've ever seen.

Apple makes the iPod,
They're truly entertainment slayers.

So go ahead and get rid of your CD's
And all of your Mp3 players.
Isabella Oram, Grade 5
Queen of All Saints Elementary School, BC

Friends
Friends are awesome, friends are cool,
Friends are kind, friends rule,
They are always there for you,
They help you when you are blue,
They are there through good and bad,
They are there when you are happy and when you are mad,
Friends laugh with you,
Friends are always true.
Bella Harrison, Grade 4
St Alphonsus School, MB

A Thousand Lives
As I fall they feel no pain,
Like a hunter to a goose.
As I speak I am not heard,
Like a mouse to a tornado.
As I walk I don't feel the rain,
Like the sun to the clouds.
As I eat there's no more taste,
Like the water to the flowers.
As I am crying they don't feel emotion,
Like a vampire to its bait.
As I try to escape they will find me in a way,
Like I'm trapped in a maze.
I am hunted like a predator to his bait.
Prisca Luyila, Grade 6
Ecole Ste-Jeanne-d'Arc, ON

The Sound of Death
The sound of death
leaves crunching under the boots of a hunter.
The sound of death
black wind whisking you away.
The sound of death
a twig snapping in the dark.
The sound of death
a fire crackling in the midnight wind.
The sound of death
a bell ringing from the midnight sky.
The sound of death is twilight.
Taylor Kraft, Grade 4
J Douglas Hogarth Public School, ON

The Rare Herd of Horses
Their manes floated in the air.
The blue sky above and the green grass below,
This kind of day was rare.
All the horses ran over the stream in a row,
Until they found a place to rest.
They grazed, mare by foal and males near.
It was, it really was the best.
And none had any fear,
Until night came and it was dark.
They slept side by side,
Then came the only sign.
The sign that showed them the time had arrived,
To ride away,
Because the sun was high in the blue sky.
Angelica Stergiopoulos, Grade 6
Morin Heights Elementary School, QC

Mmm…
Chocolate chip cookie dough
So chewy and sweet.
Every time I go to Baskin Robins
That ice cream is always taunting me.

LICK
LICK
LICK

So cold, but the minute it goes in my mouth,
MELTING begins.

The dough so thick and rich
The chocolate chips melt slowly.

I swallow, I feel as if this ice cream was
Created just for me.
CRUNCH
CRUNCH
As I take a bite out of my cone.
Now my day is complete!
Mariluz Rosero-Sanchez, Grade 6
St Maria Goretti Elementary School, ON

Taekwondo

Taekwondo is fun
You can do patterns, sparring
You can test for belts
Competitions are cool
All together, it's fun!!

Gillian Larsen, Grade 5
Pat Hardy Elementary School, AB

Who Am I?

I have only one moon,
It is small, grey and round,
It's bright in the sky like a
Rock on the ground

I am the third from the sun,
But weigh more than a ton,
I am the place to have fun,
When your work is all done,

With crystal-clear water,
And fresh air to breathe,
I am a blue ball that will
Never leave

Hundreds of satellites circle me,
Like little dots in the sky,
Who am I?

Reagan Croy, Grade 6
East Selkirk Middle School, MB

Cooperation

I wanted to play with the Wii
David threw it up in a tree
I wanted my turn
And David to learn
To cooperate with me!

Bryan Sancho, Grade 6
Walnut Road Elementary School, BC

Soft

Spilled milk from heaven
Moving in turtle speed
First a speedboat
And then a shoe
Factory smoke is not the
Same as my cloud
It's a pure gleaming white puffball
Soft and adorable
It protects me from above when
I am hot
You are a magnificent cloud
Nothing evil nothing phenomenal
Nothing but a unique little cloud.

Natalia Aguirre Cardenas, Grade 6
Blundell Elementary School, BC

Rocks

If you see a rock
a rock in the water,
a medium soft rock,
it's a water rock,
then when you squeeze it,
a waterfall
falls out of that rock.

Tia Sinclair, Grade 4
Calico Public School, ON

Hot Rod

Hot Rod
Quick, antique
Speeding, revving, leading
Goes at lightning speed
Accelerating, racing, moving
Rapid, pristine
Sports car

Michael Smith, Grade 5
St Mark Separate School, ON

Jockey

There once was a boy named Jockey
Who loved to play hockey
He shoots He scores
On the score board
Then he was hit with a clockey!

Jabes Benedict, Grade 6
Falmouth District School, NS

Trevor

I have a cat, his name is Trevor
He loves to play forever 'n ever
Sometimes we call him Wally
He often is smelly
I still like my gray cat Trevor

Braden Davis, Grade 4
Deloraine School, MB

Ibex and Wild Goats

Ibex
Wild, lively, quick
Climbing, balancing, grip
Cling to the tiniest ledges — cliffs
Wild goats

Mike Normand, Grade 6
St James Catholic School, BC

Clocks

Tick, Tock
Coocoo, Ding dong, Click click
There goes the bird
Time

Alycia Robinson, Grade 4
Good Shepherd School, AB

The Cat

Fangs of steel
Spies the mouse
By metal claws
In the house

Smooth as silk
Fast as light
Act like kids
In the night

Can be gentle
Have some fear
Can be big
Like a bear

Fangs of steel
Spies the mouse
By metal claws
In the house

Min Jae Kang, Grade 6
Sir Isaac Brock Public School, ON

Summer Rain

Leaking town houses, and cold wet faces.
Cool crisp air and water racing.
Kids are out and splashing about.
Cold rain in my mouth.
All I can taste is rain water.
People inside and by the fire.
I should go inside too.

Raven Paul, Grade 6
Ormsby School, AB

Cereal Danger!

I had a pet froot loop,
It was in my milk,
But it got goopy,
And it fell on my kilt.

My mom got mad at me,
But I said it's not my fault,
Oh ya, what was it a flea,
No, it was the salt.

Justin C. R. Demers, Grade 6
Linden Lanes School, MB

The Leaves Do Not Turn

The leaves do not turn
They don't change color when I look
But do when I don't
I want to see them change color
But they will never change for me

Vinny Andruk, Grade 6
St James Catholic School, BC

The Jungle

In the jungle
Animals forsake their families
Monkeys and snakes move around
Piranhas in the crystal blue water
Tigers hunt after monkeys and snakes after mice
While the birds fly in the creamy blue sky.

Nelson Correia, Grade 6
St Maria Goretti Elementary School, ON

The Roller Coaster!

The best and worst of rides.
Space Mountain
The dark glare and the roaring speeds.
Frightening.
The speeds slowing down as the roller coaster went up hill.
Calming.
The rattling of the tracks as the roller coaster went down hill.
Insecurity.
The fact that my older cousin beside me was shaking with fear.
Funny.
The roller coaster starts to go backwards.
Scary.
The expensive drink my dad bought me
for not crying on the roller coaster when I was only five.
Delicious.
It was the worst of rides, it was the best of rides.

Jack Brain, Grade 5
Charles Beaudoin Public School, ON

Life

For all the days you weren't here,
In my dreams you do appear,
All the days I cried in sorrow,
I'll dream of seeing you tomorrow.

You can't waste your life crying away,
You've got to live it day by day.
We have happy days yet to come,
Those solemn days are gone and done,

No more hatred,
No more homeless,
No more darkness,
Because the world would be lit
With the love in our hearts,
The everlasting source of power.

God loves us all the same,
God doesn't want us to complain,
If we brought all the love in the world together,
Love would keep going on forever.
All these little things add
Up to what's called,
Life.

Jillian Elizabeth Conrad, Grade 5
Colby Village Elementary School, NS

Terry Fox's Story

I was such a happy boy,
So glad and full of joy!
But one day my leg was taken off,
It left pain in my heart — like an awful cough!

But I saw others in pain too,
And I knew what I could do!
I'd run for the cure —
It's the perfect chance — I'm sure!

So I started running with the pain,
The sweat on my face came down like rain!
But I wouldn't stop the run for cancer —
Just keep running faster and faster!

Then finally the day came,
I couldn't handle all the pain.
A few months later, then I died,
But I wouldn't start to cry!

I wasn't running for the glory,
That's half the reason I'm writing this story!
So listen up, poem reader —
I'm not a dreamer — I'm a believer!

Laura Sullivan, Grade 5
Our Lady of Perpetual Help, BC

A Fun Filled Week

On Monday I climbed the Rocky Mountains
On Tuesday I went to Jamaica
On Wednesday I sprinted around the world
On Thursday I swam in the Black Sea
On Friday I went skating on a mountain
On Saturday I taught a class on a cloud
On Sunday I went to Costa Rica
All in all it was a fun filled week

Beth McDonald, Grade 4
David Ovans Elementary School, AB

The Evening Star

The evening star is Venus
A planet so bright
It's the first one we see
When we look up at night
The planet named after the Goddess of Love
Is the planet we see when we look up above
The planet that shines
That looks so divine
The planet we see
Glistening from afar
Is Earth's sister, Venus
The Evening Star

Andrea Olson, Grade 6
East Selkirk Middle School, MB

The Five Senses of Nature

I see spruce trees, chickadees, walking paths and whitetail deer.
I hear waves crashing against the rocks, and the gulls crying for food.
I feel the sun shining on my face, the burning hot sand under my feet and the wind blowing my hair.
I smell the smoke at the camp fire and the roasted marshmallows.
I taste sweet strawberries and sour crabapples.

Steven Pelley, Grade 4
St Alphonsus School, MB

The Moon

The moon gives us light at night. It is shining throughout the night. The moon is silver and white. Sometimes the moon is full and sometimes the moon is half. The moon is looking wonderful every night. The moon is out every night. When we sleep it's on top of our heads. The moon is very bright. Every day every night we see the moon shining bright. Sometimes there is no moon in the sky. The moon has some holes in it. There are lots of rocks on the moon. The moon follows you everywhere. The moon is there out in the night sky. The moon is nice.

Jasman Dhillon, Grade 5
Khalsa School - Old Yale Road Campus, BC

We Are Not Alone in the Universe

Here are God's words of wisdom…
speak them with confidence Remembrance and faith

While we sing our national anthem, some may not be proud,
or remember those soldiers giving up their lives for us, so we can make the world a better place

Here are God's words of wisdom…
speak them with confidence Remembrance and faith

When we wear a red flower proudly over our hearts…
stop, think, act your mind, and then reflect on what God has given us all

Here are God's words of wisdom…
speak them with confidence Remembrance and faith.

Be a peacemaker. "Treat others the way you want to be treated."

Lucas Beaton, Grade 6
St Mary Choir and Orchestra Program, ON

Imagine

Imagine…
The sky grey and cloudy, it has been raining for days.
The ground holds the bodies of my friends, now faceless in the mud.
I spit the taste of dirt out of my mouth, bitter, bland, dusty, and dry.
The sounds of gun shots fill the silence, I hold my breath; it either means loss or protection.
Further in the distance I hear the bombs, I wait for the silence; I listen for the screams.
A few seconds later the gunshots continue, loud, thundering, piercing, and echoing.
The taste in my mouth matches what I feel, the hard work of sweat,
the restlessness of tears, and the hurtfulness of blood.
I grab my friend's hand it's warm and rough.
We both know how much friends mean, support, comfort, welcoming, and caring.
We are fighting for love, in a place it's lacking.
It may be hiding but we will find it!
We always have to remember the reasons why we came,
Our country, our family, our friends, and our future!
Imagine…

Hannah Brown, Grade 6
St Mary Choir and Orchestra Program, ON

Peace Is...

Peace is...
Watching TV with my kitten on a cold, rainy day,
Having friends that care for me when I need them,
Watching movies with my best friends all night long,
Staring out the window on a hot, sunny afternoon,
Knowing that we are all safe falling asleep at night.

Hannah De Amicis, Grade 5
Bernard Elementary School, BC

Peace Is...

Peace is...
Playing video games with my friends on Saturday,
Reading books at night in my bed,
Playing K'nex at school during free time,
Going to the water slides on a hot day with my family,
Having turkey with my family on Thanksgiving.

Jeffery Toderian, Grade 5
Bernard Elementary School, BC

Leading Light

Star, shining so bright
Up in the dark midnight sky
Shine glittering star
Twinkling and sparkling each night
The star is my leading light
It guides the three wise men to baby Jesus
Star, shining so bright.

Chau Le, Grade 6
St James Catholic School, BC

Shoelace

Comes in any fashion color
Dragging along the floor
Trips you when taking a step on
Comes in any length short, long
Tied or left loose
Looped or knotted in a bow.
Shoelace

Danielle Hainz, Grade 5
Forest Hill School – Senior Campus, QC

Strawberry

S weet and sour
T ender and tart
R eally tasty
A nd has a good start
W atery and delightful
B looms in the spring
E ating this berry is my everything
R ich and great
R unny and good
Y ummy in my tummy like everything should

Lorissa Houle, Grade 6
Walnut Road Elementary School, BC

World War One

Imagine being a Canadian soldier
Separated from friends and family
Living in the cold muddy trenches
Far away from home
Fearing
Danger and death
More than 600,000 Canadians and Newfoundlanders served
More than 60,000 died in service to their country
Women at war cared for the sick and the injured
Will we be at war again?

Harlan Perchotte, Grade 6
East Selkirk Middle School, MB

A Couple of Beers

There is a girl,
Who once had a family,
She had happiness and love,
She had everything a girl needed.
But one day,
All that she had was gone,
Disappeared forever.

A dreadful car crash has taken away everything,
Her parents,
Sisters,
Brothers,
All gone...
Nothing left,
All this was gone.

The memory won't disappear,
As the doors closed,
The memory still haunts her,
And it still will every day, every second,

Because of a couple beers,
Because of a selfish adult's reasons,
Which brought misery to the pitiful girl.

Pei Lee Yap, Grade 5
Spul'u'kwuks Elementary School, BC

Cheetah Fajitas

"I want a cheetah fajita" said the boy named Scot,
"with everything on it make sure there's a lot."
Though this will be special just for me
I'll make my own secret recipe.
The bun, the fur
the cheetah goes grr
the cheetah goes grr a lot.
His toenails his whiskers
and some of my popped blisters
but I really want his black spots.
Put it on, roll it up and what does it make?
A really bad tummy ache.

Athena Kotselidis, Grade 4
Trelawny Public School, ON

My Piece of Grass

Every day means agony
From being stepped on
To being picked or cut
That is the life of grass
Dark green light green
That is how most people
Would explain grass

But I'm not talking
About any piece of grass
Just the one in my hand
The one that was in the earth
Just days ago
The one with the brown lifeless tip
The one that smells like apples
So light I can easily twirl it in my
Fingers
Small and withered dark green to brown
Randomly picked from the ground
That's how I would clarify my
Exceedingly unadorned
Piece of grass

Christian Goyette, Grade 6
Blundell Elementary School, BC

Love for Grandfather Jack

Grandfather Jack I wish I can help,
because the day you got sick,
I really wanted to do a little magic trick.
"but it was hard"
at least I gave you a Christmas card.
You became better
so I sent a little letter
Your day became brighter
and my face was a little lighter
and that's why I love you
and I hope you do too
Respect the love I have for you.

Tiana Ketlo, Grade 5
Fort Fraser Elementary School, BC

fractions are insane

fractions are like pizza,
fractions are like pie,
fractions are everywhere that i can spy,
fractions are in cooking,
fractions are in a spinner,
you can find them if you're looking,
you can find them at a dinner,
you will find them in a plant,
fractions are in lego,
fractions are in brains,
fractions are in ego waffles,
fractions are insane!

Floyd Mascarenhas, Grade 6
St Mark Separate School, ON

Fall

Children having fun and jumping like rabbits into piles of leaves.
The cool cold air of falling colorful leaves.
Crisp crunching of leaves, as loud as a stomping elephant.
Hard dry bits of falling things landing on my face.
Fresh sap from a maple tree oozing in my mouth.
Why can't I be a goose and fly south too.

Helen Ha, Grade 5
Ormsby School, AB

Paper Clips

P eople died just because they were Jewish.
A dolf Hitler assassinated 6 million Jews just because he did not admire them.
P owerful camps were made to torture those who entered.
E veryone who learns about the Holocaust's heart explodes with emotion.
R ighteous gentiles hid people so they would not perish.

C rates would be stuffed 100 Jews in one miniature crate.
L ives were lost for no known reason.
I magine being alive when the holocaust happened, imagine being cruelly tortured.
P eople that are alive now know they will never forget this horrid time.
S orrows were all over when you hear the survivors' story.

Elijah Meltzer, Grade 5
Ecole Akiva, QC

Sky

Sky, so murky, with its blue tidal waves,
so plain on clear sunny days.

Sky, so precious, the greatest sapphire no doubt,
so big that it could house a thousand trout.

Sky is like an endless expanse of blue,
towering above all that's new.
Sky is a tower to space.

Sky is a blanket, all nice and toasty,
keeping us warm on cold winter nights.

Sky is what I see, when blue eyes stare at me.

Sky is a paradise waiting to be built,
the sky is what keeps the flowers from wilt.

Sky, so mysterious with it's blue, murky depths,
the clouds like steps
lead up to this mysterious place.

Alexander Peterson, Grade 6
Barriere Elementary School, BC

The Sun

I'm so happy I smile, feeling good about the day.
As the sun is shining down on the earth around me.
What more could we ask for than the warmth it brings to the world.

Alex Hoff, Grade 6
Walnut Road Elementary School, BC

Something's Hiding

Something's hiding in the tree,
Something's hiding away from me!

Is it a snake?
Or a monster from the lake?
Does it eat cake?
Or is it *me* it will bake?

Something's hiding in the tree,
Something's hiding away from me!

Is it red? Is it green? Is it blue?
Is there one, are there three are there two?
Do they come from Tim-buck-too?

Something's hiding in the tree,
But what, oh what, could it be?

Gabrielle Drolet, Grade 5
École Renaissance, ON

Pink

Pink is spunky, fun, exhilarating.
Pink is the taste of cold, juicy watermelon on a summer day.
Pink smells like sweet, hard candy.
Pink is the sound of a ferris wheel at night.
Pink makes me feel like jumping.
Pink is happy, exciting, good.
Pink is energy.
Pink is joy.
Pink is me.

Vanessa Giovino, Grade 6
John T Tuck Public School, ON

That Basement on Willow Street...

Who is there,
And who died.
There could be anything there...
Like a 3-headed dog with one eye,
Or a guy who died.

There is a moth-eaten sofa
But not a person in sight.
Things are lying here and there,
But...there is no sign of a fight.
The curtains have scratches that look like a claw,
The walls have blood marks all over them.
What could have caused such a treacherous wreck.

If you go to that
Basement on Willow Street,
You'll get the fright of your life.
That basement on...
Willow Street
Gives everyone the creeps.

Bikramjeet Singh Bains, Grade 5
Khalsa School - Old Yale Road Campus, BC

Out of Our Respect

They came these young Canadians,
and left their lives for us.

We are grateful that they won the war,
and now our freedom is not a fuss.

We appreciate their strength and hope,
and also their trust and care.

We all know the story that happened,
without demand we must share!

From all across the country they came,
to fight for the Canadian name!

Now out of our respect,
for the Veterans living and dead.

We wear the poppy,
which is red.

On November 11th, we bow our heads and pray,
for all of those who have passed away!

Adrianna Estrada, Grade 6
St Mary Choir and Orchestra Program, ON

White Winter Snow

Snow falls,
Like white gentle cotton balls.
It tenderly kisses the ground,
Like me tiptoeing when my brother is sleeping.
I catch the snow
And it melts in my mouth.
Snow makes me feel sweet and happy!

Hannah Powell, Grade 5
Queen of All Saints Elementary School, BC

Those Spring Days

Under the shade of a big cherry tree,
In the cool of a spring day
The petals blow down from the branches.
Now down to the pond I'm skipping stones,
And the rock in my hand reminds me of you.
A year ago since I've seen your face,
Why did you leave me here? Why did you go?
You left to the war to save our country,
And I missed you so.
And I begged you, "Don't go."
But I guess everyone has to go sometime...
And soon it will be mine.
And I still think back to those days you left,
Those quiet spring days of mourning.

Jaqueline Andrews, Grade 6
St James Catholic School, BC

Snake

The snake
The snake I found on the road
The snake
That got killed because
Some human
Wouldn't
Swerve
To save its life,
And that human
Disrespects
Snakes
But I loved that
Snake.
The snake
The snake that got killed
The snake
That was
A part
Of
Me.

Jaimie Rose, Grade 5
Hamiota Elementary School, MB

Poppy Red

Poppies
Shiny apple
Ladybug
A flag in the wind
A leaf in autumn
The sound of a bell
Shiny apple
Squishy tomatoes
Shiny red raspberries
Blood, death, strawberry
Scare people
Poppy red

Graham Dunsmore, Grade 4
J Douglas Hogarth Public School, ON

The Big Race

The wind goes through my hair
When I am racing down the hill.
I hear the crowd roar.
I'm in first place.
All of a sudden it stops.
I open my eyes.
The crowd is around me.

I'm rushed to the hospital.
Two weeks later
I'm ok.
All I remember is biking down the hill.

Jason Ritchie, Grade 5
Hamiota Elementary School, MB

Mrs. H.L.

M arvelous
R espectful
S weet

H onorable
L ovable

Andrew Puim, Grade 5
Pat Hardy Elementary School, AB

Grandma

G reat to live with
w **R** ites a lot
A wesome
N o rest with her
frien **D** ly to others
like a **M** other
full of **A** rt

Kiley Rae, Grade 5
Pat Hardy Elementary School, AB

The Plane Truth

Have you ever been on a plane,
Fifteen hours straight;
Sitting in your sweaty old seat?
Have you ever been on a plane
watching a movie in Chinese,
While reading the subtitles?
Have you ever been on a plane
Fifteen hours straight?

David Wasiluk, Grade 6
Linden Lanes School, MB

Useless Things

A paper without a pencil
Fancy letters without stencils
A tick without a tock
Hands without a clock

A plate without food
A soul without a mood
A bullseye without an arrow
Cliffs that aren't narrow

A life without money
Bees without honey
Chalk without a board
A kingdom without a lord

Bread without butter
Speech without mutter
Skunk without a stink
Ice without a rink

Matthew Hoffman, Grade 6
Sir Isaac Brock Public School, ON

Sports

Sports are very fun.
Sports are cool.

Sports are sometimes very tiring
Sports can be sometimes violent

Sports can be outstanding.
Sports sometimes have trade deadlines.
Sports can be played with balls.

Sports are competitive.
Sports sometimes make you sweat.
Sports are amazing.

Sports sometimes have All-Star games
Sports sometimes have nets.

Babacar Fall, Grade 4
École Renaissance, ON

Christmas Eve

I wake up with a start
And look around,
I can't hear anything now
But I know I heard a sound.
I look out my window
Snow is twinkling bright,
Everything out there
Is covered in white.
I creep out of my room
And tiptoe to the tree,
It's lit up with lights
For Santa to see.
I can hear bells
Coming from outside,
I see Santa's sleigh
Out for a ride.
And as I walk off to bed,
I hear Santa from his flight,
Saying, "Merry Christmas to all,
And to all, a good night!"

Michelle Brooke, Grade 6
Forest Hill Public School, ON

Stars

There are billions of stars in the sky
Up very very high
They're very shiny
And look very tiny
They're fun to look at
Especially with your cat
You end up loving stars
That's just the way you are

Marc Bouchard, Grade 5
École Renaissance, ON

Imaginary Friends

Imaginary friends are…

I maginable, sunny
M ajor fun, funny,
A wesome, cool,
G rins like a mule,
I ntelligent, smart,
N appy, happy,
A nimals, people,
R espectful, careful
Y elly, and some have a big belly,

F riend, as awesome as a possum,
R esponsible, invisible,
I ncredible, great,
E asy going, nice,
N ice imaginary friends can also be mice,
D ays fun for you,
S uper fun,

Imaginary friends are…
Funny, sunny, invisible, and incredible!

Kassidy Hayes, Grade 4
Princess Elizabeth Public School, ON

Spirit

Never ending streams
Hastily rushing past me
It will never end

Jessica Dai, Grade 4
Howard De Beck Elementary School, BC

My Dog Cuddles

My dog Cuddles jumps into puddles on wet and rainy days,
she loves to be pet,
hates going to the vet,
and it's been like that since the day we met,
she gets lost in the fog,
sleeps in a log,
oh, what a strange, strange, dog.

Kaitlyn Baldwin, Grade 5
St Francis School, ON

White

White is the colour of the feather of a dove.
White is on my teeth showing love.
White is on the bellies of penguins waddling.
White is the colour of bunnies hopping.
White is on my T-shirt I wear.
White is the colour of the earrings my friends wear.
White is on the clouds flying free.
White is the colour that represents me.

Nikita Naik, Grade 6
The Valleys Senior Public School, ON

Don't Smoke

Don't smoke don't smoke
You know you might choke

They're too much money
And trust me this is not funny

Your lungs will smash
And your heart will crash

Just throw that cigarette out
Now you know for no doubt

Your teeth will turn yellow
Even the stuff you own like your beloved cello

You will drop dead
Your brain will be lead

Now you should know
Don't smoke don't smoke

John Bedggood, Grade 4
Princess Elizabeth Public School, ON

Shame and Pride

Shame
hidden, embarrassed
disgracing, degrading, confusing
mock, upset, self-respect, self-satisfaction
bragging, crowing, assuming
self-important, boastful
Pride

Malich Altman, Grade 6
Ecole Akiva, QC

The Arrival of Gunpowder

Going down the treacherous street
Were thousands of thumping feet.
The valiant king leading his battalion
Rushing ahead on his Noble stallion.

They reached the castle and burst through the gate
Taking them while they ate.
The sentry managed to activate the alarm as they came through
But there was nothing else he could do

The castle's men rushed for their swords
As their enemies burst through the doors
They swarmed the soldiers and slaughtered them all
And then they reached the king's hall

But as they opened the door,
Many fell to the floor.
All of the bodies formed a luminous beast.
That new weapon was explosive to say the least.

William Koechlin, Grade 4
Jack Miner Public School, ON

Colours
C ool
O range
L ight blue
O h! Shiny
U seful
R ed
S ilver
Jacob Aubry, Grade 4
École Renaissance, ON

Dreams/Nightmares
Dreams
Joyful, calm
Imagining, sleeping, relaxing
Happiness, peace, fear, boogeyman
Haunting, screaming, waking
Scary, unhappy
Nightmares
Connor Moore, Grade 5
Bernard Elementary School, BC

Stanley Cup Finals
puck flying across
the winner is a rocket
playoffs are finished
Owen McKerricher, Grade 6
Ormsby School, AB

Nature/City
Nature
Exquisite, lovely
Soothing, growing, swaying
Animals, water, cars, stores
Running, crashing, falling
Loud, dangerous
City
Chelsea Perkins, Grade 5
Bernard Elementary School, BC

Small
I am so small
I am not tall

I am so small
I am afraid of the mall

I don't like being mini
It's so not funny

I am so small
I am 2 cm tall

I hate being small
I can't get a ball.
Jeremy Plumb, Grade 5
École Renaissance, ON

As the Sun Sets...
As the sun sets gently above the water, waves start forming.
I sit on the blazing sand, watching the waves go by.
The waves are roller coasters bouncing up and down.
Trying to drag me onto their ride, and thrust me under the water.

I can feel the soft sand beneath me. It is tiny specks of brown sugar
Warming me up completely. Then I peer into the sky.
The sunset, an oil painting of many colours.
Dripping down the canvas, and falling into the waves.

Suddenly, my eyes are pushed back to the water.
There dancing about is a whale. A raindrop, entering a puddle.
It flies through the air, an airplane dashing about.
And the last thing I saw before it hit, was a wave, good-bye, along with the ocean.
Lauren Pawer, Grade 6
Westwind Elementary School, BC

What Is Peace?
What is Peace?
Is it a lullaby, or a kiss good night?
Is it when you hear someone cry or you stop a fight?
Is it just caring about a person?
Does it have to be more than that?
I can see what peace makers, like soldiers have in comparison to what I have
I have a bed — they have a trench
I have juice — they have dirty water
I have a cut — they have an injury

Why would someone ever decide to cause a war?
Could you imagine you having to serve in war…
You wouldn't be able to bring anything with you
You would have to say goodbye to your friends and family
Could you imagine praying and hoping every day
that you could live to see every tomorrow
Soldiers really take a risk
They do all this because they love us
Sure…they don't know us,
but risking their life for us is…love

What is Peace?
Peace is love!
Emma Paul, Grade 6
St Mary Choir and Orchestra Program, ON

Lest We Forget
R emembering the crosses that lay in the grass today.
E very soldier that fought for our country to be free.
M oms who stayed home worrying about their husbands.
E very time of the day some one could die.
M oms who had to leave their children to go home with medical issues.
B odies that are buried in the ground with crosses on top.
E arly or late they were fighting for freedom.
R ed is for poppies that we wear on top of our heart.
Breann Arndt, Grade 4
David Ovans Elementary School, AB

One Step at a Time

I opened my eyes to the world,
But I didn't have the strength to move,
So my parents helped me.
I learned how to crawl,
But I couldn't walk,
So my parents gave me balance.
I learned how to talk,
But I only knew the basics,
So my parents taught me new words.
I couldn't tie my shoes,
But I didn't like wearing either slip-ons or Velcro shoes,
So my parents taught me how to tie them.
I didn't want to go to school,
But I had to for my future,
So my parents supported me.
I am now old enough to have my own family,
But I had to go to work,
So my parents took care of my kids.
As time goes by, my parents got older,
Now I have my own kids to take care of,
Teaching them, just as my parents taught me.

Queenie Rabanes, Grade 6
St James Catholic School, BC

Under the Bed

Poor little Jimmy lost his shoe,
Glasses, hats and cats too,
He lost a bathtub and a door,
But wait there's still more.

Dogs, frogs a sewing machine,
Something in his closet that looked a bit green,
Jimmy even lost his head,
But he found everything under the bed.

A kitchen sink,
A skating rink,
An ice cream cone,
A squirrel with no home.

A little old man,
Holding peas in a can,
A pencil with no lead,
Jimmy found everything under the bed.

Christina Torrealba, Grade 5
Colby Village Elementary School, NS

Plum Trees in Flowers at Eragny

The sight of elegant trees whirling gloriously in the wind.
The sound of cheerful birds chanting playfully.
The feel of the warm sun hugging me pleasantly.
The taste of a sandy beach swaying soundlessly in the distance.
The smell of fresh nature humming melodically.
The remarkable artist Camille Pissarro.

Jillian Weinberger, Grade 6
Ecole Akiva, QC

To God

Thank you for giving me joy and smile.
Thank you for my trouble pile.

Thank you for wiping the tears off my eyes.
Thank you for showing me colorful butterflies.

Thank you for lending me your shoulders to lean.
Thank you for making my work to be seen.

Thank you for giving me the time of the day.
Thank you for your loving say.

Thank you for lending me your ear.
Thank you for being my savior.

From all this what I mean in the end
Is thank you for being my special friend.

Aakaash Arunmozhi, Grade 6
St Mary Choir and Orchestra Program, ON

The Ghosts

We are the ghosts,
As white as snow.
People can't see us,
But somehow they know.

We hear them tell stories,
About what we are.
But, they are wrong,
By very far.

They say that they see us,
Always at night.
And we even think
That we give them a fright!

We are only
Spirits from the dead.
We are the ones
Who can never go to bed.

Every day,
We can do what we want.
But, we never,
Ever, haunt!

Meredith Wanstall, Grade 6
Ecole separee Georges-Etienne-Cartier, ON

Nature

Two furry wildcats
Their fearless souls roar with might
Fear rushing in me

Maria Stamenkovic, Grade 5
Howard De Beck Elementary School, BC

Crunch Crunch Crunch
My favorite cookies are Oreo cookies.
I love the way they are just
So creamy inside.
It feels like I'm eating
Miniature white clouds of goodness.
It just melts in your mouth.

Then there is the chocolate outsides.
They are crunchy, but filled
With chocolate goodness.
It tastes as if I'm eating a
Whole chocolate bar at once.
It's hard at first then it softens up
Once you start to chew it.
It's a chocolate sandwich with
Creamy sugary icing
Mmmmm
Mmmmmmmmmm!

Are there any more??
Samantha Borges, Grade 6
St Maria Goretti Elementary School, ON

Cleo
Kitten
Fluffy, grey, fur
Sleeping, eating, playing
Is a really cute baby girl
My cat.
Alicia Logan, Grade 6
Linden Lanes School, MB

I Love Soccer
Soccer, soccer it's so fun
Soccer is the only one
Soccer is my favourite sport
You can be tall and you can be short
I'm running, running towards the net
It's raining and it's wet.
The defenses are big and tall.
And compared to them I'm so small.
I kick the ball and I score.
My teammate says do that some more.
It's the end yes we win.
And I put the trophy in a bin.
Jonathan Kazmierski, Grade 5
École Renaissance, ON

The First Days of Spring
The snow melts away
Small rivers run down the road
It must be spring time
Corey Symonds, Grade 4
Park West School, NS

War/Peace
Horrible, gun
Fighting, dying, bombing
Peace stops war everywhere
Respecting, playing, listening
Freedom, Canada
Joseph Lavoie, Grade 4
École Renaissance, ON

Animals
Animals, animals everywhere,
On the ground, in the air,
In the bush, in the park,
In the water like a shark,
Birds, fish, deer,
Even the ones you fear,
Animals, animals everywhere.
Koryssa Morgan, Grade 6
Worsley Central School, AB

Canadian Forever
Guns
Sniper
Death
Danger
Action for peace

Troops
Soldiers
Brave
Heroes
Miserable experience
Deadly
Protecting our country

Live
Challenges
A hero forever
Freedom

Veterans
Military
Fought bravely
Honorable
And wild wars
Brooke Mayo-Lagacé, Grade 6
East Selkirk Middle School, MB

Dad/Papa
Dad
Peaceful, caring, loving
In heaven
Papa
Danny Crumley, Grade 6
St James Catholic School, BC

Useless Things
A basketball without air
A bow without hair
A violin without strings
Marriage without rings

CDs without sound
Lost without found
Chess without a board
Plugs without a cord

Books without pages
Jobs without wages
Libraries without books
Restaurants without cooks
Joy Eom, Grade 6
Sir Isaac Brock Public School, ON

The History
Not an ocean, a bay
In the center
Voices whisper about the mountains
To track the time of years gone by
When the bright orange sun was not high
To penetrate the shadows
When they quivered
The people fled with fear
To escape the crushing rocks
That fell from above and tumbled
Into the river
The memory forever placed
And a story for them to tell
If someone came to find the truth
Shaylyn Kress, Grade 6
WP Sandin Composite High School, SK

Horses
I have some horses
Who run in my pasture
Thumpity, thumpity, thump.
They are fast and they are free.
And they belong to me.
Beverly Burtnick, Grade 4
Tisdale Elementary School, SK

Me in 100 Years
H undred years of life
U nder the new buildings
N o life
D readed cold
R ain seeping in
E arth on top of you
D eep in the ground
Hayley Chabot, Grade 6
Anola School, MB

Happiness

Roses are red violets are blue
I'll enjoy them I hope you do too
For happiness is in the air
And love roams the ground
With all the smiles of children
and laughing of children in the new-year
Comes with all the happiness someone would want
and more then they could buy
With the ocean songs and the singing for the king
The world is a better place.

Elizabeth Atkins, Grade 5
Oakley Park Public School, ON

Ontario Sunset

Bathed in orange sunlight
Coming quickly towards the night
Spots of pink, orange and red
Paint the sky above your head
The sun like a picture
Its glow getting bright
Pink and orange skies
Overlooking everything that lies
Peacefully setting, gentle and bright
Before the day
Turns to night
It's almost like a miracle let
Us admire the beauty of a sunset

Marisa Bordonaro, Grade 6
Our Lady of the Annunciation Catholic School, ON

Beetle

I'm a little beetle
Be careful where you step.
I'm very small.
And I need your help.
I'm upside down, grasping at anything.
I'm feeling frightened and helpless.
All of a sudden I'm flipped over onto my feet.
I'm so surprised.
I thought I was a goner.
But you saved me.
I feel very happy and thankful.
Who knows, maybe some day I will help you too.

William Norrie, Grade 5
Hamiota Elementary School, MB

War

Risking your whole life
But also knowing it's right
Then you hear Boom Bang
Thank you for all you have done
It affected all of us

Quincy Ross, Grade 5
Forest Hill School – Senior Campus, QC

Rain Shower

Splashing in puddles
I wish I brought my shampoo
I am exhausted

Jenny Liu, Grade 4
Howard De Beck Elementary School, BC

I Am

I am full of crazy ideas.
I wonder what's inside the black hole in the outer space.
I hear laughing from a newborn baby.
I see the wonders of the world.
I want to see the deepest place on earth.
I am full of crazy ideas.

I pretend I'm Albert Einstein.
I feel excited to become a gazillionaire
I touch things I haven't seen before.
I worry about people trapped in black holes.
I cry for kind people that get murdered.
I am full of crazy ideas.

I understand animal languages.
I say comforting things to sad people.
I dream about getting gold medals in the Olympics.
I try to fly into the outer space.
I hope there is peace in the world.
I am full of crazy ideas.

Tony Ma, Grade 5
Spul'u'kwuks Elementary School, BC

Yellow

Yellow is the colour of happiness and energy,
Like the hot sun on a summer day,
Like the energy you gain from encouragement and hope,
Yellow is the sound of newborn chicks chirping,
Or a frying egg in the morning at the cottage,
Yellow feels like crisp yellow leaves crunching under your feet,
Or the hot summer air,
Yellow smells like blooming lemon blossoms in spring,
Or fresh baked banana bread
Yellow is my favourite colour!

Sophia Molinaro, Grade 6
John T Tuck Public School, ON

I Am

I Am
The wind blowing the tree branches — Whoooosh
I Am
The raindrops falling on the hard concrete — Drip Drop
I Am
Tip toeing past my parents room to get milk — Shhhhhh!
I Am
Excited to open my Christmas presents — Hooray
I Am Me!

MiKaelia Miller, Grade 4
Kingswood Dr Public School, ON

Scott M.'s Weirdish Lunch

Yay buttered chicken
Oh and it's stickin'

Yuck cactus meat
It's too prickly to eat

Applesauce is always there
But this time there's a bear!

I'm not even lickin'
Except the buttered chicken!

Scott Mitchell, Grade 4
J Douglas Hogarth Public School, ON

Blue

Blue are the scary eyes
on a monster's head.
Blue are your toes when
they're frozen dead.
Blue is the sky that's
shiny and bright.
Blue is a shark that
Frightens you with all
his might.
Blue is the ocean that's
teaming with all its fish.
Blue is definitely the best
of all the rest.

John Martin, Grade 6
Mornington Central School, ON

I Wish...

I wish I were
a Shetland sheepdog
lying on hardwood flooring
chewing on a chicken-flavoured bone
happily

Netanya Zammit, Grade 5
Bernard Elementary School, BC

The Oak Tree

The oak tree stands tall
A light breeze rustles the leaves
A lot of leaves fall.

Alex Horner, Grade 6
Falmouth District School, NS

Athlete

I used to play soccer.
I was okay.
But now I play baseball
And I save day.
Because I am the pitcher
Who wins the game for us.

David McNair, Grade 4
Colby Village Elementary School, NS

Newfoundland

N ewfoundland is home to many aboriginal people.
E xplorer John Cabot came to Newfoundland in 1497.
W e mine and we can find nickel, zinc, copper, lead, silver and limestone.
F orests are found in Newfoundland.
O ceans near Newfoundland have icebergs most of the year.
U ntil airplanes were invented boats were the only way to get to Newfoundland.
N ewfoundland has many small fishing villages.
D amage was caused to the fishing business by fishing too much.
L ong range mountains is part of the Gross Monroe National Park.
A n Atlantic Puffin is found in Newfoundland.
N ewfoundland is surrounded by the Gulf of St. Lawrence.
D unes are hills of sand created by wind.

Kennedy Elcock, Grade 4
FW Gilbert School, MB

Wonders of Winter

People wearing boots, hats, gloves and scarves.
The sweat on my scarf is like hot boiled water.
People going down the hill, sledding from a mile high yelling YEAH!!
My lips all dried up it feels like it's going to burst.
The dryness of my lips is a blood factory.
I should've stayed inside for recess and played ping pong.

Asim Wahab, Grade 6
Ormsby School, AB

These Hands of Mine

These hands of mine were holding a basket of flowers down the aisle.
These hands of mine helped me get up when I fell.
These hands pet my pony.
These hands draw my first picture.

These hands help me hold a ski pole.
These hands of mine pick out clothes every day.
My hands help me type.
These hands play piano and trombone.

In my future my hands will help sick and hurt animals.
These hands will draw the plans of my house.
These hands of mine will write a book in the future.
These hands will finish an exam in college.

These Hands of Mine

Tru Gaucher, Grade 5
Forest Hill School – Senior Campus, QC

Friends

Hang with me whether it would be at the mall or watching movies
Cry with me when I'm heart broken and I just need someone to lean on
Laugh with me for laughter is good for the soul
Grow with me like family
The ones I go to for advice from boys to clothes
No matter where I am or how I might be
What would life be like if we didn't have friends?

Tyra Fitzpatrick, Grade 6
Aurora Elementary School, AB

Living in Death

As I ramble through the museum as scared as can be
I see a mummy pursuing me
As I yowl in silence
Nothing comes out
The mummy's alive but dead
No doubt
As I spring away
I hide behind a wall
The drawings move
I'm hiding patiently and the man with the bow and arrow is
watching me
Although the mummy is blind but can see I look at the mud
tracks I left behind me
All of a sudden the mummy is back where
He is supposed to be
And the hall is empty as can be

Anfal Ramadan, Grade 6
Blundell Elementary School, BC

Best Friends Forever

F is for friends to the end.
R is for remember me when I move
I is for I will remember you too.
E is for even when I am old and feel like 3000.
N is for no I will not forget you, for the 30th time.
D is for do not forget me, either.
S is for see you soon.

Ezekiel Smith, Grade 4
Tisdale Elementary School, SK

Nick

My friend Nick
got six new sticks.

His dad Rick
said, "They are as hard as a brick."

That next day Nick got six
cricket sticks.

That same day he went to go play,
he fell into some hay.

His dad, Rick said, "What happened Nick?"
"I broke my six cricket sticks."

Jack Gillis, Grade 4
Colby Village Elementary School, NS

Black Ants

Black ants
Walking in lines
Makes me want to feed them
Reminds me of dot to dot games
Tiny

Bonnie Ma, Grade 5
Howard De Beck Elementary School, BC

No War, But Peace

Think of all the veterans,
Who went to fight in war,
Even when they were young,
For peace to open a door.

Their strength, their hearts, their hope and faith
They fought for world peace,
And offered us their lives,
Another precious piece.

The family tears brought a thought,
What will happen?
Will they be caught?

Remember,
One person can make a difference.

Rachelle Eldik, Grade 6
St Mary Choir and Orchestra Program, ON

The Australian Fire

Australia was a place where nature grew
but everything changed when nobody knew.
it went from small to a forest fire
which nobody claimed, but we found a liar.

innocent animals badly hurt
from a land that was completely burnt.
smoke and flames rising in the air
but the fire fighters did their share.

destroyed houses and set out a scare
the question was, why would he dare?
over 200 lives torn apart
the man responsible was sure not smart.

Yaneka McFarland, Grade 6
Morin Heights Elementary School, QC

Night

The sun goes down for a snooze
As everything turns dark.

A frog rising from its green lily pad
Like a flower blooming.

The moon guides us at night
Like a flashlight.

The streetlights turn on
Letting us know that night is here.

And me putting this book down
And turning my light out as my mom kisses me goodnight.

Cassandra Delveaux, Grade 5
Queen of All Saints Elementary School, BC

Sun

The warm summer sun
Shining in the bright blue sky
Shining like a star
Faris Kapra, Grade 4
Park West School, NS

Get Ready

Here it comes…
It's coming towards us like a
Speeding bullet!
AAHH!
Duck and cover!
Mayday, mayday,
We're going down!
Call 911!
No, don't do that!
It's it's gone…
It's never gone…
It's quiet…
Too quiet…
AAAHHHHHH!
Here it comes again!
Hide!
It's got me!
No! Let go!
I'm too young to die!
Oh wait,
It's just my little sister…
Hannah Kvame, Grade 6
Aurora Elementary School, AB

Light in the Darkness!

Now I'm not talking,
About any ordinary star,
This one — I mean,

That's like lemon meringue pie,
as it melts in my mouth,

smooth, fuzzy, and warm,
as it sits there lighting up the sky,

the small, yellow, points
shining in the darkness
of the night,

quietly it sits there glowing,
with all the other stars.

As nights come and go,
it will continue there,
glowing.
Eveline Juce, Grade 5
Hamiota Elementary School, MB

Proud Beauty

If I were a rose
I would stand proudly and pose
I'd let myself be picked
and put in bouquets
for
sweethearts or
moms
In all different colors
and petal shapes too
You'd be proud to have me
in your garden.
Pauline Hofer, Grade 6
Milford Colony School, AB

Are You Happy?

When you're feeling blue
Find something to do!

Because not feeling happy,
Makes you all the more crappy.

Maybe a hug,
Will make you more snug.

A happy heart
A happy soul
A happy mind,
Whatever it is you should still be kind.
Rachel Sybblis, Grade 4
St Martin De Porres School, AB

My Canine Friend and I

Cute, content, tired.

My furry canine friend extends her legs
across the floor, begging for love.
Her dreamy, brown eyes hinting
at her peaceful state of mind.

Royal, elegant, furry.

She gives me a kiss
and expects nothing in return.
Slowly, lethargically,
she rises from her bed to get her ball.
My good companion
effortlessly drops the ball at my feet.

Joyful, curious, poised.

We are the best of friends,
My canine friend and I…
Sean Leighton, Grade 5
Surrey Connect School, BC

The Gingerbread Man

There once was a gingerbread man
He lived in a giant baking pan
Cooking at 350 degrees
Was what made him really say "Please!
Turn on my house's jolly good fan."
William Legault, Grade 4
Westside Academy, BC

soccer/snowshoeing

soccer
active, warm
sliding, kicking, shooting
grass, field, ice, snow
running, walking, slipping
cold, freezing
snowshoeing
Rita Hofer, Grade 5
Sunnysite Colony School, AB

Dirt Biking

D irt
I mmense
R ighteous
T alent

B laze
I ntense
K nack
E clipse
Alexander Alvarez, Grade 5
Pat Hardy Elementary School, AB

Poetry

Poetry is graceful,
Poetry is sweet,
Poetry makes people
Feel warm inside.
Poetry is loyalty,
Poetry is freedom.
If you have the gift to write poetry,
Let it free and
Write, write, write.
Erin Higgins, Grade 5
Chiganois Elementary School, NS

Curtis

C an ride a snowmobile
U ses a hockey stick
R ides a dirtbike
T rying to read every day
I like to play hockey
S kating like the wind
Curtis Stannard, Grade 4
J Douglas Hogarth Public School, ON

Remembrance Day

What does Remembrance Day mean to me?
Men and women fighting for our country.
A lot of people died for us.
And now their names are on a cross.

Remembrance Day is a special day
We say thank you in a special way.
We wear a poppie and we wear it with pride.
Thanking you for being on our side.

So what does Remembrance Day mean to me?
In one word it means we are free.

Bethany Kurtz, Grade 6
Mornington Central School, ON

Venus

Venus is a planet
A planet hot and plain
Although it has another name
It could also have quite some fame.
Morning star, morning star
See it always out so far
Shining bright, a beautiful sight
A light in the night, like a glistening kite

It's usually red like everyone said
But I think it's white as I fight to watch it in the night

Since it's next to us we should be proud
Its surface is covered by deadly clouds

Venus is known to be the goddess of love up so far above
Then I shut my eyes until the end, of my little beloved friend

Annika Ponzilius, Grade 6
East Selkirk Middle School, MB

The Big Green Monster

There once was a monster
big green and hairy
he lived in my closet
and boy did he scare me.

One day I was in bed
and he popped out and said
fear me fear me and fear me some more
for someday you will be here no more.

Just then I got an idea
before I could show anymore fear
my dog Griffin bounded through the door
I yelled take him down Griffin
well I'm saying the monster is no longer here.

Kyle Armstrong, Grade 5
Colby Village Elementary School, NS

Friends

Friends are important.
They're always there for you.
They keep your secrets.
And help you when you need it.
You should always trust them.

Kaitlin Louise Gregoire, Grade 5
Forest Hill School – Senior Campus, QC

Left Out

Once we had a party
Every child was invited
But one was left out
They were all excited about the party
But the boy was not excited
Because he was not invited.

When it was time for the party to begin
They ran and laughed as fast and as loud as they could
They just started eating
Then they heard a voice yelling
Wha! Wha! Wha!
Then they were all quiet and listened

It was the boy that was not invited
They were shocked when they saw him
"You go away," they said to the boy
The boy said, "I would like some wieners."
They said, "you get lost"
We don't want to see you.

The oldest boy at the party stood up
Ran after the boy and gave him a kick
Wha! Wha! Wha! went the boy all the way home

Laura Gross, Grade 5
Riverbend Colony School, AB

Useless Things

A boat without water teeter without totter
Words without letters worse without better,

Music and no sound square and no round
A classroom without a teacher a church without a preacher,

April without rain a world without pain
An abyss with a bottom leaves without autumn,

Paper without pencil plate without utensil
Super heroes with no powers spring with no flowers,

A show with no end a man with no friends
A doorman with no door three without four,

Sky that's not blue love that's not true
Detective with no clue me without you!

Chelsea Armstrong, Grade 6
Sir Isaac Brock Public School, ON

School

First we had a spelling test,
I started at the top.
But when I got down to banana,
I didn't know when to stop.

Then we had a math quiz,
The question 1+1,
That question is really easy,
I answered 11.

Science was the coolest,
We did experiments,
I took 3 jugs of cola,
And 6 or 7 mints.

So as you may have noticed,
I sure am not a fool,
But for some silly reason,
My teacher suggests summer school!

Graham Peters, Grade 6
Lincoln School, MB

Winter

Very freezing cold
Hockey is very awesome
Snow covers the ground

Brayden Kirkland, Grade 4
Tisdale Elementary School, SK

I Was All Ready to Practice

I was all ready to practice
I even took out my bow
But then the practice monster came
And bit me in the toe!

He huffed and puffed and grumbled
He hawed and hemmed and glared,
His eyes were red and slimy
And that got me really scared.

"Innit so pretty outside?"
The monster keenly crooned
And as the venom kicked in
My violin stopped being tuned

My motivation crumbled
My looming deadlines distant
I started wanting to ride my bike
That poison sure was potent!

So next time I go practice
I swear it won't be in vain
I'll be sure to have a hammer
So he'll never strike again!

Sandra Lin, Grade 5
Surrey Connect School, BC

If I Were in Charge of the World*

If I were in charge of the world
There would be no unfortunate, horrifying wars
The large, amazing, fun filled, world would never die
No killing or scary murdering
All people would live forever
Black people wouldn't be killed because of their unique skin color
The horrible disease of M.S. would finally be cured

If I were in charge of the world
All poor people would have a beautiful place to live
Have exotic zoo or jungle animals as pets
Get twenty dollars for every single chore you do
Live in the West Edmonton Mall with all your best friends
Be able to go wherever you want whenever you want

If I were in charge of the world
Every person in the world would live with a fabulous famous person
All awesome celebrities would take turns performing at schools
Everyone has good loyal friends they can trust and never get in fights with
Also I would make world peace
If only I were in charge of the world

Tiara Brown, Grade 6
Silver Star Elementary School, BC
*Patterned after "If I Were in Charge of the World" by Judith Viorst.

In My Life and Hers

Reader: In my life, I learned about the Holocaust
Assembly: In her life, she wished she didn't live through it
Reader: On my third birthday, all my friends were at my house
Assembly: On her third birthday, she had no friends or home
Reader: My family is a family of 5
Assembly: Her family was a family of 4
Reader: In my life, I wished I could ride a train
Assembly: In her life, the train was a death ride to a concentration camp
Reader: In my life, I read Twilight and loved it
Assembly: In her life she had no book to read and love
Reader: In my life, I went to the mall with my mom
Assembly: In her life, she entered the gas chamber with her mom
Reader: In my life I wish to make it past 97
Assembly: In her life she wished to live to the end of the day.

Hannah Brown, Grade 5
Ecole Akiva, QC

Red

Red is the roses someone just received, people giving gifts on a sunny day,
friends hugging after a long trip away from each other.
Red tastes like rich chocolate.
Red smells like fresh beautiful flowers and spicy cinnamon hearts.
Red sounds like families laughing.
Red is togetherness, Valentines decorations, and warm sunsets.
Red is love.
Red is my favourite colour.

Kayleigh Clapperton, Grade 6
John T Tuck Public School, ON

Lest We Forget

Lest we forget the people who died,
the lives that were lost and the families that cried.
Lest we forget the aches and the pains
that the soldiers got in this dangerous game.
They fought for love, peace, and hatred no more
because of this they were killed; shot to the core.
Fighting for peace is why they would die
in Flanders Fields is where they now lie,
a long time ago, sometime back then
and truly I know that all their souls went to heaven.
So lest we forget?

Britney Pagliuca, Grade 5
Nativity of Our Lord Catholic School, ON

A Dream to Remember

Terry Fox was just a teen
When cancer came to him unseen.
His leg got amputated above the knee
To keep his body cancer free.
Although no on knew for sure,
His Dr. said there was no cure.

Terry Fox was so afraid,
Then one night in bed he laid.
He dreamt that he could do much more,
By running cross Canada shore to shore.
He would run the distance with his friend,
To raise money to put this to an end.

From Newfoundland to Victoria was his dream,
It was much harder than it seemed.
His run ended in Thunder Bay,
It was much more pain than he could say.
He left us, which is a shame,
Forever we will remember his name.

Michaela Skarlicki, Grade 5
Our Lady of Perpetual Help, BC

Bounding Young Children

Bounding young children
Excited for their day
I wonder what makes them
So happy, so gay

The teacher drops her fountain pen
They stare at the clock, excited to play
Bounding young children
Excited for their day

And now and then
When the children are immersed in play
That the teacher steps out again
And decides to join the fray
Bounding young children

Katie Wickett, Grade 6
Elboya Elementary and Jr High School, AB

Harmony

You and me
Together we'll be,

Working together in harmony
We may come from a different place but
I love to see the smile on your face

We all wear clothing, we all eat food
We all dance, we all play celebrate with family

You and me together we'll be
Working together in harmony

Blood, voice, heart, special names
Harmony

Toni Linklater, Grade 6
Anola School, MB

War Is Over

The guns are put down
The horrible war has ended
Children are playing again

Grandma reminds me I am so blessed
When I listen close, I understand
Children are playing again

Soldiers fought for our country
They brought freedom and peace
Children are playing again

The courageous veterans came back
They marched tall and proud
Children are playing again

Jenna Quinn, Grade 6
St Mary Choir and Orchestra Program, ON

These Hands of Mine

My hands helped me crawl.
They helped me hold my fishing rod.
I washed myself with them
They let me swim in my pool.

They let me write.
My hands tie my shoes.
I eat with them.
I dig with my hands

My hands will let me tie my football shoes.
They will let me catch a ball.
They won't let me steal.
I will earn my living with them.

Massimo Martoccia, Grade 5
Forest Hill School – Senior Campus, QC

The Grand Canyon

There are hollow circles
Surrounded by tall mountains and deep valleys
That look like flowers and vines cascading like a waterfall
The light shines down
Making shadows that look like a jungle of birds and seaweed
There are rivers overflowing with caramel coloured water
The red clay dust smells like cinnamon
This is where I eat my dinner
Surrounded by all these magical places
This is my dining room with its marble table and bamboo shoot plants
During my dinner I traveled across the Grand Canyon
And swam with birds deep in the ocean
I may not have left my seat
But this is where I ate my dinner

Charnvir Kaur Dhillon, Grade 5
Khalsa School - Old Yale Road Campus, BC

If I Were in Charge of the World*

If I were in charge of the world
You would be able to drive before you were sixteen, cars would run on air
There would be no bills or taxes, maybe everything would even be free
There would be fuzzy lovable animals of all sorts for every child
If I were in charge of the world
You could eat all you want and not gain weight
Sweet luscious candy would be considered a healthy food
You could eat anything you want and nothing you touched would change, ice cream would never melt
If I were in charge of the world
There would be no school, people who wanted to go to school would only go for two hours
The subjects in school would be animal care and dance, there would be no rules
If I were in charge of the world
There would be no horrible bullies, everyone would be nice, no one would be lonesome
People wouldn't be jealous of others, everyone would be equal
If I were in charge of the world
Everything would run on solar power, there would be beautiful tulips and roses instead of weeds and grass
Unneeded materials would be used to make colored paper, everywhere the trees were cut down they would grow up again
If I were in charge of the world
I would have a beautiful mansion and would live in it with all my friends
Everything would fit me and look fabulous, I would have every single animal in the world as my pet
If only I were in charge of the world

Melanna Bielski, Grade 6
Silver Star Elementary School, BC
*Patterned after "If I Were in Charge of the World" by Judith Viorst.

Blue

Blue is the shining, sparkling Okanagan Lake with a mystery of a sea monster of some sort, but people still go boating.
Blue is the color of the spinning bright police sirens that tell you something terribly bad has happened.
Blue is the home of the clouds, the sky, with its incredible color; it's the place where winged birds fly.
Blue is the color of a gliding blue jay that puts sticks in its homemade nest.
Blue is the color of the felt in a marker that a kid uses to scribble with all his might.
Blue is the color of a brand new jeep rolling down a freshly paved highway, with vehicles on both sides, when you're going 75/mph and you can feel the cold breeze of freedom, which makes you feel nice.

Parker Burns, Grade 4
First Lutheran Christian School, BC

My Weird Enemy

I saw him across the street, it was my enemy.
He was trying to walk his sea anemone.
I couldn't stop laughing because it was stuck to a bunny.
Finally he saw me "What's so funny?"

The bunny ate his "pet," which made him maligned.
He chased after the bunny, but fell on his behind.
He stormed over to me, pet-less and mad.
"It's your fault it was eated!" His grammar's really bad.

We are always fighting, to see who was better.
He is good at nothing, and has ketchup on his sweater.
We decided to fight, to decide things once and for all.
We were going to get a Wii, and have a very short brawl.

I chose Kirby because he is number one.
He chose King Dedede, who looks like he weighs three tons.
We had three minutes to decide who's the best.
And who is the one who will be depressed.

I owned the whole brawl, spamming with the hammer.
Until he fell off. It's good to be a spammer.
He cried like a baby, saddened by defeat.
So I walked up to him and made him smell my feet.

Tim Wu, Grade 6
Waverley Drive Public School, ON

Four Legs, Wet Noses, and Oh So Cute!

Puppies are so cuddly and cute
I love it when they meet me as I get home
They are playful and yet gentle
It makes me mad when they roam.

I love their wet nosed kisses
If I could I would have ten
They would all need names
Like Duke, Chevy, Bingo and Ben

Maybe if I taught them
They would like to dance
I know I'd take them with me
Whenever I got the chance

They are always so playful
Puppies like to chew shoes or anything left out
But in the morning when they wake you
Watch out for their cold snout.

Do you want a puppy?
While they're brand new
Get one quick, while they're in
Someone to love you

Miranda Shannon, Grade 6
Aurora Elementary School, AB

I

I
Funny, good, weird
Brother of Sagar Deepak Patel
Lover of roller coasters
Who feels happy to learn
Who needs family, friends and video games
Who gives advice
Who fears spiders, clowns and ghosts
Who would like to be an actor
A resident of Toronto
Jay Deepak Patel

Jay Deepak Patel, Grade 4
Calico Public School, ON

These Hands of Mine

These are the hands that held my little brother's hands.

These are the hands that planted my mother's beautiful garden.
These are the hands that fed my brothers.
These hands of mine.
These are the hands that won championships.
These are the hands that fished out supper.
These are the hands that hit the notes on the clarinet.
These hands write my exams.
These hands will make cars run on water.
These hands will hold my child.
These hands will drive a fast car.
These hands of mine.

Vincentas Gudas, Grade 5
Forest Hill School – Senior Campus, QC

Cars

We use cars for every purpose and we use them every day,
Without a car our daily activities would either stop or delay.
There are Hybrid cars, new cars and old cars too,
I wish I had a smart car because it could fit for me and you.
Some are fast and some are slow,
The one I want is that never becomes old.
Cars such as Corvettes, Vipers, Ferraris, and Lamborghini
are all cool cars.
Cars are important in our lives,
Without a car we depend on the bikes.
Cars are big and cars are small,
We have the one in which we fit all.

Amritpaul S. Kooner, Grade 5
Khalsa School - Old Yale Road Campus, BC

Winter Days

Coming back inside from a long day outside.
The wind flying in my face when I close the door.
The smell I smell is a mix of chocolate and milk.
My cold cheeks became hot.
A nice taste swirling in my mouth
and a nice day I had.

Camille Taillefer, Grade 5
Forest Hill School – Senior Campus, QC

Truck/Car

Truck
huge, blue
hauling, driving
Transportation on the road
honking, speeding, racing
compact, stylish
Car

Andrew Chuang, Grade 6
Walnut Road Elementary School, BC

The Clock's Hands

Waving like humans
they tick for eternity
one second 'til home.

Frazer Connelly, Grade 6
Ormsby School, AB

When I Grow Up

When I grow up I could be a magician
or I could tell people their position
I could be an awesome cook
or I could be a writer of a huge book
I could take care of the bees,
or I could travel the seven seas,
I could take care of the homeless cats,
or I could help the helpless bats,
I could be a biologist
or I will be a school psychologist,
I could be a chef
or help the deaf
I could be a sniper or a toilet piper.
These are all the things I could be
I guess we will have to wait and see.

Trishia Martineau, Grade 6
Neilburg Composite School, SK

Spring Is...

Nice in every way
The sun is usually out
Can't wait for our first rain
The snow does not want to leave
There are always puddles to splash in.
Rose, violet, buttercup
All the pretty flowers!!

Sara Samida, Grade 4
Tisdale Elementary School, SK

One Window Is All I Need

One window is all I need
To see what is all around me
To see the people playing in parks
To see the people grieving in loss
To see that someone needs my help
To see what the world can be.

Jill Northcott, Grade 6
Strathcona-Tweedsmuir School, AB

My Friend

I loved you so much.
You were my friend; you were with me from start to end.
I haven't seen you in a year or two,
You have been in my heart from midnight to noon.
I miss your laughter, I miss your cry,
I need you now right by my side.
You were with me and I was with you,
Why did you leave me like you do?
You played our song in the summer day.
I miss you, you miss me,
I hope to run and see you like you used to be.

Elizabeth Humphrey, Grade 6
St James Catholic School, BC

It's a Worry

When they start to change
It is a worry.
When they start to stretch
It is a worry.
When the coin is thrown
It is a worry.
When he puts on Asham curling gloves
It is a worry.
When his Asham curling boots touch the ice
It's a worry.
When Dad's Asham curling broom touches the ice
It's a worry.
When his rock glides down the ice, we all stop breathing
It's a worry.
When the skip yells, "Sweep!"
It's a worry.
When it's the last end and it's 3-1
It's a worry.
So if you don't have a curler in your family,
Just remember the worries that some people have to go through.

Chelsea Lawn, Grade 5
Hamiota Elementary School, MB

My Life and His

When I was born, it felt like a miracle.
When he was born, everyone said he'd need a miracle to survive.
When I was 13, I was happy Canada was a free country.
When he was 13, he had already forgotten what free meant.
When I got married, I stamped on a glass.
When he got married, he stamped on fire because the building was lit.
When I turned 40, I thought I was old.
When he turned 40, he thought he was too young to die.
When I turned 50, I retired.
When he turned 50, he was forced to join the army.
When I died, people put rocks over my grave.
When he died, his grave was a bunch of blasted rocks.
At my funeral, everyone mourned.
At his funeral, there was no one left to mourn.

Jacob Laxer, Grade 5
Ecole Akiva, QC

The Dude

A lean cowboy rode down the lane
With nothing to spare.
Then he heard voices
In the thin night air.
He rode a little more,
When he got shot at from the right.
Then he rode off into the darkness of the night.

Cole Gisi, Grade 4
Tisdale Elementary School, SK

Bullies

Bullying is when people call you names
or make fun of what you wear of what you look like
Sometimes how you talk even how you walk
Where you live and where you sleep.

Bullying is when people tell you to do things
That you don't want to do then you say "No"
And they make fun of you.

Bullying makes people miserable
scared, mad, and sad
And it makes people act
The way they don't normally act.

If the bullies were treated
The way they treated people
They would feel the same way.

Jessie Fillmore, Grade 5
Chiganois Elementary School, NS

You Had a Lot of Courage

Peace to the heavens
Peace to the earth
Peace to all who remember

In Flanders Field is where we remember
All the soldiers who died in November

You had a lot of courage to go out there
Now a poppy is what we all wear

Just for you
And for the soldiers too

We will remember what you did
Don't think that we will close the lid
On what you have done for us

Peace to the heavens
Peace to the earth
Peace to all who remember

Susannah Kingo, Grade 6
St Mary Choir and Orchestra Program, ON

Mickey Mouse

Mickey Mouse lives in a house
Mickey Mouse is of course a Mouse
Mickey Mouse lives with Minney Mouse
Mickey Mouse is my friend
Mickey Mouse's friend is Fred
Fred does not have a bed
The reason that Fred
does not have a bed
is because he is all in Mickey's head
He is in Mickey's head because he made him up
Mickey made Fred look like a duck
That is the end of Mickey's life
I hope you enjoyed it now good night!!!

Michelle Pellerin, Grade 5
École Renaissance, ON

This Little Light of Mine

I used to hide my little light, I put in on a shelf.
The light was for my eyes-only, me and no one else.
Nobody knew the real me, she was deep within my heart.
Tried to find my place but I did not know where to start.
Every page of my story was blank; there were no written words.
Wanted to go out there but it was such a big and scary world.
But then I took the little light out there for all to see.
Then I knew what I had to do, show the real me.
A fire burned inside my heart, everything was clear.
As the flame grew brighter it chased away all fear.
My story unfolded page by page, every chapter was adventure.
Then the real me came out and everybody met her.
Now I'll turn my life around light everybody's fire.
I will never ever stop until everybody is inspired.
I'll venture far beyond the limits, keep going 'till I've reached my goal.
I'll be the change I want to see and let everybody know.
All of us must band together and make this world a better place.
The best award to get is simply just a smiling face.
These fantasies may be far off; you may say that I'm out of my mind,
But if I fail a million times at least I know I've tried.

Shannon Egan, Grade 6
St Mark Separate School, ON

Grades K-1-2-3

Top Poem Grades K-1-2-3

The Butterfly

I saw a beautiful
butterfly
in the world.
Every time
I see her
she looks
different.
I realize that she
changed.
The sun
gives her
new clothes.

Hanifa Beni-Asaf, Grade 1
Islamic Foundation School, ON

Top Poem Grades K-1-2-3

Green

The blazing sun outside crowds
the clouds beyond and the
wondrous flowers stand with pride.

My daily journey in the garden
leads me through a flurry of
ruffled petals and a crowd of
waltzing leaves.

I stroll past a cluster of frilly
scarlet tulips and a patch of
quiet lily-of-the-valley.

Then, to my surprise, I see,
hiding in a bundle of dahlias
a bee disguised in a dreamy
dazzling petal-full gown.

From across the garden I
smell the intoxicating scent
of a stream of hyacinths.

This is the present that my precious
garden gave me today — tomorrow, even better!

Ariana Dancu, Grade 3
Greendale School, QC

Top Poem Grades K-1-2-3

Tweet, Tweet, Tweet!

Blue bird,
Blue bird,
Listen to your tweet!
Who is sitting in the big oak tree!
Your tweet fills the town with all happiness!

Blue bird,
Blue bird,
Just listen to your tweet!

In the town,
People are dancing because
They love your tweet!
The tweet is your music!

Blue bird,
Blue bird,
Just listen to your tweet!

Aisha Farman Khan, Grade 3
Islamic Foundation School, ON

Top Poem Grades K-1-2-3

Spring

In the spring time
Fish splash.
Splash! Splash!
Green leaves grow.
Grow! Grow!
The flowers spring.
Spring! Spring!

The sun is warm.
A rainbow is shining
Through the fuzzy clouds.

Abby Levy, Grade 2
Falmouth District School, NS

Top Poem Grades K-1-2-3

In the Forest

When the moon is shining up so white,
And the stars are glowing very bright,
An owl hoots from above,
Then nudges her babies with care and love.
A coyote passes by,
And then I see some fireflies.
Two deer run in the shadow of a tree,
The two deer turn and look at me.
One small raccoon goes into its den,
I point this out to my smiling friend.
Then I look up into the sky,
And what do I see, painted so high?
What a breathtaking sunrise I see,
That wonderful sight was lovely to me.

Amanda Lim, Grade 3
Dr George M Weir Elementary School, BC

Top Poem Grades K-1-2-3

Jungle Party

In the jungle
The leopards dance,
While the zebras prance!
The monkeys swing from tree to tree.
I think the crocodile likes me!

The snakes slither here and there.
Ants are crawling everywhere!
What a jungle party!

Ellen Moore, Grade 2
Falmouth District School, NS

Top Poem Grades K-1-2-3

Rain

Rain, rain up from the sky.
Please don't ever stop.

I like the pitter, patter coming from the sky.
Drip, drop, drip.

Come and play in the rain.
Splish splash, splish splash.

Everyone plays in the rain.
Swick swick swick.

Everyone in their rubber boots.
SPLASH!

BOOM! BOOM! BOOM! It's thunder.
Everybody let's go inside.

Swick swick
Let's take our rubber boots off.

Michael Opoku, Grade 3
Kingswood Dr Public School, ON

Top Poem Grades K-1-2-3

Loons

Two loons
Gliding on the calm water,
Beady red eyes
Staring ahead of them,
Brown fluffy baby
Leading mother,
With her white necklace
On her long
Black neck
And dark green
Head.

Brooklyn Roach, Grade 3
Mary Montgomery School, MB

Top Poem Grades K-1-2-3

Seaweed

I got a fish from the sea
She told her name to me
Her name was Seaweed
She could talk and she could read
I put her in a giant shell
She was happy I could tell
She was like a rainbow
And we loved each other so

Laura Schultz, Kindergarten
Trelawny Public School, ON

Top Poem Grades K-1-2-3

Those Who Gave

Bombs crashing
Tanks firing
Mothers crying
Tears falling
Poppies shining
Angels glowing
Thanks to those who gave!

Cassie Tam, Grade 3
Ranch Park Elementary School, BC

Orangie

Orange is like green stemmed pumpkins
And juicy oranges rolling and rolling.
It bounces like basketballs.
The color says "howdy" to me every day.
It smells like freshly squeezed oranges.
My color tastes like orange, sticky, lollipops.
Alexandra Nichols, Grade 2
The Country Day School, ON

My Home

My home is busy.
My home is confusing.
At my home I have two dogs and two cats.
My home is CRAZY!!!
Tyler Horne, Grade 2
Falmouth District School, NS

Hot Pink

My favorite color is hot pink
My color moves back and forth
like a flower when the wind blows on it
My color smells like cotton candy
Hot pink tastes like a strawberry smoothie
Ashley Iacobelli, Grade 2
The Country Day School, ON

Friends Are…

Friends are considerate,
Friends are cool.
Friends are awesome and so are you.
Sometimes they are mean!
But we never stay mad.
And that's what friends are for!
Brandy Macnab, Grade 3
McKenzie School, ON

Spring Rocks

I was at the golf course on a par five.
I took my driver and hit the ball
I heard a swish.
When I was driving to the hole
I felt the wind in my face.
Spring rocks!
Noah Kader, Grade 3
Ecole Akiva, QC

Food

Some foods are yummy.
Some foods are yucky!
Strawberries, beans, chocolate,
Tomatoes, cabbage, carrots,
Peppers, eggplants, ice cream.
FOOD! FOOD! FOOD!
Makayla Sexton, Grade 2
Falmouth District School, NS

Storm

The storm has hit!
BOOM!
CRASH!
Oh my goodness!
There you go again!
BOOM!
CRASH!

Then it is silent.
The loud creature is gone.
Maggy Burbidge, Grade 2
Falmouth District School, NS

Snowflakes

Snowflakes fall everywhere.
Snowflakes fall on trees.
Snowflakes fall on houses.
Snowflakes fall on the ground.
Snowflakes fall on benches.
Snowflakes fall for you to share.
Snowflakes fall everywhere!
Melissa Hoffman, Grade 3
Sir Isaac Brock Public School, ON

My Mommy's Mad

I broke a vase,
and mommy's mad.
Then she said,
that I'm so bad.
She said, I'm grounded
for a week.
Go to your room,
and don't you speak!
Marcus Duerr, Grade 2
Trelawny Public School, ON

When I Grow Up…

I want to be happy.
I will have a large family.
My wife will be lovely,
and we will have three children.
I want to be happy.

I want to be happy.
I will be a video game designer.
My video game will be called Slime.
I will make ten more.
I want to be happy.

I want to be happy.
I want to be rich.
I will have $10,000.
I will have a giant house.
I want to be happy.
Aidan Cole Rubin, Grade 2
Ecole Akiva, QC

Birds

B ack from migration.
I n my nest.
R esting.
D anger is on the ground.
S o I stay up!
Sarah Saunders, Grade 2
Trelawny Public School, ON

When I Grow Up

I want to be happy
I want a nice family
I will have a nice husband
I want to be happy
I want to be happy
I want to be happy
I want to be a teacher
I will have 22 children
I will be a very nice teacher
I want to be happy
I want to be happy
I want to be a violin teacher
I want to be a very nice violin teacher
I want to be happy
Clara Grenier, Grade 2
Ecole Akiva, QC

Chocolate! Chocolate!

Chocolate! chocolate!
I love you so much.
Chocolate! chocolate!
You're the food I love to eat.
Chocolate!chocolate!
I could take you into bed.
Chocolate! chocolate!
Melting in your mouth.
Chocolate! chocolate!
So sweet and so good
Chocolate! chocolate!
It could melt in your hand.
Chocolate! chocolate!
So good in every form.
Chocolate! chocolate!
Smelling so sweet and tasty
Chocolate! chocolate!
No one will throw you in the garbage.
Oh, chocolate! chocolate!
Dustin Larsen, Grade 3
River Valley School, AB

Ice Cream

I love ice cream
Taste so many flavours
Chocolate, vanilla, strawberry
Yum yum!
Hillary Wolfe, Grade 2
Kingswood Dr Public School, ON

Underground Railroad*

U pset masters have
N o slaves left.
D inner is near.
E very slave escaped
R ight when masters' backs were turned.
G reat danger lurks ahead
R ocks smash under feet
O ver the hills
U nder the stars
N orth to Canada
D etermined to go on

R unning, running
A ll through the night
I n horror we hear
L oud noises
R un faster
O ur hearts beat faster
A t last, we are free
D one running time to rest

Oskar Kaune, Grade 3
Central Public School, ON
*Based on the book "Under the Quilt of Night"
by Deborah Hopkins and James E. Rensome

Run

Karrina and I are having a race
If you win you get a vase
I am going on a trip and bringing my case.

Charli Morrison, Grade 1
Helen Gorman Elementary School, BC

Nachos, Nachos

Nachos, nachos
I love you so much
Nachos, nachos
You're the food I love to eat
You're salty, juicy, crunchy, cheesy, colorful and meaty
Nachos, nachos
I ask my mom for nachos every night
I don't look forward to my last bite.
Nachos, nachos
Your cheese is so hot, sticky, and better every bite
Nachos, nachos
You're covered in cheese with all your vegetables.

Jordon Graville, Grade 3
River Valley School, AB

Orange

Orange is the color of the sunset.
It smells like freshly squeezed orange juice.
It moves like clouds soaring through the sky.
Orange tastes like tangerines.
I really love the color orange!

Ella Nadalini, Grade 2
The Country Day School, ON

Hareem

H areem likes to play with her friends.
A pples are my favourite fruit.
R unning is my favourite hobby.
E lephants are my second favourite animal.
E xploring is my favourite adventure.
M aitreyi is my best friend.

Hareem Hashmi, Grade 2
Trelawny Public School, ON

All In Fall

In fall
The
Leaves
Fall
While the
Wind
Blows
Like wings
In the
Sky

Shoshana Cutler, Grade 1
Dublin Heights Elementary & Middle School, ON

Hockey

H is for hockey
O is for offside
C is for captain
K is for keeping the puck in the other end
E is for energy
Y is for you having fun!

Cameron Kevin Waddington, Grade 3
McKenzie School, ON

Hot, Hot Pink

Hot pink tastes like sweet lemonade,
Like cotton candy.
It tastes warm and smooth melting in your mouth.
Some people can't see hot pink,
but it smells like sugar floating in the air.
It gives you a cozy feeling inside of you.
Worms are hot pink.
Hot pink feels like jelly in your hands.

Alisha Papazian, Grade 2
The Country Day School, ON

Snow

Snow is white.
Snow is light.
We make snowmen.
We always make ten.
We always name them Ben.
Snow is cold.
We wear extra clothes.
Snow is fun with everyone.

Gurjot S. Gill, Grade 2
Khalsa School - Old Yale Road Campus, BC

Spring

S pring is nice.
P laying in spring.
R ain in spring.
I n spring new bugs.
N ew grass grows.
G reen grass grows.

Sarah Larson, Grade 1
Sparling School, AB

Love

Love is something
You can't forget.

Without love
Your life can't be fun.

Ryan Coleski, Grade 2
Falmouth District School, NS

Spring Is...

Catching butterflies in the meadow.
Swimming at the pool.
Planting flowers.
And finding Easter eggs.
Noticing that the bunny puts
an egg on my chair.
Spring is wonderful!

Alexa Friesen, Grade 3
Tisdale Elementary School, SK

Snakes

I like snakes
They have scales.
They are cool
And can slither.
They have small eyes.
They are awesome!
I like snakes!

Drew Heaman, Grade 3
Mary Montgomery School, MB

Under the Rainbow

Under the rainbow
Where the leprechauns guard their gold

Under the rainbow
Where pixies fly

Under the rainbow
Where shamrocks glow

Under the rainbow
Where the fairy princess lives

Under the rainbow

Rayannah Hwang, Grade 2
Falmouth District School, NS

Hockey

Hockey is fun.
I score.
We win.
When I play
Road hockey
With my
Friends
I can deke
Around three
Players.
I pass.
Only Declan
Grabs the puck.
I can
Skate hard.
Hockey is
So much
Fun!

Michael Krochak, Grade 3
Mary Montgomery School, MB

Wintertime

In the cold winter.
When the animals are cold.
Many are sleeping.

Jake Walters, Grade 2
A J McLellan Elementary School, BC

Green

Green is slow like a brontosaurus
Flower stems
So beautiful
So minty fresh
So green.
The beauty of the Earth
The bumpiness of a crocodile
Juicy like grapes
The color green.

Jeremy Garbe, Grade 2
The Country Day School, ON

The Freezing Cat

"Brr," said the cat
"I thought it was summer
It's June, but I am freezing
My feet are numb
My ears have frostbite
My eyes are droopy
My feet are dragging
If I slept a little bit longer...
Maybe it will be warm
I'll crawl into bed and get cozy
When I wake up, I hope
I can chase mice in the sun!"

Kayla Killam, Grade 3
River Valley School, AB

I Love Dogs!

I love dogs.
I adore dogs.
I love fluffy dogs.
I like all dogs.
Even poor dogs.
I love dogs.

Aleksis Holt, Grade 2
A J McLellan Elementary School, BC

Loons

One loon
With two babies
On her back,
Floating
On the cool calm water.
White spots
On her back
With a
White necklace
And
Two red eyes.

Taylor Masson, Grade 3
Mary Montgomery School, MB

Halloween!

Halloween is candy
yum yum yum.
Halloween is fun
fun fun fun.
Halloween is costumes
boo boo boo.
Halloween is darkness
ooh ooh ooh.
Halloween is trick or treating.
AHHHHHH!!!!!!!

Joshua Kanai, Grade 2
A J McLellan Elementary School, BC

The Place I Like to Go

I like a place to go
Can you guess what is that
There are no toys
So I cannot play there
But still I like to go there
There is no food
So I cannot eat there
But still I like to go there
There are no beds
So I cannot sleep there
But still I like to go there
There are all books
So I can read a lot
But I know now you guessed it
"Yes it's a library"

Anittha Mappanasingam, Grade 3
St Isaac Jogues Catholic School, ON

The Forest

I see the creeping crawling animals in the woods. I look at a huge maple-leafed tree.
Lions roaring so loud that trees are s-h-a-k-i-n-g (every one in the forest!!!).

I hear the rustling, giant animals in the green bushes.
The snakes slithering and hissing through the yellow grass. Cheetahs pouncing and bursting out of the long grass.

I feel the rough ground beneath my feet.
The shiny, slippery, brown worm in the deep ground. A piece of brown, rough bark from a huge tree.

I smell the delicious blackberries picked freshly from a bush.
The wet leaves that have just been rained on. A sticky, icky snail on the dirty, wet ground.

I taste the raspberries with one green leaf from a green bush.
The dirty, wet, brown soil. A squirmy worm going through the dirt.

The forest appeals to all my senses don't you see? That's why it's my favourite place to be!

Charlotte Kriwez, Grade 2
St Frances Cabrini School, ON

The Beach

I see the waves crashing in the beautiful, dark blue water.
There are red crabs nipping at my feet. In the sky, the bright, yellow sun is shining on me.

I hear white, wonderful seagulls chomping on fish like crazy.
Green, tall trees blowing in the air. The waves roaring in the deep, blue sea.

I feel the wet, brown sand sticking to my burning hot feet.
Waves splashing so fast on my hands. Lots of greasy lotion getting spread on my skin.

I smell seagulls gushy poop on the wet sand.
Green, stinky seaweed laying on the light brown sand. Some fresh, blue water swishing in my mouth.

I taste the freezing cold water I accidentally swallowed. Hard sand stuck in between my white teeth.
The beach appeals to all my senses don't you see? That's why it's my favourite place to be!

Lana Hodgson, Grade 2
St Frances Cabrini School, ON

The Library

I see about a zillion animal books on the shelf.
A series of Captain Underpants — traa laa laa! 25 GIANT Pickachu Pokemon chapter books.

I hear the silent wind of the pages swishing in the air. Myself reading the GIGANTIC words of animal books,
for example, camouflage. GIANT Pokemon names, for example, Houndoom.

I feel the pages that are as soft as a polar bear's fur.
The fabulous cover of the Pokemon chapter book, *Return of the Squirtle Squad*.

I smell the fantastic new pages from the new books. The GIANT book cover of the *Animal Encyclopedia*.
I can almost smell the animal fur straight from the book *Wild, Wild World*.

I taste the juicy words from the excellent Pokemon and animal books.
I can almost taste the book covers and pages that are in front of me.

The library appeals to all my senses don't you see? That's why it's my favourite place to be!

Jackson Grant, Grade 2
St Frances Cabrini School, ON

Cheese

Mr. Cheese,

I am not pleased because
you gave me processed cheese!
Now I have a cheese disease
that even a squeeze won't decrease!

I know you have expertise on
ancient cheese,
processed cheese and eye disease.
Now I have a spirited debate to
send grated cheese through a gate.

Now help me would you,
my first mate,
as I assist you to a crate,
to know that you're sent away!

Aisha Saadiah, Grade 3
Islamic Foundation School, ON

Hockey

H ockey is fun
O ut in an ice arena
C anucks rock
K ick the puck
E asy sport
Y ipee, we scored a goal!

Elliott Marshall, Grade 2
A J McLellan Elementary School, BC

Spring Is Here!

Spring is here, spring is here !
Chirping birds, croaking frogs,
All the animals come and play.
Spring is here, spring is here!
Flowers bloom, flowers grow,
Baby animals eat and grow.
Spring is here, spring is here!
Now it's time to come out of your homes!
Let's go play, let's go play!
Birds are chirping, frogs are croaking.
Spring is here, spring is here!
Swing and slide, swing and slide!
All the animals come and play.
Spring is here, spring is here!

Bilan Mohamud, Grade 3
Islamic Foundation School, ON

Funny Mom

love Mom
fun Mom
likable Mom
good Mom
my Mom

Brandon Johnson-Martin, Grade 1
Sparling School, AB

The Easter Bunny Is Coming

He likes to jump up and down,
He is nice and furry and round,
He creeps at night,
To bring us Easter eggs.

Jasmine Martinez-Mannella, Grade 3
McKenzie Public School, ON

Squirrels

Squirrels in the chimney!
Squirrels in the barn!
Squirrels in the house!
Squirrels are everywhere!
Some squirrels are fat.
Some squirrels are skinny.
Some squirrels are tall and big.
Some squirrels are short and small.
Squirrels can be mean.
Squirrels can be nice.
Squirrels can be wild.
Squirrels can be tame.
Some squirrels like to glide.
Some squirrels like to jump.
Some squirrels like to climb high.
Some squirrels like to climb low.
Squirrels are everywhere!

Katharina Schramm, Grade 3
River Valley School, AB

Black of the Black

Black feels like a woolly sweater
It tastes like an Oreo
It looks like the night sky
And my polished shoes
Black tiptoes like a mouse

Massimo Sardo, Grade 2
The Country Day School, ON

My Dog Buckley

Buckley! Buckley! Buckley!
He's a very special dog
Buckley! Buckley! Buckley!
He's nothing like a frog
Buckley! Buckley! Buckley!
He likes to jump around
Buckley! Buckley! Buckley!
He also likes to bound
Buckley! Buckley! Buckley!
He's an awesome dog
Buckley! Buckley! Buckley!
I'd be sad if I lost him in the fog
Buckley! Buckley! Buckley!
You are an orange colour
Buckley! Buckley! Buckley!
He likes to eat cauliflower

Grace Johnson, Grade 3
River Valley School, AB

It's Spring

It's the first flower
And the flower grew in spring
While the blue birds sing.

Sage Soetisna, Grade 2
A J McLellan Elementary School, BC

School Construction

Building
Bang! Bang! Bang! Bang!
Construction workers work
When is it going to be done?
It's done!

Faizan Shaikh, Grade 2
Kingswood Dr Public School, ON

Weather

Weather is wonderful, weather is great.
It makes hurricanes rip off a gate.
It makes breezes blow
and clouds being to snow.
Thunder roars! Lightning crashes!
It turns everything into ashes!

Claudia Rando, Grade 2
Trelawny Public School, ON

When I Grow Up...

I want to be beautiful and happy.
I will dress well.
There will always be a smile on my face,
and I will always wear lip-gloss.
I want to be beautiful and happy.

I want to be beautiful and happy.
I want to be a beading-lady.
There will be fifteen smiley faces.
Everyone will do beading.
I want to be beautiful and happy.

I want to be beautiful and happy.
I will be married.
There will be about three children.
Everyone will be calm.
I want to be beautiful and happy.

Sarah Suzanna Moghrabi, Grade 2
Ecole Akiva, QC

Puppies

Cute
Playful
Cuddly
Sleepy
Lovable
Soft
Puppies!

Madeline Shanks, Grade 2
Falmouth District School, NS

Winter

I feel cold winds,
They whistle through naked trees
Making delicate noises.
As I walk down the street,
I feel icy fingers tickling down my back.
When I get home,
I am welcomed by small lights and warmth
Between the love of me and my parents.
After I warm up,
I get dressed to go out again into the deadly winter.
This time I hear church bells singing,
And I start to enjoy myself.
It is getting dark,
I want to go home, but I'm lost.
Suddenly I start to recognize where I am.
I am outside my house.
It is getting colder, and whiter.
My parents find me,
Inside I melt
I am put to bed.
Good night!

Grace Pawlik, Grade 3
Busby School, AB

Leaves

Leaves grow in the tree
then the leaves fall
down
down
down
down
down the tree

Claudia Ramilo, Grade 1
Dublin Heights Elementary & Middle School, ON

Soldiers Fight

I am a soldier,
I fight to help my country stay free
Children are lucky; they do not need to fight.
Children have to remember.

Nicole Boire, Grade 3
McKenzie School, ON

Summer Day

S ummer is when we go out to play on swings.
U se your feet to walk.
M ove your body, get into shape.
M ake your soccer coach happy.
E verybody goes to camp.
R ide your scooter.

D rink a lot.
A t soccer make sure your cleats are tied.
Y ou are the best player.

Jared Boidman, Grade 2
Ecole Akiva, QC

High

My parrot goes high in the sky.
It goes down to the town,
and finds a crab on the sand.
It goes up high in the sky again.
He could see a tree under him.

Harjap S. Dhaliwal, Grade 2
Khalsa School - Old Yale Road Campus, BC

My Gift

What would I give
The boy that I am?
If I were an athlete
I would give the homeless anything they need.
I would do my part with the government
But what would I give?
I would give with my HEART.

Reece Dickinson, Grade 3
Ranch Park Elementary School, BC

The Library

The library is filled with fun,
Fun for everyone.
We take out books and read about crooks.

Computers are number 1
'Cause they are so much fun.
Magazines on my knees,
I fall asleep
Reading about sheep.

I love the library
'Cause I think and think so much.

Bridget Halko, Grade 2
St Gabriel, AB

Surprisingly

Surprisingly my lamp broke and no one was around.
Surprisingly my dog ate my homework.
Surprisingly I had a sleepover.
Surprisingly I went skating.
Surprisingly I got a present for free
Surprisingly

Sung Won Kim, Grade 2
A J McLellan Elementary School, BC

Colors

Colors are pretty.
They are orange, yellow, green and pink.
They are colorful to your eyes.
They shine in the sun.
Colors you pick can be your favorite.
Or, if you don't like it then don't use it.
I love colors. Usually they are all nice.
I hope you like colors!

Alyssa Carry, Grade 2
Heritage Heights School, AB

When I Grow Up…

I want to be happy.
I will have a medium sized family.
There will be a generous husband
and four children.
I want to be happy.
I want to be happy.
I will be an artist.
There will be beautiful pictures
in the world.
Everyone will be happy.
I want to be happy.
I want to be happy.
I also want to be a singer.
I want to be rich
with love!
I am happy.

Hannah Faith Kalin, Grade 2
Ecole Akiva, QC

When I Grow Up

I want to be a businessman at Servomax.
I will have a medium sized family.
There will be a quiet wife.
I will have four kids.
I want to be a businessman.
I want to be a businessman at Servomax.
I will take over Servomax from my dad.
I will be the boss of Servomax.
I will be rich.
I want to be a businessman at Servomax.
I want to be a businessman at Servomax.
My brother Dustin will be my partner.
I will have 192 people working for me.
I want to be a businessman at Servomax.

Jonah Koifman, Grade 2
Ecole Akiva, QC

Turtles

Turtles are fun.
Turtles are snappers.
I like turtles.

Dawson Riley, Grade 2
Falmouth District School, NS

Baby

I am getting a new baby brother
Or maybe a new baby sister
And I don't know what to do.
I have an older brother
And I don't know what to do.
I have a mom and a dad and a stepdad
And I don't know what to do.
Love them!
I love my family.

Jonathan Chandler, Grade 2
Falmouth District School, NS

Skating

People skating on the ice
Having fun and falling down
Playing hockey
Scoring in nets
Learning to skate
Having fun!
I love skating
It's so fun!

Krista Hall, Grade 3
Mary Montgomery School, MB

Words

Look at words!
They look normal
But wait…
They're adjectives, nouns
Or even verbs!
Now I like words even better
Because…
They're interesting!

Natalie Wilson, Grade 3
McKenzie School, ON

The Sea

Fish as tiny as dimes
Octopus bigger than elephants
Dolphins 100 in a pod
Sharks with sharp teeth
Plankton as small as tennis balls
Catfish with the biggest whiskers
You have ever seen!

Julia Strickey, Grade 2
Falmouth District School, NS

Pony

There once was a black pony.
She went by the name Tony.

One day I decided to braid her hair.
She looked so pretty, we went to the fair.

I love to see Tony the pony.
Even more than eating macaroni.

Quinlan Nowoczin, Grade 3
Westside Academy, BC

Miss Kirkness

Miss Kirkness is a friend.
Miss Kirkness is nice.
Miss Kirkness is smart.
Miss Kirkness is pretty.
Miss Kirkness is joyful.
Miss Kirkness is here till the end.
Miss Kirkness is a friend.

Cassidy McDonald, Grade 3
Sir Isaac Brock Public School, ON

Hockey

I play hockey
I am number 3
I play defense
I play for the Virden Kings
I get lots of goals
I can deke
I wrist shot
Hockey is fun
It is my favourite sport.
I love hockey!

Declan Cosgrove, Grade 3
Mary Montgomery School, MB

I Like Cats!

I love cats.
I adore cats.
Fluffy cats.
Puffy cats.
Even mean cats.
I have a very nice cat.

Mihayla Schlecker, Grade 2
A J McLellan Elementary School, BC

Wind

Cold wind.
Wind is fun
I wear a jacket
Wind.

Cassidy Bannister, Grade 1
Sparling School, AB

School Is Driving Me Crazy

School is driving me crazy
there is science,
math, E.L.A. and more
all we do is work,
work and more work
so that was it
I didn't do my homework,
I didn't do my tests,
I didn't listen to the teacher
and YIPEE! I was out of school forever.

Mattea Becker, Grade 3
Tisdale Elementary School, SK

Green

It is a hot greeny color
Colors with green fly in the sky
The smell is like tall plants
Plants are light green
When the wind blows on the grass
The air smells green
Sometimes green smells like cream soda
Green eats money

Ian Rokas, Grade 2
The Country Day School, ON

Ski Racing

S kiing is very fun.
K nowing friends to ski with is great
I n skiing there are many different types.

R acing is very different than free skiing.
A medal is what you get if you win.
C old days need a good cup of hot chocolate.
I love to ski in the winter.
N ight skiing is cool.
G ood skiers win races.

Taylor Rosenbloom, Grade 2
Ecole Akiva, QC

Belonging

I feel like I belong
When I hear my mom calling me.
I feel like I belong
When I see the cat scratch in gymnastics.
I feel like I belong
When I smell my wacky melon shampoo.
I feel like I belong
When I taste my delicious birthday cake.
I feel like I belong
When I touch my dog, kittens, cats and horses.

Tia Webb, Grade 3
Mary Montgomery School, MB

Spring

Birds come out and sing,
Flowers bloom, here comes spring.
The sun shines bright, butterflies come out,
Rain pours, a rainbow comes out.
No more snow boots' chance,
Kids come out and dance.
Flowers bloom, here comes spring.
We have fun in spring.

Naaz K. Gill, Grade 2
Khalsa School - Old Yale Road Campus, BC

Summer

In summer it is very hot.
And we can go to the beach.
We put on sun-cream so that our
Skin doesn't get burned.
It's lot of fun in summer.
In summer, girls wear dresses,
And boys wear shorts.
Summer is the fourth season.
Summer is the sunniest season.
And it's the warmest season.
Most people in the world like summer.
In summer, we don't wear warm clothes.
In summer lots of plants grow.
Some butterflies hatch from the chrysalis.

Jasmeen K. Gill, Grade 2
Khalsa School - Old Yale Road Campus, BC

Hands

My hands allow me to hold a book and keep my spot.
My hands give me strength to write mysteries and poems.
Because of my hands, I can hold a G1 license.
My hands can wrap a present for my best friend's birthday.
My stupendous hands give a hug to my mom and dad.

Zan Qureshi, Grade 2
Kingswood Dr Public School, ON

Freedom!*

U nder the quilt, the
N orth star guiding you.
D ogs barking for
E very man that's running.
R oad by road, following the
G ourd.
R acing
O n the trail to freedom.
U nder the
N ight sky.
D aring to go on.

R ocks
A t my feet.
I n the light of the moon,
L ooking for the boat.
R owing across the
O hio River.
A t the end of the river
D anger is behind us. Only freedom is ahead.

Madeline Chinnery, Grade 3
Central Public School, ON
*Based on the book "Under the Quilt of Night"
by Deborah Hopkins and James E. Rensome

Soldier

I am a soldier,
I am never scared of enemies.
I do my work as my master says.
We practice our drills.
Our pilots drop us there.
I want to save my world from enemies.
I love to be a Canadian soldier.

Josh Paul S. Clair, Grade 2
Khalsa School - Old Yale Road Campus, BC

Harmony

Harmony is not…
Kicking, punching, shooting and drugs.
If you do these things, you will get in big trouble!

Harmony is…
Being good to the Earth.
Harmony is being good to people.
Harmony will get you friends!

William Carr, Grade 3
McKenzie School, ON

Poor Little Boy

There once was a poor little boy,
Who didn't have any parents,
He had no home or toys,
No one to share his trials or joys.

He had no clothes or food,
Begging was all he knew
People passed him by,
Not even sharing a smile.

Winter came, snow was on the ground,
And there he was still sitting,
Shivering in the frigid weather,
Nobody seemed to notice his misery.

One morning as the crowds passed by,
He was no longer there,
They searched and found him,
He was lying still and cold.

Now he has gone to heaven,
And he will be an angel,
He will wear a golden crown,
And live with Jesus forever.
Pauline W. Decker, Grade 3
Riverbend Colony School, AB

Mrs. Blue

The color blue soars across the ocean.
The color blue is the sky.
Apples are red,
Grapes are purple,
An iris is blue and Smarties are too.
Blue tastes like juicy blueberries.
Blue is warm and cozy.
Blue is like the softness of the air.
Mira Cantor, Grade 2
The Country Day School, ON

My Mom

M y mom is special
Y ellow is her favorite color

M om is special
O ranges are her favorite fruit
M opping is her favorite thing to do

I love my mom
S he loves to play with me

M y mom is mine
I n the sun we swim
N o one messes with her
E at, eat she says
Vienna Mracovcic, Grade 3
Westside Academy, BC

Peace

P eace is important in the world.
E very country should never have a war.
A nimals can get killed.
C an you help make peace?
E ven some little kids say it is easy.
Mikaela Barry, Grade 2
Ecole Akiva, QC

Canada

Canada is a fun place to live.
Canada is also a free country.
And Canada is the best place
For anyone in the whole world!
If you live in Canada,
You can do whatever you want!
Amanda Lynn Beaulieu, Grade 3
McKenzie School, ON

Red

Red is flames
Red is roses
Red is like raspberry jam
Red smells like steam from a fire
Red tastes like strawberries
Nicholas Suriwka, Grade 2
The Country Day School, ON

When I Grow Up…

I want to be rich!
I will buy three dogs.
I will walk them every day
and feed them too.
I want to be rich!

I want to be rich!
I will buy an airplane.
I will fly to San Francisco
and meet my cousins.
I want to be rich!

I want to be rich!
I will buy a very fast car.
I will race with my car
and get a trophy.
I want to be rich!
Dolev Faitelis, Grade 2
Ecole Akiva, QC

My Friend Brock

Brown eyes,
nice manner,
is funny,
is nice,
fast runner.
Kenneth Gabourie, Grade 1
Sparling School, AB

Books!

Books are here
Books are there
Books are everywhere.

Books are scary.
Books are green
Books can be very mean.

Books are happy.
Books are bad.
Books I read are sometimes sad.
Isabella Hepner, Grade 2
A J McLellan Elementary School, BC

Spring

I like spring because I feel
the colors
it makes me happy
everyone else wants
to ride their bikes
the breeze on my face
feels good.
And I like to
run around.
Jordan Edelstein, Grade 3
Ecole Akiva, QC

The Dragon

I saw a dragon.
The dragon saw me.
I started to run, and he ate me.

D ragons are orange and red
R oar and are meat-eaters
A dragon likes to stalk his prey
G oing fast and munching along the way.
O n and off they hunt and hunt and
N ow dragons are extinct.
Seth Walton, Grade 3
McKenzie School, ON

Bouncy Balls

Balls bounce most everywhere
Some bouncy balls are hard
Some are squishy
But every bouncy ball bounces.
I love bouncy balls!
Jakob Cooper-Brown, Grade 3
Mary Montgomery School, MB

War

Please stop the war now.
Why does war even exist?
Bring the soldiers home!
Dante JamsaBabcock, Grade 3
McKenzie School, ON

In the Night Garden
In the night garden
I hear a sound.
Whoo-whoo!
It's only an owl!

Creeeeek!
What's that hiding in the tree?
It's only a cat looking at me.

Listen for noises in your garden!
Kiya McDow, Grade 2
Falmouth District School, NS

Spring Is…
Spring is here!
It sounds like birds chirping in my ear.
Spring is here!
It smells like spring flowers in the air.
Spring is here!
It looks like a bright view everywhere.
Spring is here!
It tastes like chocolate ice cream.
Spring is here!
It makes me feel happy.
Spring is here!
Ryley Norum, Grade 3
Tisdale Elementary School, SK

It's Lost!
I looked in my closet
I looked in my dresser
I looked everywhere
It's lost! It's lost!
This is not fair!
I even looked in my hair
And it's not there!
Oh well, I'll have to go without it
I'm not wearing…
UNDERWEAR!

Kendra Janz, Grade 3
River Valley School, AB

I Am a Dog
I am a dog
Running, jumping, playing
With my owner.

I am a dog
Eating, barking, whining,
A very cute dog.

I am a dog
Digging, sniffing, resting
Under a shady tree.
Emma Brooks, Grade 2
A J McLellan Elementary School, BC

I Know It's Spring
When I see flowers starting to bloom I know it is spring.
I see a rainbow when I look out the window.
I hear the birds chirping at me.
I love the spring.

Julia Goodman, Grade 3
Ecole Akiva, QC

I'm Glad It's Spring
I feel great when I go outside in spring after it rains.
Seeing the flowers blooming and the trees turn green.
Smelling the nice fresh smell.
I'm glad it's spring.

Joelle Nadler, Grade 3
Ecole Akiva, QC

Autumn
Autumn looks like squirrels hiding in the trees.
Autumn smells like winter.
Autumn sounds like kids jumping in leaves.
Autumn feels like warm and cold.
Autumn.

Jacob Dowell, Grade 3
Ranch Park Elementary School, BC

Mr. Blue
Mr. Blue bounces up and down when he walks.
He tastes like yummy berries
And smells like the salty ocean.
He shimmers like the glittering sky.

Julian Pasquali, Grade 2
The Country Day School, ON

Overdreaming
Overdreaming means you see inside your dream
You go to sleep in your dream
And then you can see the dream from inside
Even though you are already dreaming
I did it only once and once
When it happened
That was a long time ago
In that dream inside a dream
When I overdreamed
I saw myself inside my dream inside another dream
I saw myself inside two dreams
All at the same time
And when I was inside one dream already
I was late for a basketball game
The whole place was yellow
And when I wasn't in the basketball game yet
The whole room was very dark
And there were doors all over.
Sometimes it is something that is left from what happened in your life.
Sometimes it can be something that was left from your life.

Mahto Boneshirt, Grade 1
Garibaldi Elementary School, BC

The End of the River
The end of the river
Frogs croak!
The end of the river
Grasshoppers chirp!
The end of the river
Fish swim.
The end of the river
The wind blows!
How will I get to sleep?
Sydney Baker, Grade 2
Falmouth District School, NS

Spring
Buzz buzz
Reports come home
Summer break is coming
Yeah yeah yeah! School's over soon!
Let's play
Nirmpaul Moondi, Grade 3
Kingswood Dr Public School, ON

Rain
R aindrops falling
A t the window.
I nside, I'm safe
N o rain will get me.
Jovana Haag, Grade 2
Trelawny Public School, ON

Christmas
Just see the bells at the stores.
Just hear church bells ringing.
Just smell the sugar cookies baking.
Just feel the warm scarf.
Just taste the candy canes.
And then I know it's Christmas
Breanna Carter, Grade 2
A J McLellan Elementary School, BC

On the Beach
On the beach there are many seashells,
In the water too.
Lots of people go swimming there,
And are having fun too.
Lots of kids are in the water,
Splashing at each other.
And grown-ups are having fun too.
Emilie-Jade Pakrashi, Grade 3
McKenzie School, ON

Water
Water is peaceful.
Reflection is on water.
It is very warm.
Kate Morrow, Grade 3
Westside Academy, BC

A Friend
Lovable, loyal
Shares her secrets
Someone to laugh with
Caring
Sonia Gauld, Grade 3
Sir Isaac Brock Public School, ON

A Loon
A loon looking backwards
Over the peaceful water
A loon resting
On the smooth water
A loon feeling
The breeze
In its feathers
A loon feeling
The water push against it.
Phoenix Pennycook, Grade 3
Mary Montgomery School, MB

Birds
B eautiful birds
I n the trees
R ain falling too.
D o they have musical ears?
S inging birds!
Saiba Anand, Grade 2
Trelawny Public School, ON

Springtime
Drip drop
It is raining
I feel soggy, sleepy
I want to get to school on time
Drip drop
Ulrich Meyer, Grade 3
Kingswood Dr Public School, ON

Seasons
Spring!
When you see birds and bees
And when it rains, rains, rains

Summer!
When it becomes hot
When everyone drinks lemonade

Fall!
When it becomes cold
And leaves fall off the trees

Winter!
When it snows
And everyone drinks hot chocolate
Sarah Lynch, Grade 2
Falmouth District School, NS

My Kitten Candy
I know a little kitten
She is brown and white.
She eats a lot of mice.
She stays out all night.
She has an older sister.
She has another friend.
A frisky Border Collie
Who chases her to the end!
Candy, Candy
You're a good kitten.
I take care of you every day.
You like to play
You like to chew on leather
Candy, Candy
You go out in any weather.
Codi Wilson, Grade 3
River Valley School, AB

Lions
Lions can jump high
Lions eat good food and you
Lions can roar loud
Teagen Gosling, Grade 1
Sparling School, AB

Mouse in the House
I saw a small mouse.
Inside my house.

I set up a trap.
But it just went snap.

I tried a big box.
But captured a fox.

I let out the cat.
But it caught a rat.

What will I do with this mouse?
When it is inside my house?
Emma Van Dinter, Grade 3
Westside Academy, BC

At the Beach
At the beach
The hermit crab hides in its shell.
At the beach
The baby sharks come to the shore.
At the beach
The sand is blowing like dust.
At the beach
When the tide goes out
Islands reappear.
At the beach.
MacKenzie Miller, Grade 2
Falmouth District School, NS

When I Grow Up...

I want to be happy
I will have a big dog
Like Edison
It will be a golden doodle
I want to be happy

I want to be happy
I will be a veterinarian
I will take care of a lot of dogs
I want to be happy

I want to be happy
I will play with my dog
I will name it Edison
He will be allowed to sit on my bed
I want to be happy

Laura Fishko, Grade 2
Ecole Akiva, QC

Skidooing in the Fields

Skidoos zoom cross fields
Like lightning
Turn sharp
Do small wheelies
Big wheelies
Two kinds of skidoos racing
And having fun.
I love skidooing!

Max Wegner, Grade 3
Mary Montgomery School, MB

The Pencil

It lets
me write
words
and letters.
It feels hard.
It is made of wood.
I think
the pencil
is smiling at me.

Mawiz Hassan, Grade 1
Islamic Foundation School, ON

Sad Day

Today I was
so grouchy.
I broke my
favourite toy
by accident.
I started to cry
until I realized,
today was
a field trip!

Leeya Chohan, Grade 1
Islamic Foundation School, ON

Spring Is...

When baby animals are born
When flowers start to blossom
When the snow is gone
When the sun is shining
When the warm is coming
When summer is almost here
When trees began to grow
Spring is.

Weier Fan, Grade 3
Tisdale Elementary School, SK

Muddy Shoes

My muddy shoes
Give me a frown
When I am colouring brown.
When I am upside down,
My smile turns into a frown.
My feet stick to the ground.
That makes me slow down,
Fall down
Into the muddy,
Muddy,
Muddy
Mud.

Dawson Masluk, Grade 2
St Gabriel, AB

Easter

Easter is chocolate eggs,
Easter is egg salad,
Easter is finding Easter eggs,
Easter is my sister's birthday
on the 12th
I like the big jackpots hidden
so my cousins can't find them,
But I can.

Rohan Bajwa, Grade 2
A J McLellan Elementary School, BC

The Cottonball

The cottonball
Looks like snow.
It is round
It is white
It looks like snow!

Zoha Dadabhoy, Grade 1
Islamic Foundation School, ON

Spring

Pop, pop!
Blowing bubbles
with my friends, together.
When I wake up I blow bubbles.
It's fun.

Areesha Mahmood, Grade 2
Kingswood Dr Public School, ON

At the Beach

At the beach
the water laps on the sand,
the people wade in the water,
the fish swim around,
the lobsters feed on fish,
and the people swim
at the beach.

Jeremy Davison, Grade 2
Falmouth District School, NS

I Am a Cat

I am a cat
Black, white, gray
Living in a house.

I am a cat
Playing, running, jumping
Climbing up trees

I am a cat
Eating, sleeping, meowing
Climbing up fences.

Madelin Long, Grade 2
A J McLellan Elementary School, BC

Sonia

Sonia is a great friend.
Sonia is very caring.
Sonia is a very pretty girl.
Sonia is very smart.

Madison Mitchinson, Grade 3
Sir Isaac Brock Public School, ON

The Cottonball

Looks like a
soft pillow.
The soft pillow
is fluffy.
It
feels
smooshy.

Khadija Desai, Grade 1
Islamic Foundation School, ON

Edible Rainbow

R ed as an apple
O range as an apricot
Y ellow as a mango
G reen as a pear
B lue as a berry
I ndigo like the plums
V iolet like a grape

A rainbow to eat.

Katie Kleinsasser, Grade 3
Milford Colony School, AB

Popcorn

Popcorn, popcorn
I love popcorn.
It pops and it pops
POP, POP, POP!
I love popcorn.
Popcorn, popcorn, popcorn!
It smells soooo good as it pops.
Adam Jillett, Grade 2
Falmouth District School, NS

Stars at Night

Stars at night shine in your eyes.
Stars at night glide through the air.
Stars at night shoot above the sky.
Wish! Make a wish!
Stars at night so gracefully in the sky.
Stars at night come down
To take you up to outer space.
Stars at night are so sleepy.
Stars at night say good night.
Emma Tupper, Grade 2
Falmouth District School, NS

In Spring

In spring I love going to my aunt's pool.
When I come out of the pool I get cold.
Later I have a snack beside the pool.
I love spring.
Daniella Schwartz, Grade 3
Ecole Akiva, QC

Look Outside and See the World

Look outside and see the world,
Many colours,
Green, brown and blue,
Looks colourful
Children running,
Sounds nice
Roses, jasmines, tulips,
Smells sweet
Trees shaking,
Feels breezy
So much to smell, see, hear and feel,
Look outside and see the world.
Barakah Nana, Grade 3
Islamic Foundation School, ON

Spring

S pring has flowers.
P apa gives me slushes.
R ain comes.
I smell flowers.
N o snow.
G o to the spray park.
Sierra Sellin-King, Grade 1
Sparling School, AB

A Crazy Feather

Oh that crazy feather!
Just looking at me
on a crazy bird.
Oh that crazy feather
on that crazy bird dancing.
Wait a second…
Don't you know
feathers can't dance!
Aamina Anjum, Grade 1
Islamic Foundation School, ON

My Name Is Hanna, Just Hanna

My name is Hanna,
not banana,
or even that other
word Savannah.

And although she is
quite divine,
Hannah Montana
is another rhyme.

The bandana is for
your head you see.
It has nothing at all
to do with me.

I like my name,
it's who I am.
Do you have these problems
if your name is Sam?

My name is Hanna.
Just Hanna.
Hanna Johannesen, Grade 1
Ecole Baker, BC

Ice Cream Cone

You put ice cream in
a cone.
It is crunchy.
Very yummy,
delicious,
what is it?
An ice cream cone!
Safiya Patel, Grade 1
Islamic Foundation School, ON

Come to My House

My house
Come to my house
I am waiting for you
I am waiting for you to come
Playtime
Namoos Fatima, Grade 2
Kingswood Dr Public School, ON

Chicken Wings

Chicken wings, chicken wings
All sticky and such,
Chicken wings, chicken wings
I love you so much
You can be salty or sweet
You're the only one I want to eat
Chicken wings, chicken wings
You're made out of meat
Chicken wings, chicken wings
You can't be beat!
Lexus FirstRider, Grade 3
River Valley School, AB

Ice Fishing

I go ice fishing
You have to
Get a drill
Drill a hole
Put a fishing rod
In the hole
Wait until a fish bites
It will
YANK your fishing rod!
Hang on tight to the rod!
Ahh! Fish for supper!
Ansel Wu, Grade 3
Mary Montgomery School, MB

Purple

Purple glides over grapes
It's tasty when it's frozen.
Purple feels as soft as silk.
If purple could talk
I think it would say peace.
Ethan Steck, Grade 2
The Country Day School, ON

Jasper

Skiing
in Jasper
skiing in paradise
skiing in the mountains
down the hill we go
on skis
in Jasper
going through the trees
going off jumps
in Jasper
we stayed in a cabin
me and my family
a very nice cabin
a very warm cabin
in Jasper.
Luka Gader, Grade 2
St Gabriel, AB

Leaves Falling Down

Leaves are
Falling down
Falling down
In fall
We are
Happy now
We are
Happy still

Josselyn Estrada-Pedroza, Grade 1
Dublin Heights Elementary & Middle School, ON

Dreams

In my dreams
I see a long patch of ice
With banners flying in the air
Shouting from people as the players come out
Uniforms with bright colours
Lights are directed to the center of the ice
Players are down and set to go!
What's in my dreams?
A hockey player!

Cameron Casselman, Grade 3
River Valley School, AB

Hooray

Hooray spring is finally here!
I am so excited for the pretty flowers to bloom!

I'm jumping in the puddles,
laughing in the rain.

The sun is out.
I smell the new flowers.

Hear the rain go pitter patter outside!

Isabelle Rachel Shtern, Grade 3
Ecole Akiva, QC

When I Grow Up

I want to be nice.
I want a medium sized family.
I want a handsome husband and two kids.
I want them to be happy.
I want to be nice.
I want to be nice.
I will be a teacher.
There will be twenty-five singing people.
There will be a lot of competitions for math.
I want to be nice.
I want to be nice.
In my spare time I will do work and make jewelry.
I will sell them to stores.
I want to give some jewelry to poor people.
I want to be nice.

Maggie Fayer, Grade 2
Ecole Akiva, QC

I'd Love to Be Invisible

I'd love to be invisible if even for a week
I'd go to the swimming pool and jump off the diving board.
I'd love to be invisible if even for a day.
I'd sneak into Eli's room and mess up his bookshelf.
I'd watch him take out his secret drawer.
I'd love to be invisible if even for an hour
I'd walk to Matthew's house and play his Wii
We'd play a soccer game and I'd get all the goals
Because he wouldn't see me coming.
I'd love to be invisible if even for a minute
I'd pinch Josh on April Fool's Day
I'd hide Josh's toothbrush
I'd pick up a ball and throw it
So Jene my dog would chase it
Too bad the spell of invisibility wore off in a flash!

Nathanael Waters, Grade 3
River Valley School, AB

Dinosaurs

Dinosaurs lived long ago.
There were big ones,
Small ones,
Medium and tall ones,
Some had teeth,
Some didn't.
They used their tails to balance.
Some walked on four legs,
Some walked on two,
Some swallowed stones to help them chew.
Dinosaurs are cool!
That's what I know.

Isabella Giancola, Grade 2
The Country Day School, ON

Red Flower

You are a red flower
On red leaves,
On red stalks,
And on red branches.

Gavin Ghag, Grade 2
Khalsa School - Old Yale Road Campus, BC

My Penguin

My penguin has a white body and a stomach that's black.
He never stops traveling, so he never looks back.
His hair is the reddest of all red,
And at midnight, he goes right to his bed!
Just the other day, we went to the zoo
My penguin got quite scared
When the lion said "Boo!"
He exercises half of the day.
Then we go up to Hudson's Bay!
This penguin was sleeping and now just awoke.
This poem is a big, huge, gigantic penguin JOKE!

Lucas Vancuren, Grade 3
River Valley School, AB

The Magic
Look up high
Look at the snow
See
Look around
Bunch of snowflakes
Falling from the sky
If only I could fly
I would do my best
If it was possible
To catch a snowflake
From way up high
That would be magic
Sean Brundrett, Grade 2
Surrey Connect School, BC

Pickle
Pickle
Bumpy, Lumpy
Crunching, munching, lunching,
Cucumbers makin' you pucker.
Gherkin.
Nicholas Exelby, Grade 2
A J McLellan Elementary School, BC

Run
My dog and I like to run
We always have lots of fun
We stop and talk to everyone.
Saje Doobay-Janisch, Grade 1
Helen Gorman Elementary School, BC

Hockey
Hockey
Hockey is fun
Feel free to play hockey
Hockey is energetic, fun
Have fun
Jake Allen, Grade 2
Kingswood Dr Public School, ON

Peace at Last
Soldiers were killed for us
They now lie peacefully in the graveyard
Where crosses stand at rest.
Jordan Kleinsasser, Grade 3
Milford Colony School, AB

Springtime
Good times
Spring is fun too
Birds are always chirping
I like to ride my bicycle
It's fun!
Nakul Mistry, Grade 2
Kingswood Dr Public School, ON

Spring
S horter days
P retty flowers.
R ed roses
I n the spring it gets warmer.
N o snow
G reat time in the spring!
Madelin Stroebel, Grade 2
Trelawny Public School, ON

Breezy Wind
Wind is
strong.
It has
a lot of force!
It is
sometimes
strong.
It can
blow you
away!
Yasein Hussein, Grade 1
Islamic Foundation School, ON

Two Swimming Loons
Two little loons
Floating
In the cool calm water
Looking at each other
As they swim
On the great lake!
Tristan MacDonald, Grade 3
Mary Montgomery School, MB

Last Night I Dreamed of Hypo
I dreamed of a dog just last night,
And his name was Hypo.
Hypo was a Border Collie
He was really good at agility.
He has a favorite ability.
He's really good at herding sheep
Oh, did I mention
Hypo is a very hyper dog.
Just last night I found him,
Bounding up and down
He bounded on the red bed
And began to dance around.
But when I awoke this morning
Hypo wasn't bounding up and down
He wasn't dancing around
And he wasn't herding sheep.
I think he was just in my dreams.
I guess I'll just have to wait until tonight
To see him once again.
Araya Simington, Grade 3
River Valley School, AB

Winter!!
In winter we play.
In winter we run.
In winter we have
A lot of fun.

In winter we sled.
In winter we ski
In winter the snow
Falls down on me!
Liam Knight, Grade 2
A J McLellan Elementary School, BC

Run
I like to run
It's lots of fun
It's good to walk in the sun.
Piper MacDonell, Grade 1
Helen Gorman Elementary School, BC

Sad Friend
I know my friend's feelings
About his mom and dad,
They got separated
And he is feeling bad.
I don't see him smiling like before,
He is not playing with others anymore.
He looks sad
And often doesn't see his dad.
I feel sorry for my friend.
I see him unhappy on the pavement,
Since that day he is late for school
And sometimes absent.
Durjoy Munshi, Grade 3
George R Allan Jr Public School, ON

Joe
Joe
Happy, good
Bites, licks, scratches
Jumps on people a lot
FRIENDS!
Victoria Johnston, Grade 3
Sir Isaac Brock Public School, ON

Hockey
Hockey is an awesome sport
Especially because you can score goals
I like to pass in hockey
But I like to shoot the little puck
Into the big net
But it is hard to score
With a goalie in the huge net
I think playing hockey is sweet!
Tanner Andrew, Grade 3
Mary Montgomery School, MB

Wrestling

Wrestling, wrestling is my favorite thing.
You start to fight when the bell goes DING!
The other man throws out a punch and…
He takes his buddies and goes out for lunch.
When he goes back to the wrestling ring,
He scores 2 points
Now it is 2-2, last score is the winner.
The guy punches and he wins 2-3!
Wrestling, wrestling is my favorite thing.

Sheldon Oliver Nummikoski, Grade 3
McKenzie School, ON

Belonging

I feel like I belong
When I hear my mom's soft voice.
I feel like I belong
When I see my mom and dad walking with me.
I feel like I belong
When I smell Mom's freshly baked buns.
I feel like I belong
When I taste my mom's chocolate chip cookies.
I feel like I belong
When I touch my rabbit Tinka.

Anneliese Schelesnak, Grade 3
Mary Montgomery School, MB

Books, Books, Everywhere!

Books are the best. Books rule.
If you read one, you'll be cool.
To read a book, you'll need to know your alphabet.
Fiction, nonfiction and religion books.
Books everywhere!
Books are round or square.
Big and tall.
Skinny and small.
You can find them in libraries, school, and at home.
I love to read books, and I hope you do too!

Abdullah Zahid, Grade 3
Islamic Foundation School, ON

Plants

Plants are great plants are fun,
Full of colours for everyone.
Start from seeds and grow,
Into rows of red, green, orange and blue.
Beautiful, living, breathtaking creatures,
In colours of a rainbow.
I love my plant as sweet as can be,
Soon will grow as big as me.
Roots as long as they can grow to be,
Please be a tall tree for me.
Here is some food, yum what a treat!
Not for me, but for my tiny plant,
I named 'Planty.'

Areej Ahmed, Grade 3
Islamic Foundation School, ON

Spring

Spring is great.
Spring is the best.
Everybody likes spring.
Spring is nine days.
Let us celebrate.

Tarunjot S. Toor, Grade 2
Khalsa School - Old Yale Road Campus, BC

Friendship

Kicking, punching, and screaming
is not how you get friends.
If you play in harmony,
then your friends will come over and over,
and your friendship will get bigger and bigger!

Jamie Stewart, Grade 3
McKenzie School, ON

Mini Trees

Broccoli are
mini trees
for a bug
but they can
munch munch
munch it.

Celina Cayabyab, Grade 1
Dublin Heights Elementary & Middle School, ON

Blue

Waves splash
Blueberries are soft
Blue soars above the mellow sky
Blue ink is dark like the middle of the ocean
Blue is a very natural color
Now you know my color is blue!

Connor Wilkes, Grade 2
The Country Day School, ON

When I Grow Up…

I want to be happy.
I will be an author.
A lot of my books will be published.
Some will be fiction and some will be nonfiction.
I want to be happy.
I want to be happy.
I will be a famous author.
I will be in the newspaper.
I will have some gold medals on some of my books.
I want to be happy.
I want to be happy.
My books will be in stores.
For two ninety-nine.
Smiling children will buy my books.
I want to be happy.

Talia Kliot, Grade 2
Ecole Akiva, QC

Spring
S wimming in spring
P laying in spring
R unning in spring
I tan in spring
N ew leaves
G rows in spring
Desyrae LeClercq, Grade 1
Sparling School, AB

Teachers
Teachers help kids learn.
Teachers are fun.
I like my teachers.
They take us outside for a run.

Students study hard.
Students like to play.
Teachers like their students.
For the whole day.
Grace Messmer, Grade 2
A J McLellan Elementary School, BC

Bunnies
Bunnies are cute
And I love them.
Bunnies can be brown
And black and white and gray.
Bunnies are cute.
Bunnies love carrots and carrot tops.
Madison Sabean, Grade 2
Falmouth District School, NS

Birds
B eautiful birds
I n spring.
R obins fly back from
D own
S outh.
Dante Budhan, Grade 2
Trelawny Public School, ON

Brownies
The colour brown
Is like planting a garden.
The softness of the dirt
Sprinkles off my hands.
The smell of the flowers
Speaks to me.
The wind blows in my hair
And it feels so good.
Brown is the colour of brownies and
I like that!
Kitt Empey, Grade 2
The Country Day School, ON

Soccer
Kick, kick, kick.
The ball goes
And I have a goal!
Yes, I have a goal!
I love soccer very much.
Madison Hebb, Grade 2
Falmouth District School, NS

Family of Loons
Mama loon floating
With baby following Mama
While splashing
Around the lake
Savannah Matthewson, Grade 3
Mary Montgomery School, MB

When I Grow Up…
I want to be nice
I will be a gym teacher
There will be 25 people
And I teacher
I want to be nice

I want to be nice
I will be an artist
Drawing good stuff
And having nice pictures
I want to be nice

I want to be nice
I will be a doctor
I will take care of people
And make them feel better
I want to be nice
Joey Elkabas, Grade 2
Ecole Akiva, QC

When I Grow Up
I want to be good at hockey.
My friends and I will play hockey.
We will meet three times a week.
We will practice hard.
I want to be good at hockey.
I want to be good at hockey.
I will be a goalie.
I will try to save a lot of shots.
I use red equipment.
I want to be good at hockey.
I want to be good at hockey.
I will rob the players.
I will have a red net.
I want to be good at hockey.
Josh Jacobson, Grade 2
Ecole Akiva, QC

I Am Nature
I am nature
Beautiful, alive, green
Living everywhere.

I am nature
Growing, sweet smelling, natural
Bigger every day.

I am nature
Cooling, shading, red
A beautiful sight.
Braedan Kanai, Grade 2
A J McLellan Elementary School, BC

Spring
When I play soccer I score a goal.
When I play soccer I get an assist.
When I play soccer I run as fast as I can.
When I play soccer I feel good.
Jackson Cooper, Grade 3
Ecole Akiva, QC

Butterfly
B eautiful
U sually flying
T winkling in the sunshine
T wirling
E xtremely attractive
R eady to dance
F luttering
L ifting up in the sky
Y ellow spots
Lucinda Nelson, Grade 3
Bella Coola Adventist Academy, BC

Hockey
Puck shoots!
I stride.
Buzzer buzzes.
Scratching skates.
People cheering!
Skating on the ice.
Bailey Peach, Grade 2
Falmouth District School, NS

Family
F amilies are people you love.
A nd people you care for.
M ommy is the one you came from.
I really love my sister.
L ove your Daddy.
Y eah now we are going for lunch.
Ben Tannenbaum, Grade 2
Ecole Akiva, QC

My Hands
My hands can bring me to level 16 in TMNT
My hands allow me to hold the steering wheel driving with Dad
My hands allow me to type on the computer with my brother
Hands help me enjoy junk food with my dad…it has lots of sugar!
My hands can bring me to level 16 in TMNT

Jaskaran Bola, Grade 2
Kingswood Dr Public School, ON

Soldier
As a soldier I am brave and strong and fight against what's wrong.
I fought for you. Now you are safe and sound in Canada.
I lie in Flanders Fields with poppies all around me.
I am a soldier brave and strong and fight against what's wrong.

Annika Maki, Grade 3
McKenzie School, ON

Two Little Girls
They were funny little girls
When there were playing with a ball
when they were playing catch but I wasn't thinking of the whole story. But I'll go on I will think of it it was really fun writing the story. I liked how it is funny and silly they were having fun playing catch. I will think more of it. They were with the ball playing when they went sleeping at night. The next morning they woke up they went playing again with the ball but they couldn't find him anymore the ball the two little girls went into the house crying Wha-wha-wha their mothers asked them why are you crying, they just said the right answer. When their mothers decided to go out to look for their ball. She went down to look in the garbage but it wasn't there she decided to look in the garage, there she found it. Then the two little girls were happy they laughed ha-ha-ha.
They were as friendly as ever they could be,
they played catch again they were so friendly as ever.

Sarah Gross, Grade 2
Riverbend Colony School, AB

Chunky
My horse, Chunky, lets me sit on him and ride him in the pen and across the field.
My mom and dad help me feed him. Hay, grain, and cookies (horse cookies, of course).
Chunky is deep, dark brown, with a white star and charlotte mane.
Charlotte? Yes, Charlotte.
He lets me pet him for hours.
I love my Chunky.
He neighs across the fence:
Merherher, merherher, merherher.

Rachel Chatham, Grade 1
Bella Coola Adventist Academy, BC

Underwater
Hi, my name is Mia. I'm a girl and I live in Montreal. I have 2 brothers, a mom, and a dad. We all live in one house. The only thing that keeps me alive is my diary. It's a bit funny. Every time my mind goes out of my head, I travel with my friends. Today I want to go swimming in the ocean. Wow, look at all these fish! Splash! There goes a dolphin jumping up beautifully, well that was awesome. Now let's see a shark coming with its sharp teeth. It look so hungry. Oh phew, it turned. OH, what do I see swimming towards me? It is so shiny and pretty and it seems to sparkle. Ouch. What was that? I just got stung by something. Now I know that it was a jelly fish. Wow! What's that singing voice that I hear? It's getting louder. Look, it is a killer whale. OH, I'm going to ride on you, yahoo! That was fun! What's that? It looks like a group of turtles. They are beautiful! Look at how they twist and turn as they swim. Wonderful! I wish I could do that. Anyway, look at that seal. It is swimming so fast. You should have seen that. It caught a fish. The seal must be having so much fun as it glides through the water.
"Mia! Wake up! You have been daydreaming again, it is time for bed." Goodnight.

Tara Mintzberg, Grade 2
Ecole Akiva, QC

Books

I love to read books
I read in the morning
I read at night time
I borrow books from the library.
I LOVE BOOKS.
Bella Old, Grade 2
A J McLellan Elementary School, BC

Homework

Homework, homework
Please stop it now!
More work, more work
I can't take it much longer!
Just STOP IT!
STOP IT!
Just stop it NOW!

Back to school...
More homework!
Carmen Bastarache, Grade 2
Falmouth District School, NS

Love

I love my family.
I love my dad.
I love my mom.
I love my sister.
I love my cousin.
I love my dogs.
I love my cats.
I love my name.
I love my bed.
I love my room.
Natalie Peach, Grade 2
Falmouth District School, NS

Spring

S pring is fun
P laying in spring
R ain in spring
I like spring
N ests in spring
G oats are in spring
Madison Cole, Grade 1
Sparling School, AB

The Loons

Four black and white loons
Are swimming
Facing forwards
With red eyes
And white collars
Danny Makarchuk, Grade 3
Mary Montgomery School, MB

I Am a Killer Whale

I am a Killer whale
Jumping, splashing, training
Living in the ocean

I am a Killer whale
Swimming, playing, hunting
Part of the mammal family.

I am a Killer whale
Flipping, eating, diving
Having a baby.
Saiya Phagoora, Grade 2
A J McLellan Elementary School, BC

When I Grow Up

I will be very happy.
My wife and I will have a big family.
I will have two children.
My wife will be very beautiful.
I will be very happy.

I will be very happy.
I want to have a good family.
Everyone will be happy.
Everyone will have smiling faces.
I will be very happy.

I will be very happy.
I will be rich.
I will buy a big house and
Have a staff for my family.
I will be very happy.
Justin Goodman, Grade 2
Ecole Akiva, QC

Our Playground

In our playground
Some play around
Chasing a ball
Makes some fall
Some start to run
For a little fun
Some like to walk
With a secret talk
Some like to stand
On their two hands
Some jump rope
With a good hope
Some do nothing
Still watch everything
We all play a lot
It makes us so hot
Anusha Mappanasingam, Grade 3
St Isaac Jogues Catholic School, ON

The Rock

It is hard.
It is shiny.
It is gold.
It is silver.
It is very strong.
Mohammed Fadeel, Grade 1
Islamic Foundation School, ON

When I Grow Up...

I want to be a star.
I want to be famous.
I want to be a singer.
I could go in a limousine.
I want to be a star.
I want to be a star.
I want to play hockey.
I want to score.
I want to be on the Hab's team.
I want to be a star.
I want to be a star.
I want to have a baby girl.
She's going to sleep with me.
I'm going to feed her.
I want to be a star.
Yoan Cohen, Grade 2
Ecole Akiva, QC

Spring

In the springtime I see
the green grass growing.
I hear the birds singing.
I smell the air after it rains.
I feel happy that spring is here.
Samuel Maislin, Grade 3
Ecole Akiva, QC

Tree of Life

The leaves on a tree fall off
The branches break off
The birds start to fly away
People drink root beer
The squirrel scatters away
The sprouts do not grow
...In the fall
Sophie Heroux, Grade 1
Garibaldi Elementary School, BC

Spring

In my backyard I dig for worms.
The earth makes my fingers gooey.
Sometimes we fill it up with water.
It is always so much fun.
Jeremy Schachter, Grade 3
Ecole Akiva, QC

Belonging

I feel like I belong
When I hear the clapping
In the theatre after my dance.
I feel like I belong
When I see my dad fixing cars.
I feel like I belong
When I smell my gramma's haystacks.
I feel like I belong
When I taste my gramma's chocolate chip cookies.
I feel like I belong
When I touch my blanket
When I'm going to sleep.

Teyanna Beltz, Grade 3
Mary Montgomery School, MB

Puppies

P uppies are cute,
   They play the flute.

U nder the towel,
   They like to howl

P uppies are fun,
   They like the sun

P uppies are funny,
   I named mine Honey

I n the house
   Mine chased a mouse

E verything gets chewed in the path of a puppy
   I have another one his name is Nuppie

S illy, silly puppies are silly
   I have one his name is Billy

Megan Stillwell, Grade 3
Westside Academy, BC

What Does the Sun Shine On?

The sun shines on us brightly.
So bright like a sparkling star at night.
It shines on nature to make it grow,
it shines on flowers to make them bloom.
It shines on the world so much to make it bright,
like a shining star at night.
With no sun, it will be freezing.
No more sun rises or sunsets.
It will be dark as black,
may be darker than that.
Look what the sun does for us all,
that is why we all need the sun!

Najat Halane, Grade 3
Islamic Foundation School, ON

Spring Is Here

In the spring I love to bike ride in the park.
I always smell the beautiful flowers by my side.
I just heard the chirping birds on the tree tops.
I see my friends playing volleyball.
I really feel spring is here!

Lauren Rotholz, Grade 3
Ecole Akiva, QC

Index

Author Autograph Page

Author Autograph Page

Author Autograph Page

Author Autograph Page

Author Autograph Page